Google's PageRank and Beyond:
The Science of Search Engine Rankings

PRINCETON

Princeton University Press
Princeton and Oxford

NEW AGE

Google's PageRank and Beyond: The Science of Search Engine Rankings

Amy N. Langville and Carl D. Meyer

PUBLISHING FOR ONE WORLD

NEW AGE INTERNATIONAL (P) LIMITED, PUBLISHERS

New Delhi • Bangalore • Chennai • Cochin • Guwahati • Hyderabad

Jalandhar • Kolkata • Lucknow • Mumbai • Ranchi

Visit us at **www.newagepublishers.com**

First Indian Sub-Continent Edition : 2010
by New Age International (P) Ltd., Publishers

This special low-priced edition is for sale in **India, Bangladesh, Bhutan, Myanmar (Burma), Sri Lanka, Nepal and Pakistan only.**

Originally Published by *Princeton University Press, USA.*

Branches:

- No. 37/10, 8th Cross (Near Hanuman Temple), Azad Nagar, Chamrajpet, **Bangalore**-560 018. Tel.: (080) 2675 6823, Telefax: 2675 6820, E-mail: bangalore@newagepublishers.com
- 26, Damodaran Street, T. Nagar, **Chennai**-600 017. Tel.: (044) 24353401, Telefax: 24351463, E-mail: chennai@newagepublishers.com
- CC-39/1016, Carrier Station Road, Ernakulam South, **Cochin**-682 016, Tel.: (0484) 2377004, Telefax: 4051303. E-mail: cochin@newagepublishers.com
- Hemsen Complex, Mohd. Shah Road, Paltan Bazar, Near Starline Hotel, **Guwahati**-781 008. Tel.: (0361) 2513881. Telefax: 2543669, E-mail: guwahati@newagepublishers.com
- No. 105, 1st Floor, Madhiray Kaveri Tower, 3-2-19, Azam Jahi Road, Nimboliadda, **Hyderabad**-500 027. Tel.: (040) 24652456, Telefax: 24652457, E-mail:hyderabad@newagepublishers.com
- RDB Chambers (Formerly Lotus Cinema)106A, 1st Floor, S.N. Banerjee Road, **Kolkata**-700 014. Tel.: (033) 22273773, Telefax: 22275247, E-mail:kolkata@newagepublishers.com
- 16-A, Jopling Road, **Lucknow**-226 001. Tel.: (0522) 2209578, 4045297, Telefax: 2204098, E-mail: lucknow@newagepublishers.com
- 142C, Victor House, Ground Floor, N.M. Joshi Marg, Lower Parel, **Mumbai**-400 013. Tel.: (022) 24927869. Telefax: 24915415, E-mail: mumbai@newagepublishers.com
- 22, Golden House, Daryaganj, **New Delhi**-110 002. Tel.: (011) 23262370, 23262368, Telefax: 43551305. E-mail: sales@newagepublishers.com

Printed in India at Glorious Printers, Delhi
C-10-05-4745

ISBN: 978-81-224-3129-2
Original Edition Price: $ 39.50
Indian Edition Price: Rs. 395.00

PUBLISHING FOR ONE WORLD
NEW AGE INTERNATIONAL (P) LIMITED, PUBLISHERS
4835/24, Ansari Road, Daryaganj, New Delhi-110002
Visit us at **www.newagepublishers.com**

Contents

Preface

Purpose

As teachers of linear algebra, we wanted to write a book to help students and the general public appreciate and understand one of the most exciting applications of linear algebra today—the use of link analysis by web search engines. This topic is inherently interesting, timely, and familiar. For instance, the book answers such curious questions as: How do search engines work? Why is Google so good? What's a Google bomb? How can I improve the ranking of my homepage in Teoma?

We also wanted this book to be a single source for material on web search engine rankings. A great deal has been written on this topic, but it's currently spread across numerous technical reports, preprints, conference proceedings, articles, and talks. Here we have summarized, clarified, condensed, and categorized the state of the art in web ranking.

Our Audience

We wrote this book with two diverse audiences in mind: the general science reader and the technical science reader. The title echoes the technical content of the book, but in addition to being informative on a technical level, we have also tried to provide some entertaining features and lighter material concerning search engines and how they work.

The Mathematics

Our goal in writing this book was to reach a challenging audience consisting of the general scientific public as well as the technical scientific public. Of course, a complete understanding of link analysis requires an acquaintance with many mathematical ideas. Nevertheless, we have tried to make the majority of the book accessible to the general scientific public. For instance, each chapter builds progressively in mathematical knowledge, technicality, and prerequisites. As a result, Chapters 1-4, which introduce web search and link analysis, are aimed at the general science reader. Chapters 6, 9, and 10 are particularly mathematical. The last chapter, Chapter 15, "The Mathematics Guide," is a condensed but complete reference for every mathematical concept used in the earlier chapters. Throughout the book, key mathematical concepts are highlighted in shaded boxes. By postponing the mathematical definitions and formulas until Chapter 15 (rather than interspersing them throughout the text), we were able to create a book that our mathematically sophisticated readers will also enjoy. We feel this approach is a compromise that allows us to serve both audiences: the general and technical scientific public.

Asides

An enjoyable feature of this book is the use of Asides. Asides contain entertaining news stories, practical search tips, amusing quotes, and racy lawsuits. Every chapter, even the particularly technical ones, contains several asides. Often times a light aside provides the perfect break after a stretch of serious mathematical thinking. Brief asides appear in shaded boxes while longer asides that stretch across multiple pages are offset by horizontal bars and italicized font. We hope you enjoy these breaks—we found ourselves looking forward to writing them.

Computing and Code

Truly mastering a subject requires experimenting with the ideas. Consequently, we have incorporated Matlab code to encourage and jump-start the experimentation process. While any programming language is appropriate, we chose Matlab for three reasons: (1) its matrix storage architecture and built-in commands are particularly suited to the large sparse link analysis matrices of this text, (2) among colleges and universities, Matlab is a market leader in mathematical software, and (3) it's very user-friendly. The Matlab programs in this book are intended to be instruction, not production, code. We hope that, by playing with these programs, readers will be inspired to create new models and algorithms.

Acknowledgments

We thank Princeton University Press for supporting this book. We especially enjoyed working with Vickie Kearn, the Senior Editor at PUP. Vickie, thank you for displaying just the right combination of patience and gentle pressure. For a book with such timely material, you showed amazing faith in us. We thank all those who reviewed our manuscripts and made this a better book. Of course, we also thank our families and friends for their encouragement. Your pride in us is a powerful driving force.

Dedication

We dedicate this book to mentors and mentees worldwide. The energy, inspiration, and support that is sparked through such relationships can inspire great products. For us, it produced this book, but more importantly, a wonderful synergistic friendship.

Chapter One

Introduction to Web Search Engines

1.1 A SHORT HISTORY OF INFORMATION RETRIEVAL

Today we have museums for everything—the museum of baseball, of baseball players, of crazed fans of baseball players, museums for world wars, national battles, legal fights, and family feuds. While there's no shortage of museums, we have yet to find a museum dedicated to this book's field, a museum of information retrieval and its history. Of course, there are related museums, such as the Library Museum in Boras, Sweden, but none concentrating on information retrieval. **Information retrieval**[1] is the process of searching within a document collection for a particular information need (called a **query**). Although dominated by recent events following the invention of the computer, information retrieval actually has a long and glorious tradition. To honor that tradition, we propose the creation of a museum dedicated to its history. Like all museums, our museum of information retrieval contains some very interesting artifacts. Join us for a brief tour.

The earliest document collections were recorded on the painted walls of caves. A cave dweller interested in searching a collection of cave paintings to answer a particular information query had to travel by foot, and stand, staring in front of each painting. Unfortunately, it's hard to collect an artifact without being gruesome, so let's fast forward a bit.

Before the invention of paper, ancient Romans and Greeks recorded information on papyrus rolls. Some papyrus artifacts from ancient Rome had tags attached to the rolls. These tags were an ancient form of today's Post-it Note, and make an excellent addition to our museum. A tag contained a short summary of the rolled document, and was attached in order to save readers from unnecessarily unraveling a long irrelevant document. These abstracts also appeared in oral form. At the start of Greek plays in the fifth century B.C., the chorus recited an abstract of the ensuing action. While no actual classification scheme has survived from the artifacts of Greek and Roman libraries, we do know that another elementary information retrieval tool, the table of contents, first appeared in Greek scrolls from the second century B.C. Books were not invented until centuries later, when necessity required an alternative writing material. As the story goes, the Library of Pergamum (in what is now Turkey) threatened to overtake the celebrated Library of Alexandria as the best library in the world, claiming the largest collection of papyrus rolls. As a result, the Egyptians ceased the supply of papyrus to Pergamum, so the Pergamenians invented an alternative writing material, parchment, which is made from thin layers of animal skin. (In fact, the root of the word *parchment* comes from the word *Pergamum*.) Unlike papyrus,

[1]The boldface terms that appear throughout the book are also listed and defined in the Glossary, which begins on page 201.

parchment did not roll easily, so scribes folded several sheets of parchment and sewed them into books. These books outlasted scrolls and were easier to use. Parchment books soon replaced the papyrus rolls.

The heights of writing, knowledge, and documentation of the Greek and Roman periods were contrasted with their lack during the Dark and Middle Ages. Precious few documents were produced during this time. Instead, most information was recorded orally. Document collections were recorded in the memory of a village's best storyteller. Oral traditions carried in poems, songs, and prayers were passed from one generation to the next. One of the most legendary and lengthy tales is *Beowulf*, an epic about the adventures of a sixth-century Scandinavian warrior. The tale is believed to have originated in the seventh century and been passed from generation to generation through song. Minstrels often took poetic license, altering and adding verses as the centuries passed. An inquisitive child wishing to hear stories about the monster Grendel waited patiently while the master storyteller searched his memory to find just the right part of the story. Thus, the result of the child's search for information was biased by the wisdom and judgement of the intermediary storyteller. Fortunately, the invention of paper, the best writing medium yet, superior to even parchment, brought renewed acceleration to the written record of information and collections of documents. In fact, Beowulf passed from oral to written form around A.D. 1000, a date over which scholars still debate. Later, monks, the possessors of treasured reading and writing skills, sat in scriptoriums working as scribes from sunrise to sunset. The scribes' works were placed in medieval libraries, which initially were so small that they had no need for classification systems. Eventually the collections grew, and it became common practice to divide the holdings into three groups: theological works, classical authors of antiquity, and contemporary authors on the seven arts. Lists of holdings and tables of contents from classical books make nice museum artifacts from the medieval period.

Other document collections sprung up in a variety of fields. This dramatically accelerated with the re-invention of the printing press by Johann Gutenberg in 1450. The wealthy proudly boasted of their private libraries, and public libraries were instituted in America in the 1700s at the prompting of Benjamin Franklin. As library collections grew and became publicly accessible, the desire for focused search became more acute. Hierarchical classification systems were used to group documents on like subjects together. The first use of a hierarchical organization system is attributed to the Roman author Valerius Maximus, who used it in A.D. 30 to organize the topics in his book, *Factorum ac dictorum memorabilium libri IX* (Nine Books of Memorable Deeds and Sayings). Despite these rudimentary organization systems, word of mouth and the advice of a librarian were the best means of obtaining accurate quality information for a search. Of course, document collections and their organization expanded beyond the limits of even the best librarian's memory. More orderly ways of maintaining records of a collection's holdings were devised. Notable artifacts that belong in our information retrieval museum are a few lists of individual library holdings, sorted by title and also author, as well as examples of the Dewey decimal system (1872), the card catalog (early 1900s), microfilm (1930s), and the MARC (MAchine Readable Cataloging) system (1960s).

These inventions were progress, yet still search was not completely in the hands of the information seeker. It took the invention of the digital computer (1940s and 1950s) and the subsequent inventions of computerized search systems to move toward that goal. The first computerized search systems used special syntax to automatically retrieve book and article information related to a user's query. Unfortunately, the cumbersome syntax kept search largely in the domain of librarians trained on the systems. An early representative of computerized search such as the Cornell SMART system (1960s) [146] deserves a place in our museum of information retrieval.

In 1989 the storage, access, and searching of document collections was revolutionized by an invention named the World Wide Web by its founder Tim Berners-Lee [79]. Of course, our museum must include artifacts from this revolution such as a webpage, some HTML, and a hyperlink or two. The invention of linked document collections was truly original at this time, despite the fact that Vannevar Bush, once Director of the Office of Scientific Research and Development, foreshadowed its coming in his famous 1945 essay, "As We May Think" [43]. In that essay, he describes the memex, a futuristic machine (with shocking similarity to today's PC and Web) that mirrors the cognitive processes of humans by leaving "trails of association" throughout document collections. Four decades of progress later, remnants of Bush's memex formed the skeleton of Berners-Lee's Web. A drawing of the memex (Figure 1.1) by a graphic artist and approved by Bush was included in *LIFE* magazine's 1945 publishing of Bush's prophetic article.

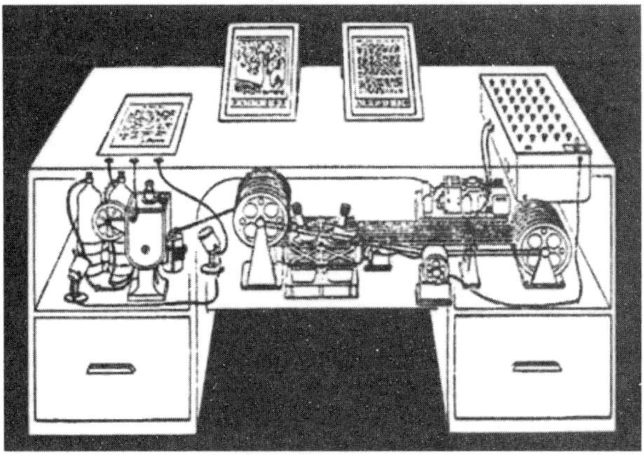

Figure 1.1 Drawing of Vannevar Bush's memex appearing in *LIFE*. Original caption read: "Memex in the form of a desk would instantly bring files and material on any subject to the operator's fingertips. Slanting translucent screens supermicrofilm filed by code numbers. At left is a mechanism which automatically photographs longhand notes, pictures, and letters, then files them in the desk for future reference."

The World Wide Web became the ultimate signal of the dominance of the Information Age and the death of the Industrial Age. Yet despite the revolution in information storage and access ushered in by the Web, users initiating web searches found themselves floundering. They were looking for the proverbial needle in an enormous, ever-growing information haystack. In fact, users felt much like the men in Jorge Luis Borges' 1941 short story [35], "The Library of Babel", which describes an imaginary, infinite library.

> When it was proclaimed that the Library contained all books, the first impression was one of extravagant happiness. All men felt themselves to be the masters of an intact and secret treasure. There was no personal or world problem whose eloquent solution did not exist in some hexagon.

> . . . As was natural, this inordinate hope was followed by an excessive depression. The certitude that some shelf in some hexagon held precious books and that these precious books were inaccessible seemed almost intolerable.

Much of the information in the Library of the Web, like that in the fictitious Library of Babel, remained inaccessible. In fact, early web search engines did little to ease user frustration; search could be conducted by sorting through hierarchies of topics on Yahoo, or by sifting through the many (often thousands of) webpages returned by the search engine, clicking on pages to personally determine which were most relevant to the query. Some users resorted to the earliest search techniques used by ancient queriers—word of mouth and expert advice. They learned about valuable websites from friends and linked to sites recommended by colleagues who had already put in hours of search effort.

All this changed in 1998 when **link analysis** hit the information retrieval scene [40, 106]. The most successful search engines began using link analysis, a technique that exploited the additional information inherent in the hyperlink structure of the Web, to improve the quality of search results. Web search improved dramatically, and web searchers religiously used and promoted their favorite engines like Google and AltaVista. In fact, in 2004 many web surfers freely admit their obsession with, dependence on, and addiction to today's search engines. Below we include the comments [117] of a few Google fans to convey the joy caused by the increased accessibility of the Library of the Web made possible by the link analysis engines. Incidentally, in May 2004 Google held the largest share of the search market with 37% of searchers using Google, followed by 27% using the Yahoo conglomerate, which includes AltaVista, AlltheWeb, and Overture.[2]

- "It's not my homepage, but it might as well be. I use it to ego-surf. I use it to read the news. Anytime I want to find out anything, I use it."—Matt Groening, creator and executive producer, *The Simpsons*
- "I can't imagine life without Google News. Thousands of sources from around the world ensure anyone with an Internet connection can stay informed. The diversity of viewpoints available is staggering."—Michael Powell, chair, Federal Communications Commission
- "Google is my rapid-response research assistant. On the run-up to a deadline, I may use it to check the spelling of a foreign name, to acquire an image of a particular piece of military hardware, to find the exact quote of a public figure, check a stat, translate a phrase, or research the background of a particular corporation. It's the Swiss Army knife of information retrieval."—Garry Trudeau, cartoonist and creator, *Doonesbury*

Nearly all major search engines now combine link analysis scores, similar to those used by Google, with more traditional information retrieval scores. In this book, we record the history of one aspect of *web* information retrieval. That aspect is the link analysis or *ranking* algorithms underlying several of today's most popular and successful search

---

[2]These market share statistics were compiled by comScore, a company that counted the number of searches done by U.S. surfers in May 2004 using the major search engines. See the article at `http://searchenginewatch.com/reports/article.php/2156431`.

engines, including Google and Teoma. Incidentally, we'll add the **PageRank** link analysis algorithm [40] used by Google (see Chapters 4-10) and the **HITS** algorithm [106] used by Teoma (see Chapter 11) to our museum of information retrieval.

1.2 AN OVERVIEW OF TRADITIONAL INFORMATION RETRIEVAL

To set the stage for the exciting developments in link analysis to come in later chapters, we begin our story by distinguishing **web information retrieval** from **traditional information retrieval**. Web information retrieval is search within the world's largest and linked document collection, whereas traditional information retrieval is search within smaller, more controlled, nonlinked collections. The traditional nonlinked collections existed before the birth of the Web and still exist today. Searching within a university library's collection of books or within a professor's reserve of slides for an art history course—these are examples of traditional information retrieval.

These document collections are nonlinked, mostly static, and are organized and categorized by specialists such as librarians and journal editors. These documents are stored in physical form as books, journals, and artwork as well as electronically on microfiche, CDs, and webpages. However, the mechanisms for searching for items in the collections are now almost all computerized. These computerized mechanisms are referred to as search engines, virtual machines created by software that enables them to sort through virtual file folders to find relevant documents. There are three basic computer-aided techniques for searching traditional information retrieval collections: Boolean models, vector space models, and probabilistic models [14]. These search models, which were developed in the 1960s, have had decades to grow, mesh, and morph into new search models. In fact, as of June 2000, there were at least 3,500 different search engines (including the newer web engines) [37], which means that there are possibly 3,500 different search techniques. Nevertheless, since most search engines rely on one or more of the three basic models, we describe these in turn.

1.2.1 Boolean Search Engines

The **Boolean model** of information retrieval, one of the earliest and simplest retrieval methods, uses the notion of exact matching to match documents to a user query. Its more refined descendents are still used by most libraries. The adjective Boolean refers to the use of Boolean algebra, whereby words are logically combined with the Boolean operators AND, OR, and NOT. For example, the Boolean AND of two logical statements x and y means that both x AND y must be satisfied, while the Boolean OR of these two statements means that at least one of these statements must be satisfied. Any number of logical statements can be combined using the three Boolean operators. The Boolean model of information retrieval operates by considering which keywords are present or absent in a document. Thus, a document is judged as relevant or irrelevant; there is no concept of a partial match between documents and queries. This can lead to poor performance [14]. More advanced fuzzy set theoretic techniques try to remedy this black-white Boolean logic by introducing shades of gray. For example, a title search for `car` AND `maintenance` on a Boolean engine causes the virtual machine to return all documents that use both words in the title. A relevant document entitled "Automobile Maintenance" will not be returned. Fuzzy Boolean engines use fuzzy logic to categorize this document as somewhat relevant and return it to the user.

The car maintenance query example introduces the main drawbacks of Boolean search engines; they fall prey to two of the most common information retrieval problems, **synonymy** and **polysemy**. Synonymy refers to multiple words having the same meaning, such as car and automobile. A standard Boolean engine cannot return semantically related documents whose keywords were not included in the original query. Polysemy refers to words with multiple meanings. For example, when a user types `bank` as their query, does he or she mean a financial center, a slope on a hill, a shot in pool, or a collection of objects [24]? The problem of polysemy can cause many documents that are irrelevant to the user's actual intended query meaning to be retrieved. Many Boolean search engines also require that the user be familiar with Boolean operators and the engine's specialized syntax. For example, to find information about the phrase `iron curtain`, many engines require quotation marks around the phrase, which tell the search engine that the entire phrase should be searched as if it were just one keyword. A user who forgets this syntax requirement would be surprised to find retrieved documents about interior decorating and mining for iron ore.

Nevertheless, variants of the Boolean model do form the basis for many search engines. There are several reasons for their prevalence. First, creating and programming a Boolean engine is straightforward. Second, queries can be processed quickly; a quick scan through the keyword files for the documents can be executed in parallel. Third, Boolean models scale well to very large document collections. Accommodating a growing collection is easy. The programming remains simple; merely the storage and parallel processing capabilities need to grow. References [14, 75, 107] all contain chapters with excellent introductions to the Boolean model and its extensions.

1.2.2 Vector Space Model Search Engines

Another information retrieval technique uses the **vector space model** [147], developed by Gerard Salton in the early 1960s, to sidestep some of the information retrieval problems mentioned above. Vector space models transform textual data into *numeric vectors* and *matrices*, then employ *matrix analysis*[3] techniques to discover key features and connections in the document collection. Some advanced vector space models address the common text analysis problems of synonymy and polysemy. Advanced vector space models, such as LSI [64] (Latent Semantic Indexing), can access the hidden semantic structure in a document collection. For example, an LSI engine processing the query `car` will return documents whose keywords are related semantically (in meaning), e.g., `automobile`. This ability to reveal hidden semantic meanings makes vector space models, such as LSI, very powerful information retrieval tools.

Two additional advantages of the vector space model are **relevance scoring** and **relevance feedback**. The vector space model allows documents to partially match a query by assigning each document a number between 0 and 1, which can be interpreted as the likelihood of relevance to the query. The group of retrieved documents can then be sorted by degree of relevancy, a luxury not possible with the simple Boolean model. Thus, vector space models return documents in an ordered list, sorted according to a relevance score. The first document returned is judged to be most relevant to the user's query.

[3]Mathematical terms are defined in Chapter 15, the Mathematics Chapter, and are italicized throughout.

Some vector space search engines report the relevance score as a relevancy percentage. For example, a 97% next to a document means that the document is judged as 97% relevant to the user's query. (See the Federal Communications Commission's search engine, `http://www.fcc.gov/searchtools.html`, which is powered by *Inktomi*, once known to use the vector space model. Enter a query such as `taxes` and notice the relevancy score reported on the right side.) Relevance feedback, the other advantage of the vector space model, is an information retrieval tuning technique that is a natural addition to the vector space model. Relevance feedback allows the user to select a subset of the retrieved documents that are useful. The query is then resubmitted with this additional relevance feedback information, and a revised set of generally more useful documents is retrieved.

A drawback of the vector space model is its computational expense. At query time, distance measures (also known as similarity measures) must be computed between each document and the query. And advanced models, such as LSI, require an expensive singular value decomposition [82, 127] of a large matrix that numerically represents the entire document collection. As the collection grows, the expense of this matrix decomposition becomes prohibitive. This computational expense also exposes another drawback—vector space models do not scale well. Their success is limited to small document collections.

Understanding Search Engines

The informative little book by Michael Berry and Murray Browne, *Understanding Search Engines: Mathematical Modeling and Text Retrieval* [23], provides an excellent explanation of vector space models, especially LSI, and contains several examples and sample code. Our mathematical readers will enjoy this book and its application of linear algebra algorithms in the context of traditional information retrieval.

1.2.3 Probabilistic Model Search Engines

Probabilistic models attempt to estimate the probability that the user will find a particular document relevant. Retrieved documents are ranked by their odds of relevance (the ratio of the probability that the document is relevant to the query divided by the probability that the document is not relevant to the query). The probabilistic model operates recursively and requires that the underlying algorithm guess at initial parameters then iteratively tries to improve this initial guess to obtain a final ranking of relevancy probabilities.

Unfortunately, probabilistic models can be very hard to build and program. Their complexity grows quickly, deterring many researchers and limiting their scalability. Probabilistic models also require several unrealistic simplifying assumptions, such as independence between terms as well as documents. Of course, the independence assumption is restrictive in most cases. For instance, in this document the most likely word to follow `information` is the word `retrieval`, but the independence assumption judges each word as equally likely to follow the word `information`. On the other hand, the probabilistic framework can naturally accommodate a priori preferences, and thus, these models do offer promise of tailoring search results to the preferences of individual users. For example, a user's query history can be incorporated into the probabilistic model's initial guess, which generates better query results than a democratic guess.

1.2.4 Meta-search Engines

There's actually a fourth model for traditional search engines, meta-search engines, which combines the three classic models. **Meta-search engines** are based on the principle that while one search engine is good, two (or more) are better. One search engine may be great at a certain task, while a second search engine is better at another task. Thus, meta-search engines such as *Copernic* (`www.copernic.com`) and *SurfWax* (`www.surfwax.com`) were created to simultaneously exploit the best features of many individual search engines. Meta-search engines send the query to several search engines at once and return the results from all of the search engines in one long unified list. Some meta-search engines also include subject-specific search engines, which can be helpful when searching within one particular discipline. For example, *Monster* (`www.monster.com`) is an employment search engine.

1.2.5 Comparing Search Engines

Annual information retrieval conferences, such as TREC [3], SIGIR, CIR [22] (for traditional information retrieval), and WWW [4] (for web information retrieval), are used to compare the various information retrieval models underlying search engines and help the field progress toward better, more efficient search engines. The two most common ratings used to differentiate the various search techniques are precision and recall. **Precision** is the ratio of the number of relevant documents retrieved to the total number of documents retrieved. **Recall** is the ratio of the number of relevant documents retrieved to the total number of relevant documents in the collection. The higher the precision and recall, the better the search engine is. Of course, search engines are tested on document collections with known parameters. For example, the commonly used test collection Medlars [6], containing 5,831 keywords and 1,033 documents, has been examined so often that its properties are well known. For instance, there are exactly 24 documents relevant to the phrase `neoplasm immunology`. Thus, the denominator of the recall ratio for a user query on `neoplasm immunology` is 24. If only 10 documents were retrieved by a search engine for this query, then a recall of $10/24 = .41\overline{6}$ is reported. Recall and precision are information retrieval-specific performance measures, but, of course, when evaluating any computer system, time and space are always performance issues. All else held constant, quick, memory-efficient search engines are preferred to slower, memory-inefficient engines. A search engine with fabulous recall and precision is useless if it requires 30 minutes to perform one query or stores the data on 75 supercomputers. Some other performance measures take a user-centered viewpoint and are aimed at assessing user satisfaction and frustration with the information system. A book by Robert Korfhage, *Information Storage and Retrieval* [107], discusses these and several other measures for comparing search engines. Excellent texts for information retrieval are [14, 75, 163].

1.3 WEB INFORMATION RETRIEVAL

1.3.1 The Challenges of Web Search

Tim Berners-Lee and his World Wide Web entered the information retrieval world in 1989 [79]. This event caused a branch that focused specifically on search within this new document collection to break away from traditional information retrieval. This branch is called **web information retrieval**. Many web search engines are built on the techniques of traditional search engines, but they differ in many important ways. We list the properties that make the Web such a unique document collection. The Web is:

- huge,
- dynamic,
- self-organized, and
- hyperlinked.

The Web is indeed huge! In fact, it's so big that it's hard to get an accurate count of its size. By January 2004, it was estimated that the Web contained over 10 billion pages, with an average page size of 500KB [5]. With a world population of about 6.4 billion, that's almost 2 pages for each inhabitant. The early exponential growth of the Web has slowed recently, but it is still the largest document collection in existence. The Berkeley information project, "How Much Information," estimates that the amount of information on the Web is about 20 times the size of the entire Library of Congress print collection [5]. Bigger still, a company called BrightPlanet sells access to the so-called Deep Web, which they estimate to contain over 92,000TB of data spread over 550 billion pages [1]. BrightPlanet defines the Deep Web as the hundreds of thousands of publicly accessible databases that create a collection over 500 times larger than the Surface Web. Deep webpages can not be found by casual, routine surfing. Surfers must request information from a particular database, at which point, the relevant pages are served to the user dynamically within a matter of seconds. As a result, search engines cannot easily find these dynamic pages since they do not exist before or after the query. However, Yahoo appears to be the first search engine aiming to index parts of the Deep Web.

The Web is dynamic! Contrast this with traditional document collections which can be considered static in two senses. First, once a document is added to a traditional collection, it does not change. The books sitting on a bookshelf are well behaved. They don't change their content by themselves, but webpages do, very frequently. A study by Junghoo Cho and Hector Garcia-Molina [52] in 2000 reported that 40% of all webpages in their dataset changed within a week, and 23% of the .com pages changed daily. In a much more extensive and recent study, the results of Fetterly et al. [74] concur. About 35% of all webpages changed over the course of their study, and also pages that were larger in size changed more often and more extensively than their smaller counterparts. Second, for the most part, the size of a traditional document collection is relatively static. It is true that abstracts are added to MEDLINE each year, but how many? Hundreds, maybe thousands. These are minuscule additions by Web proportions. Billions of pages are added to the Web each year. The dynamics of the Web make it tough to compute relevancy scores for queries when the collection is a moving, evolving target.

The Web is self-organized! Traditional document collections are usually collected and categorized by trained (and often highly paid) specialists. However, on the Web, anyone can post a webpage and link away at will. There are no standards and no gatekeepers policing content, structure, and format. The data are volatile; there are rapid updates, broken links, and file disappearances. One 2002 U.S. study reporting on "link rot" suggested that up to 50% of URLs cited in articles in two information technology journals were inaccessible within four years [1]. The data is heterogeneous, existing in multiple formats, languages, and alphabets. And often this volatile, heterogeneous data is posted multiple times. In addition, there is no editorial review process, which means errors, falsehoods, and invalid statements abound. Further, this self-organization opens the door for sneaky **spammers** who capitalize on the mercantile potential offered by the Web. *Spammers* was the name originally given to those who send mass advertising emails. With one click of the send button, spammers can send their advertising message to thousands of potential customers in a matter of seconds. With web search and online retailing, this name was broadened to include those using deceptive webpage creation techniques to rank highly in web search listings for particular queries. Spammers resorted to using minuscule text font, hidden text (white on a white background), and misleading **metatag** descriptions to fool early web search engines (like those using the Boolean technique of traditional information retrieval). The self-organization of the Web also means that webpages are created for a variety of different purposes. Some pages are aimed at surfers who are shopping, others at surfers who are researching. In fact, search engines must be able to answer many types of queries, such as transactional queries, navigational queries, and informational queries. All these features of the Web combine to make the job for web search engines Herculean.

Ah, but the Web is hyperlinked! This linking feature, the foundation of Vannevar Bush's memex, is the saving grace for web search engines. Hyperlinks make the new national pastime of surfing possible. But much more importantly, they make focused, effective searching a reality. This book is about ways that web search engines exploit the additional information available in the Web's sprawling link structure to improve the quality of their search results. Consequently, we focus on just one aspect of the web information retrieval process, but one we believe is the most exciting and important. However, the advantages resulting from the link structure of the Web did not come without negative side effects. The most interesting side effects concern those sneaky spammers. Spammers soon caught wind of the link analysis employed by major search engines, and immediately set to work on link spamming. Link spammers carefully craft hyperlinking strategies in the hope of increasing traffic to their pages. This has created an entertaining game of cat and mouse between the search engines and the spammers, which many, the authors included, enjoy spectating. See the asides on pages 43 and 52.

An additional information retrieval challenge for any document collection, but especially pertinent to the Web, concerns precision. Although the amount of accessible information continues to grow, a user's ability to look at documents does not. Users rarely look beyond the first 10 or 20 documents retrieved [94]. This user impatience means that search engine precision must increase just as rapidly as the number of documents is increasing. Another dilemma unique to web search engines concerns their performance measurements and comparison. While traditional search engines are compared by running tests on familiar, well studied, controlled collections, this is not realistic for web engines. Even small web collections are too large for researchers to catalog, count, and create estimates of the precision and recall numerators and denominators for dozens of queries. Comparing two search engines is usually done with user satisfaction studies and market share measures in addition to the baseline comparison measures of speed and storage requirements.

1.3.2 Elements of the Web Search Process

This last section of the introductory chapter describes the basic elements of the web information retrieval process. Their relationship to one another is shown in Figure 1.2. Our purpose in describing the many elements of the search process is twofold: first, it helps emphasize the focus of this book, which is the ranking part of the search process, and second, it shows how the ranking process fits into the grand scheme of search. Chapters 3-12 are devoted to the shaded parts of Figure 1.2, while all other parts are discussed briefly in Chapter 2.

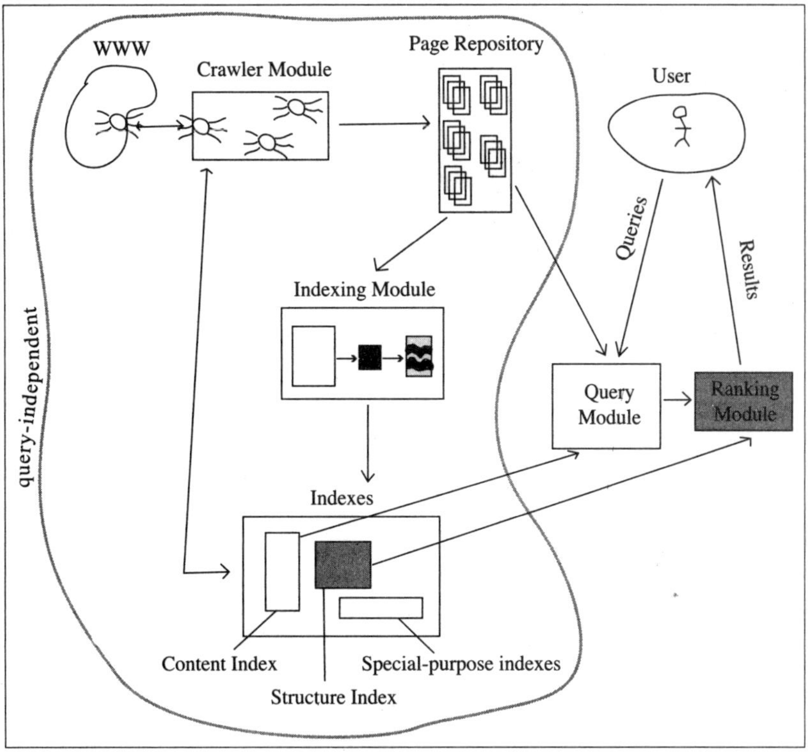

Figure 1.2 Elements of a search engine

- **Crawler Module.** The Web's self-organization means that, in contrast to traditional document collections, there is no central collection and categorization organization. Traditional document collections live in physical warehouses, such as the college's library or the local art museum, where they are categorized and filed. On the other hand, the web document collection lives in a cyber warehouse, a virtual entity that is not limited by geographical constraints and can grow without limit. However, this geographic freedom brings one unfortunate side effect. Search engines must do the data collection and categorization tasks on their own. As a result, all web search engines have a crawler module. This module contains the software that collects and categorizes the web's documents. The crawling software creates virtual robots, called **spiders**, that constantly scour the Web gathering new information and webpages and returning to store them in a central repository.

- **Page Repository.** The spiders return with new webpages, which are temporarily stored as full, complete webpages in the page repository. The new pages remain in the repository until they are sent to the indexing module, where their vital information is stripped to create a compressed version of the page. Popular pages that are repeatedly used to serve queries are stored here longer, perhaps indefinitely.

- **Indexing Module.** The indexing module takes each new uncompressed page and extracts only the vital descriptors, creating a compressed description of the page that is stored in various indexes. The indexing module is like a black box function that takes the uncompressed page as input and outputs a "Cliffnotes" version of the page. The uncompressed page is then tossed out or, if deemed popular, returned to the page repository.

- **Indexes.** The indexes hold the valuable compressed information for each webpage. This book describes three types of indexes. The first is called the **content index**. Here the content, such as keyword, title, and anchor text for each webpage, is stored in a compressed form using an **inverted file** structure. Chapter 2 describes the inverted file in detail. Further valuable information regarding the hyperlink structure of pages in the search engine's index is gleaned during the indexing phase. This link information is stored in compressed form in the **structure index**. The crawler module sometimes accesses the structure index to find uncrawled pages. **Special-purpose indexes** are the final type of index. For example, indexes such as the image index and pdf index hold information that is useful for particular query tasks.

The four modules above (crawler, page repository, indexers, indexes) and their corresponding data files exist and operate independent of users and their queries. Spiders are constantly crawling the Web, bringing back new and updated pages to be indexed and stored. In Figure 1.2 these modules are circled and labeled as **query-independent**. Unlike the preceding modules, the query module is **query-dependent** and is initiated when a user enters a query, to which the search engine must respond in **real-time**.

- **Query Module.** The query module converts a user's natural language query into a language that the search system can understand (usually numbers), and consults the various indexes in order to answer the query. For example, the query module consults the content index and its inverted file to find which pages use the query terms. These pages are called the relevant pages. Then the query module passes the set of relevant pages to the ranking module.

- **Ranking Module.** The ranking module takes the set of relevant pages and ranks them according to some criterion. The outcome is an ordered list of webpages such that the pages near the top of the list are most likely to be what the user desires. The ranking module is perhaps the most important component of the search process because the output of the query module often results in too many (thousands of) relevant pages that the user must sort through. The ordered list filters the less relevant pages to the bottom, making the list of pages more manageable for the user. (In contrast, the similarity measures of traditional information retrieval often do not filter out enough irrelevant pages.) Actually, this ranking which carries valuable, discriminatory power is arrived at by combining two scores, the **content score** and the **popularity score**. Many rules are used to give each relevant page a relevancy or content score. For example, many web engines give pages using the query word in the title or description a higher content score than pages using the query word in the body of the page [39]. The popularity score, which is the focus of this book, is determined from an analysis of the Web's hyperlink structure. The content score is combined with the popularity score to determine an **overall score** for each relevant page [30]. The set of relevant pages resulting from the query module is then presented to the user in order of their overall scores.

Chapter 2 gives an introduction to all components of the web search process, except the ranking component. The ranking component, specifically the popularity score, is the subject of this book. Chapters 3 through 12 provide a comprehensive treatment of the ranking problem and its suggested solutions. Each chapter progresses in depth and mathematical content.

Chapter Two

Crawling, Indexing, and Query Processing

Spiders are the building blocks of search engines. Decisions about the design of the crawler and the capabilities of its spiders affect the design of the other modules, such as the indexing and query processing modules.

So in this chapter, we begin our description of the basic components of a web search engine with the crawler and its spiders. We purposely exclude one component, the ranking component, since it is the focus of this book and is covered in the remaining chapters. The goals and challenges of web crawlers are introduced in section 2.1, and a simple program for crawling the Web is provided. Indexing a collection of documents as enormous as the Web creates special storage challenges (section 2.2), and also has search engines constantly increasing the size of their indexes (see the aside on page 20). The size of the Web makes the real-time processing of queries an astounding feat, and section 2.3 describes the structures and mechanisms that make this possible.

2.1 CRAWLING

The crawler module contains a short software program that instructs robots or spiders on how and which pages to retrieve. The crawling module gives a spider a root set of URLs to visit, instructing it to start there and follow links on those pages to find new pages. Every crawling program must address several issues. For example, which pages should the spiders crawl? Some search engines focus on specialized search, and as a result, conduct specialized crawls, through only `.gov` pages, or pages with images, or blog files, etc. For instance, Bernhard Seefeld's search engine, search.ch, crawls only Swiss webpages and stops at the geographical borders of Switzerland. Even the most comprehensive search engine indexes only a small portion of the entire Web. Thus, crawlers must carefully select which pages to visit.

How often should pages be crawled? Since the Web is dynamic, last month's crawled page may contain different content this month. Therefore, crawling is a never-ending process. Spiders return exhausted, carrying several new and many updated pages, only to be immediately given another root URL and told to start over. Theirs is an endless task like Sisyphus's uphill ball-rolling. However, some pages change more often than others, so a crawler must decide which pages to revisit and how often. Some engines make this decision democratically, while others refresh pages in proportion to their perceived freshness or importance levels. In fact, some researchers have proposed a crawling strategy that uses the PageRank measure of Chapters 3 and 4 to decide which pages to update [31].

How should pages be crawled ethically? When a spider visits a webpage, it consumes resources, such as bandwidth and hits quotas, belonging to the page's host and the

Internet at large. Like outdoor activists who try to "leave no trace," polite spiders try to minimize their impact. The Robots Exclusion Protocol was developed to define proper spidering activities and punish obnoxious, disrespectful spiders. In fact, website administrators can use a `robots.txt` file to block spiders from accessing parts of their sites.

How should multiple spiders coordinate their activities to avoid coverage overlap? One crawler can set several spiders loose on the Web, figuring parallel crawling can save time and effort. However, an optimal crawling policy is needed to insure websites are not visited multiple times, and thus significant overhead communication is required.

Regardless of the ways a crawling program addresses these issues, spiders return with URLs for new or refreshed pages that need to be added to or updated in the search engine's indexes. We discuss one index in particular, the content index, in the next section.

Submitting a Site to Search Engines

Like a castaway stranded on a tiny island, many webpage authors worry that a search engine spider might never find their webpage. This is certainly possible, especially if the page is about an obscure topic, and contains little content and few inlinks. Authors hosting a new page can check if spiders such as Googlebot have visited their site by viewing their web server's log files. Most search engines have mechanisms to calm the fears of castaway authors. For example, Google offers authors a submission feature. Every webpage author can submit his or her site through a web form (`http://www.google.com/addurl.html`), which adds the site to Google's list of to-be-crawled URLs. While Google offers no guarantees on if or when the site will be crawled, this service does help both site authors and the Google crawler. Almost all major search engines offer a "Submit Your Site" feature, although some require small fees in exchange for a listing, featured listing, or sponsored listing in their index.

Spidering Hacks

Readers interested in programming their own special purpose crawler will find the O'Reilly book, *Spidering Hacks* [93], useful. This book contains 100 tips and tools for training a spider to do just about anything. With these tricks, your spider will be able to do more than just sit, roll over, and play dead; he'll go find news stories about an actor, retrieve stock quotes, run an email discussion group, or find current topical trends on the Web.

Matlab Crawler m-file

With Cleve Moler's permission, we display the guts of his Matlab spider here. If you're a programmer or curious reader who's not squeamish around spiders or Matlab code, please feel free to dissect. Squeamish, code-averse readers should skip ahead to section 2.2.

Versions 6.5 and later of MATLAB contain two commands, `urlread` and `urlwrite`, that enable one to write simple m-files that crawl the Web. The m-file below, `surfer.m`, begins a web crawl at a `root` page and continues until `n` pages have been crawled. The program creates two outputs, `U`, a list of the `n` crawled URLs, and `L`, a sparse binary *adjacency matrix* containing the link structure of the `n` pages. (The `L` matrix is related to the **H** PageRank matrix of Chapter 4.) The command `urlwrite` can then be used to save the contents of each retrieved URL to a file, which can then be sent to the indexing module of the search engine for compression. (This m-file can be downloaded from the website for Cleve's book *Numerical Computing with Matlab* [132], `http://www.mathworks.com/moler/ncmfilelist.html`.)

```
function [U,L] = surfer(root,n);

% SURFER  Create the adjacency matrix of a portion of the Web.
%    [U,L] = surfer(root,n) starts at the URL root and follows
%    Web links until it forms an n-by-n adjacency matrix of links.
%    The output U is a cell array of the URLs visited and
%    L is a sparse matrix with L(i,j) = 1 if url{i} links to url{j}.
%
%    Example:  [U,L] = surfer('http://www.ncsu.edu',500);
%
%    This function currently has two defects.  (1) The algorithm for
%    finding links is naive.  We just look for the string 'http:'.
%    (2) An attempt to read from a URL that is accessible, but very
%    slow, might take an unacceptably long time to complete.  In
%    some cases, it may be necessary to have the operating system
%    terminate MATLAB. Key words from such URLs can be added to the
%    skip list in surfer.m.

% Initialize

U = cell(n,1);
hash = zeros(n,1);
L = logical(sparse(n,n));
m = 1;
U{m} = root;
hash(m) = hashfun(root);

for j = 1:n

   % Try to open a page.
```

```
try
   disp(['open ' num2str(j) ' ' U{j}])
   page = urlread(U{j});
catch
   disp(['fail ' num2str(j) ' ' U{j}])
   continue
end

% Follow the links from the open page.

for f = findstr('http:',page);

   % A link starts with 'http:' and ends with next double quote.

   e = min(findstr('"',page(f:end)));
   if isempty(e), continue, end
   url = deblank(page(f:f+e-2));
   url(url<' ') = '!';    % Nonprintable characters
   if url(end) == '/', url(end) = []; end

   % Look for links that should be skipped.

   skips = {'.gif','.jpg','.pdf','.css','lmscadsi','cybernet',...
            'search.cgi','.ram','www.w3.org', ...
            'scripts','netscape','shockwave','webex','fansonly'};
   skip = any(url=='!') | any(url=='?');
   k = 0;
   while ~skip & (k < length(skips))
      k = k+1;
      skip = ~isempty(findstr(url,skips{k}));
   end
   if skip
      if isempty(findstr(url,'.gif')) & ...
         isempty(findstr(url,'.jpg'))
           disp(['     skip ' url])
      end
      continue
   end

   % Check if page is already in url list.

   i = 0;
   for k = find(hash(1:m) == hashfun(url))';
      if isequal(U{k},url)
         i = k;
         break
      end
   end

   % Add a new url to the graph there if are fewer than n.

   if (i == 0) & (m < n)
      m = m+1;
      U{m} = url;
      hash(m) = hashfun(url);
      i = m;
   end

   % Add a new link.
```

```
        if i > 0
            disp(['      link ' int2str(i) ' ' url])
            L(i,j) = 1;
        end
    end
end

%------------------------
function h = hashfun(url)
% Almost unique numeric hash code for pages already visited.
h = length(url) + 1024*sum(url);
```

2.2 THE CONTENT INDEX

Each new or refreshed page that a spider brings back is sent to the indexing module, where software programs parse the page content and strip it of its valuable information, so that only the essential skeleton of the page is passed to the appropriate indexes. Valuable information is contained in title, description, and **anchor text** as well as in bolded terms, terms in large font, and hyperlinks. One important index is the content index, which stores the textual information for each page in compressed form. An inverted file, which is used to store this compressed information, is like the index in the back of a book. Next to each term is a list of all locations where the term appears. In the simplest case, the location is the page identifier. An inverted file might look like:

- term 1 (aardvark) - 3, 117, 3961

  ⋮

- term 10 (aztec) - 3, 15, 19, 101, 673, 1199
- term 11 (baby) - 3, 31, 56, 94, 673, 909, 11114, 253791

  ⋮

- term m (zymurgy) - 1159223

This means that term 1 is used in webpages 3, 117, and 3961. It is clear that an advantage of the inverted file is its use as a quick lookup table. Processing a query on term 11 begins by consulting the inverted list for term 11.

The simple inverted file, a staple in traditional information retrieval [147], does pose some challenges for web collections. Because multilingual terms, phrases, and proper names are used, the number of terms m, and thus the file size, is huge. Also, the number of webpages using popular broad terms such as *weather* or *sports* is large. Therefore, the number of page identifiers next to these terms is large and consumes storage. Further, page identifiers are usually not the only descriptors stored for each term. See section 2.3. Other descriptors such as the location of the term in the page (title, description, or body) and the appearance of the term (bolded, large font, or in anchor text) are stored next to each page identifier. Any number of descriptors can be used to aid the search engine in retrieving relevant documents. In addition, as pages change content, so must their compressed representation in the inverted file. Thus, an active area of research is the design of methods for efficiently updating indexes. Lastly, the enormous inverted file must be stored on a distributed architecture, which means strategies for optimal partitioning must be designed.

ASIDE: Indexing Wars

While having a larger index of webpages accessed does not necessarily make one search engine better than another, it does mean the "bigger" search engine has a better opportunity to return a longer list of relevant results, especially for unusual queries. As a result, search engines are constantly battling for the title of "The World's Largest Index." Reporters writing for The Search Engine Showdown *or* Search Engine Watch *enjoy charting the changing leaders in the indexing war. Figure 2.1 shows how self-reported search engine sizes have changed over the years.*

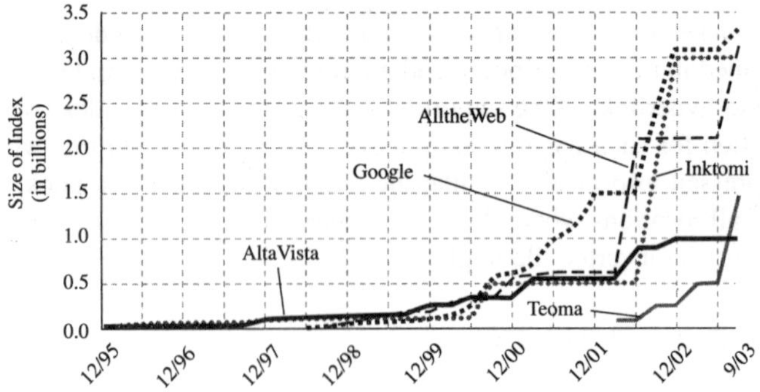

Figure 2.1 Growth of index for major search engines

Google, whose name is a play on googol, the word for the number 10^{100}*, entered the search market in 1998 and immediately grew, dethroning AltaVista and claiming the title of the World's Largest Index. In 2002, AlltheWeb snatched the title from Google by declaring it had reached the two billion mark. Google soon regained the lead by indexing three billion pages. AlltheWeb and Inktomi quickly upped their sizes to hit this same mark. The search latecomer Teoma has been steadily growing its index since its debut in early 2002. Web search engines use elaborate schemes, structures, and machines to store their massive indices. In fact, in 2003, Google used a network of over 15,000 computers to store their index [19], which in November 2004 jumped from 4.3 billion to 8.1 billion webpages. The number of servers used today is at least an order of magnitude higher. Figure 2.2 shows part of the server system that is housed in the Googleplex Mountain View, California site. Google history buffs can see the dramatic evolution of Google's server system by viewing pictures of their original servers that used a Lego-constructed cabinet to house disk drives and cooling fans (*`http://www-db.stanford.edu/pub/voy/museum/pictures/display/0-4-Google.htm`*).*

Figure 2.2 Google servers

The Internet Archive Project

In 1996 a nonprofit organization called the Internet Archive took on the arduous task of archiving the Web's contents–pages, images, video files, audio files, etc. This project archives old versions of pages, pages that are now extinct, as well as current pages. For example, to view the previous versions of author Carl Meyer's homepage, use the Internet Archive's Wayback Machine (`http://web.archive.org/`). Enter the address for Carl's current homepage, `http://meyer.math.ncsu.edu/`, and the Wayback machine returns archived versions and the dates of updates to this page. A temporary addition to the Archive website was a beta version of Anna Patterson's Recall search engine. Because this engine was tailored to archival search, it had some novel features such as time-series plots of the relevancy of search terms over time. (Perhaps such features will become commonplace in mainstream engines, as Patterson now works for Google.) One of the archive's goals is to make sure information on ephemeral pages is not lost forever because valuable trends and cultural artifacts exist in such pages. The archive also allows for systematic tracking of the Web's evolution. Of course, as the Internet Archive Project continues to grow and receive support, it will inevitably claim the undisputed title of Index King, and hold the world's largest document collection.

2.3 QUERY PROCESSING

Unlike the crawler and indexing modules of a search engine, the query module's operations depend on the user. The query module must process user queries in real-time, and return results in milliseconds. In February 2003, Google reported serving 250 million searches per day, while Overture and Inktomi handled 167 and 80 million, respectively [156]. Google likes to keep their processing time under half a second. In order to process a query this quickly, the query module accesses precomputed indexes such as the content index and the structure index.

Consider an example that uses the inverted file below, which is copied from section 2.2.

- term 1 (aardvark) — 3, 117, 3961

  ⋮

- term 10 (aztec) — 3, 15, 19, 101, 673, 1199
- term 11 (baby) — 3, 31, 56, 94, 673, 909, 11114, 253791

  ⋮

- term m (zymurgy) — 1159223

Suppose a user enters the unusual query of `aztec baby`, and the search engine assumes the Boolean AND is used. Then the query module consults the inverted lists for `aztec`, which is term 10, and `baby`, which is term 11. The resulting set of "on topic" or relevant pages is {3, 673} because these pages use both query terms. Many traditional search engines stop here, returning this list to the user. However, for broad queries on the vast web collection, this set of relevant pages can be huge, containing hundreds of thousands of pages. Therefore, rankings are imposed on the pages in this set to make the list of retrieved pages more manageable. Consequently, the query module passes its list of relevant pages to the ranking module, which creates the list of pages ordered from most relevant to least relevant. The ranking module accesses precomputed indexes to create a ranking at query-time. In Chapter 1, we mentioned that search engines combine content scores for relevant pages with popularity scores to generate an overall score for each page. Relevant pages are then sorted by their overall scores.

We describe the creation of the content score with an example that also shows how the inverted file can be expanded to include more information. Suppose document 94 is updated by its author and now contains information about term 10 (`aztec`). This means that the inverted file must be updated, with the document identifier of 94 added to the list of pages recorded next to term 10. However, suppose that rather than storing just the document identifier, we decide to store three additional pieces of information. First, we record whether the term in question (`aztec`) appears in the title. Second, we record the term's appearance (or not) in the description metatag. Finally, we record a count of the number of times the term appears in the page. One way to record this information is to append a vector to the document identifier for page 94 as follows:

$$\text{term 10 (aztec)} — \ 3, 15, 19, 94\,[1, 0, 7], 101, 673, 1199.$$

In the vector $[1, 0, 7]$, the 1 means that term 10 appears in the title tag of page 94, the 0 means that term 10 does not appear in the description tag of page 94, and the 7 means that term 10 occurred seven times in page 94. Similar information must be added to each element in the inverted file. That is, for every term, a three-dimensional vector must be inserted after each page identifier. While more work must be done by the indexing module and more storage used by the content index, the additional content information makes the search engine much better at processing queries. This is achieved by creating a content score for each page in the relevant set, which is now $\{3, 94, 673\}$ in our example. At query time, the query module consults the inverted file, and for each document in the relevant set, pulls off the document identifier along with its appended three-dimensional vector. Suppose the result is:

$$\text{term 10 (aztec)} - 3\,[1, 1, 27], 94\,[1, 0, 7], 673\,[0, 0, 3]$$
$$\text{term 11 (baby)} - 3\,[1, 1, 10], 94\,[0, 0, 5], 673\,[1, 1, 14]$$

Heuristics or rules are now applied to determine an content score for documents 3, 94, and 673. One elementary heuristic adds the values in the three-dimensional vector for term 10/page 3 and multiplies this by the sum of the values in the vector for term 11/page 3. Thus, the content scores for the three relevant pages are:

$$\text{content score (page 3)} = (1 + 1 + 27) \times (1 + 1 + 10) = 348,$$
$$\text{content score (page 94)} = (1 + 0 + 7) \times (0 + 0 + 5) = 40,$$
$$\text{content score (page 673)} = (0 + 0 + 3) \times (1 + 1 + 14) = 48.$$

Different schemes exist with many other factors making up the content score [30].

The content score can be computed solely from the content index and its inverted file, and is query-dependent. On the other hand, the popularity score is computed solely from the structure index, and is usually query-independent. The remainder of this book is devoted to the popularity score, so we postpone its description and computation until later. For now, we merely state that each page on the Web has a popularity score, which is independent of user queries and which gives a global measure of that page's popularity within the search engine's entire index of pages. This popularity score is then combined with the content score, for example, by multiplication, to create an overall score for each relevant page for a given query.

Lord Campbell's Motion to Index

John Campbell (1799–1861) was a Scottish lawyer and politician who became Lord Chancellor of Great Britain in 1859. In the preface to volume 3 of his book, *Lives of the Chief Justices* [45], Lord Campbell writes:

> So essential do I consider an Index to be to every book, that I proposed to bring a Bill into Parliament to deprive an author who publishes a book without an Index of the privilege of copyright; and, moreover, to subject him, for his offence, to a pecuniary penalty.

Unfortunately, his bill was never enacted, perhaps because Parliamentary members and their constituents wanted to shirk the responsibility and effort associated with creating a good index.

Appeals similar to Lord Campbell's have been made by the web community and its indexers. W3C, the World Wide Web Consortium, has been pushing for a more rigorous structure for HTML documents (e.g., XML documents and RSS code) that will allow the indexers of search engines to more accurately and quickly pull the essential elements from documents. On the other hand, the Web's lack of structure is recognized universally as a source of its strength and a major contributor to its many creative uses. In an attempt to outline a balance between structure and freedom, in July 1997, former President Bill Clinton wrote the "Framework for Global Electronic Commerce," which advocated a laissez-faire attitude toward web legislation and regulation.

Chapter Three

Ranking Webpages by Popularity

Nobody wants to be picked last for teams in gym class. Likewise, nobody wants their webpage to appear last in the list of relevant pages for a search query. As a result, many grown-ups transfer their high school wishes to be the "Most Popular" to their webpages. The remainder of this book is about the popularity contests that search engines hold for webpages. Specifically, it's about the popularity score, which is combined with the traditional content score of section 2.3 to rank retrieved pages by relevance. By 1998, the traditional content score was buckling under the Web's massive size and the death grip of spammers. In 1998, the popularity score came to the rescue of the content score. The popularity score became a crucial complement to the content score and provided search engines with impressively accurate results for all types of queries. The popularity score, also known as the importance score, harnesses the information in the immense graph created by the Web's hyperlink structure. Thus, models exploiting the Web's hyperlink structure are called link analysis models. The impact that these link analysis models have had is truly awesome. Since 1998, the use of web search engines has increased dramatically. In fact, an April 2004 survey by Websense, Inc., reported that half of the respondents would rather forfeit their habitual morning cup of coffee than their connectivity. That's because today's search tools allow users to answer in seconds queries that were impossible just a decade ago (from fun searches for pictures, quotes, and snooping amateur detective work to more serious searches for academic research papers and patented inventions). In this chapter, we introduce the intuition behind the classic link analysis systems of PageRank [40] and HITS [106].

3.1 THE SCENE IN 1998

The year 1998 was a busy year for link analysis models. At IBM Almaden in Silicon Valley, a young scientist named Jon Kleinberg, now a professor at Cornell University, was working on a Web search engine project called HITS, an acronym for Hypertext Induced Topic Search. His algorithm used the hyperlink structure of the Web to improve search engine results, an innovative idea at the time, as most search engines used only textual content to return relevant documents. He presented his work [106], begun a year earlier at IBM, in January 1998 at the Ninth Annual ACM-SIAM Symposium on Discrete Algorithms held in San Francisco, California.

Very nearby, at Stanford University, two computer science doctoral candidates were working late nights on a similar project called PageRank. Sergey Brin and Larry Page had been collaborating on their Web search engine since 1995. By 1998, things were really starting to accelerate for these two scientists. They were using their dorm rooms as offices for their fledgling business, which later became the giant Google. By August 1998, both Brin (right) and Page (left) took a leave of absence from Stanford in order to focus on their growing business. In a public presentation at the Seventh International World Wide Web conference (WWW98) in Brisbane, Australia, their paper "The anatomy of a large-scale hypertextual Web search engine" [39] made small ripples in the information science community that quickly turned into waves. It appears that HITS and PageRank were developed independently despite the close geographic and temporal proximity of the discoveries. The connections between the two models are striking (see [110]). Nevertheless, since that eventful year, PageRank has emerged as the dominant link analysis model, partly due to its query-independence (see section 3.3), its virtual immunity to spamming, and Google's huge business success. Kleinberg was already making a name for himself as an innovative academic, and unlike Brin and Page did not try to develop HITS into a company. However, later entrepreneurs did, thus giving HITS its belated and deserving claim to commercial success. The search engine Teoma uses an extension of the HITS algorithm as the basis of its underlying technology [150]. Incidentally, Google has kept Brin and Page famously busy and wealthy enough to remain on leave from Stanford, as well as make their debut break into People's June 28th List of the 50 Hottest Bachelors of 2004.

3.2 TWO THESES

In this section, we describe the theses underlying both PageRank and HITS. In order to do that, we need to define the Web as a graph. The Web's **hyperlink** structure forms a massive directed graph. The nodes in the graph represent webpages and the directed arcs or links represent the hyperlinks. Thus, hyperlinks into a page, which are called **inlinks**, point into nodes, while **outlinks** point out from nodes. Figure 3.1 shows a tiny, artificial document collection consisting of six webpages.

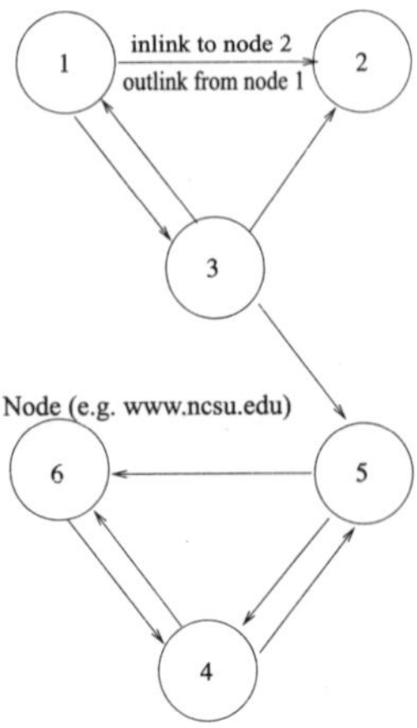

Figure 3.1 Directed graph representing web of six pages

Maps of the Web Graph

The massive web graph has little resemblance to the clean tiny graph of Figure 3.1. Instead, the Web's nodes and arcs create a jumbled mess that's a headache to untangle and present in a visually appealing and meaningful way. Fortunately, many researchers have succeeded. *The Atlas of Cyberspace* [62] presents over 300 colorful, informative maps of cyberactivities. With permission, we present a hyperlink graph that was the graduate work of Stanford's Tamara Munzner. She used three-dimensional hyperbolic spaces to produce the map on the left side of Figure 3.2. Munzner's ideas were implemented by Young Hyun in his Java software program called Walrus (even though the pictures it draws look like jellyfish.) The right side of Figure 3.2 is one of Hyun's maps with 535,102 nodes and 601,678 links.

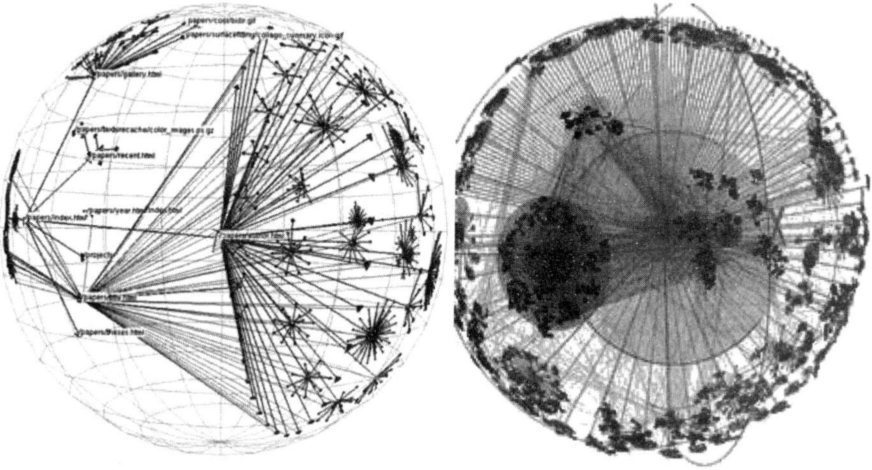

Figure 3.2 Munzner's and Hyun's maps of subsets of the Web

3.2.1 PageRank

Before 1998, the web graph was largely an untapped source of information. While researchers like Kleinberg and Brin and Page recognized this graph's potential, most people wondered just what the web graph had to do with search engine results. The connection is understood by viewing a hyperlink as a recommendation. A hyperlink from my homepage to your page is my endorsement of your page. Thus, a page with more recommendations (which are realized through inlinks) must be more important than a page with a few inlinks. However, similar to other recommendation systems such as bibliographic citations or letters of reference, the status of the recommender is also important. For example, one personal endorsement from Donald Trump probably does more to strengthen a job application than 20 endorsements from 20 unknown teachers and colleagues. On the other hand, if the job interviewer learns that Donald Trump is very free and generous with his praises of employees, and he (or his secretary) has written over 40,000 recommendations in his life, then his recommendation suddenly drops in weight. Thus, weights signifying the status of a recommender must be lowered for recommenders with little discrimination. In fact, the weight of each endorsement should be tempered by the total number of recommendations made by the recommender.

Actually, this is exactly how Google's PageRank popularity score works. This PageRank score is very famous, even notoriously so (see the asides on pages 52 and 112). Literally hundreds of papers have been written about it, and this book is one of the first of the undoubtedly many that is devoted to PageRank's methodology, mechanism, and computation. In the coming chapters we will reveal many reasons why PageRank has become so popular, but one of the most convincing reasons for studying the PageRank score is Google's own admission of its impact on their successful technology. According to the Google website (`http://www.google.com/technology/index.html`) "the heart of [Google's] software is PageRank . . . [which] continues to provide the basis for all of [our] web search tools."

In short, *PageRank's thesis is that a webpage is important if it is pointed to by other important pages.* Sounds circular, doesn't it? We will see in Chapter 4 that this can be formalized in a beautifully simple mathematical formula.

Google Toolbar

Comparing the PageRank scores for two pages gives an indication of the relative importance of the two pages. However, Google guards the exact PageRank scores for the pages in its index very carefully, and for good reason. (See the aside on page 52.) Google does graciously provide public access to a very rough approximation of their PageRank scores. These approximations are available through the Google toolbar, which can be downloaded at `http://toolbar.google.com/`. The toolbar, which then resides on the browser, displays a lone bar graph showing the approximate PageRank for the current page. The displayed PageRank is an integer from 0 to 10, with the most important pages receiving a PageRank of 10. The toolbar automatically updates this display for each page you visit. Thus, it must send information about the page you're viewing to the Google servers. Google's privacy policy states that it does not collect information that directly identifies you (e.g., your name or email address) and will not sell any information. For those still concerned with their privacy, Google allows users to disable the PageRank feature while still maintaining the functionality of the other toolbar features. There's a way to access the approximate PageRank scores without getting the Toolbar—visit `http://www.seochat.com/seo-tools/PageRank-search/`, enter a query, and view the PageRank bar graphs next to the results. Readers can get a feel for PageRank by locating high PageRank pages (e.g., `www.espn.com` with a 9/10 score) and low PageRank pages (`http://www.csc.ncsu.edu:8080/nsmc2003/` with a 0/10 score). Google's homepage (`www.google.com`) has a PageRank of 10, perhaps automatically set. Google sets the PageRank of pages identified to be authored by spammers to 0 [160], a value known among spammers as the horrifying **PR0**.

3.2.2 HITS

Kleinberg's HITS method for ranking pages is very similar to PageRank, but it uses both inlinks and outlinks to create two popularity scores for each page. HITS defines hubs and authorities. A page is considered a hub if, similar in some respects to an airline hub, it contains many outlinks. With an equally descriptive term, a page is called an authority if it has many inlinks. Of course, a page can be both a hub and an authority, just as the Hartsfield–Jackson Atlanta airport has many incoming and outgoing flights each hour. Thus, HITS assigns both a hub score and an authority score to each page. Very similar to PageRank's lone circular thesis, HITS has a pair of interdependent circular theses: *a page is a good hub (and therefore deserves a high hub score) if it points to good authorities, and a page is a good authority if it is pointed to by good hubs*. Like PageRank, these circular definitions create simple mathematical formulas. Readers will have to wait until Chapter 11 to hear the details of HITS. Although developed during 1997–1998, HITS was not incorporated into a commercial search engine until 2001 when the search newcomer Teoma adopted it as the heart of its underlying technology [150]. Check out Teoma at `www.teoma.com`, and notice that the pages listed as "Results" correspond to HITS authorities and the pages listed under "Resources" correspond to HITS hubs.

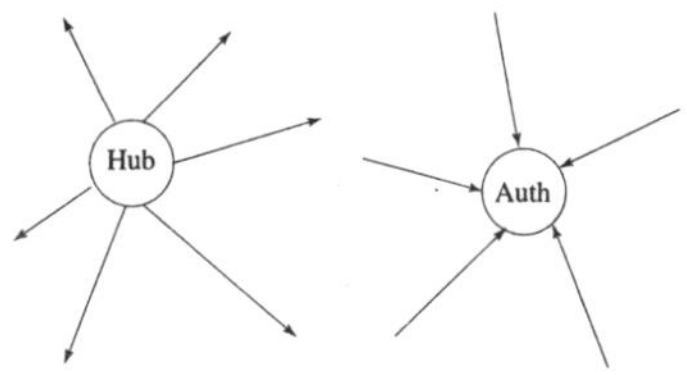

Figure 3.3 A hub node and an authority node

Inlink Feature

Of course, every webpage author knows exactly how many outlinks his or her page has and to which pages these outlinks point. However, getting a hold on inlink counts and inlinking pages is not as obvious. Fortunately, with the help of third party services, it is equally easy to uncover this inlink information. For example, Google's `link:` feature can be used to see how many and which, if any, important pages point to yours. Try typing `link:http://www4.ncsu.edu:8030/~anlangvi` into Google's input box and notice the modest number of inlinks to Amy's homepage. (If you like this book and our research, you can help both of us improve our popularity scores with recommendations through hyperlinks. We prefer inlinks from authors of important pages. Of course, we joke in this parenthetical comment but our comments foreshadow some of the exciting and serious side effects associated with link analysis. See the asides on search engine optimization and link farms on pages 43 and 52, respectively.) To find out how many inlinks your page has in the indexes of other search engines, go to `http://www.top25web.com/cgi-bin/linkpop.cgi`. This website also provides other tools, such as a ranking report and PageRank score that reports the Toolbar scores for several pages at once.

3.3 QUERY-INDEPENDENCE

It is now time to emphasize the word *query-independence*. A ranking is called query-independent if the popularity score for each page is determined off-line, and remains constant (until the next update) regardless of the query. This means at query time, when milliseconds are precious, no time is spent computing the popularity scores for relevant pages. The scores are merely "looked up" in the previously computed popularity table. This can be contrasted with the traditional information retrieval scores of section 2.3, which are query-dependent. We will see that popularity scoring systems can be classified as either query-independent or query-dependent. This classification is important because it immediately reveals a system's advantages and disadvantages. PageRank is query-independent, which means it produces a global ranking of the importance of all pages in Google's index of 8.1 billion pages. On the other hand, HITS in its original version is query-dependent. Both PageRank and HITS can be modified to change their classifications. See Chapter 11.

Who Links to Whom

The science of who links to whom has extended beyond the Web to a variety of other networks that collectively go by the name of complex systems. Graph techniques have successfully been applied to learn valuable information about networks ranging from the AIDS transmission and power grid networks to terrorist and email networks. The recent book by Barabasi, *Linked: The New Science of Networks* [16], contains a fascinating and entertaining introduction to these complex systems.

Chapter Four

The Mathematics of Google's PageRank

The famous and colorful mathematician Paul Erdos (1913–96) talked about The Great Book, a make-believe book in which he imagined God kept the world's most elegant and beautiful proofs. In 2002, Graham Farmelo of London's Science Museum edited and contributed to a similar book, a book of beautiful equations. *It Must Be Beautiful: Great Equations of Modern Science* [73] is a collection of 11 essays about the greatest scientific equations, equations like $E = hf$ and $E = mc^2$. The contributing authors were invited to give their answers to the tough question of what makes an equation great. One author, Frank Wilczek, included a quote by Heinrich Hertz regarding Maxwell's equation:

> One cannot escape the feeling that these mathematical formulae have an independent existence and an intelligence of their own, that they are wiser than we are, wiser even than their discoverers, that we get more out of them than was originally put into them.

While we are not suggesting that the PageRank equation presented in this chapter,

$$\boldsymbol{\pi}^T = \boldsymbol{\pi}^T(\alpha\mathbf{S} + (1-\alpha)\mathbf{E}),$$

deserves a place in Farmelo's book alongside Einstein's theory of relativity, we do find Hertz's statement apropos. One can get a lot of mileage from the simple PageRank formula above—Google certainly has. Since beauty is in the eye of the beholder, we'll let you decide whether or not the PageRank formula deserves the adjective *beautiful*. We hope the next few chapters will convince you that it just might.

In Chapter 3, we used words to present the PageRank thesis: a page is important if it is pointed to by other important pages. It is now time to translate these words into mathematical equations. This translation reveals that the PageRank importance scores are actually the stationary values of an enormous Markov chain, and consequently Markov theory explains many interesting properties of the elegantly simple PageRank model used by Google.

This is the first of the mathematical chapters. Many of the mathematical terms in each chapter are explained in the Mathematics Chapter (Chapter 15). As terms that appear in the Mathematics Chapter are introduced in the text, they are italicized to remind you that definitions and more information can be found in Chapter 15.

4.1 THE ORIGINAL SUMMATION FORMULA FOR PAGERANK

Brin and Page, the inventors of PageRank,[1] began with a simple summation equation, the roots of which actually derive from bibliometrics research, the analysis of the citation structure among academic papers. The PageRank of a page P_i, denoted $r(P_i)$, is the sum of the PageRanks of all pages pointing into P_i.

$$r(P_i) = \sum_{P_j \in B_{P_i}} \frac{r(P_j)}{|P_j|}, \tag{4.1.1}$$

where B_{P_i} is the set of pages pointing into P_i (backlinking to P_i in Brin and Page's words) and $|P_j|$ is the number of outlinks from page P_j. Notice that the PageRank of inlinking pages $r(P_j)$ in equation (4.1.1)) is tempered by the number of recommendations made by P_j, denoted $|P_j|$. The problem with equation (4.1.1) is that the $r(P_j)$ values, the PageRanks of pages inlinking to page P_i, are unknown. To sidestep this problem, Brin and Page used an iterative procedure. That is, they assumed that, in the beginning, all pages have equal PageRank (of say, $1/n$, where n is the number of pages in Google's index of the Web). Now the rule in equation (4.1.1) is followed to compute $r(P_i)$ for each page P_i in the index. The rule in equation (4.1.1) is successively applied, substituting the values of the previous iterate into $r(P_j)$. We introduce some more notation in order to define this *iterative procedure*. Let $r_{k+1}(P_i)$ be the PageRank of page P_i at iteration $k+1$. Then,

$$r_{k+1}(P_i) = \sum_{P_j \in B_{P_i}} \frac{r_k(P_j)}{|P_j|}. \tag{4.1.2}$$

This process is initiated with $r_0(P_i) = 1/n$ for all pages P_i and repeated with the hope that the PageRank scores will eventually converge to some final stable values. Applying equation (4.1.2) to the tiny web of Figure 4.1 gives the following values for the PageRanks after a few iterations.

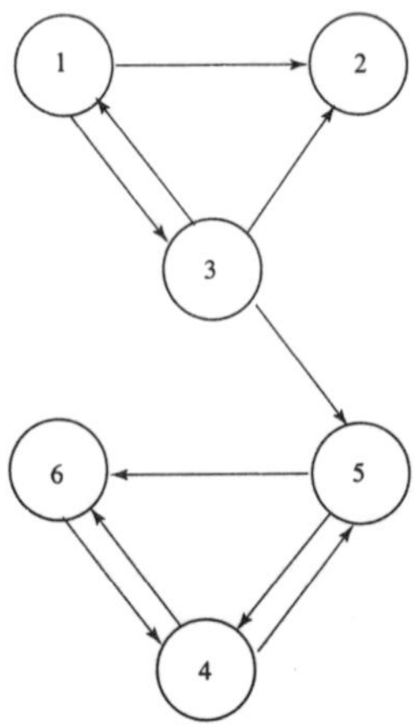

Figure 4.1 Directed graph representing web of six pages

[1]The patent for PageRank was filed in 1998 by Larry Page and granted in 2001 (US Patent #6285999), and thus the name PageRank has a double reference to both webpages and one of its founding fathers.

Table 4.1 First few iterates using (4.1.2) on Figure 4.1

Iteration 0	Iteration 1	Iteration 2	Rank at Iter. 2
$r_0(P_1) = 1/6$	$r_1(P_1) = 1/18$	$r_2(P_1) = 1/36$	5
$r_0(P_2) = 1/6$	$r_1(P_2) = 5/36$	$r_2(P_2) = 1/18$	4
$r_0(P_3) = 1/6$	$r_1(P_3) = 1/12$	$r_2(P_3) = 1/36$	5
$r_0(P_4) = 1/6$	$r_1(P_4) = 1/4$	$r_2(P_4) = 17/72$	1
$r_0(P_5) = 1/6$	$r_1(P_5) = 5/36$	$r_2(P_5) = 11/72$	3
$r_0(P_6) = 1/6$	$r_1(P_6) = 1/6$	$r_2(P_6) = 14/72$	2

4.2 MATRIX REPRESENTATION OF THE SUMMATION EQUATIONS

Equations (4.1.1) and (4.1.2) compute PageRank one page at a time. Using *matrices*, we replace the tedious $\sum$ symbol, and at each iteration, compute a PageRank vector, which uses a single $1 \times n$ *vector* to hold the PageRank values for all pages in the index. In order to do this, we introduce an $n \times n$ matrix $\mathbf{H}$ and a $1 \times n$ row vector $\boldsymbol{\pi}^T$. The matrix $\mathbf{H}$ is a row normalized *hyperlink* matrix with $\mathbf{H}_{ij} = 1/|P_i|$ if there is a link from node i to node j, and 0, otherwise. Although $\mathbf{H}$ has the same nonzero structure as the binary *adjacency matrix* for the graph (called `L` in the Matlab Crawler m-file on page 17), its nonzero elements are probabilities. Consider once again the tiny web graph of Figure 4.1.

The $\mathbf{H}$ matrix for this graph is

$$\mathbf{H} = \begin{array}{c} \\ P_1 \\ P_2 \\ P_3 \\ P_4 \\ P_5 \\ P_6 \end{array} \begin{array}{c} \begin{array}{cccccc} P_1 & P_2 & P_3 & P_4 & P_5 & P_6 \end{array} \\ \begin{pmatrix} 0 & 1/2 & 1/2 & 0 & 0 & 0 \\ 0 & 0 & 0 & 0 & 0 & 0 \\ 1/3 & 1/3 & 0 & 0 & 1/3 & 0 \\ 0 & 0 & 0 & 0 & 1/2 & 1/2 \\ 0 & 0 & 0 & 1/2 & 0 & 1/2 \\ 0 & 0 & 0 & 1 & 0 & 0 \end{pmatrix} \end{array}.$$

The nonzero elements of row i correspond to the outlinking pages of page i, whereas the nonzero elements of column i correspond to the inlinking pages of page i. We now introduce a row vector $\boldsymbol{\pi}^{(k)T}$, which is the PageRank vector at the kth iteration. Using this matrix notation, equation (4.1.2) can be written compactly as

$$\boldsymbol{\pi}^{(k+1)T} = \boldsymbol{\pi}^{(k)T}\mathbf{H}. \tag{4.2.1}$$

If you like, verify with the example of Figure 4.1 that the iterates of equation (4.2.1) match those of equation (4.1.2).

Matrix equation (4.2.1) yields some immediate observations.

1. Each iteration of equation (4.2.1) involves one vector-matrix multiplication, which generally requires $O(n^2)$ *computation*, where n is the size of the square matrix $\mathbf{H}$.

2. $\mathbf{H}$ is a very *sparse* matrix (a large proportion of its elements are 0) because most webpages link to only a handful of other pages. Sparse matrices, such as the one shown in Figure 4.2, are welcome for several reasons. First, they require minimal storage, since sparse storage schemes, which store only the nonzero elements of the

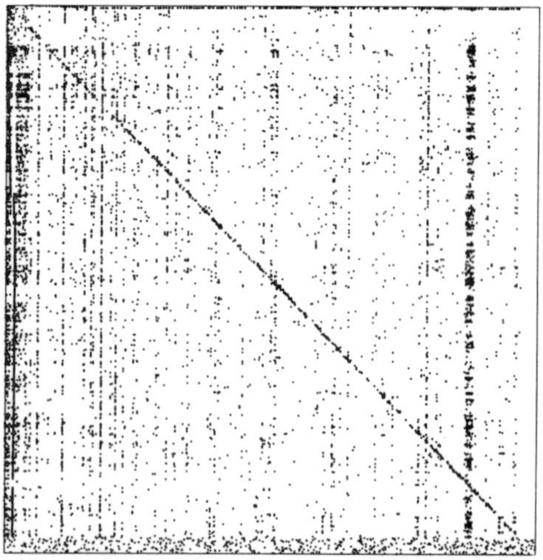

Figure 4.2 Example of a sparse matrix. The nonzero elements are indicated by pixels.

matrix and their location [145], exist. Second, vector-matrix multiplication involving a sparse matrix requires much less effort than the $O(n^2)$ *dense* computation. In fact, it requires $O(nnz(\mathbf{H}))$ computation, where $nnz(\mathbf{H})$ is the number of nonzeros in $\mathbf{H}$. Estimates show that the average webpage has about 10 outlinks, which means that $\mathbf{H}$ has about $10n$ nonzeros, as opposed to the n^2 nonzeros in a completely dense matrix. This means that the vector-matrix multiplication of equation (4.2.1) reduces to $O(n)$ effort.

3. The iterative process of equation (4.2.1) is a simple *linear stationary process* of the form studied in most numerical analysis classes [82, 127]. In fact, it is the classical *power method* applied to $\mathbf{H}$.

4. $\mathbf{H}$ looks a lot like a *stochastic transition probability matrix* for a *Markov chain.* The **dangling nodes** of the network, those nodes with no outlinks, create 0 rows in the matrix. All the other rows, which correspond to the nondangling nodes, create stochastic rows. Thus, $\mathbf{H}$ is called *substochastic.*

These four observations are important to the development and execution of the PageRank model, and we will return to them throughout the chapter. For now, we spend more time examining the iterative matrix equation (4.2.1).

4.3 PROBLEMS WITH THE ITERATIVE PROCESS

Equation (4.2.1) probably caused readers, especially our mathematical readers, to ask several questions. For example,

- Will this iterative process continue indefinitely or will it converge?
- Under what circumstances or properties of $\mathbf{H}$ is it guaranteed to converge?

- Will it converge to something that makes sense in the context of the PageRank problem?
- Will it converge to just one vector or multiple vectors?
- Does the convergence depend on the starting vector $\pi^{(0)T}$?
- If it will converge eventually, how long is "eventually"? That is, how many iterations can we expect until convergence?

We'll answer these questions in the next few sections. However, our answers depend on how Brin and Page chose to resolve some of the problems they encountered with their equation (4.2.1).

Brin and Page originally started the iterative process with $\pi^{(0)T} = 1/n\,\mathbf{e}^T$, where $\mathbf{e}^T$ is the row vector of all 1s. They immediately ran into several problems when using equation (4.2.1) with this initial vector. For example, there is the problem of **rank sinks**, those pages that accumulate more and more PageRank at each iteration, monopolizing the scores and refusing to share. In the simple example of Figure 4.3, the dangling node 3 is a rank sink. In the more complicated example of Figure 4.1, the cluster of nodes 4, 5,

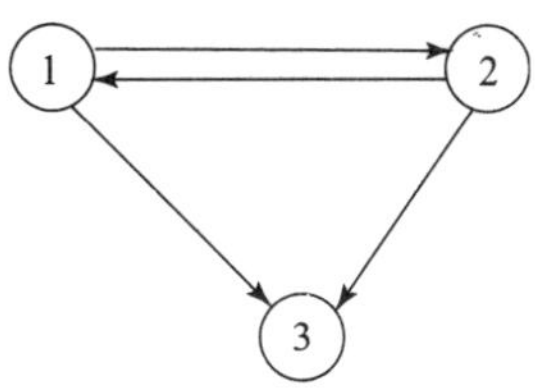

Figure 4.3 Simple graph with rank sink

and 6 conspire to hoard PageRank. After just 13 iterations of equation (4.2.1), $\pi^{(13)T} = (\,0 \quad 0 \quad 0 \quad 2/3 \quad 1/3 \quad 1/5\,)$. This conspiring can be malicious or inadvertent. (See the asides on search engine optimization and link farms on pages 43 and 52, respectively.) The example with $\pi^{(13)T}$ also shows another problem caused by sinks. As nodes hoard PageRank, some nodes may be left with none. Thus, ranking nodes by their PageRank values is tough when a majority of the nodes are tied with PageRank 0. Ideally, we'd prefer the PageRank vector to be positive, i.e., contain all positive values.

There's also the problem of **cycles**. Consider the simplest case in Figure 4.4. Page

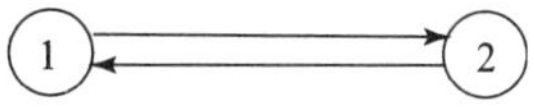

Figure 4.4 Simple graph with cycle

1 only points to page 2 and vice versa, creating an infinite loop or cycle. Suppose the iterative process of equation (4.2.1) is run with $\pi^{(0)T} = (\,1 \quad 0\,)$. The iterates will not converge no matter how long the process is run. The iterates $\pi^{(k)T}$ flip-flop indefinitely between $(\,1 \quad 0\,)$ when k is even and $(\,0 \quad 1\,)$ when k is odd.

4.4 A LITTLE MARKOV CHAIN THEORY

Before we get to Brin and Page's adjustments to equation (4.2.1), which solve the problems of the previous section, we pause to introduce a little theory for Markov chains. (We urge readers who are less familiar with Markov chains to read the Mathematics Chapter, Chapter 15, before proceeding.) In observations 3 and 4, we noted that equation (4.2.1) resembled the power method applied to a Markov chain with *transition probability matrix* $\mathbf{H}$. These observations are very helpful because the theory of Markov chains is well developed,[2] and very applicable to the PageRank problem. With Markov theory we can make adjustments to equation (4.2.1) that insure desirable results, convergence properties, and encouraging answers to the questions on page 34. In particular, we know that, for any starting vector, the power method applied to a Markov matrix $\mathbf{P}$ converges to a unique positive vector called the *stationary vector* as long as $\mathbf{P}$ is *stochastic, irreducible*, and *aperiodic*. (Aperiodicity plus irreducibility implies primitivity.) Therefore, the PageRank convergence problems caused by sinks and cycles can be overcome if $\mathbf{H}$ is modified slightly so that it is a Markov matrix with these desired properties.

Markov properties affecting PageRank

A unique positive PageRank vector exists when the Google matrix is stochastic and irreducible. Further, with the additional property of aperiodicity, the power method will converge to this PageRank vector, regardless of the starting vector for the iterative process.

4.5 EARLY ADJUSTMENTS TO THE BASIC MODEL

In fact, this is exactly what Brin and Page did. They describe their adjustments to the basic PageRank model in their original 1998 papers. It is interesting to note that none of their papers used the phrase "Markov chain," not even once. Although, most surely, if they were unaware of it in 1998, they now know the connection their original model has to Markov chains, as Markov chain researchers have excitedly and steadily jumped on the PageRank bandwagon, eager to work on what some call the grand application of Markov chains.

Rather than using Markov chains and their properties to describe their adjustments, Brin and Page use the notion of a **random surfer**. Imagine a web surfer who bounces along randomly following the hyperlink structure of the Web. That is, when he arrives at a page with several outlinks, he chooses one at random, hyperlinks to this new page, and continues this random decision process indefinitely. In the long run, the proportion of time the random surfer spends on a given page is a measure of the relative importance of that page. If he spends a large proportion of his time on a particular page, then he must have, in randomly following the hyperlink structure of the Web, repeatedly found himself returning to that page. Pages that he revisits often must be important, because they must be pointed to by other important pages. Unfortunately, this random surfer encounters some problems. He gets caught whenever he enters a dangling node. And on the Web there are plenty of nodes dangling, e.g., pdf files, image files, data tables, etc. To fix this, Brin and Page define

[2] Almost 100 years ago in 1906, Andrei Andreyevich Markov invented the chains that after 1926 bore his name [20].

their first adjustment, which we call the **stochasticity adjustment** because the $\mathbf{0}^T$ rows of $\mathbf{H}$ are replaced with $1/n\,\mathbf{e}^T$, thereby making $\mathbf{H}$ stochastic. As a result, the random surfer, after entering a dangling node, can now hyperlink to any page at random. For the tiny 6-node web of Figure 4.1, the **stochastic matrix** called $\mathbf{S}$ is

$$\mathbf{S} = \begin{pmatrix} 0 & 1/2 & 1/2 & 0 & 0 & 0 \\ 1/6 & 1/6 & 1/6 & 1/6 & 1/6 & 1/6 \\ 1/3 & 1/3 & 0 & 0 & 1/3 & 0 \\ 0 & 0 & 0 & 0 & 1/2 & 1/2 \\ 0 & 0 & 0 & 1/2 & 0 & 1/2 \\ 0 & 0 & 0 & 1 & 0 & 0 \end{pmatrix}.$$

Writing this stochasticity fix mathematically reveals that $\mathbf{S}$ is created from a *rank-one update* to $\mathbf{H}$. That is, $\mathbf{S} = \mathbf{H} + \mathbf{a}(1/n\,\mathbf{e}^T)$, where $a_i = 1$ if page i is a dangling node and 0 otherwise. The binary vector $\mathbf{a}$ is called the **dangling node vector**. $\mathbf{S}$ is a combination of the raw original hyperlink matrix $\mathbf{H}$ and a rank-one matrix $1/n\,\mathbf{a}\mathbf{e}^T$.

This adjustment guarantees that $\mathbf{S}$ is stochastic, and thus, is the transition probability matrix for a Markov chain. However, it alone cannot guarantee the convergence results desired. (That is, that a unique positive $\boldsymbol{\pi}^T$ exists and that equation (4.2.1) will converge to this $\boldsymbol{\pi}^T$ quickly.) Brin and Page needed another adjustment–this time a **primitivity adjustment**. With this adjustment, the resulting matrix is stochastic and *primitive*. A primitive matrix is both irreducible and aperiodic. Thus, the stationary vector of the chain (which is the PageRank vector in this case) exists, is unique, and can be found by a simple power iteration. Brin and Page once again use the random surfer to describe these Markov properties.

The random surfer argument for the primitivity adjustment goes like this. While it is true that surfers follow the hyperlink structure of the Web, at times they get bored and abandon the hyperlink method of surfing by entering a new destination in the browser's URL line. When this happens, the random surfer, like a Star Trek character, "teleports" to the new page, where he begins hyperlink surfing again, until the next teleportation, and so on. To model this activity mathematically, Brin and Page invented a new matrix $\mathbf{G}$, such that

$$\mathbf{G} = \alpha\mathbf{S} + (1-\alpha)1/n\,\mathbf{e}\mathbf{e}^T,$$

where α is a scalar between 0 and 1. $\mathbf{G}$ is called the **Google matrix**. In this model, α is a parameter that controls the proportion of time the random surfer follows the hyperlinks as opposed to teleporting. Suppose $\alpha = .6$. Then 60% of the time the random surfer follows the hyperlink structure of the Web and the other 40% of the time he teleports to a random new page. The teleporting is random because the teleportation matrix $\mathbf{E} = 1/n\,\mathbf{e}\mathbf{e}^T$ is uniform, meaning the surfer is equally likely, when teleporting, to jump to any page.

There are several consequences of the primitivity adjustment.

- $\mathbf{G}$ is *stochastic*. It is the *convex combination* of the two stochastic matrices $\mathbf{S}$ and $\mathbf{E} = 1/n\,\mathbf{e}\mathbf{e}^T$.

- $\mathbf{G}$ is *irreducible*. Every page is directly connected to every other page, so irreducibility is trivially enforced.
- $\mathbf{G}$ is *aperiodic*. The self-loops ($\mathbf{G}_{ii} > 0$ for all i) create aperiodicity.
- $\mathbf{G}$ is *primitive* because $\mathbf{G}^k > 0$ for some k. (In fact, this holds for $k = 1$.) This implies that a unique positive $\boldsymbol{\pi}^T$ exists, and the power method applied to $\mathbf{G}$ is guaranteed to converge to this vector.
- $\mathbf{G}$ is completely *dense*, which is a very bad thing, computationally. Fortunately, $\mathbf{G}$ can be written as a *rank-one update* to the very sparse hyperlink matrix $\mathbf{H}$. This is computationally advantageous, as we show later in section 4.6.

$$\begin{aligned}\mathbf{G} &= \alpha\mathbf{S} + (1-\alpha)1/n\,\mathbf{e}\mathbf{e}^T \\ &= \alpha(\mathbf{H} + 1/n\,\mathbf{a}\mathbf{e}^T) + (1-\alpha)\,1/n\,\mathbf{e}\mathbf{e}^T \\ &= \alpha\mathbf{H} + (\alpha\mathbf{a} + (1-\alpha)\mathbf{e})\,1/n\,\mathbf{e}^T.\end{aligned}$$

- $\mathbf{G}$ is artificial in the sense that the raw hyperlink matrix $\mathbf{H}$ has been twice modified in order to produce desirable convergence properties. A stationary vector (thus, a PageRank vector) does not exist for $\mathbf{H}$, so Brin and Page creatively cheated to achieve their desired result. For the twice-modified $\mathbf{G}$, a unique PageRank vector exists, and as it turns out, this vector is remarkably good at giving a global importance value to webpages.

Notation for the PageRank Problem

$\mathbf{H}$	very sparse, raw substochastic hyperlink matrix
$\mathbf{S}$	sparse, stochastic, most likely reducible matrix
$\mathbf{G}$	completely dense, stochastic, primitive matrix called the Google Matrix
$\mathbf{E}$	completely dense, rank-one teleportation matrix
n	number of pages in the engine's index = order of $\mathbf{H}, \mathbf{S}, \mathbf{G}, \mathbf{E}$
α	scaling parameter between 0 and 1
$\boldsymbol{\pi}^T$	stationary row vector of $\mathbf{G}$ called the PageRank vector
$\mathbf{a}^T$	binary dangling node vector

In summary, Google's adjusted PageRank method is

$$\boldsymbol{\pi}^{(k+1)T} = \boldsymbol{\pi}^{(k)T}\mathbf{G}, \tag{4.5.1}$$

which is simply the *power method* applied to $\mathbf{G}$.

We close this section with an example. Returning again to Figure 4.1, for $\alpha = .9$, the stochastic, primitive matrix $\mathbf{G}$ is

$$\mathbf{G} = .9\mathbf{H} + (.9 \begin{pmatrix} 0 \\ 1 \\ 0 \\ 0 \\ 0 \\ 0 \end{pmatrix} + .1 \begin{pmatrix} 1 \\ 1 \\ 1 \\ 1 \\ 1 \\ 1 \end{pmatrix}) \, 1/6 \, (1 \quad 1 \quad 1 \quad 1 \quad 1 \quad 1)$$

$$= \begin{pmatrix} 1/60 & 7/15 & 7/15 & 1/60 & 1/60 & 1/60 \\ 1/6 & 1/6 & 1/6 & 1/6 & 1/6 & 1/6 \\ 19/60 & 19/60 & 1/60 & 1/60 & 19/60 & 1/60 \\ 1/60 & 1/60 & 1/60 & 1/60 & 7/15 & 7/15 \\ 1/60 & 1/60 & 1/60 & 7/15 & 1/60 & 7/15 \\ 1/60 & 1/60 & 1/60 & 11/12 & 1/60 & 1/60 \end{pmatrix}.$$

Google's PageRank vector is the stationary vector of $\mathbf{G}$ and is given by

$$\begin{matrix} & & 1 & 2 & 3 & 4 & 5 & 6 \\ \boldsymbol{\pi}^T & = & (.03721 & .05396 & .04151 & .3751 & .206 & .2862). \end{matrix}$$

The interpretation of $\pi_1 = .03721$ is that 3.721% of the time the random surfer visits page 1. Therefore, the pages in this tiny web can be ranked by their importance as $(4 \quad 6 \quad 5 \quad 2 \quad 3 \quad 1)$, meaning page 4 is the most important page and page 1 is the least important page, according to the PageRank definition of importance.

4.6 COMPUTATION OF THE PAGERANK VECTOR

The PageRank problem can be stated in two ways:

1. Solve the following *eigenvector* problem for $\boldsymbol{\pi}^T$.

$$\boldsymbol{\pi}^T = \boldsymbol{\pi}^T \mathbf{G},$$
$$\boldsymbol{\pi}^T \mathbf{e} = 1.$$

2. Solve the following *linear homogeneous system* for $\boldsymbol{\pi}^T$.

$$\boldsymbol{\pi}^T (\mathbf{I} - \mathbf{G}) = \mathbf{0}^T,$$
$$\boldsymbol{\pi}^T \mathbf{e} = 1.$$

In the first system, the goal is to find the normalized *dominant left-hand eigenvector* of $\mathbf{G}$ corresponding to the *dominant eigenvalue* $\lambda_1 = 1$. ($\mathbf{G}$ is a stochastic matrix, so $\lambda_1 = 1$.) In the second system, the goal is to find the normalized left-hand null vector of $\mathbf{I} - \mathbf{G}$. Both systems are subject to the normalization equation $\boldsymbol{\pi}^T \mathbf{e} = 1$, which insures that $\boldsymbol{\pi}^T$ is a probability vector. In the example in section 4.5, $\mathbf{G}$ is a 6×6 matrix, so we used Matlab's `eig` command to solve for $\boldsymbol{\pi}^T$, then normalized the result (by dividing the vector by its sum) to get the PageRank vector. However, for a web-sized matrix like Google's, this will not do. Other more advanced and computationally efficient methods must be used. Of course, $\boldsymbol{\pi}^T$ is the stationary vector of a Markov chain with transition matrix $\mathbf{G}$, and much research has been done on computing the stationary vector for a general Markov chain. See William J. Stewart's book *Introduction to the Numerical Solution of Markov Chains* [154], which contains over a dozen methods for finding $\boldsymbol{\pi}^T$. However, the specific features of the

PageRank matrix **G** make one numerical method, the power method, the clear favorite. In this section, we discuss the power method, which is the original method proposed by Brin and Page for finding the PageRank vector. We describe other more advanced methods in Chapter 9.

The World's Largest Matrix Computation

Cleve Moler, the founder of Matlab, wrote an article [131] for his October 2002 newsletter *Matlab News* that cited PageRank as "The World's Largest Matrix Computation." Then Google was applying the power method to a sparse matrix of order 2.7 billion. Now it's up to 8.1 billion!

The power method is one of the oldest and simplest iterative methods for finding the *dominant eigenvalue and eigenvector* of a matrix.[3] Therefore, it can be used to find the stationary vector of a Markov chain. (The stationary vector is simply the dominant left-hand eigenvector of the Markov matrix.) However, the power method is known for its tortoise-like speed. Of the available iterative methods (Gauss-Seidel, Jacobi, restarted GMRES, BICGSTAB, etc. [18]), the power method is generally the slowest. So why did Brin and Page choose a method known for its sluggishness? There are several good reasons for their choice.

First, the power method is simple. The implementation and programming are elementary. (See the box on page 42 for a Matlab implementation of the PageRank power method.) In addition, the power method applied to **G** (equation (4.5.1)) can actually be expressed in terms of the very sparse **H**.

$$\begin{aligned}\boldsymbol{\pi}^{(k+1)T} &= \boldsymbol{\pi}^{(k)T}\mathbf{G} \\ &= \alpha\,\boldsymbol{\pi}^{(k)T}\mathbf{S} + \frac{1-\alpha}{n}\,\boldsymbol{\pi}^{(k)T}\,\mathbf{e}\,\mathbf{e}^T \\ &= \alpha\,\boldsymbol{\pi}^{(k)T}\mathbf{H} + (\alpha\,\boldsymbol{\pi}^{(k)T}\mathbf{a} + 1 - \alpha)\,\mathbf{e}^T/n. \end{aligned} \tag{4.6.1}$$

The vector-matrix multiplications ($\boldsymbol{\pi}^{(k)T}\mathbf{H}$) are executed on the extremely sparse **H**, and **S** and **G** are never formed or stored, only their rank-one components, **a** and **e**, are needed. Recall that each vector-matrix multiplication is $O(n)$ since **H** has about 10 nonzeros per row. This is probably the main reason for Brin and Page's use of the power method in 1998. But why is the power method still the predominant method in PageRank research papers today, and why have most improvements been novel modifications to the PageRank power method, rather than experiments with other methods? The other advantages of the PageRank power method answer these questions.

The power method, like many other iterative methods, is matrix-free, which is a term that refers to the storage and handling of the coefficient matrix. For matrix-free methods, the coefficient matrix is only accessed through the vector-matrix multiplication routine. No manipulation of the matrix is done. Contrast this with direct methods, which manipulate elements of the matrix during each step. Modifying and storing elements of the Google

[3]The power method goes back at least to 1913. With the help of James H. Wilkinson, the power method became the standard method in the 1960s for finding the eigenvalues and eigenvectors of a matrix with a digital computer [152, p. 69–70].

matrix is not feasible. Even though $\mathbf{H}$ is very sparse, its enormous size and lack of structure preclude the use of direct methods. Instead, matrix-free methods, such as the class of iterative methods, are preferred.

The power method is also storage-friendly. In addition to the sparse matrix $\mathbf{H}$ and the dangling node vector $\mathbf{a}$, only one vector, the current iterate $\boldsymbol{\pi}^{(k)T}$, must be stored. This vector is completely dense, meaning n real numbers must be stored. For Google, $n = 8.1$ billion, so one can understand their frugal mentality when it comes to storage. Other iterative methods, such as GMRES or BICGSTAB, while faster, require the storage of multiple vectors. For example, a restarted GMRES(10) requires the storage of 10 vectors of length n at each iteration, which is equivalent to the amount of storage required by the entire $\mathbf{H}$ matrix, since $nnz(\mathbf{H}) \approx 10n$.

The last reason for using the power method to compute the PageRank vector concerns the number of iterations it requires. Brin and Page reported in their 1998 papers, and others have confirmed, that only 50-100 power iterations are needed before the iterates have converged, giving a satisfactory approximation to the exact PageRank vector. Recall that each iteration of the power method requires $O(n)$ effort because $\mathbf{H}$ is so sparse. As a result, it's hard to find a method that can beat 50 $O(n)$ power iterations. Algorithms whose run time and computational effort are linear (or sublinear) in the problem size are very fast, and rare.

The next logical question is: why does the power method applied to $\mathbf{G}$ require only about 50 iterations to converge? Is there something about the structure of $\mathbf{G}$ that indicates this speedy convergence? The answer comes from the theory of Markov chains. In general, the *asymptotic rate of convergence* of the power method applied to a matrix depends on the ratio of the two eigenvalues that are largest in magnitude, denoted λ_1 and λ_2. Precisely, the asymptotic convergence rate is the rate at which $|\lambda_2/\lambda_1|^k \rightarrow 0$. For stochastic matrices such as $\mathbf{G}$, $\lambda_1 = 1$, so $|\lambda_2|$ governs the convergence. Since $\mathbf{G}$ is also primitive, $|\lambda_2| < 1$. In general, numerically finding λ_2 for a matrix requires computational effort that one is not willing to spend just to get an estimate of the asymptotic rate of convergence. Fortunately, for the PageRank problem, it's easy to show [127, p. 502], [90, 108] that if the respective spectrums are $\sigma(\mathbf{S}) = \{1, \mu_2, \ldots, \mu_n\}$ and $\sigma(\mathbf{G}) = \{1, \lambda_2, \ldots, \lambda_n\}$, then

$$\lambda_k = \alpha\mu_k \quad \text{for} \quad k = 2, 3, \ldots, n.$$

(A short proof of this statement is provided at the end of this chapter.) Furthermore, the link structure of the Web makes it very likely that $|\mu_2| = 1$ (or at least $|\mu_2| \approx 1$), which means that $|\lambda_2(\mathbf{G})| = \alpha$ (or $|\lambda_2(\mathbf{G})| \approx \alpha$). As a result, the convex combination parameter α explains the reported convergence after just 50 iterations. In their papers, Google founders Brin and Page use $\alpha = .85$, and at last report, this is still the value used by Google. $\alpha^{50} = .85^{50} \approx .000296$, which implies that at the 50th iteration one can expect roughly 2-3 *places of accuracy* in the approximate PageRank vector. This degree of accuracy is apparently adequate for Google's ranking needs. Mathematically, ten places of accuracy may be needed to distinguish between elements of the PageRank vector (see Section 8.3), but when PageRank scores are combined with content scores, high accuracy may be less important.

Subdominant Eigenvalue of the Google Matrix

For the Google matrix $\mathbf{G} = \alpha\mathbf{S} + (1-\alpha)1/n\,\mathbf{e}\mathbf{e}^T$,

$$|\lambda_2(\mathbf{G})| \leq \alpha.$$

- For the case when $|\lambda_2(\mathbf{S})| = 1$ (which occurs often due to the reducibility of the web graph), $|\lambda_2(\mathbf{G})| = \alpha$. Therefore, the asymptotic rate of convergence of the PageRank power method of equation (4.6.1) is the rate at which $\alpha^k \to 0$.

We can now give positive answers to the six questions of section 4.3. With the stochasticity and primitivity adjustments, the power method applied to $\mathbf{G}$ is guaranteed to converge to a unique positive vector called the PageRank vector, regardless of the starting vector. Because the resulting PageRank vector is positive, there are no undesirable ties at 0. Further, to produce PageRank scores with approximately τ digits of accuracy about $-\tau/log_{10}\alpha$ iterations must be completed.

Matlab m-file for PageRank Power Method

This m-file is a Matlab implementation of the PageRank power method given in equation (4.6.1).

```
function [pi,time,numiter]=\hbox{PageRank}(pi0,H,n,alpha,epsilon);

% \hbox{PageRank}  computes the \hbox{PageRank} vector for an n-by-n Markov
%           matrix H with starting vector pi0 (a row vector)
%           and scaling parameter alpha (scalar).  Uses power
%           method.
%
% EXAMPLE:  [pi,time,numiter]=\hbox{PageRank}(pi0,H,1000,.9,1e-8);
%
% INPUT:   pi0 = starting vector at iteration 0 (a row vector)
%          H = row-normalized hyperlink matrix (n-by-n sparse matrix)
%          n = size of H matrix (scalar)
%          alpha = scaling parameter in \hbox{PageRank} model (scalar)
%          epsilon = convergence tolerance (scalar, e.g. 1e-8)
%
% OUTPUT:    pi = \hbox{PageRank} vector
%            time = time required to compute \hbox{PageRank} vector
%            numiter = number of iterations until convergence
%
% The starting vector is usually set to the uniform vector,
% pi0=1/n*ones(1,n).
% NOTE: Matlab stores sparse matrices by columns, so it is faster
%       to do some operations on H', the transpose of H.
```

```
% get "a", the dangling node vector, where a(i)=1, if node i
%   is dangling node and 0, o.w.

rowsumvector=ones(1,n)*H';
nonzerorows=find(rowsumvector);
zerorows=setdiff(1:n,nonzerorows); l=length(zerorows);
a=sparse(zerorows,ones(l,1),ones(l,1),n,1);


k=0;
residual=1;
pi=pi0;
tic;

while (residual >= epsilon)
  prevpi=pi;
  k=k+1;
  pi=alpha*pi*H + (alpha*(pi*a)+1-alpha)*((1/n)*ones(1,n));
  residual=norm(pi-prevpi,1);
end
numiter=k;
time=toc;
```

Search within a Site

In the competitive business of search, Google is refreshingly generous at times. For example, at no charge, Google lets website authors employ its technology to search within their site. (Clicking on the "more" button on Google's home page will lead you to the latest information on their services.) For queries within a site, Google restricts the set of relevant pages to only in-site pages. These in-site relevant pages are then ranked using the global PageRank scores. In essence, this in-site search extracts the site from Google's massive index of billions of pages and untangles the part of the Web pertaining to the site. Looking at an individual subweb makes for a much more manageable hyperlink graph.

ASIDE: Search Engine Optimization

As more and more sales move online, large and small businesses alike turn to search engine optimizers (SEOs) to help them boost profits. SEOs carefully craft webpages and links in order to "optimize" the chances that their clients' pages will appear in the first few pages of search engine results. SEOs can be classified as ethical or unethical. Ethical SEOs are good netizens, citizens of the net, who offer only sound advice, such as the best way to display text and label pictures and tags. They encourage webpage authors to maintain good content, as page rankings are the combination of the content score and the popularity score. They also warn authors that search engines punish pages they perceive as deliberately spamming. Ethical SEOs and search engines consider themselves partners who, by exchanging information and tips, together improve search quality. Unethical SEOs, on the other hand, intentionally try to outwit search engines and promote spamming techniques. See the aside on page 52 for a specific case of unethical SEO practices. Since the Web's infancy, search engines have been embroiled in an eternal battle with unethical SEOs. The battle rages all over the Web, from visible webpage content to hidden metatags, from links to anchor text, and from inside servers to out on link farms (again, see the aside on page 52).

SEOs had success against the early search engines by using term spamming and hiding techniques [84]. In term spamming, spam words are included in the body of the page, often times repeatedly, in the title, metatags, anchor text, and URL text. Hiding techniques use color schemes and cloaking to deceive search engines. For example, using white text on a white background makes spam invisible to human readers, which means search engines are less likely to receive helpful complaints about pages with hidden spam. Cloaking refers to the technique of returning one spam-loaded webpage for normal user requests and another spam-free page for requests from search engine crawlers. As long as authors can clearly identify web crawling agents, they can send the agent away with a clean, spam-free page. Because these techniques are so easy for webpage authors to use, search engines had to retaliate. They did so by increasing the IQ of their spiders and indexers. Many spiders and indexers are trained to ignore metatags, since by the late 1990s these rarely held accurate page information. They also ignore repeated keywords. However, cloaking is harder to counteract. Search engines request help from users to stop cloaking. For example, Google asks surfers to act as referees and to blow the whistle whenever they find a suspicious page that instantaneously redirects them to a new page.

In 1998, search engines added link analysis to their bag of tricks. As a result, content spam and cloaking alone could no longer fool the link analysis engines and garner spammers unjustifiably high rankings. Spammers and SEOs adapted by learning how link analysis works. The SEO community has always been active—its members, then and now, hold conferences, write papers and books, host weblogs, and sell their secrets. The most famous and informative SEO papers were written by Chris Ridings, "PageRank explained: Everything you've always wanted to know about PageRank" [143] and "PageRank uncovered" [144]. These papers offer practical strategies for hoarding PageRank and avoiding such undesirable things as PageRank leak. Search engines constantly tune their algorithms in order to stay one step ahead of the SEO gamers. While search engines consider unethical SEOs to be adversaries, some web analysts call them an essential part of the web food chain, because they drive innovation and research and development.

ASIDE: How Do Search Engines Make Money?

We are asked this question often. It's a good question. Search engines provide free and unlimited access to their services, so just where do the billions of dollars in search revenue come from? Search engines have multiple sources of income. First, there's the inclusion fee that some search engines charge website authors. Some impatient authors want a guarantee that their new site will be indexed soon (in a day or two) rather than in a month or two, when a spider finally gets to it in the to-be-crawled URL list. Search engines supply this guarantee for a small fee, and for a slightly larger fee, authors can guarantee that their site be reindexed on a more frequent, perhaps monthly, basis.

Most search engines also generate revenue by selling profile data to interested parties. Search engines collect enormous amounts of user data on a daily basis. This data are used to improve the quality of search and predict user needs, but it is also sold in an aggregate form to various companies. For example, search engine optimization companies who are interested in popular query words or the percentage of searches that are commercial in nature can buy this information directly from a search engine.

While search engines do not sell access to their search capabilities to individual users, they do sell search services to companies. For example, Netscape pays Google to use Google search as the default search provided by its browser. At one point, GoTo (which was bought by Overture, which is now part of Yahoo) sold its top seven results for each query term to Yahoo and AltaVista, who, in turn, used the seven results as their top results.

Despite these sources of income, by far the most profitable and fastest-growing revenue source for search engines is advertising. It is estimated that in 2004 $3 billion in search revenue will be generated from advertising. Google's IPO filing on June 21, 2004 made the company's dependence on advertising very clear: advertising accounted for over 97% of their 2003 revenue. Many search engines sell banner ads that appear on their homepages and results pages. Others sell pay-for-placement ads. These controversial ads allow a company to buy their way to the top of the ranking. Many web analysts argue that these pay-for-placement ads pollute the search results. However, search engines using this technique (GoTo is a prime example) retort that this method of ranking is excellent for commercial searches. Since recent surveys estimate that 15-30% of all searches are commercial in nature, engines like Overture provide a valuable service for this class of queries. On the other hand, many searches are research-oriented, and the results of pay-for-placement engines frustrate these users.

Google takes a different approach to advertisements and rankings. They present the unpaid results in a main list while pay-for-placement sites appear separately on the side as "sponsored links." Google, and now Yahoo, are the only remaining companies not to mingle paid links with pure links. Google uses a cost-per-click advertising scheme to present sponsored links. Companies choose a keyword associated with their product or service, and then bid on a price they are willing to pay each time a searcher clicks on their link. For example, a bike shop in Raleigh may bid 5 cents for every query on "bike Raleigh." The bike shop is billed only if a searcher actually clicks on their ad. However, another company may bid 17 cents for the same query. The ad for the second company is likely to appear first because, although there is some fine tuning and optimization, sponsored ads generally are listed in order from the highest bid to the lowest bid.

Cost-per-click advertising is an innovation in marketing. Small businesses who traditionally spent little on advertising are now spending much more on web advertising because cost-per-click advertising is so cost-effective. If a searcher clicks on the link, he or she is indicating an intent to buy, something that other means of advertising such as billboards or mail circulars cannot deliver. Interestingly, like many other things on the Web, it was only a matter of time before cost-per-click advertising turned into a battleground between competitors. Without protection (which can be purchased in the form of a software program) naive companies buying cost-per-click advertising can easily be sabotaged by competitors. Competitors repeatedly click on the naive company's ads, running up their tab and exhausting the company's advertising budget.

4.7 THEOREM AND PROOF FOR SPECTRUM OF THE GOOGLE MATRIX

In this chapter, we defined the Google matrix as $\mathbf{G} = \alpha\mathbf{S} + (1-\alpha)1/n\,\mathbf{e}\mathbf{e}^T$. However, in the Section 5.3 of the next chapter, we broaden this to include a more general Google matrix, where the fudge factor matrix $\mathbf{E}$ changes from the uniform matrix $1/n\,\mathbf{e}\mathbf{e}^T$ to $\mathbf{e}\mathbf{v}^T$, where $\mathbf{v}^T > \mathbf{0}$ is a probability vector. In this section, we present the theorem and proof for the second eigenvalue of this more general Google matrix.

Theorem 4.7.1. *If the spectrum of the stochastic matrix* $\mathbf{S}$ *is* $\{1, \lambda_2, \lambda_3, \ldots, \lambda_n\}$, *then the spectrum of the Google matrix* $\mathbf{G} = \alpha\mathbf{S} + (1-\alpha)\mathbf{e}\mathbf{v}^T$ *is* $\{1, \alpha\lambda_2, \alpha\lambda_3, \ldots, \alpha\lambda_n\}$, *where* $\mathbf{v}^T$ *is a probability vector.*

Proof. Since $\mathbf{S}$ is stochastic, $(1, \mathbf{e})$ is an eigenpair of $\mathbf{S}$. Let $\mathbf{Q} = (\mathbf{e} \;\; \mathbf{X})$ be a nonsingular matrix that has the eigenvector $\mathbf{e}$ as its first column. Let $\mathbf{Q}^{-1} = \begin{pmatrix} \mathbf{y}^T \\ \mathbf{Y}^T \end{pmatrix}$. Then $\mathbf{Q}^{-1}\mathbf{Q} = \begin{pmatrix} \mathbf{y}^T\mathbf{e} & \mathbf{y}^T\mathbf{X} \\ \mathbf{Y}^T\mathbf{e} & \mathbf{Y}^T\mathbf{X} \end{pmatrix} = \begin{pmatrix} 1 & 0 \\ \mathbf{0} & \mathbf{I} \end{pmatrix}$, which gives two useful identities, $\mathbf{y}^T\mathbf{e} = 1$ and $\mathbf{Y}^T\mathbf{e} = \mathbf{0}$. As a result, the similarity transformation

$$\mathbf{Q}^{-1}\mathbf{S}\mathbf{Q} = \begin{pmatrix} \mathbf{y}^T\mathbf{e} & \mathbf{y}^T\mathbf{S}\mathbf{X} \\ \mathbf{Y}^T\mathbf{e} & \mathbf{Y}^T\mathbf{S}\mathbf{X} \end{pmatrix} = \begin{pmatrix} 1 & \mathbf{y}^T\mathbf{S}\mathbf{X} \\ 0 & \mathbf{Y}^T\mathbf{S}\mathbf{X} \end{pmatrix}$$

reveals that $\mathbf{Y}^T\mathbf{S}\mathbf{X}$ contains the remaining eigenvalues of $\mathbf{S}$, $\lambda_2, \ldots, \lambda_n$. Applying the similarity transformation to $\mathbf{G} = \alpha\mathbf{S} + (1-\alpha)\mathbf{e}\mathbf{v}^T$ gives

$$\begin{aligned}
\mathbf{Q}^{-1}(\alpha\mathbf{S} + (1-\alpha)\mathbf{e}\mathbf{v}^T)\mathbf{Q} &= \alpha\mathbf{Q}^{-1}\mathbf{S}\mathbf{Q} + (1-\alpha)\mathbf{Q}^{-1}\mathbf{e}\mathbf{v}^T\mathbf{Q} \\
&= \begin{pmatrix} \alpha & \alpha\mathbf{y}^T\mathbf{S}\mathbf{X} \\ 0 & \alpha\mathbf{Y}^T\mathbf{S}\mathbf{X} \end{pmatrix} + (1-\alpha)\begin{pmatrix} \mathbf{y}^T\mathbf{e} \\ \mathbf{Y}^T\mathbf{e} \end{pmatrix}(\mathbf{v}^T\mathbf{e} \;\; \mathbf{v}^T\mathbf{X}) \\
&= \begin{pmatrix} \alpha & \alpha\mathbf{y}^T\mathbf{S}\mathbf{X} \\ 0 & \alpha\mathbf{Y}^T\mathbf{S}\mathbf{X} \end{pmatrix} + \begin{pmatrix} (1-\alpha) & (1-\alpha)\mathbf{v}^T\mathbf{X} \\ \mathbf{0} & \mathbf{0} \end{pmatrix} \\
&= \begin{pmatrix} 1 & \alpha\mathbf{y}^T\mathbf{S}\mathbf{X} + (1-\alpha)\mathbf{v}^T\mathbf{X} \\ \mathbf{0} & \alpha\mathbf{Y}^T\mathbf{S}\mathbf{X} \end{pmatrix}.
\end{aligned}$$

Therefore, the eigenvalues of $\mathbf{G} = \alpha\mathbf{S} + (1-\alpha)\mathbf{e}\mathbf{v}^T$ are $\{1, \alpha\lambda_2, \alpha\lambda_3, \ldots, \alpha\lambda_n\}$. ∎

Chapter Five

Parameters in the PageRank Model

My grandfather, William H. Langville, Sr., loved fiddling with projects in his basement workshop. Down there he had a production process for making his own shad darts for fishing. He poured lead into a special mold, let it cool, then applied bright paints. He manufactured those darts by the dozens, which was good because on each fishing trip my brothers, cousins, and I always lost at least three each to trees, underwater boots, poor knot-tying, and of course, really big, sharp-toothed fish. Grandpop kept meticulous fishing records of where, when, how many, and which type of fish he caught each day. He also noted the style of dart he'd used. He looked for success patterns. It wasn't long before he started fiddling with his manufacturing process, making big darts, small darts, green darts, orange darts, two-toned darts, feathered darts, darts with sinks, and darts with spinners. He found the fiddling fun—hypothesizing, testing, and reporting what happened if he tweaked this parameter that way, that parameter this way.

We agree with Grandpop. The fun is in the fiddling. In this chapter, we introduce the various methods for fiddling with the basic PageRank model of Chapter 4, and then, like Grandpop, consider the implications of such changes.

5.1 THE α FACTOR

In Chapter 4, we introduced the scaling parameter $0 < \alpha < 1$ to create the Google matrix $\mathbf{G} = \alpha\mathbf{S} + (1-\alpha)\mathbf{E}$. The constant α clearly controls the priority given to the Web's natural hyperlink structure as opposed to the artificial teleportation matrix $\mathbf{E}$. In their early papers [39, 40], Brin and Page, the founders of Google, suggest setting $\alpha = .85$. Like many others, we wonder why .85? Why not .9? Or .95? Or .6? What effect does α have on the PageRank problem? In Chapter 4, we mentioned that the scaling parameter controlled the asymptotic rate of convergence of the PageRank power method. Reviewing the conclusion there, as $\alpha \to 1$, the expected number of iterations required by the power method increases dramatically. See Table 5.1 below.

For $\alpha = .5$, only about 34 iterations are expected before the power method has *converged to a tolerance of* 10^{-10}. As $\alpha \to 1$, this number becomes prohibitive. Even using $\alpha = .85$, this choice of α still requires several days of computation before satisfactory convergence due to the scale of the matrices and vectors involved. This means that Google engineers are forced to perform a delicate balancing act—as $\alpha \to 1$, the artificiality introduced by the teleportation matrix $\mathbf{E} = 1/n\ \mathbf{e}\mathbf{e}^T$ reduces, yet the computation time increases.

It seems that setting $\alpha = .85$ strikes a workable compromise between efficiency and effectiveness. Interestingly, this constant α controls more than just the convergence of the

Table 5.1 Effect of α on expected number of power iterations

α	Number of Iterations
.5	34
.75	81
.8	104
.85	142
.9	219
.95	449
.99	2,292
.999	23,015

PageRank method; it affects the sensitivity of the resulting PageRank vector. Specifically, as $\alpha \rightarrow 1$, the PageRankings become much more volatile, and fluctuate noticeably for even small changes in the Web's structure. The Web's dynamic nature, which we emphasized in Chapter 1, makes sensitivity an important issue. Ideally, we'd like to produce a ranking that is stable despite such small changes. The sensitivity issue, especially α's effect on it, is treated in depth in the next chapter.

5.2 THE HYPERLINK MATRIX $\mathbf{H}$

Another part of the PageRank model that can be adjusted is the $\mathbf{H}$ matrix itself. Brin and Page originally suggested a uniform weighting scheme for filling in elements in $\mathbf{H}$. That is, all outlinks from a page are given equal weight in terms of the random surfer's hyperlinking probabilities. While fair, democratic, and easy to implement, equality may not be best for webpage rankings. In fact, the random surfer description may not be accurate at all. Rather than hyperlinking to new pages by randomly selecting one of the outlinking pages, perhaps surfers select new pages by choosing outlinking pages with a lot of valuable content or pertinent descriptive anchor text. (To understand the importance of anchor text, see the aside on Google bombs on page 54.) In this case, take the random surfer who plays eeni-meeni-meini-mo to decide which page to visit next and replace him with an **intelligent surfer** who upon arriving at a new page pulls a calculator from his chest pocket and pecks away until he decides which page is most appropriate to visit next (based on current location, interests, history, and so on). For example, the intelligent surfer may be more likely to jump to content-filled pages, so these pages should be given more probabilistic weight than brief advertisement pages.

A practical approach to filling in $\mathbf{H}$'s elements is to use access logs to find actual surfer tendencies. For example, a webmaster can study his access logs and find that surfers on page P_1 are twice as likely to hyperlink to P_2 as they are to P_3. Thus, outlinking probabilities in row 1 of $\mathbf{H}$ can be adjusted accordingly. For the webgraph from Figure 4.1, the original hyperlink matrix using the random surfer description,

$$\mathbf{H} = \begin{array}{c} \\ P_1 \\ P_2 \\ P_3 \\ P_4 \\ P_5 \\ P_6 \end{array} \begin{array}{c} \begin{array}{cccccc} P_1 & P_2 & P_3 & P_4 & P_5 & P_6 \end{array} \\ \begin{pmatrix} 0 & 1/2 & 1/2 & 0 & 0 & 0 \\ 0 & 0 & 0 & 0 & 0 & 0 \\ 1/3 & 1/3 & 0 & 0 & 1/3 & 0 \\ 0 & 0 & 0 & 0 & 1/2 & 1/2 \\ 0 & 0 & 0 & 1/2 & 0 & 1/2 \\ 0 & 0 & 0 & 1 & 0 & 0 \end{pmatrix} \end{array},$$

changes to

$$\mathbf{H} = \begin{array}{c} \\ P_1 \\ P_2 \\ P_3 \\ P_4 \\ P_5 \\ P_6 \end{array} \begin{array}{c} \begin{array}{cccccc} P_1 & P_2 & P_3 & P_4 & P_5 & P_6 \end{array} \\ \begin{pmatrix} 0 & 2/3 & 1/3 & 0 & 0 & 0 \\ 0 & 0 & 0 & 0 & 0 & 0 \\ 1/3 & 1/3 & 0 & 0 & 1/3 & 0 \\ 0 & 0 & 0 & 0 & 1/2 & 1/2 \\ 0 & 0 & 0 & 1/2 & 0 & 1/2 \\ 0 & 0 & 0 & 1 & 0 & 0 \end{pmatrix} \end{array},$$

when the intelligent surfer description is applied to page P_1.
PageRank

researchers have presented many other methods for filling in the elements of raw hyperlink matrix $\mathbf{H}$ [13, 26, 27, 142, 159]. These methods use heuristic rules to create the nonzero elements of $\mathbf{H}$ by combining measures concerning the location of the outlinks in a page, the length of the anchor text associated with the outlinks, and the content similarity between the two documents connected by a link. For example, row 4 of the above matrix shows that page P_4 links to pages P_5 and P_6. The probabilities in $\mathbf{H}_{45}$ and $\mathbf{H}_{46}$ can be determined by computing the angle similarity measure between pages P_4 and P_5 and P_4 and P_6, respectively. The angle similarity measure is an important part of a traditional information retrieval model, the vector space model of Chapter 1 [23]. Regardless of how $\mathbf{H}$ is created, it is important, in the context of the Markov chain, that the resulting matrix be nearly stochastic. That is, the rows corresponding to nondangling nodes (pages with at least one outlink) sum to 1, while rows for dangling nodes sum to 0. If this is not the case, the rows must be normalized. We will discuss other non-Markovian ranking models in Chapters 11 and 12.

5.3 THE TELEPORTATION MATRIX $\mathbf{E}$

One of the first modifications to the basic PageRank model that founders Brin and Page suggested was a change to the teleportation matrix $\mathbf{E}$. Rather than using $1/n\,\mathbf{e}\mathbf{e}^T$, they used $\mathbf{e}\mathbf{v}^T$, where $\mathbf{v}^T > 0$ is a *probability vector* called the **personalization** or **teleportation vector**. Since $\mathbf{v}^T$ is a probability vector with positive elements, every node is still directly connected to every other node; thus, $\mathbf{G}$ is primitive, which means that a unique stationary vector for the Markov chain exists and is the PageRank vector. Using $\mathbf{v}^T$ in place of $1/n\,\mathbf{e}^T$ means that the teleportation probabilities are no longer uniformly distributed. Instead, each time a surfer teleports, he or she follows the probability distribution given in $\mathbf{v}^T$ to jump to the next page. This slight modification retains the advantageous properties of the power method. When $\mathbf{G} = \alpha\mathbf{S} + (1-\alpha)\mathbf{e}\mathbf{v}^T$, the power method becomes

$$\begin{aligned}\boldsymbol{\pi}^{(k+1)T} &= \boldsymbol{\pi}^{(k)T}\mathbf{G}\\ &= \alpha\,\boldsymbol{\pi}^{(k)T}\mathbf{S} + (1-\alpha)\,\boldsymbol{\pi}^{(k)T}\mathbf{e}\,\mathbf{v}^T\\ &= \alpha\,\boldsymbol{\pi}^{(k)T}\mathbf{H} + (\alpha\,\boldsymbol{\pi}^{(k)T}\mathbf{a} + 1 - \alpha)\,\mathbf{v}^T. \end{aligned} \tag{5.3.1}$$

Compare equation (5.3.1) with equation (4.6.1) on page 40, which uses the original democratic teleportation matrix $\mathbf{E} = 1/n\,\mathbf{ee}^T$. Since only the constant vector added at each iteration changes from $\mathbf{e}^T/n$ to $\mathbf{v}^T$, nearly all our Chapter 4 discoveries concerning the PageRank power method still apply. Specifically, the asymptotic rate of convergence, sparse vector-matrix multiplications, minimal storage, and coding simplicity are preserved. However, one thing that does change is the PageRank vector itself. Different personalization vectors produce different PageRankings [158]. That is, $\boldsymbol{\pi}^T(\mathbf{v}^T)$ is a function of $\mathbf{v}^T$.

Recognizing the uses of $\mathbf{v}^T$ is liberating. Think about it. Why should we all be subject to the same ranking of webpages? That single global, query-independent ranking $\boldsymbol{\pi}^T$ (which uses $\mathbf{v}^T = 1/n\,\mathbf{e}^T$) says nothing about me and my preferences. As Americans, aren't we all entitled to our own individual ranking vector—one that knows our personal preferences regarding pages and topics on the Web. If you like to surf for pages about news and current events, simply bias your $\mathbf{v}^T$ vector, so that v_i is large for pages P_i about news and current events and v_j is nearly 0 for all other pages, and then compute the PageRank vector that's tailored to your needs. Politicians can add another phrase to their campaign promises: "a car in every garage, a computer in every home, and a personalization vector $\mathbf{v}^T$ for every web surfer."

This seems to have been Google's original intent in introducing the personalization vector [38]. However, it makes the once query-independent, user-independent PageRanks user-dependent and more calculation-laden. Tailoring rankings for each user sounds wonderful in theory, yet doing this in practice is computationally impossible. Remember, it takes Google days to compute just one $\boldsymbol{\pi}^T$ corresponding to one $\mathbf{v}^T$ vector, the democratic personalization vector $\mathbf{v}^T = 1/n\,\mathbf{e}^T$.

Motivated in part by the fact that many see personalized engines as the future of search, several researchers have ignored the claims of computational impossibility and have created pseudo-personalized PageRanking systems [58, 88, 91, 99, 142]. We say pseudo because these systems do not deliver rankings that are customized for each and every user, but rather groups of users.

One such system was the product of Taher Haveliwala, while he was a graduate student at Stanford. He adapted the standard, query-independent PageRank to create a topic-sensitive PageRank [88, 89]. He created a finite number of PageRank vectors $\boldsymbol{\pi}^T(\mathbf{v}_i^T)$, each biased toward some particular topic i. For his experiments, Haveliwala chose the 16 top-level topics from the Open Directory Project (ODP) classification of webpages. For example, suppose $\boldsymbol{\pi}^T(\mathbf{v}_1^T)$ is the PageRank vector for Arts, the first ODP topic, while $\boldsymbol{\pi}^T(\mathbf{v}_2^T)$ is the PageRank vector for Business, the second ODP topic. $\boldsymbol{\pi}^T(\mathbf{v}_1^T)$ is biased toward Arts because $\mathbf{v}_1^T$ has significant probabilities only for pages pertaining to Arts, the remaining probabilities are nearly 0. The 16 biased PageRank vectors are precomputed. Then at query time, the trick is to quickly combine these biased vectors in a way that mimics the interests of the user and meanings of the query. Haveliwala forms his topic-sensitive, query-dependent PageRank vector as a convex combination of the 16 biased

PageRank vectors. That is,

$$\pi^T = \beta_1 \pi^T(\mathbf{v}_1^T) + \beta_2 \pi^T(\mathbf{v}_2^T) + \cdots + \beta_{16} \pi^T(\mathbf{v}_{16}^T),$$

where $\sum_i \beta_i = 1$. For instance, a query on `science project ideas` falls between the ODP categories of Kids and Teens (category 7), Reference (category 10), and Science (category 12). Logically, the PageRank vectors associated with these topics should be given more weight, or even all the weight, so that β_7, β_{10}, and β_{12} are large compared to the other coefficients. Haveliwala uses a Bayesian classifier to compute the β_i's for his experiments, but there are other options. When all this is done, the topic-sensitive popularity score is combined with the traditional content score from Chapter 1. Of course, if a finer gradation of personalization is desired, more than 16 topics can be used to better bias the rankings toward the user's query and interests.

It seems this little personalization vector $\mathbf{v}^T$ has potentially more significant side effects. Some speculate that Google can use this personalization vector to control spamming done by the so-called link farms. See the aside, SearchKing vs. Google, on page 52.

Kaltix's Personalized Web Search

It didn't take Google long to recognize the value of personalized search. In fact, Google snatched up Kaltix, a personalized search startup, just three months after its inception. Kaltix technology was created by Glen Jeh, Sepandar Kamvar, and Taher Haveliwala in the summer of 2003, while the three were on leaves of absence from the Stanford Computer Science Department. The Kaltix guys worked 20 hours a day that summer, literally working their fingers to the bone, falling asleep some nights with ice packs on their overworked wrists. The hard work paid off. Google bought Kaltix in September 2003, and the three moved into the Google headquarters to continue the project. In March 2004, Google labs released Personalized Search in beta version (`http://labs.google.com/personalized`). A user creates a profile by setting check boxes in a hierarchical listing of categories of interest. A personalization vector is created from this profile. Then when a query is entered into the Personalized Search box, the results are presented in the standard ranked list. However, in addition, a slider bar allows one to turn up the level of customization and increase the effect of the personalization vector.

Matlab m-file for Personalized PageRank Power Method

The Matlab implementation of the PageRank power method on page 42 used a uniform personalization vector $\mathbf{v}^T = \mathbf{e}^T/n$. This m-file, which is a simple one-line change in that code, implements a more general PageRank power method, allowing the personalization vector to vary as input. Therefore, the m-file below implements the PageRank power method applied to $\mathbf{G} = \alpha\mathbf{S} + (1-\alpha)\mathbf{e}\mathbf{v}^T$.

```
function [pi,time,numiter]=\hbox{PageRank}(pi0,H,v,n,alpha,epsilon);

% \hbox{PageRank}  computes the \hbox{PageRank} vector for an n-by-n Markov
%           matrix H with starting vector pi0 (a row vector),
%           scaling parameter alpha (scalar), and teleportation
%           vector v (a row vector).  Uses power method.
%
% EXAMPLE:[pi,time,numiter]=\hbox{PageRank}(pi0,H,v,900,.9,1e-8);
%
% INPUT:  pi0 = starting vector at iteration 0 (a row vector)
%         H = row-normalized hyperlink matrix (n-by-n sparse matrix)
%         v = teleportation vector (1-by-n row vector)
%         n = size of P matrix (scalar)
%         alpha = scaling parameter in \hbox{PageRank} model (scalar)
%         epsilon = convergence tolerance (scalar, e.g. 1e-8)
%
% OUTPUT:   pi = \hbox{PageRank} vector
%           time = time required to compute \hbox{PageRank} vector
%           numiter = number of iterations until convergence
%
% The starting vector is usually set to the uniform vector,
% pi0=1/n*ones(1,n).
% NOTE: Matlab stores sparse matrices by columns, so it is faster
%       to do some operations on H', the transpose of H.


% get "a" vector, where a(i)=1, if row i is dangling node
%   and 0, o.w.

rowsumvector=ones(1,n)*H';
nonzerorows=find(rowsumvector);
zerorows=setdiff(1:n,nonzerorows); l=length(zerorows);
a=sparse(zerorows,ones(1,l),ones(1,l),n,1);


k=0;
residual=1;
pi=pi0;
tic;

while (residual >= epsilon)
  prevpi=pi;
  k=k+1;
  pi=alpha*pi*H + (alpha*(pi*a)+1-alpha)*v;
  residual=norm(pi-prevpi,1);
end
numiter=k;
time=toc;
```

ASIDE: SearchKing vs. Google

Link farms are set up by spammers to fool information retrieval systems into increasing the rank of their clients' pages. One client who made it onto the front page of the Wall Street Journal is Joy Holton, the owner of an online store (`exoticleatherwear.com`*) that sells provocative leather clothing [160]. Using metatags and HTML coding, she was able to attract a modest number of surfers to her store. However, an email from the search* engine optimization company, AutomatedLinks, convinced Holman to pay the $22 annual fee to use their rank-boosting service. (See the aside on search engine optimization on page 43.) AutomatedLinks' sole efforts are aimed at increasing the PageRank (and ranking among other search engines) of their clients' pages. AutomatedLinks accomplishes this with link farms. Knowing that PageRank increases when the number of important inlinks to a client's page increases, optimizers add such links to a client's page. Link farms have several interconnected nodes about important topics and with significant PageRanks. These interconnected nodes then link to a client's page, thus, in essence, sharing some of their PageRank with the client's page. Holman's $22 investment with AutomatedLinks brought her over 26,000 visitors a month and thousands of dollars in revenue.

Most link farms use a link exchange program or reciprocal linking policy to boost the rank of client's pages, but there are other scenarios for doing this [28, 29]. Of course, link farms are very troublesome for search engines who are concerned with the integrity of their rankings. Search engines employ several techniques to sniff out link farms. First, they ask surfers to be tattletales and report any suspicious pages. Second, they use algorithms to identify tightly connected subgraphs of the Web with a high density of reciprocal links. And third, they manually inspect the algorithm's results to determine whether suspected sites play fair or foul. Google discourages link spamming by threatening to ban or drop the ranking of suspected sites and their neighbors.

Google's devalueing of the PageRank of link farmers created a legal stir during 2002 and 2003. The search engine optimization company, SearchKing, was running smoothly from February 2001 until August 2002, in part because it had a high PageRank, which it then shared with its clients. Clients with high PageRank had more traffic, and thus happily paid SearchKing for its rank-boosting service. However, in the few months after August 2002, Bob Massa, president of SearchKing, watched the PageRank estimate reported on his Google Toolbar (see the box on page 28) drop from PR8 to PR4, then from PR2 to PR0. Of course, his clients were affected as well. They complained and many jumped ship. Furious, Bob Massa took action on October 17, 2002, by filing a suit against Google with the U.S. District Court for the Western District of Oklahoma. SearchKing's legal team sued Google, demanding $75,000 in lost revenue plus court fees, the restoration of its and its clients' previous PageRanks, and the disclosure of the source code for the PageRank algorithm used by Google from August to October 2002. Both parties knew the import of the case. Its outcome would set a precedent for the relationship between optimization companies and search engines. SearchKing pushed for an early response, Google delayed. By December 30, 2002, Google had prepared a powerful, convincing, and well-researched response to SearchKing's motion for a preliminary injunction, and further added a motion to dismiss. There were two main arguments to Google's response. First, Google argued that PageRanks are opinions, the company's judgment of the value of webpages. These opinions are protected by the First Amendment. In fact, the Google defense team cited a precedent for a similar ranking, the rankings created by credit agencies. In 1999 in Jefferson County School District # R-I vs. Moody's Investors Service, Inc., the same court ruled that Moody's low credit ranking of the school's district, while possibly harming the district's perceived housing and schooling value in the public's eye, was just an opinion and was protected by the First Amendment. Similarly, the Google defense team argued:

> The PageRank values assigned by Google are not susceptible to being proved true or false by objective evidence. How could SearchKing ever "prove" that its ranking should "truly" be a 4 or a 6 or a 8? Certainly, SearchKing is not suggesting that each one of the billions of web pages ranked by Google are subject to another "truer" evaluation? If it believes so, it is certainly free to develop its own search services using the criteria it deems most appropriate.

Google also mentioned that its crawlers index just a small part of the Web, and therefore, Google is not entitled to index SearchKing's page in the first place, much less rank it.

The second part of Google's argument concerns the "irreparable harm" that could be done by SearchKing's demand to see the PageRank source code. A motion for preliminary injunction can be granted if the plaintiff shows (among other required things) that not doing so causes irreparable harm to the plaintiff as SearchKing claimed, due to its loss of clients. On the other hand, a motion for a preliminary injunction cannot be granted if it causes the defendant irreparable harm. Google presented the affidavit of Matthew Cutts, Google's software engineer who works on the PageRank quality team. Regarding the irreparable harm issue, Cutts stated:

> *Google's source code for its internally developed software is kept confidential by Google and has great value to the ongoing business of Google. Indeed, the technology that it encodes constitutes one of Google's most valuable assets . . . . If an entity were in possession of Google's proprietary source code and wanted to manipulate or to abuse Google's guidelines or relevance, Google could suffer irreparable damage as the integrity of, and the public's confidence in, Google's quality and scoring would be seriously jeopardized.*

Thus, Google made a much stronger case for possible irreparable harm.

On May 27, 2003, the Court denied SearchKing's motion for a preliminary injunction, and instead, granted Google's motion to dismiss. The court concluded that Google's PageRanks are entitled to full constitutional protection. Google won this one of their many legal battles of late. (See the aside on censorship and privacy on page 147.) Those of us engaging in hard-fought ethical search engine optimization rejoiced that justice was served. Unethical rank-boosting reminds us of a similar unfair practice from our elementary school days—line-butting at the water fountain. Nonbutters dislike both the butters (SearchKing clients) and the enabler (Bob Massa). Nonbutters feel safer when a teacher is watching. Rest assured that Google and other search engines are watching as often as they can. However, some netizens argue that the Oklahoma court ruling only plays into the disturbing and growing **Googleopoly** *(see the aside on page 112).*

It is not clear exactly how Google devalued SearchKing's PageRank, whether algorithmically or in an ad-hoc ex postfacto way. One way to incorporate such devaluation algorithmically into the PageRank model is through the personalization vector $\mathbf{v}^T$ *. The elements in* $\mathbf{v}^T > 0$ *corresponding to suspected or known link farming pages can be set to a very small number, close to 0. As the iterative PageRank algorithm proceeds, such pages will be devalued slightly, as the surfer will be less likely to teleport there. Of course, the simpler way to devalue spammers' pages is to assign them* **PR0** *after the PageRank calculation is completed. The much harder part of the spam problem is the identification of spam pages.*

ASIDE: Google Bombs

Friday, April 6, 2001, G-Day: Adam Mathes, then a computer science major at Stanford, launches the first **Google bomb** operation. Adam uses his Filler Friday web article to encourage his readers to help deploy the first ever international Google bomb. Readers are instructed to make a hyperlink to the homepage of Adam's friend, Andy Pressman. Adam reported that the anchor text of the hyperlink was the key to the Google bomb. Adam's readers were instructed to make "talentless hack" the anchor text of their new hyperlink, which pointed to

Andy Pressman's page. Adam Mathes had cleverly discovered a loophole in Google's use of anchor text. Given enough links to Andy Pressman's page with anchor text describing that page as "talentless hack," Google assumes that page really is about talentless hack, even though the words may never once appear on Andy's page. Google added Andy's page to its index under the terms "talentless" and "hack." From the beginning, Google rightfully noticed the descriptive power of anchor text. In fact, anchor text is useful in synonym association. If several pages point to a page about autos, but use the term car, the auto page should also be indexed under car. Of course, Google bombs have a slow-deploying mechanism—it takes an accumulation of links with descriptive anchor text, and thus, time until the content of those pages are updated in Google's index before the bomb explodes.

Monday, October 27, 2003: *George Johnston uses his* **blog** *(which is an interactive online diary) to set off the most famous Google bomb, the "miserable failure" bomb aimed at President George W. Bush. Johnston reported that his mission as bomb detonator had been accomplished by late November 2003. In December, entering the query "miserable failure" into Google showed the official White House Biography of the President as the number 1 result. One reporter noticed that of the over 800 links pointing to the Bush biography, only 32 used the phrase "miserable failure" in the anchor text, which meant Google bombing was not only fun, it was easy. By January 2004, bombers using the phrase "miserable failure" had to compete; results showed Michael Moore, President Bush, Jimmy Carter, and Hillary Clinton in the top four positions. And of course, other phrases were used by pranksters such as "French military victories," which brought up a Typo Correction page asking "did you mean: French military defeats," and "weapons of mass destruction," which showed an error page similar to the "404 Page Not Found" error page.*

Google's Reaction: *Google initially took a disinterested stance toward Google bombs, claiming that such games only affected obscure, goofy queries and not their typical serious queries. Besides, they claimed that their rankings reflected accurate opinions on the Web; obviously, many webpage authors agreed with Johnston that Bush really was a miserable failure. But with their June 21, 2004 IPO filing, Google mentioned that the war with spammers including these bombers, is "ongoing and increasing," and that they were stepping up tactics to outsmart the spammers and defuse the bombs.*

Chapter Six

The Sensitivity of PageRank

Psychologists say that a person's sensitivities give insights into the personality. They say sensitivity to name-calling might indicate a maligned childhood. Sensitivity to injury, a pampered, spoiled upbringing; a short fuse with the boss, anger toward parents, and so on. It seems the same is true for the PageRank model. The sensitivities of the PageRank model reveal quite a bit about the popularity scores it produces. For example, when α gets very close to 1 (its upperbound), it seems to really get PageRank's goat. In this chapter, we explain exactly how PageRank reacts to changes like this.

In fact, the sensitivity of the PageRank vector can be analyzed by examining each parameter of the Google matrix $\mathbf{G}$ separately. In Chapter 5, we emphasized $\mathbf{G}$'s dependence on three specific parameters: the scaling parameter α, the hyperlink matrix $\mathbf{H}$, and the personalization vector $\mathbf{v}^T$. We discuss the effect of each of these on the PageRank vector in turn in this chapter.

6.1 SENSITIVITY WITH RESPECT TO α

In this section, we use the derivative to show the effect of changes in α on $\boldsymbol{\pi}^T$. The derivative is a classical tool for answering questions of sensitivity. The derivative of $\boldsymbol{\pi}^T$ with respect to α, written $d\boldsymbol{\pi}^T(\alpha)/d\alpha$, tells how much the elements in the PageRank vector $\boldsymbol{\pi}^T$ vary when α varies slightly. If element j of $d\boldsymbol{\pi}^T(\alpha)/d\alpha$, denoted $d\pi_j(\alpha)/d\alpha$, is large in magnitude, then we can conclude that as α increases slightly, π_j (the PageRank for page P_j) is very sensitive to small changes in α. The signs of the derivatives also give important information; if $d\pi_j(\alpha)/d\alpha > 0$, then small increases in α imply that the PageRank for P_j will increase. And similarly, $d\pi_j(\alpha)/d\alpha < 0$ implies the PageRank decreases. It is important to remember that $d\boldsymbol{\pi}^T(\alpha)/d\alpha$ is only an *approximation* of how elements in $\boldsymbol{\pi}^T$ change when α changes, and does not describe *exactly* how they change. Nevertheless, analyzing this derivative can reveal important information about how changes in α affect $\boldsymbol{\pi}^T$.

Even though the parameter α is usually set to .85, it can theoretically vary between $0 < \alpha < 1$. Of course, $\mathbf{G}$ depends on α, and so, $\mathbf{G}(\alpha) = \alpha\mathbf{S} + (1-\alpha)\mathbf{e}\mathbf{v}^T$. The question about how sensitive $\boldsymbol{\pi}^T(\alpha)$ is to changes in α can be answered precisely if the derivative $d\boldsymbol{\pi}^T(\alpha)/d\alpha$, which gives the rate of change of $\boldsymbol{\pi}^T(\alpha)$ with respect to small changes in α, can be evaluated. But before attempting to differentiate we should be sure that this derivative is well defined. The distribution $\boldsymbol{\pi}^T(\alpha)$ is a *left-hand eigenvector* for $\mathbf{G}(\alpha)$, but eigenvector components need not be differentiable (or even continuous) functions of the entries of $\mathbf{G}(\alpha)$ [127, p. 497], so the existence of $d\boldsymbol{\pi}^T(\alpha)/d\alpha$ is not a slam dunk. The following theorem provides what is needed. (We have postponed all proofs in this chapter until the last section, section 6.5.)

Theorem 6.1.1. *The PageRank vector is given by*

$$\boldsymbol{\pi}^T(\alpha) = \frac{1}{\sum_{i=1}^{n} D_i(\alpha)} \big(D_1(\alpha),\, D_2(\alpha),\, \ldots,\, D_n(\alpha)\big),$$

where $D_i(\alpha)$ is the ith principal minor determinant of order $n-1$ in $\mathbf{I}-\mathbf{G}(\alpha)$. Because each principal minor $D_i(\alpha) > 0$ is just a sum of products of numbers from $\mathbf{I}-\mathbf{G}(\alpha)$, it follows that each component in $\boldsymbol{\pi}^T(\alpha)$ is a differentiable function of α on the interval $(0,1)$.

The theorem below provides an upperbound on the individual components of the derivative vector as well as an upperbound on the sum of these individual components, denoted by the *1-norm*.

Theorem 6.1.2. *If $\boldsymbol{\pi}^T(\alpha) = \big(\pi_1(\alpha), \pi_2(\alpha), \ldots \pi_n(\alpha)\big)$ is the PageRank vector , then*

$$\left|\frac{d\pi_j(\alpha)}{d\alpha}\right| \le \frac{1}{1-\alpha} \qquad \text{for each } j = 1, 2, \ldots, n, \tag{6.1.1}$$

and

$$\left\|\frac{d\boldsymbol{\pi}^T(\alpha)}{d\alpha}\right\|_1 \le \frac{2}{1-\alpha}. \tag{6.1.2}$$

The utility of Theorem 6.1.2 is limited to smaller values of α. For smaller values of α, Theorem 6.1.2 insures that PageRanks are not overly sensitive as a function of the Google parameter α. However, as $\alpha \to 1$, the upperbound (6.1.1) of $1/(1-\alpha) \to \infty$. Thus, the bound becomes increasingly useless because there is no guarantee that it is attainable.

But the larger values of α are the ones of most interest because they give more weight to the true link structure of the Web while smaller values of α increase the influence of the artificial probability vector $\mathbf{v}^T$. Since the PageRank concept is predicated on taking advantage of the Web's link structure, it is natural to choose α closer to 1. Again, it is been reported that Google uses $\alpha \approx .85$ [39, 40]. Therefore, more analysis is needed to decide on the degree of sensitivity of PageRank to larger values of α. The following theorem provides a clear and more complete understanding.

Theorem 6.1.3. *If $\boldsymbol{\pi}^T(\alpha)$ is the PageRank vector associated with the Google matrix $\mathbf{G}(\alpha) = \alpha\mathbf{S} + (1-\alpha)\mathbf{e}\mathbf{v}^T$, then*

$$\frac{d\boldsymbol{\pi}^T(\alpha)}{d\alpha} = -\mathbf{v}^T(\mathbf{I}-\mathbf{S})(\mathbf{I}-\alpha\mathbf{S})^{-2}. \tag{6.1.3}$$

In particular, the limiting values of this derivative are

$$\lim_{\alpha\to 0} \frac{d\boldsymbol{\pi}^T(\alpha)}{d\alpha} = -\mathbf{v}^T(\mathbf{I}-\mathbf{S}) \quad \text{and} \quad \lim_{\alpha\to 1} \frac{d\boldsymbol{\pi}^T(\alpha)}{d\alpha} = -\mathbf{v}^T(\mathbf{I}-\mathbf{S})^{\#},$$

where $(\star)^{\#}$ denotes the group inverse [46, 122].

The dominant eigenvalue $\lambda_1 = 1$ of all stochastic matrices is *semisimple* [127, p. 696], so, when $\mathbf{S}$ is reduced to *Jordan form* by a *similarity transformation*, the result is

$$\mathbf{J} = \mathbf{X}^{-1}\mathbf{S}\mathbf{X} = \begin{pmatrix} \mathbf{I} & \mathbf{0} \\ \mathbf{0} & \mathbf{C} \end{pmatrix},\ 1 \notin \sigma(\mathbf{C}), \implies (\mathbf{I}-\mathbf{S}) = \mathbf{X}\begin{pmatrix} \mathbf{0} & \mathbf{0} \\ \mathbf{0} & \mathbf{I}-\mathbf{C} \end{pmatrix}\mathbf{X}^{-1}$$

and

$$(\mathbf{I}-\mathbf{S})^{\#} = \mathbf{X}\begin{pmatrix} \mathbf{0} & \mathbf{0} \\ \mathbf{0} & (\mathbf{I}-\mathbf{C})^{-1} \end{pmatrix}\mathbf{X}^{-1}.$$

Matrix $\mathbf{C}$ is composed of *Jordan blocks* $\mathbf{J}_\star$ associated with eigenvalues $\lambda_k \neq 1$, and the corresponding blocks in $(\mathbf{I}-\mathbf{C})^{-1}$ are $(\mathbf{I}-\mathbf{J}_\star)^{-1}$. Combining this with Theorem 6.1.3 makes it clear that the sensitivity of $\boldsymbol{\pi}^T(\alpha)$ as $\alpha \to 1$ is governed by the size of the entries of $(\mathbf{I}-\mathbf{S})^{\#}$. $\|(\mathbf{I}-\mathbf{S})^{\#}\| \leq \kappa(\mathbf{X})\|(\mathbf{I}-\mathbf{C})^{-1}\|$, where $\kappa(\mathbf{X})$ is the *condition number* of $\mathbf{X}$. Therefore, the sensitivity of $\boldsymbol{\pi}^T(\alpha)$ as $\alpha \to 1$ is governed primarily by the size of $\|(\mathbf{I}-\mathbf{C})^{-1}\|$, which is driven by the size of $|1-\lambda_2|^{-1}$ (along with the index of λ_2), where $\lambda_2 \neq 1$ is the eigenvalue of $\mathbf{S}$ that is closest to $\lambda_1 = 1$. *In other words, the closer λ_2 is to $\lambda_1 = 1$, the more sensitive $\boldsymbol{\pi}^T(\alpha)$ is when α is close to 1.*

Generally speaking, stochastic matrices having a subdominant eigenvalue near to 1 are those that represent *nearly uncoupled chains* [85] (also known as nearly completely decomposable chains). These are chains whose states form clusters such that the states within each cluster are strongly linked to each other, but the clusters themselves are only weakly linked—i.e., the states can be ordered so that the transition probability matrix has the form $\mathbf{S} = \mathbf{D} + \epsilon\mathbf{E}$, where $\mathbf{D}$ is block diagonal, $\|\mathbf{E}\| \leq 1$, and $0 \leq \epsilon < 1$ is small relative to 1.

The chain defined by the link structure of the Web is almost certainly nearly uncoupled (weakly linked clusters of closely coupled nodes abound due to specialized interests, regional interests, geographical considerations, etc.), so the matrix $\mathbf{S}$ can be expected to have a subdominant eigenvalue very close to $\lambda_1 = 1$. Therefore, as α grows, the PageRank vector becomes increasingly sensitive to changes in α, and when $\alpha \approx 1$, PageRank is extremely sensitive. Putting all of these observations together produces the following conclusions.

Summary of PageRank Sensitivity

As a function of the parameter α, the sensitivity of the PageRank vector $\boldsymbol{\pi}^T(\alpha)$ to small changes in α is as follows.

- For small α, PageRank is insensitive to slight variations in α.
- As α becomes larger, PageRank becomes increasingly more sensitive to small perturbations in α.
- For α close to 1, PageRank is very sensitive to small changes in α. The degree of sensitivity is governed by the degree to which $\mathbf{S}$ is nearly uncoupled.

The Balancing Act

Larger values of α give more weight to the true link structure of the Web while smaller values of α increase the influence of the artificial probability vector $\mathbf{v}^T$. Because the PageRank concept is predicated on trying to take advantage of the Web's link structure, it's more desirable to choose α close to 1. But this is where PageRank becomes most sensitive, so moderation is necessary—it has been reported that Google uses $\alpha \approx .85$ [39, 40].

We close this section with a numerical example whereby we examine the eigenvalues and PageRank vectors of the matrices associated with two related web graphs.

EXAMPLE 1 A small web graph is pictured in Figure 6.1.

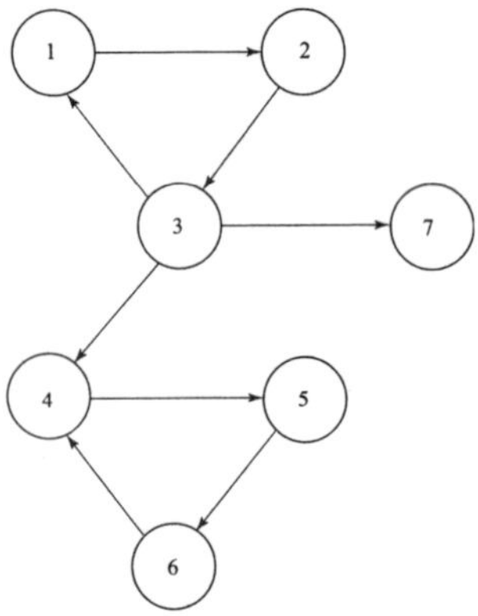

Figure 6.1 Directed graph for web of seven pages

Table 6.1 shows the eigenvalues (sorted by magnitude) for the three matrices associated with this graph: the raw hyperlink matrix $\mathbf{H}$, the stochastic matrix $\mathbf{S}$, and the Google matrix $\mathbf{G}$. It also shows the PageRank values and rank for different values of α.

Table 6.1 Eigenvalues and PageRank vector for 7-node graph of Figure 6.1

		$\alpha = .8$			$\alpha = .9$			$\alpha = .99$		
$\sigma(\mathbf{H})$	$\sigma(\mathbf{S})$	$\sigma(\mathbf{G})$	$\boldsymbol{\pi}^T$	Rank	$\sigma(\mathbf{G})$	$\boldsymbol{\pi}^T$	Rank	$\sigma(\mathbf{G})$	$\boldsymbol{\pi}^T$	Rank
1	1	1	.0641	6	1	.0404	6	1	.0054	6
-.50+.87i	-.50+.87i	-.40+.69i	.0871	5	-.45+.78i	.0558	5	-.50+.86i	.0075	5
-.50-.87i	-.50-.87i	-.40-.69i	.1056	4	-.45-.78i	.0697	4	-.50+.86i	.0096	4
-.35+.60i	**.7991**	.6393	.2372	1	.7192	.2720	1	.7911	.3253	1
-.35-.60i	-.33+.61i	-.26+.49i	.2256	2	-.30+.55i	.2643	2	-.33+.60i	.3240	2
.6934	-.33-.61i	-.26-.49i	.2164	3	-.30-.55i	.2573	3	-.33-.60i	.3231	3
0	0	0	.0641	6	0	.0404	6	0	.0054	6

According to PageRank, the pages are ordered from most important to least important as $(4 \quad 5 \quad 6 \quad 3 \quad 2 \quad 1 \quad 7)$. Table 6.1 reveals several facts. First, $|\lambda_2(\mathbf{G})| = \alpha$ since $\mathbf{S}$ has several eigenvalues on the unit circle, a consequence of the reducibility and periodicity of the graph. Second, as $\alpha \to 1$, the PageRank values do change noticeably, however; in this example, the actual ranks do not change. Other experiments on larger graphs show that the ranks can also change as $\alpha \to 1$ [158]. (We discuss the issue of sensitivity of PageRank *values* versus PageRank *ranks* later, in Section 6.4). Third, the second largest in magnitude eigenvalue of $\mathbf{S}$ is .7991. In this section, we emphasized that this value (which also measures the degree of coupling of the Markov chain) governs the sensitivity of the PageRank vector. Since .7991 is not close to 1, we expect this chain to be rather insensitive to small changes. Let's check this hypothesis. We perturb the chain by adding one hyperlink from page 6 to page 5. Thus, row 6 of $\mathbf{H}$ changes, so that $\mathbf{H}_{64} = \mathbf{H}_{65} = .5$. Table 6.2 shows the changes in the eigenvalues and PageRanks.

After the addition of just one hyperlink the pages are now ordered from most important to least important as $(5 \quad 6 \quad 4 \quad 3 \quad 2 \quad 1 \quad 7)$. Comparing this with the original

Table 6.2 Eigenvalues and PageRank vector for perturbed 7-node graph of Figure 6.1

		$\alpha = .8$			$\alpha = .9$			$\alpha = .99$		
$\sigma(\mathbf{H})$	$\sigma(\mathbf{S})$	$\sigma(\mathbf{G})$	$\boldsymbol{\pi}^T$	Rank	$\sigma(\mathbf{G})$	$\boldsymbol{\pi}^T$	Rank	$\sigma(\mathbf{G})$	$\boldsymbol{\pi}^T$	Rank
1	1	1	.0641	6	1	.0404	6	1	.0054	6
-.50+.50i	.7991	.6393	.0871	5	.7192	.0558	5	.7911	.0075	5
-.50-.50i	-.50+.50i	-.40+.40i	.1056	4	-.45+.45i	.0697	4	-.50+.50i	.0096	4
.6934	-.50-.50i	-.40-.40i	.1637	3	-.45-.45i	.1765	3	-.50-.50i	1968	3
-.35+.60i	-.33+.61i	-.26-.49i	.2664	1	-.30+.55i	.3145	1	-.33+.60i	.3885	1
-.35-.60i	-.33-.61i	-.26-.49i	.2491	2	-.30-.55i	.3025	2	-.33-.60i	.3848	2
0	0	0	.0641	6	0	.0404	6	0	.0054	6

ordering, we see that page 4 has moved down the ranked list from first place to third place. Comparing the PageRank values for the original chain with those for the perturbed chain, we see that only the PageRank values for pages 4, 5, and 6 have changed (again, a consequence of the reducibility of the chain).

In Example 2, we consider a related graph in which the second largest in magnitude eigenvalue of $\mathbf{S}$ is closer to 1. In this case, we expect the PageRank vector to be more sensitive to small changes than the PageRank vector for Example 1.

EXAMPLE 2 In this example, we apply the intelligent surfer model of section 5.2 rather than the democratic random surfer model to the same graph from Example 1. Suppose an intelligent surfer determines new hyperlinking probabilities for page 3. See Figure 6.2.

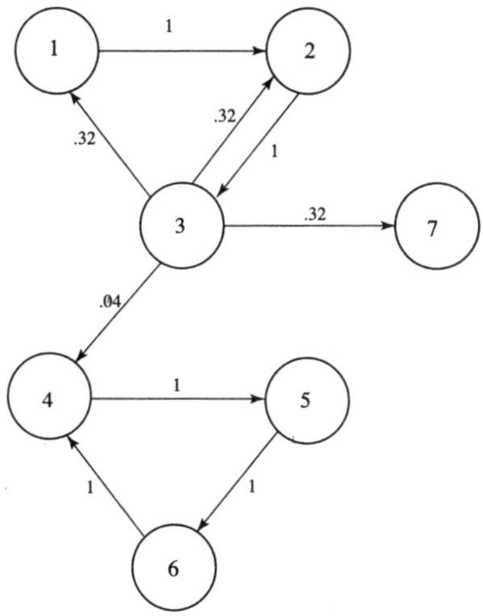

Figure 6.2 Intelligent surfer's graph for web of seven pages

Notice that the intelligent surfer decides to increase the hyperlinking probabilities of pages inside the cluster of pages 1, 2, 3, and 7, while drastically decreasing the probability of jumping to the other cluster of pages 4, 5, and 6. As a result, the stochastic matrix $\mathbf{S}$ is much more uncoupled. Of course, we purposely designed this example so that the second largest in magnitude eigenvalue of $\mathbf{S}$ is closer to 1. The increased degree of coupling is apparent—$\lambda_2(\mathbf{S}) = .9193$ in this example versus .7991 in Example 1. Table 6.3 shows the eigenvalues and PageRank vectors associated with this new graph.

Table 6.3 Eigenvalues and PageRank vector for intelligent surfer graph of Figure 6.2

		$\alpha = .8$			$\alpha = .9$			$\alpha = .99$		
$\sigma(\mathbf{H})$	$\sigma(\mathbf{S})$	$\sigma(\mathbf{G})$	$\boldsymbol{\pi}^T$	Rank	$\sigma(\mathbf{G})$	$\boldsymbol{\pi}^T$	Rank	$\sigma(\mathbf{G})$	$\boldsymbol{\pi}^T$	Rank
1	1	1	.0736	6	1	.0538	6	1	.0099	6
-.50+.870i	-.50+.87i	-.40+.70i	.1324	5	-.45+.78i	.1022	5	-.50+.86i	.0197	5
-.50-.87i	-.50-.87i	-.40-.70i	.1429	4	-.45-.78i	.1132	4	-.50+.86i	.0224	4
.8378	**.9193**	.7354	.1943	1	.8274	.2271	1	.9101	.3130	1
-.42+.43i	-.39+.44i	-.31+.36i	.1924	2	-.35+.40i	.2256	2	-.38+.44i	.3127	2
-.42-.43i	-.39-.44i	-.31-.36i	.1909	3	-.35-.40i	.2242	3	-.38+.44i	.3124	3
0	0	0	.0736	6	0	.0538	6	0	.0099	6

Notice that the pages in Figure 6.2 are ordered from most important to least important as $(4 \quad 5 \quad 6 \quad 3 \quad 2 \quad 1 \quad 7)$. Now let's make the same perturbation that we did in Example 1 (add a hyperlink from page 6 to page 5, making $\mathbf{H}_{64} = \mathbf{H}_{65} = .5$). Table 6.4 shows the effect on the PageRank vector.

Table 6.4 Eigenvalues and PageRank vector for perturbed intelligent surfer graph of Figure 6.2

		$\alpha = .8$			$\alpha = .9$			$\alpha = .99$		
$\sigma(\mathbf{H})$	$\sigma(\mathbf{S})$	$\sigma(\mathbf{G})$	$\boldsymbol{\pi}^T$	Rank	$\sigma(\mathbf{G})$	$\boldsymbol{\pi}^T$	Rank	$\sigma(\mathbf{G})$	$\boldsymbol{\pi}^T$	Rank
1	1	1	.0736	6	1	.0538	6	1	.0099	6
.8378	.9193	.7354	.1324	4	.8274	.1022	5	.9101	.0197	5
-.50+.50i	-.50+.50i	-.40+.40i	.1429	3	-.45+.45i	.1132	4	-.50+.50i	.0224	4
-.50-.50i	-.50-.50i	-.40-.40i	.1294	5	-.45-.45i	.1439	3	-.50-.50i	.1889	3
-.42+.45i	-.39+.44i	-.31+.36i	.2284	1	-.35+.40i	.2694	1	-.38+.44i	.3750	1
-.42-.45i	-.39-.44i	-.31-.36i	.2197	2	-.35-.40i	.2636	2	-.38-.44i	.3741	2
0	0	0	.0736	6	0	.0538	6	0	.0099	6

After the perturbation, the pages are ordered from most important to least important as $(5 \quad 6 \quad 3 \quad 2 \quad 4 \quad 1 \quad 7)$. Page 4 slides much farther down the ranked list. Both the rankings and the PageRank values are more sensitive in Example 2 than Example 1 to the same small perturbation. This clearly demonstrates the effect of $\lambda_2(\mathbf{S})$ on the sensitivity of the PageRank vector.

Very recently, researchers from the University of Southern California have studied the behavior of PageRank with respect to changes in α in order to detect link spammers [164]. Their results are promising. Their technique is successful in identifying "colluding" pages, pages that are in collusion to boost each other's PageRank through a link farm or link exchange scheme. They also define a slightly modified PageRank algorithm that decreases the value of links from the identified colluding pages.

Italian researchers have extended work on the sensitivity of PageRank with respect to α by examining higher-order derivatives than the simple first-order derivatives of this section [32].

6.2 SENSITIVITY WITH RESPECT TO H

The question in this section is: how sensitive is $\boldsymbol{\pi}^T$ to changes in the $\mathbf{H}$? Traditional perturbation results [121] say that for a Markov chain with transition matrix $\mathbf{P}$ and stationary vector $\boldsymbol{\pi}^T$

$$\boldsymbol{\pi}^T \text{is sensitive to perturbations in } \mathbf{P} \iff |\lambda_2(\mathbf{P})| \approx 1.$$

For the PageRank problem, we know that $|\lambda_2(\mathbf{G})| \leq \alpha$, and further, for a reducible $\mathbf{S}$, $\lambda_2(\mathbf{G}) = \alpha$. Therefore, as $\alpha \rightarrow 1$, the PageRank vector becomes more and more sensitive to changes in $\mathbf{G}$, a result from the previous section. However, $\mathbf{G}$ depends on α, $\mathbf{H}$, and $\mathbf{v}^T$, so in this section we would like to isolate the effect of hyperlink changes (the effect of changes to $\mathbf{H}$ on the sensitivity of the PageRank vector). We can squeeze a little more information about the sensitivity with respect of hyperlink changes by computing another derivative.

$$\frac{d\boldsymbol{\pi}^T(h_{ij})}{dh_{ij}} = \alpha\pi_i(\mathbf{e}_j^T - \mathbf{v}^T)(\mathbf{I} - \alpha\mathbf{S})^{-1}. \tag{6.2.1}$$

The effect of α is clear. As $\alpha \rightarrow 1$, the elements of $(\mathbf{I} - \alpha\mathbf{S})^{-1}$ approach infinity, and the PageRank vector is more sensitive to small changes in the structure of the web graph. But another result appears, a rather common sense result: adding a link or increasing the weight of a link from an important page (i.e., π_i is high) has a greater effect on the sensitivity of the PageRank vector than changing a link from an unimportant page.

6.3 SENSITIVITY WITH RESPECT TO $\mathbf{V}^T$

Lastly, we consider the effect of changes in the personalization vector $\mathbf{v}^T$. We begin by computing the derivative of $\boldsymbol{\pi}^T$ with respect to $\mathbf{v}^T$.

$$\frac{d\boldsymbol{\pi}^T(\mathbf{v}^T)}{d\mathbf{v}^T} = (1 - \alpha + \alpha\sum_{i\in D}\pi_i)(\mathbf{I} - \alpha\mathbf{S})^{-1}, \tag{6.3.1}$$

where D is the set of dangling nodes.

Equation 6.3.1 gives two insights into the sensitivity of $\boldsymbol{\pi}^T$ with respect to $\mathbf{v}^T$. First, there is the dependence on α. As $\alpha \rightarrow 1$, the elements of $(\mathbf{I} - \alpha\mathbf{S})^{-1}$ approach infinity. Again, we conclude that as $\alpha \rightarrow 1$, $\boldsymbol{\pi}^T$ becomes increasingly sensitive. Nothing new there. However, the second interpretation gives a bit more information. If the dangling nodes combine to contain a large proportion of the PageRank (i.e., $\sum_{i\in D}\pi_i$ is large), then the PageRank vector is more sensitive to changes in the personalization vector $\mathbf{v}^T$. This agrees with common sense. If collectively the set of dangling nodes is important, then the random surfer revisits them often and thus follows the teleportation probabilities given in $\mathbf{v}^T$ more often. Therefore, the random surfer's actions, and thus the distribution of PageRanks, are sensitive to changes in the teleportation vector $\mathbf{v}^T$.

A Fundamental Matrix for the PageRank problem

Because the matrix $(\mathbf{I}-\alpha\mathbf{S})^{-1}$ plays a fundamental role in the PageRank problem, both in the sensitivity analysis of this chapter and the linear system formulation of the next chapter, we call it the **fundamental matrix** of the PageRank problem.

6.4 OTHER ANALYSES OF SENSITIVITY

Three other research groups have examined the sensitivity and stability of the PageRank vector; Ng et al. at the University of California at Berkeley, Bianchini et al. in Siena, Italy and Borodin et al. at the University of Toronto. All three groups have computed some version of the following bound on the difference between the old PageRank vector $\boldsymbol{\pi}^T$ and the new, updated PageRank vector $\tilde{\boldsymbol{\pi}}^T$ [29, 113, 133].

$$\|\boldsymbol{\pi}^T - \tilde{\boldsymbol{\pi}}^T\|_1 \leq \frac{2\alpha}{1-\alpha}\sum_{i\in U}\pi_i,$$

where U is the set of all pages that have been updated. (The proof is given in section 6.5, p. 69.) This bound gives another sensitivity interpretation: as long as α is not close to 1 and the updated pages do not have high PageRank, then the updated PageRank values do not change much. Let's consider the two factors of the bound, $2\alpha/(1-\alpha)$ and $\sum_{i\in U}\pi_i$.

As an example, suppose $\alpha = .8$ and the sum of the old PageRanks for all updated pages, $\sum_{i\in U}\pi_i$, is 10^{-6}. Then the multiplicative constant $2\alpha/(1-\alpha) = 8$, which means that the 1-norm of the difference between the old PageRank vector and the updated PageRank vector, $\|\boldsymbol{\pi}^T - \tilde{\boldsymbol{\pi}}^T\|_1$, is at most 8×10^{-6}. Consequently, in this case, the PageRank values are rather insensitive to the Web's updates. As $\alpha \to 1$, the bound becomes increasingly useless. The utility of the bound is governed by how much $\sum_{i\in U}\pi_i$ can offset the growth of $2\alpha/(1-\alpha)$. Two things affect the size of $\sum_{i\in U}\pi_i$: the number of updated pages and the PageRanks of those updated pages. This exposes another limitation of the bound. It provides no help with the more interesting and natural question of "what happens to PageRank when the high PageRank pages are updated?" For example, how do changes to a popular, high rank page like the Amazon webpage affect the rankings? Section 6.2 provided a more complete answer to this question.

PageRank and Link Spamming

The difference between the old PageRank vector $\boldsymbol{\pi}^T$ and the updated PageRank vector $\tilde{\boldsymbol{\pi}}^T$ can be bounded as follows:

$$\|\boldsymbol{\pi}^T - \tilde{\boldsymbol{\pi}}^T\|_1 \leq \frac{2\alpha}{1-\alpha}\sum_{i\in U}\pi_i, \tag{6.4.1}$$

where U is the set of all pages that have been updated.

- This bound is useful when α is small and the set of updated pages have small aggregate PageRank. It implies that as long as α is not close to 1 and the updated pages do not have high PageRank, then the updated PageRank values do not differ greatly from the original PageRank values.
- On the other hand, the bound does not tell us how sensitive PageRank is to changes in popular, high PageRank pages.
- Using the bound of (6.4.1), researchers [29] have made the following statement about the effectiveness of link spamming:

  > ... a nice property of PageRank [is] that a community can only make a very limited change to the overall PageRank of the Web. Thus, regardless of the way they change, non-authoritative communities cannot affect significantly the global PageRank.

This bound reinforces the philosophy that the optimizing game is to either get several high PageRank pages or many lower PageRank pages to point to your page. See [12] for other mathematically optimal linking strategies regarding PageRank.

A fourth group of researchers recently joined the stability discussion. Ronny Lempel and Shlomo Moran, the inventors of the SALSA algorithm [114] (see Chapter 12), have added a further distinction to the definition of stability. In [115], they note that the stability of an algorithm, which concerns volatility of the *values* assigned to pages, has been well studied. What has not been studied is the notion of rank-stability (first defined and studied by Borodin et al. [36]), which addresses how volatile the *rankings* of pages are with respect to changes in the underlying graph. As an example, suppose

$$\boldsymbol{\pi}^T = (\,.198 \quad .199 \quad .20 \quad .201 \quad .202\,) \quad \text{and}$$
$$\tilde{\boldsymbol{\pi}}^T = (\,.202 \quad .201 \quad .20 \quad .199 \quad .198\,).$$

The original and updated PageRank values have not changed much, $\|\boldsymbol{\pi}^T - \tilde{\boldsymbol{\pi}}^T\|_1 = .012$, and yet the *rankings* have flipped. Lempel and Moran show that stability of PageRank values does not imply rank-stability. In fact, they provide a small example demonstrating that a change in just one outlink of a very low ranking page can turn the entire ranking upside down! They also introduce the interesting concept of running-time stability, challenging researchers to examine the effect of small perturbations in the graph on an algorithm's running time.

REMARK: From the start of the book, we've emphasized the Web's dynamics. However, while the content of webpages does change very often, we are concerned only with changes to the graph structure of the Web. Graph changes affect the PageRank vector, whereas content changes affect the inverted index of Chapters 1 and 2. Updates to the Web's graph can be of two types: link updates or node updates. The analyses of sensitivity and updating in this chapter all assume that the Web's updates are only link updates, which refers to the addition or removal of hyperlinks. Node updates, the addition or removal of webpages, are not considered. Analyzing node updates is a much harder problem, which we postpone until Chapter 10.

ASIDE: RankPulse

The website `www.rankpulse.com` *uses Google's Web Application Programming Interface (Web API, see the aside on page 97) to monitor the pulse of the top ten rankings for 1,000 queries. Even though exact PageRank values are not available, the RankPulse authors have developed a clever workaround. They track only the first page of Google results (the top ten list) for a query like "basketball," noticing how the ten sites jockey for position. Every day they record the websites and their positions in the top ten list. Then they plot these rankings over time. Figure 6.3 shows a RankPulse chart for "basketball" on July 26, 2004.*

We have included only the plots for five of the available 10 websites to reduce the clutter on the chart. The sites `www.nba.com` *and* `www.basketball.com` *are historical fixtures in the top two spots, while* `www.basketball.ca` *bounces in and out of the bottom part of the top ten. The other two sites,* `www.fiba.com` *and* `www.wnba.com` *fluctuate among the top ten. The fluctuations for the WNBA site can be explained by the league's seasonal schedule and frequent updates—big college tournaments in March, predictions for and the lead up to the April draft, then the May through September season.*

Since Google's overall rankings are a combination of content scores and PageRank popularity scores, it is hard to isolate the sensitivity of PageRank in the RankPulse charts.

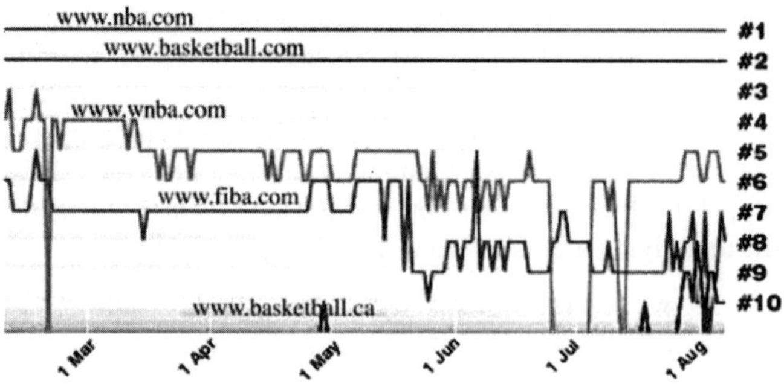

Figure 6.3 RankPulse chart for `basketball`

Nevertheless, these charts give some approximation to the sensitivity of Google rankings for select pages.

6.5 SENSITIVITY THEOREMS AND PROOFS

Theorem 6.1.1 *The PageRank vector is given by*

$$\boldsymbol{\pi}^T(\alpha) = \frac{1}{\sum_{i=1}^{n} D_i(\alpha)} \big(D_1(\alpha),\, D_2(\alpha),\, \ldots,\, D_n(\alpha)\big),$$

where $D_i(\alpha)$ is the ith principal minor determinant of order $n-1$ in $\mathbf{I}-\mathbf{G}(\alpha)$. Because each principal minor $D_i(\alpha) > 0$ is just a sum of products of numbers from $\mathbf{I}-\mathbf{G}(\alpha)$, it follows that each component in $\boldsymbol{\pi}^T(\alpha)$ is a differentiable function of α on the interval $(0,1)$.

Proof. For convenience, let $\mathbf{G} = \mathbf{G}(\alpha)$, $\boldsymbol{\pi}^T(\alpha) = \boldsymbol{\pi}^T$, $D_i = D_i(\alpha)$, and set $\mathbf{A} = \mathbf{I}-\mathbf{G}$. If adj $(\mathbf{A})$ denotes the the transpose of the matrix of cofactors (often called the adjugate or adjoint), then

$$\mathbf{A}[\text{adj}\,(\mathbf{A})] = \mathbf{0} = [\text{adj}\,(\mathbf{A})]\mathbf{A}.$$

It follows from the Perron–Frobenius theorem that $rank\,(\mathbf{A}) = n-1$, and as a result $rank\,(\text{adj}\,(\mathbf{A})) = 1$. Furthermore, Perron–Frobenius insures that each column of $[\text{adj}\,(\mathbf{A})]$ is a multiple of $\mathbf{e}$, so $[\text{adj}\,(\mathbf{A})] = \mathbf{e}\mathbf{w}^T$ for some vector $\mathbf{w}$. But $[\text{adj}\,(\mathbf{A})]_{ii} = D_i$, so $\mathbf{w}^T = (D_1,\, D_2,\, \ldots,\, D_n)$. Similarly, $[\text{adj}\,(\mathbf{A})]\mathbf{A} = \mathbf{0}$ insures that each row in $[\text{adj}\,(\mathbf{A})]$ is a multiple of $\boldsymbol{\pi}^T$ and hence $\mathbf{w}^T = \alpha\boldsymbol{\pi}^T$ for some α. This scalar α cannot be zero; otherwise $[\text{adj}\,(\mathbf{A})] = \mathbf{0}$, which is impossible. Therefore, $\mathbf{w}^T\mathbf{e} = \alpha \neq 0$, and $\mathbf{w}^T/(\mathbf{w}^T\mathbf{e}) = \mathbf{w}^T/\alpha = \boldsymbol{\pi}^T$. ∎

Theorem 6.1.2 *If $\boldsymbol{\pi}^T(\alpha) = \big(\pi_1(\alpha), \pi_2(\alpha), \ldots \pi_n(\alpha)\big)$ is the PageRank vector, then*

$$\left|\frac{d\pi_j(\alpha)}{d\alpha}\right| \leq \frac{1}{1-\alpha} \qquad \text{for each } j = 1, 2, \ldots, n, \tag{6.1.1}$$

and

$$\left\|\frac{d\boldsymbol{\pi}^T(\alpha)}{d\alpha}\right\|_1 \leq \frac{2}{1-\alpha}. \tag{6.1.2}$$

Proof. First compute $d\boldsymbol{\pi}^T(\alpha)/d\alpha$ by noting that $\boldsymbol{\pi}^T(\alpha)\mathbf{e} = 1$ implies

$$\frac{d\boldsymbol{\pi}^T(\alpha)}{d\alpha}\mathbf{e} = 0.$$

Using this while differentiating both sides of

$$\boldsymbol{\pi}^T(\alpha) = \boldsymbol{\pi}^T(\alpha)\big(\alpha\mathbf{S} + (1-\alpha)\mathbf{e}\mathbf{v}^T\big)$$

yields

$$\frac{d\boldsymbol{\pi}^T(\alpha)}{d\alpha}(\mathbf{I} - \alpha\mathbf{S}) = \boldsymbol{\pi}^T(\alpha)(\mathbf{S} - \mathbf{e}\mathbf{v}^T).$$

Matrix $\mathbf{I} - \alpha\mathbf{S}(\alpha)$ is nonsingular because $\alpha < 1$ guarantees that $\rho\big(\alpha\mathbf{S}(\alpha)\big) < 1$, so

$$\frac{d\boldsymbol{\pi}^T(\alpha)}{d\alpha} = \boldsymbol{\pi}^T(\alpha)(\mathbf{S} - \mathbf{e}\mathbf{v}^T)(\mathbf{I} - \alpha\mathbf{S})^{-1}. \tag{6.5.1}$$

The proof of (6.1.1) hinges on the following inequality. For every real $\mathbf{x} \in \mathbf{e}^\perp$ (the orthogonal complement of $span\{\mathbf{e}\}$), and for all real vectors $\mathbf{y}_{n\times 1}$,

$$|\mathbf{x}^T\mathbf{y}| \le \|\mathbf{x}\|_1 \left(\frac{y_{\max} - y_{\min}}{2}\right). \tag{6.5.2}$$

This is a consequence of Hölder's inequality because for all real α,

$$|\mathbf{x}^T\mathbf{y}| = \|\mathbf{x}^T(\mathbf{y} - \alpha\mathbf{e})| \le \|\mathbf{x}\|_1\|\mathbf{y} - \alpha\mathbf{e}\|_\infty,$$

and $\min_\alpha \|\mathbf{y} - \alpha\mathbf{e}\|_\infty = (y_{\max} - y_{\min})/2$, where the minimum is attained when $\alpha = (y_{\max} + y_{\min})/2$. It follows from (6.5.1) that

$$\frac{d\pi_j(\alpha)}{d\alpha} = \boldsymbol{\pi}^T(\alpha)(\mathbf{S} - \mathbf{e}\mathbf{v}^T)(\mathbf{I} - \alpha\mathbf{S})^{-1}\mathbf{e}_j,$$

where $\mathbf{e}_j$ is the jth standard basis vector (i.e, the jth column of $\mathbf{I}_{n\times n}$). Since it's true that $\boldsymbol{\pi}^T(\alpha)(\mathbf{S} - \mathbf{e}\mathbf{v}^T)\mathbf{e} = 0$, inequality (6.5.2) may be applied with

$$\mathbf{y} = (\mathbf{I} - \alpha\mathbf{S})^{-1}\mathbf{e}_j$$

to obtain

$$\left|\frac{d\pi_j(\alpha)}{d\alpha}\right| \le \|\boldsymbol{\pi}^T(\alpha)(\mathbf{S} - \mathbf{e}\mathbf{v}^T)\|_1 \left(\frac{y_{\max} - y_{\min}}{2}\right).$$

But $\|\boldsymbol{\pi}^T(\alpha)(\mathbf{S} - \mathbf{e}\mathbf{v}^T)\|_1 \le 2$, so

$$\left|\frac{d\pi_j(\alpha)}{d\alpha}\right| \le y_{\max} - y_{\min}.$$

Now use the fact that $(\mathbf{I} - \alpha\mathbf{S})^{-1} \ge \mathbf{0}$ together with the observation that

$$(\mathbf{I} - \alpha\mathbf{S})\mathbf{e} = (1-\alpha)\mathbf{e} \implies (\mathbf{I} - \alpha\mathbf{S})^{-1}\mathbf{e} = (1-\alpha)^{-1}\mathbf{e}$$

to conclude that $y_{\min} \ge 0$ and

$$y_{\max} \le \max_{i,j}\left[(\mathbf{I} - \alpha\mathbf{S})^{-1}\right]_{ij} \le \|(\mathbf{I} - \alpha\mathbf{S})^{-1}\|_\infty = \|(\mathbf{I} - \alpha\mathbf{S})^{-1}\mathbf{e}\|_\infty = \frac{1}{1-\alpha}.$$

Consequently,

$$\left|\frac{d\pi_j(\alpha)}{d\alpha}\right| \leq \frac{1}{1-\alpha},$$

which is (6.1.1). Inequality (6.1.2) is a direct consequence of (6.5.1), along with the above observation that

$$\|(\mathbf{I}-\alpha\mathbf{S})^{-1}\|_\infty = \|(\mathbf{I}-\alpha\mathbf{S})^{-1}\mathbf{e}\|_\infty = \frac{1}{1-\alpha}. \quad \blacksquare$$

Theorem 6.1.3 *If $\boldsymbol{\pi}^T(\alpha)$ is the PageRank vector associated with the Google matrix $\mathbf{G}(\alpha) = \alpha\mathbf{S} + (1-\alpha)\mathbf{e}\mathbf{v}^T$, then*

$$\frac{d\boldsymbol{\pi}^T(\alpha)}{d\alpha} = -\mathbf{v}^T(\mathbf{I}-\mathbf{S})(\mathbf{I}-\alpha\mathbf{S})^{-2}. \tag{6.1.3}$$

In particular, the limiting values of this derivative are

$$\lim_{\alpha\to 0}\frac{d\boldsymbol{\pi}^T(\alpha)}{d\alpha} = -\mathbf{v}^T(\mathbf{I}-\mathbf{S}) \quad \textit{and} \quad \lim_{\alpha\to 1}\frac{d\boldsymbol{\pi}^T(\alpha)}{d\alpha} = -\mathbf{v}^T(\mathbf{I}-\mathbf{S})^{\#},$$

where $(\star)^{\#}$ denotes the group inverse [46, 122].

Proof. Multiplying $\mathbf{0}^T = \boldsymbol{\pi}^T(\alpha)\big(\mathbf{I} - \alpha\mathbf{S} - (1-\alpha)\mathbf{e}\mathbf{v}^T\big)$ on the right by $(\mathbf{I}-\alpha\mathbf{S})^{-1}$ yields

$$\mathbf{0}^T = \boldsymbol{\pi}^T(\alpha)\big(\mathbf{I} - (1-\alpha)\mathbf{e}\mathbf{v}^T(\mathbf{I}-\alpha\mathbf{S})^{-1}\big) \implies \boldsymbol{\pi}^T(\alpha) = (1-\alpha)\mathbf{v}^T(\mathbf{I}-\alpha\mathbf{S})^{-1}.$$

Using the formula $d\mathbf{A}(\alpha)^{-1}/d\alpha = -\mathbf{A}^{-1}(\alpha)[d\mathbf{A}(\alpha)/d\alpha]\mathbf{A}^{-1}(\alpha)$ for differentiating an inverse matrix [127, p. 130] together with the fact that $(\mathbf{I}-\mathbf{S})$ commutes with $(\mathbf{I}-\alpha\mathbf{S})^{-1}$ produces

$$\begin{aligned}\frac{d\boldsymbol{\pi}^T(\alpha)}{d\alpha} &= (1-\alpha)\mathbf{v}^T(\mathbf{I}-\alpha\mathbf{S})^{-1}\mathbf{S}(\mathbf{I}-\alpha\mathbf{S})^{-1} - \mathbf{v}^T(\mathbf{I}-\alpha\mathbf{S})^{-1}\\ &= -\mathbf{v}^T(\mathbf{I}-\alpha\mathbf{S})^{-1}\left[\mathbf{I} - (1-\alpha)\mathbf{S}(\mathbf{I}-\alpha\mathbf{S})^{-1}\right]\\ &= -\mathbf{v}^T(\mathbf{I}-\alpha\mathbf{S})^{-1}(\mathbf{I}-\alpha\mathbf{S}-(1-\alpha)\mathbf{S})(\mathbf{I}-\alpha\mathbf{S})^{-1}\\ &= -\mathbf{v}^T(\mathbf{I}-\alpha\mathbf{S})^{-1}(\mathbf{I}-\mathbf{S})(\mathbf{I}-\alpha\mathbf{S})^{-1}\\ &= -\mathbf{v}^T(\mathbf{I}-\mathbf{S})(\mathbf{I}-\alpha\mathbf{S})^{-2}.\end{aligned}$$

By definition, matrices $\mathbf{Y}$ and $\mathbf{Z}$ are group inverses of each other if and only if $\mathbf{YZY} = \mathbf{Y}$, $\mathbf{ZYZ} = \mathbf{Z}$, and $\mathbf{YZ} = \mathbf{ZY}$, so it's clear that if

$$\mathbf{Y}(\alpha) = (\mathbf{I}-\mathbf{S})(\mathbf{I}-\alpha\mathbf{S})^{-2}\mathbf{Z}(\alpha) = (\mathbf{I}-\mathbf{S})^{\#}(\mathbf{I}-\alpha\mathbf{S})^2,$$

then

$$\mathbf{Z}^{\#}(\alpha) = \begin{cases}\mathbf{Y}(\alpha) & \text{for } \alpha < 1,\\ \mathbf{I}-\mathbf{S} & \text{for } \alpha = 1.\end{cases}$$

Therefore, by continuity properties of group inversion [46, p. 232], it follows that

$$\lim_{\alpha\to 1}\mathbf{Y}(\alpha) = \lim_{\alpha\to 1}\left[\mathbf{Z}^{\#}(\alpha)\right] = \left[\lim_{\alpha\to 1}\mathbf{Z}(\alpha)\right]^{\#} = (\mathbf{I}-\mathbf{S})^{\#},$$

and thus

$$\lim_{\alpha\to 1}\frac{d\boldsymbol{\pi}^T(\alpha)}{d\alpha} = -\mathbf{v}^T(\mathbf{I}-\mathbf{S})^{\#}. \quad \blacksquare$$

Theorem 6.5.1. *Suppose* $\mathbf{G} = \alpha\mathbf{S} + (1-\alpha)\mathbf{e}\mathbf{v}^T$ *is the Google matrix with PageRank vector* $\boldsymbol{\pi}^T$ *and* $\tilde{\mathbf{G}} = \alpha\tilde{\mathbf{S}} + (1-\alpha)\mathbf{e}\mathbf{v}^T$ *is the updated Google matrix (of the same size) with corresponding PageRank vector* $\tilde{\boldsymbol{\pi}}^T$. *Then*

$$\|\boldsymbol{\pi}^T - \tilde{\boldsymbol{\pi}}^T\|_1 \leq \frac{2\alpha}{1-\alpha}\sum_{i\in U}\pi_i,$$

where U *is the set of all pages that have been updated.*

Proof. Let $\mathbf{F}$ be the matrix representing the perturbation between the two stochastic matrices $\mathbf{S}$ and $\tilde{\mathbf{S}}$. Thus, $\mathbf{F} = \mathbf{S} - \tilde{\mathbf{S}}$. Then,

$$\begin{aligned}\boldsymbol{\pi}^T - \tilde{\boldsymbol{\pi}}^T &= \alpha\tilde{\boldsymbol{\pi}}^T\mathbf{S} - \alpha\boldsymbol{\pi}^T\tilde{\mathbf{S}}\\ &= \alpha\boldsymbol{\pi}^T\mathbf{S} - \alpha(\tilde{\boldsymbol{\pi}}^T - \boldsymbol{\pi}^T + \boldsymbol{\pi}^T)\tilde{\mathbf{S}}\\ &= \alpha\boldsymbol{\pi}^T\mathbf{S} - \alpha\boldsymbol{\pi}^T\tilde{\mathbf{S}} + \alpha(\boldsymbol{\pi}^T - \tilde{\boldsymbol{\pi}}^T)\tilde{\mathbf{S}}\\ &= \alpha\boldsymbol{\pi}^T\mathbf{F} + \alpha(\boldsymbol{\pi}^T - \tilde{\boldsymbol{\pi}}^T)\tilde{\mathbf{S}}.\end{aligned}$$

Solving for $\boldsymbol{\pi}^T - \tilde{\boldsymbol{\pi}}^T$ gives

$$\boldsymbol{\pi}^T - \tilde{\boldsymbol{\pi}}^T = \alpha\boldsymbol{\pi}^T\mathbf{F}(\mathbf{I} - \alpha\tilde{\mathbf{S}})^{-1}.$$

Computing norms, we obtain

$$\begin{aligned}\|\boldsymbol{\pi}^T - \tilde{\boldsymbol{\pi}}^T\|_1 &\leq \alpha\|\boldsymbol{\pi}^T\mathbf{F}\|_1\|(\mathbf{I} - \alpha\tilde{\mathbf{S}})^{-1}\|_\infty\\ &= \frac{\alpha}{1-\alpha}\|\boldsymbol{\pi}^T\mathbf{F}\|_1.\end{aligned}$$

See [108] for theorems and proofs showing that $\mathbf{I} - \alpha\tilde{\mathbf{S}}$ is nonsingular and has row sums of $1/(1-\alpha)$. Now reorder $\mathbf{F}$ (and $\boldsymbol{\pi}^T$) so that the rows corresponding to updated pages (nonzero rows) are at the top of the matrix. Then

$$\boldsymbol{\pi}^T\mathbf{F} = \begin{pmatrix}\boldsymbol{\pi}_1^T & \boldsymbol{\pi}_2^T\end{pmatrix}\begin{pmatrix}\mathbf{F}_1\\ \mathbf{0}\end{pmatrix} = \boldsymbol{\pi}_1^T\mathbf{F}_1.$$

Therefore, $\|\boldsymbol{\pi}^T\mathbf{F}\|_1 = \|\boldsymbol{\pi}_1^T\mathbf{F}_1\|_1 \leq \|\boldsymbol{\pi}_1^T\|_1\|\mathbf{F}_1\|_\infty$. And $\|\mathbf{F}_1\|_\infty = \|\mathbf{S}_1 - \tilde{\mathbf{S}}_1\|_\infty \leq \|\mathbf{S}_1\|_\infty + \|\tilde{\mathbf{S}}_1\|_\infty = 2$, where $\mathbf{S}_1$ and $\tilde{\mathbf{S}}_1$ also correspond to the updated pages. Therefore, $\|\boldsymbol{\pi}^T\mathbf{F}\|_1 \leq 2\sum_{i\in U}\pi_i$. Finally,

$$\|\boldsymbol{\pi}^T - \tilde{\boldsymbol{\pi}}^T\|_1 \leq \frac{2\alpha}{1-\alpha}\sum_{i\in U}\pi_i. \quad \blacksquare$$

Chapter Seven

The PageRank Problem as a Linear System

Abraham Lincoln, in his humorous, self-deprecating style, said "If I were two-faced, would I be wearing this one?" Honest Abe wasn't, but the PageRank problem is two-faced. There's the eigenvector face it was given by its parents, Brin and Page, at birth, and there's the linear system face, which can be arrived at with a little cosmetic surgery in the form of algebraic manipulation. Because Brin and Page originally conceived of the PageRank problem as an eigenvector problem (find the dominant eigenvector for the Google matrix), the eigenvector face has received much more press and fanfare. However, the normalized eigenvector problem $\boldsymbol{\pi}^T(\alpha\mathbf{S} + (1-\alpha)\mathbf{e}\mathbf{v}^T) = \boldsymbol{\pi}^T$ can be rewritten, with some algebra as,

$$\boldsymbol{\pi}^T(\mathbf{I} - \alpha\mathbf{S}) = (1-\alpha)\mathbf{v}^T. \tag{7.0.1}$$

This linear system is always accompanied by the normalization equation $\boldsymbol{\pi}^T\mathbf{e} = 1$. The question is: which face should PageRank be wearing, or does it even matter? By the end of the chapter we will answer these questions about the two-faced PageRank.

7.1 PROPERTIES OF $(\mathbf{I} - \alpha\mathbf{S})$

In Chapter 4 we learned a lot about PageRank by discussing the properties of the Google Markov matrix $\mathbf{G}$ in the eigenvector problem. Now it's time to carefully examine the linear system formulation of equation (7.0.1). Below are some interesting properties of the coefficient matrix in this equation. (The proofs of these statements are very straightforward. See the books by Berman and Plemmons [21], Golub and Van Loan [82] or Meyer [127].)

Properties of $(\mathbf{I} - \alpha\mathbf{S})$:

1. $(\mathbf{I} - \alpha\mathbf{S})$ is an $\mathbf{M}$-*matrix*.
2. $(\mathbf{I} - \alpha\mathbf{S})$ is nonsingular.
3. The row sums of $(\mathbf{I} - \alpha\mathbf{S})$ are $1-\alpha$.
4. $\|\mathbf{I} - \alpha\mathbf{S}\|_\infty = 1 + \alpha$.
5. Since $(\mathbf{I} - \alpha\mathbf{S})$ is an $\mathbf{M}$-matrix, $(\mathbf{I} - \alpha\mathbf{S})^{-1} \geq 0$.
6. The row sums of $(\mathbf{I} - \alpha\mathbf{S})^{-1}$ are $(1-\alpha)^{-1}$. Therefore, $\|(\mathbf{I} - \alpha\mathbf{S})^{-1}\|_\infty = (1-\alpha)^{-1}$.
7. Thus, the *condition number* $\kappa_\infty(\mathbf{I} - \alpha\mathbf{S}) = (1+\alpha)/(1-\alpha)$.

These are nice properties for $(\mathbf{I} - \alpha\mathbf{S})$. However, recall that $(\mathbf{I} - \alpha\mathbf{S})$ can be pretty dense, whenever the number of dangling nodes is large because these completely sparse rows are replaced with completely dense rows. We like to operate, whenever possible, on the very sparse $\mathbf{H}$ matrix. And so we wonder if similar properties hold for $(\mathbf{I} - \alpha\mathbf{H})$.

7.2 PROPERTIES OF $(\mathbf{I} - \alpha\mathbf{H})$

Using the rank-one dangling node trick (i.e., $\mathbf{S} = \mathbf{H} + \mathbf{a}\mathbf{v}^T$), we can once again write the PageRank problem in terms of the very sparse hyperlink matrix $\mathbf{H}$. The linear system of equation (7.0.1) can be rewritten as

$$\boldsymbol{\pi}^T(\mathbf{I} - \alpha\mathbf{H} - \alpha\mathbf{a}\mathbf{v}^T) = (1-\alpha)\mathbf{v}^T.$$

If we let $\boldsymbol{\pi}^T\mathbf{a} = \gamma$, then the linear system becomes

$$\boldsymbol{\pi}^T(\mathbf{I} - \alpha\mathbf{H}) = (1-\alpha+\alpha\gamma)\mathbf{v}^T.$$

The scalar γ holds the aggregate PageRank for all the dangling nodes. Since the normalization equation $\boldsymbol{\pi}^T\mathbf{e} = 1$ will be applied at the end, we can arbitrarily choose a convenient value for γ, say $\gamma = 1$ [55, 80, 109, 138]. We arrive at the following conclusion.

Theorem 7.2.1 (Linear System for Google problem). *Solving the linear system*

$$\mathbf{x}^T(\mathbf{I} - \alpha\mathbf{H}) = \mathbf{v}^T \tag{7.2.1}$$

and letting $\boldsymbol{\pi}^T = \mathbf{x}^T/\mathbf{x}^T\mathbf{e}$ *produces the PageRank vector.*

In addition, $(\mathbf{I} - \alpha\mathbf{H})$ has many of the same properties as $(\mathbf{I} - \alpha\mathbf{S})$.

Properties of $(\mathbf{I} - \alpha\mathbf{H})$:

1. $(\mathbf{I} - \alpha\mathbf{H})$ is an $\mathbf{M}$-matrix.
2. $(\mathbf{I} - \alpha\mathbf{H})$ is nonsingular.
3. The row sums of $(\mathbf{I} - \alpha\mathbf{H})$ are either $1-\alpha$ for nondangling nodes or 1 for dangling nodes.
4. $\|\mathbf{I} - \alpha\mathbf{H}\|_\infty = 1 + \alpha$.
5. Since $(\mathbf{I} - \alpha\mathbf{H})$ is an $\mathbf{M}$-matrix, $(\mathbf{I} - \alpha\mathbf{H})^{-1} \geq 0$.
6. The row sums of $(\mathbf{I} - \alpha\mathbf{H})^{-1}$ are equal to 1 for the dangling nodes and less than or equal to $\frac{1}{1-\alpha}$ for the nondangling nodes.
7. The condition number $\kappa_\infty(\mathbf{I} - \alpha\mathbf{H}) \leq \frac{1+\alpha}{1-\alpha}$.
8. The row of $(\mathbf{I} - \alpha\mathbf{H})^{-1}$ corresponding to dangling node i is $\mathbf{e}_i^T$, where $\mathbf{e}_i$ is the ith column of the identity matrix.

Linear System for PageRank problem

The sparse linear system formulation of the PageRank problem is

$$\mathbf{x}^T(\mathbf{I} - \alpha\mathbf{H}) = \mathbf{v}^T \quad \text{with} \quad \pi^T = \mathbf{x}/\mathbf{x}^T\mathbf{e}.$$

Like the eigenvector formulation, the PageRank problem has a very *sparse* linear system formulation (with at least eight nice properties). Solve both and you get the same vector, the PageRank vector. So what's the point? There are several good reasons for remembering that PageRank is two-faced. First, for a small problem, such as computing a ranking for a company Intranet, a direct method applied to the linear system is much faster than the power method. Try this out with Matlab. Compare the PageRank power method code from page 51 with some of Matlab's built-in linear system solvers, e.g., `pi=v/(eye(n)-alpha*H)`. Second, in Chapter 5 we warned that as $\alpha \to 1$, the power method takes an increasing amount of time to converge. However, the solution time of the direct method is unaffected by the parameter α. So α can be increased to capture the true essence of the Web, giving less weight to the artificial teleportation matrix. But, don't forget the sensitivity issues of Chapter 6. Unfortunately, the PageRank vector is sensitive as $\alpha \to 1$ regardless of the problem formulation [100]. Third, thinking about PageRank as a linear system opens new research doors. Nearly all PageRank research has focused on solving the eigenvector problem. Researchers have recently begun experimenting with new PageRank techniques such as preconditioners, multigrid methods, and reorderings [55, 80, 109]. In fact, a group from Yahoo! recently tried popular linear system iterative methods such as BiCGSTAB and GMRES on several large web graphs [80]. The preliminary results for some of these methods look promising; see Section 8.4.

Google Hacks

The O'Reilly book, *Google Hacks: 100 Industrial-Strength Tips and Tools* [44], shows readers that there's more to Google than most people know. Google provides a customizable interface as well as an even more flexible programming interface (Google's Web API; see the aside on page 97) that allows users to exercise their creativity with Google. If you know how to use it and *Google Hacks* helps, Google is, to name just a few, an entertainment, research, social, informational, news, archival, spelling, calculating, shopping, and email tool all rolled into one user-friendly package.

7.3 PROOF OF THE PAGERANK SPARSE LINEAR SYSTEM

Theorem 7.3.1. *Solving the linear system*

$$\mathbf{x}^T(\mathbf{I} - \alpha\mathbf{H}) = \mathbf{v}^T \tag{7.3.1}$$

and letting $\pi^T = \mathbf{x}^T/\mathbf{x}^T\mathbf{e}$ *produces the PageRank vector.*

Proof. $\boldsymbol{\pi}^T$ is the PageRank vector if it satisfies $\boldsymbol{\pi}^T\mathbf{G} = \boldsymbol{\pi}^T$ and $\boldsymbol{\pi}^T\mathbf{e} = 1$. Clearly, $\boldsymbol{\pi}^T\mathbf{e} = 1$. Showing $\boldsymbol{\pi}^T\mathbf{G} = \boldsymbol{\pi}^T$ is equivalent to showing $\boldsymbol{\pi}^T(\mathbf{I} - \mathbf{G}) = \mathbf{0}^T$, which is equivalent to showing $\mathbf{x}^T(\mathbf{I} - \mathbf{G}) = \mathbf{0}^T$.

$$\begin{aligned}\mathbf{x}^T(\mathbf{I} - \mathbf{G}) &= \mathbf{x}^T(\mathbf{I} - \alpha\mathbf{H} - \alpha\mathbf{a}\mathbf{v}^T - (1-\alpha)\mathbf{e}\mathbf{v}^T) \\ &= \mathbf{x}^T(\mathbf{I} - \alpha\mathbf{H}) - \mathbf{x}^T(\alpha\mathbf{a} + (1-\alpha)\mathbf{e})\mathbf{v}^T \\ &= \mathbf{v}^T - \mathbf{v}^T = \mathbf{0}^T.\end{aligned}$$

The above line results from the fact that $\mathbf{x}^T(\alpha\mathbf{a} + (1-\alpha)\mathbf{e})\mathbf{v}^T = 1$ because

$$\begin{aligned}1 &= \mathbf{v}^T\mathbf{e} \\ &= \mathbf{x}^T(\mathbf{I} - \alpha\mathbf{H})\mathbf{e} \\ &= \mathbf{x}^T\mathbf{e} - \alpha\mathbf{x}^T\mathbf{H}\mathbf{e} \\ &= \mathbf{x}^T\mathbf{e} - \alpha\mathbf{x}^T(\mathbf{e} - \mathbf{a}) \\ &= (1-\alpha)\mathbf{x}^T\mathbf{e} + \alpha\mathbf{x}^T\mathbf{a}. \quad \blacksquare\end{aligned}$$

Chapter Eight

Issues in Large-Scale Implementation of PageRank

On two occasions, I have been asked [by members of Parliament], 'Pray, Mr. Babbage, if you put into the machine wrong figures, will the right answers come out?' I am not able to rightly apprehend the kind of confusion of ideas that could provoke such a question. –Charles Babbage, designer of the Analytical Machine, a prototype of the first computer

That's a funny quote, but of course, for us the question is: if you put the right (in our case, arbitrary) figures into the PageRank machine, do you get the right answers out? Simple enough to answer. Just check that, for any input $\pi^{(0)T}$, the output satisfies $\pi^{(k)T}\mathbf{G} = \pi^{(k)T}$ up to some tolerance. However, when the problem size grows dramatically, crazy things can happen and simple questions aren't so simple. It's hard to even put numbers into the machine, it's hard to make the machine start running, and it's hard to know whether you have the right answer.

We've all had firsthand experiences with problems of scale. Things don't always scale up nicely. Strategies for babysitting two or three kids just don't work when you're counseling 15-20 campers. Translating teaching strategies for 35 students to 120 students doesn't work either. (At least one of your authors found this out the hard way.) In this chapter, we'll talk about important issues that arise when researchers scale the PageRank model up to web-sized proportions. For instance, how do you store $\mathbf{G}$ when it's of order 8.1 billion? How accurate should the PageRank solution be? And how should dangling nodes be handled? These are substantial issues at the scale of the World Wide Web.

8.1 STORAGE ISSUES

Every adequate search engine requires huge storage facilities for archiving information such as webpages and their locations; inverted indexes and image indexes; content score information; PageRank scores; and the hyperlink graph. The 1998 paper by Brin and Page [39] and more recent papers by Google engineers [19, 78] provide detailed discussions of the many storage schemes used by the Google search engine for all parts of its information retrieval system. The excellent survey paper by Arasu et al. [9] also provides a section on storage schemes needed by any web search engine. Since this book deals with mathematical link analysis algorithms, we focus only on the storage of the mathematical components, the matrices and vectors, used in the PageRank part of the Google system.

Computing the PageRank vector requires access to the items in Table 8.1. Here $nnz(\mathbf{H})$ is the number of nonzeros in $\mathbf{H}$, $|\mathrm{D}|$ is the number of dangling nodes, and n is the number of pages in the web graph. When $\mathbf{v}^T$, the personalization vector, is the uniform vector ($\mathbf{v}^T = \mathbf{e}^T/n$), no storage is required for $\mathbf{v}^T$.

Table 8.1 Storage requirements for the PageRank problem

Entity	Description	Storage
$\mathbf{H}$	sparse hyperlink matrix	$nnz(\mathbf{H})$ doubles
$\mathbf{a}$	sparse binary dangling node vector	$\lvert\mathcal{D}\rvert$ integers
$\mathbf{v}^T$	dense personalization vector	n doubles
$\boldsymbol{\pi}^{(k)T}$	dense current iterate of PageRank power method	n doubles

Since there are roughly 10 outlinks per page on average, $nnz(\mathbf{H})$ is about $10n$, which means that of the entities in Table 8.1, the sparse hyperlink matrix $\mathbf{H}$ requires the most storage. Thus, we begin our discussion of storage for the PageRank problem with $\mathbf{H}$. The size of this matrix makes its storage nontrivial, and at times, requires some creativity. The first thing to determine about $\mathbf{H}$ is whether or not it will fit in the main memory of the available computer system.

For small subsets of the Web, when $\mathbf{H}$ fits in main memory, computation of the PageRank vector can be implemented in the usual fashion (e.g., using code similar to the Matlab programs given on pages 42 and 51). However, when the $\mathbf{H}$ matrix does not fit in main memory, a little more ingenuity (and complexity) is required. When a large hyperlink matrix exceeds a machine's memory, there are two options: compress the data needed so that the compressed representation fits in main memory, then creatively implement a modified version of PageRank on this compressed representation, or keep the data in its uncompressed form and develop I/O (input/output)-efficient implementations of the computations that must take place on the large, uncompressed data.

Even for modest web graphs for which the hyperlink matrix $\mathbf{H}$ can be stored in main memory (meaning compression of the data is not essential), minor storage techniques should still be employed to reduce the work involved at each iteration. For example, for the random surfer model only, the $\mathbf{H}$ matrix can be decomposed into the product of the inverse of the diagonal matrix $\mathbf{D}$ holding outdegrees of the nodes and the adjacency matrix $\mathbf{L}$ of 0's and 1's. First, the simple decomposition $\mathbf{H} = \mathbf{D}^{-1}\mathbf{L}$, where $[\mathbf{D}^{-1}]_{ii} = 1/d_{ii}$ if i is a nondangling node, 0 otherwise, saves storage. Rather than storing $nnz(\mathbf{H})$ real numbers in double precision, we can store n integers (for $\mathbf{D}$) and $nnz(\mathbf{H})$ integers (for the locations of 1's in $\mathbf{L}$). Integers require less storage than doubles. Second, $\mathbf{H} = \mathbf{D}^{-1}\mathbf{L}$ reduces the work at each PageRank power iteration . Each power iteration is executed as

$$\boldsymbol{\pi}^{(k+1)T} = \alpha\boldsymbol{\pi}^{(k)T}\mathbf{H} + (\alpha\boldsymbol{\pi}^{(k)T}\mathbf{a} + 1 - \alpha)\mathbf{v}^T.$$

The most expensive part, the vector-matrix multiplication $\boldsymbol{\pi}^{(k)T}\mathbf{H}$, requires $nnz(\mathbf{H})$ multiplications and $nnz(\mathbf{H})$ additions. Using the vector $diag(\mathbf{D}^{-1})$, $\boldsymbol{\pi}^{(k)T}\mathbf{H}$ can be accomplished as $\boldsymbol{\pi}^{(k)T}\mathbf{D}^{-1}\mathbf{L} = (\boldsymbol{\pi}^{(k)T}).*(diag(\mathbf{D}^{-1}))\mathbf{L}$, where $.*$ represents componentwise multiplication of the elements in the two vectors. The first part, $(\mathbf{x}^T).*(diag(\mathbf{D}^{-1}))$ requires n multiplications. Since $\mathbf{L}$ is an adjacency matrix, $(\boldsymbol{\pi}^{(k)T}).*(diag(\mathbf{D}^{-1}))\mathbf{L}$ now requires a total of n multiplications and $nnz(\mathbf{H})$ additions. Thus, using the $\mathbf{H} = \mathbf{D}^{-1}\mathbf{L}$ decomposition saves $nnz(\mathbf{H}) - n$ multiplications. Unfortunately, this decomposition is limited to the random surfer model. For the intelligent surfer model, other compact storage schemes [18], such as compressed row storage or compressed column storage, may be used. Of course, each compressed format, while saving some storage, requires a bit more overhead for matrix operations.

As mathematicians, we see things as matrices and vectors, and so like to think of $\mathbf{H}$, $\boldsymbol{\pi}^{(k)T}$, $\mathbf{v}^T$, and $\mathbf{a}$ as stored in matrix or compressed matrix form. However, computer scientists see arrays, stacks, and lists, and therefore, store our matrices as *adjacency lists*.

The web-sized implementations of the PageRank model store the $\mathbf{H}$ (or $\mathbf{L}$) matrix in an adjacency list of the columns of the matrix [139]. In order to compute the PageRank vector, the PageRank power method requires vector-matrix multiplications of $\boldsymbol{\pi}^{(k)T}\mathbf{H}$ at each iteration k. Therefore, quick access to the columns of the matrix $\mathbf{H}$ (or $\mathbf{L}$) is essential to algorithm speed. Column i contains the inlink information for page i, which, for the PageRank system of ranking webpages, is more important than the outlink information contained in the rows of $\mathbf{H}$ (or $\mathbf{L}$). Table 8.2 is an adjacency list representation of the columns of $\mathbf{L}$ for the tiny 6-node web in Figure 8.1.

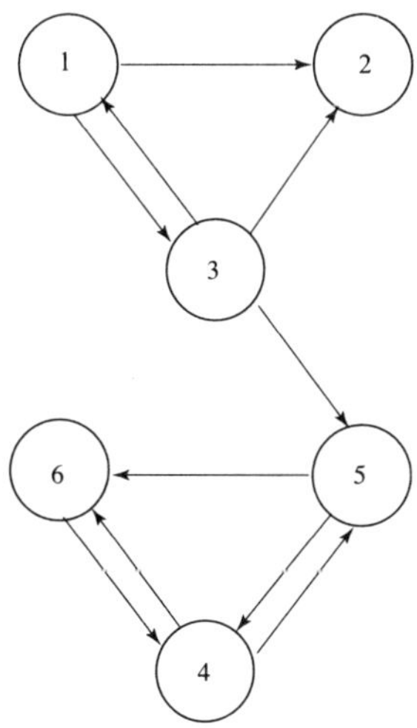

Figure 8.1 Tiny 6-node web

Table 8.2 Adjacency list for random surfer model of Figure 8.1

Node	Inlinks from
1	3
2	1, 3
3	1
4	5, 6
5	3, 4
6	4, 5

Exercise 2.24 of Cleve Moler's recent book *Numerical Computing with Matlab* [132] gives one possible implementation of the PageRank power method applied to an adjacency list, along with sample Matlab code (`PageRankpow.m`) that can be downloaded from `http://www.mathworks.com/moler/`. When the adjacency list does not fit in

main memory, references [139, 141] suggest methods for compressing the data.

Because of their potential and promise, we briefly discuss two methods for compressing the information in an adjacency list, the gap technique [25] and the reference encoding technique [140, 141]. The gap method exploits the locality of hyperlinked pages. Locality refers to the fact that the source and destination pages for a hyperlink are often close to each other lexicographically. A page labeled 100 often has inlinks from pages nearby lexicographically such as pages 112, 113, 116, and 117 rather than pages 924 and 4,931,010. Based on this locality principle, the information in an adjacency list for page 100 is stored as below.

Node	Inlinks from
100	112 0 2 0

The label for the first page inlinking to page 100, which is page 112, is stored. After that, only the gaps between subsequent inlinking pages are stored. Since these gaps are usually nice, small integers, they require less storage.

The other graph compression method, reference encoding, exploits the similarity between webpages. If pages P_i and P_j have similar adjacency lists, it is possible to compress the adjacency list of P_j by representing it in terms of the adjacency list of P_i, in which case P_i is called a reference page for P_j. Pages within the same domain might often share common outlinks, making the reference encoding technique attractive. Consider the example in Figure 8.2, taken from [141]. The adjacency list for page P_j looks a lot like the

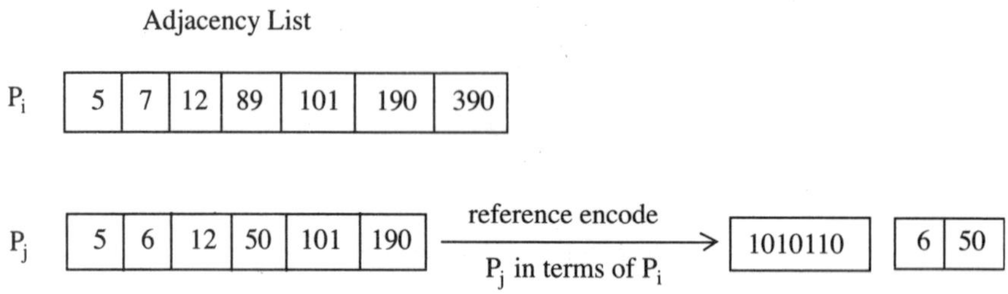

Figure 8.2 Reference encoding example

adjacency list for P_i. In fact, both pages have outlinks to pages 5, 12, 101, and 190. In order to take advantage of this repetition, we need to create two vectors: a sharing vector of 1's and 0's and a dissimilarity vector of integers. The binary sharing vector has the same size as the adjacency list of P_i, and contains a 1 in the kth position if entry k of P_i's adjacency list appears in P_j's adjacency list. The second vector in the reference encoding is a list of all entries in the adjacency list of P_j that are not found in the adjacency list of its reference P_i. Of course, the sharing vector for P_j requires less storage than the adjacency list for P_j. Therefore, the effectiveness of reference encoding depends on the number of dissimilar pages. P_i is a good reference page for P_j if the overlap between the adjacency lists for the two pages is high, which means the dissimilarity vector is short. However, it's not easy to determine a reference page for each page in the index, so some guidelines are given in [140]. Both the gap method and the reference encoding method are used, along with other compression techniques, to impressively compress the information in a standard web graph. These techniques are freely available in the efficient graph compression tool WebGraph, which is produced by Paolo Boldi and Sebastiano Vigna [33, 34].

References [47, 86] take the other approach; rather than compressing the matrix information, they suggest I/O-efficient implementations of PageRank. In addition, because the PageRank vector itself is large and completely dense, containing over 4.3 billion pages, and must be consulted in order to process each user query, Haveliwala [87] has suggested a technique to compress the PageRank vector. This encoding of the PageRank vector hopes to keep the ranking information cached in main memory, thus speeding query processing.

8.2 CONVERGENCE CRITERION

The power method applied to $\mathbf{G}$ is the predominant method for finding the PageRank vector. Being an iterative method, the power method continues until some termination criterion is met. In Chapter 4, we mentioned the traditional termination criterion for the power method: stop when the residual (as measured by the difference of successive iterates) is less than some predetermined tolerance (i.e., $\|\boldsymbol{\pi}^{(k+1)T} - \boldsymbol{\pi}^{(k)T}\|_1 < \tau$). However, PageRank researcher Taher Haveliwala [86] has rightfully noted that the exact values of the PageRank vector are not as important as the correct ordering of the values in this vector. That is, iterate until the ordering of the approximate PageRank vector obtained by the power method converges. Considering the scope of the PageRank problem, saving just a handful of iterations is praiseworthy. Haveliwala's experiments show that the savings could be even more substantial on some datasets. As few as 10 iterations produced a good approximate ordering, competitive with the exact ordering produced by the traditional convergence measure. This raises several interesting issues: How do you measure the difference between two orderings? How do you determine when an ordering has converged satisfactorily? Or better yet, is it possible to write a "power method" that operates on and stores only orderings, rather than PageRank values, at each iteration? Several papers [65, 68, 69, 86, 88, 120] have provided a variety of answers to the question of comparing rank orderings, using such measures as Kendall's Tau, rank aggregation, and set overlap.

8.3 ACCURACY

Another implementation issue is the accuracy of PageRank computations. We do not know the accuracy with which Google works, but it at least has to be high enough to differentiate between the often large list of ranked pages that Google commonly returns. Since $\boldsymbol{\pi}^T$ is a probability vector, each π_i will be between 0 and 1. Suppose $\boldsymbol{\pi}^T$ is a 1 by 4 billion vector. Since the PageRank vector is known to follow a *power law* or Zipfian distribution [16, 70, 136], it is possible that a small section of the tail of this vector, ranked in decreasing order, might look like:

$$\boldsymbol{\pi}^T = (\cdots \quad .000001532 \quad .0000015316 \quad .0000015312 \quad .0000015210 \quad \cdots).$$

Accuracy *at least* on the order of 10^{-9} is needed to distinguish among the elements of this ranked subvector. However, comparisons are made only among a subset of elements of this ranked vector. While the elements of the entire global PageRank vector may be tightly packed in some sections of the (0,1) interval, elements of the subset related to a particular query are much less densely packed. Therefore, extreme accuracy on the order of 10^{-12} is most likely unnecessary for this application.

The fact that Brin and Page report reasonable estimates for $\boldsymbol{\pi}^T$ after only 50 iterations of the power method on a matrix of order 322, 000, 000 has one of two implications: either (1) their estimates of π^T are not very accurate or (2) the subdominant eigenvalue of the iteration matrix is far removed from $\lambda_1 = 1$. The first statement is a claim that outsiders not privy to inside information can never verify, as Google has never published information about their convergence tests. The implication of the second statement is that the "fudge factor" matrix $\mathbf{E} = \mathbf{e}\mathbf{v}^T$ must carry a good deal of weight and perhaps α is lowered to .8 in order to increase the eigengap and speed convergence. By decreasing α and simultaneously increasing the weight of the fudge factor, the transition probability matrix moves farther from the Web's original hyperlink structure.

8.4 DANGLING NODES

When you begin large-scale implementation of PageRank, you must make a design decision about how you're going to deal with dangling nodes, and this decision will affect the PageRanks you produce. Every webpage is either a dangling node or a nondangling node. We first encountered dangling nodes in Chapter 4–the pages with no outlinks that caused the problem of rank sinks. All other pages, having at least one outlink, are called nondangling nodes. Dangling nodes exist in many forms. For example, a page of data, a page with a postscript graph, a page with jpeg pictures, a pdf document, a page that has been fetched by a crawler but not yet explored–these are all examples of possible dangling nodes. The more ambitious the crawl, the bigger the proportion of dangling nodes because the set of fetched but uncrawled pages grows quickly. In fact, for some subsets of the Web, dangling nodes make up 80% of the collection's pages.

The presence of these dangling nodes causes both philosophical and computational issues for the PageRank problem. To understand this, let's recap how the PageRank model addresses dangling nodes. Google founders Brin and Page suggested replacing $\mathbf{0}^T$ rows of the sparse hyperlink matrix $\mathbf{H}$ with dense vectors (the uniform vector $\mathbf{e}^T/n$ or the more general $\mathbf{v}^T$ vector) to create the stochastic matrix $\mathbf{S}$. Of course, if this suggestion were to be implemented explicitly, storage requirements would increase dramatically. Instead, we showed in Chapter 4 how the stochasticity fix can be modeled implicitly with the construction of one vector, the dangling node vector $\mathbf{a}$. Element $a_i = 1$ if row i of $\mathbf{H}$ corresponds to a dangling node, and 0, otherwise. Then $\mathbf{S}$ (and also $\mathbf{G}$) can be written as a rank-one update of $\mathbf{H}$.

$$\mathbf{S} = \mathbf{H} + \mathbf{a}\mathbf{v}^T, \quad \text{and therefore,} \quad \mathbf{G} = \alpha\,\mathbf{S} + (1-\alpha)\,\mathbf{e}\mathbf{v}^T$$
$$= \alpha\,\mathbf{H} + (\alpha\,\mathbf{a} + (1-\alpha)\,\mathbf{e})\mathbf{v}^T.$$

The PageRank power method

$$\boldsymbol{\pi}^{(k+1)T} = \alpha\,\boldsymbol{\pi}^{(k)T}\mathbf{H} + (\alpha\,\boldsymbol{\pi}^{(k)T}\mathbf{a} + 1 - \alpha)\,\mathbf{v}^T \tag{8.4.1}$$

is then applied to compute the PageRank vector. (The Matlab code for the PageRank power method is given in the box on page 51.) However, this is not exactly the way that Brin and Page originally dealt with dangling nodes [38, 40]. Instead, they suggest "removing dangling nodes during the computation of PageRank, then adding them back in after the PageRanks have converged" [38], presumably for the final few iterations [102].

This brings us to the philosophical issue of dangling nodes. To dangle or not to dangle: that is the question. And it's not an easy one to answer. We warn you—answer carefully or face discrimination charges. Leaving dangling nodes out somehow feels morally wrong. Arguing in a utilitarian vein that dangling nodes can't be that important anyway certainly is scientifically wrong. A dangling node with lots of inlinks from important pages has just as much right to a high PageRank as a nondangling node, and shouldn't be tossed aside (the way Brin and Page suggested) as matter of algorithmic convenience. Indeed, this was confirmed experimentally by Kevin McCurley, one of the first scientists to boldly explore the Web Frontier (Kevin's name for the set of dangling nodes, since many dangling nodes are yet to-be-crawled pages). He showed on small graphs as well as enormous graphs that some dangling nodes can have higher rank than nondangling nodes [66]. Removing the dangling nodes completely can cause even more problems. The process of removing these nodes can itself produce new dangling nodes. If this process is repeated until no dangling nodes remain, it's possible in theory (although unlikely) that no nodes remain. Further, removing the dangling nodes amounts to unnecessarily removing a great deal of useful data.

Excluding the dangling nodes from the start, then trying to make it up to them later (Brin and Page's solution) also feels wrong. In fact, the dangling node gets a treatment similar to the Native American. Further, the exclusion/correction procedure biases all the PageRank values of nondangling and dangling nodes alike, and unnecessarily so.

A better solution is to treat all nodes fairly from the start. Include the dangling nodes, but be aware of their unique talents. That's exactly the solution proposed by three groups of researchers, Lee et al. [112], McCurley et al. [66], and yours truly (authors Carl and Amy) [109]. We note that our first solution to the PageRank problem (represented by the power method of equation 8.4.1 and the linear system of equation 7.2.1) treats all nodes fairly from the start, but doesn't capitalize on the unique potential of the dangling nodes. We describe this potential in the next few paragraphs.

Stanford graduate student Chris Lee and his colleagues noticed that, for the most part, all dangling nodes look alike; at least their rows in $\mathbf{H}$ (and $\mathbf{S}$ and $\mathbf{G}$) do [112]. And further, whenever the random surfer arrives at a dangling node, he always behaves the same. Regardless of the particular dangling node he's currently at, he always teleports immediately to a new page (at random if $\mathbf{v}^T = \mathbf{e}^T/n$ or according to the given teleportation distribution if $\mathbf{v}^T \neq \mathbf{e}^T/n$). If that's the case, Lee et al. thought, why not lump the individual dangling nodes together into one new state, a teleportation state. This reduces the size of the problem greatly, especially if the proportion of dangling nodes is high. However, solving the smaller $(|\text{ND}| + 1) \times (|\text{ND}| + 1)$ system, where $|\text{ND}|$ is the number of nondangling nodes, creates two new problems. First, ranking scores are available only for the nondangling pages plus the one lumped teleportation state. Second, this smaller set of rankings is biased. The question is: how can we recover the scores for each dangling node and remove the bias in the ranks? While Lee et al.'s answer to this question can be explained by the mathematical techniques of aggregation [51, 56, 92, 151, 154, 155] and stochastic complementation [125], we present an alternative answer, which is easier to follow and was inspired by the linear system formulation of McCurley et al. [112].

Suppose the rows and columns of $\mathbf{H}$ are permuted (i.e., the indices are reordered) so that the rows corresponding to dangling nodes are at the bottom of the matrix.

$$\mathbf{H} = \begin{matrix} \\ \text{ND} \\ \text{D} \end{matrix} \begin{matrix} \text{ND} & \text{D} \\ \left(\begin{matrix} \mathbf{H}_{11} \\ \mathbf{0} \end{matrix}\right. & \left.\begin{matrix} \mathbf{H}_{12} \\ \mathbf{0} \end{matrix}\right) \end{matrix},$$

where ND is the set of nondangling nodes and D is the set of dangling nodes. The coefficient matrix in the sparse linear system formulation of Chapter 7 (i.e., $\mathbf{x}^T(\mathbf{I} - \alpha\mathbf{H}) = \mathbf{v}^T$ with $\boldsymbol{\pi}^T = \mathbf{x}/\mathbf{x}^T\mathbf{e}$) becomes

$$(\mathbf{I} - \alpha\mathbf{H}) = \begin{pmatrix} \mathbf{I} - \alpha\mathbf{H}_{11} & -\alpha\mathbf{H}_{12} \\ \mathbf{0} & \mathbf{I} \end{pmatrix},$$

and the inverse of this matrix is

$$(\mathbf{I} - \alpha\mathbf{H})^{-1} = \begin{pmatrix} (\mathbf{I} - \alpha\mathbf{H}_{11})^{-1} & \alpha(\mathbf{I} - \alpha\mathbf{H}_{11})^{-1}\mathbf{H}_{12} \\ \mathbf{0} & \mathbf{I} \end{pmatrix}.$$

Therefore, the unnormalized PageRank vector $\mathbf{x}^T = \mathbf{v}^T(\mathbf{I} - \alpha\mathbf{H})^{-1}$ can be written as

$$\mathbf{x}^T = (\,\mathbf{v}_1^T(\mathbf{I} - \alpha\mathbf{H}_{11})^{-1} \;\;|\;\; \alpha\mathbf{v}_1^T(\mathbf{I} - \alpha\mathbf{H}_{11})^{-1}\mathbf{H}_{12} + \mathbf{v}_2^T\,),$$

where the personalization vector $\mathbf{v}^T$ has been partitioned accordingly into nondangling ($\mathbf{v}_1^T$) and dangling ($\mathbf{v}_2^T$) sections. Note that $\mathbf{I} - \alpha\mathbf{H}_{11}$ inherits many of the properties of $\mathbf{I} - \alpha\mathbf{H}$ from Chapter 7, most especially nonsingularity. In summary, we now have an algorithm that computes the PageRank vector using only the nondangling portion of the web, exploiting the rank-one structure (and therefore lumpability) of the dangling node fix.

DANGLING NODE PAGERANK ALGORITHM

1. Solve for $\mathbf{x}_1^T$ in $\mathbf{x}_1^T(\mathbf{I} - \alpha\mathbf{H}_{11}) = \mathbf{v}_1^T$.
2. Compute $\mathbf{x}_2^T = \alpha\mathbf{x}_1^T\mathbf{H}_{12} + \mathbf{v}_2^T$.
3. Normalize $\boldsymbol{\pi}^T = [\mathbf{x}_1^T \;\; \mathbf{x}_2^T]/\|[\mathbf{x}_1^T \;\; \mathbf{x}_2^T]\|_1$.

This algorithm is much simpler and cleaner, but equivalent to the specialized iterative method proposed by Lee et al. [112], which exploits the dangling nodes to reduce computation of the PageRank vector by a factor of 1/5 on a graph in which 80% of the nodes are dangling. While this solution to the problem of dangling nodes gives them fair treatment and capitalizes on their unique properties, we can do even better.

Inspired by the dangling node PageRank algorithm above, we wondered if a deeper search for "sub-dangling" nodes might help further. That is, if the presence of dangling nodes, and therefore, $\mathbf{0}^T$ rows in $\mathbf{H}$ is so advantageous, can we find more $\mathbf{0}^T$ rows in submatrices of $\mathbf{H}$? In fact, in [109], we proposed that the process of locating zero rows be repeated recursively on smaller and smaller submatrices of $\mathbf{H}$, continuing until a submatrix is created that has no zero rows. For example, consider executing such a process on a hyperlink matrix $\mathbf{H}$ that has 9664 rows and columns and contains 16773 nonzero entries in the positions indicated in the left-hand side of Figure 8.3. The process amounts to a simple reordering of the states of the Markov chain. The left pane shows the nonzero pattern in

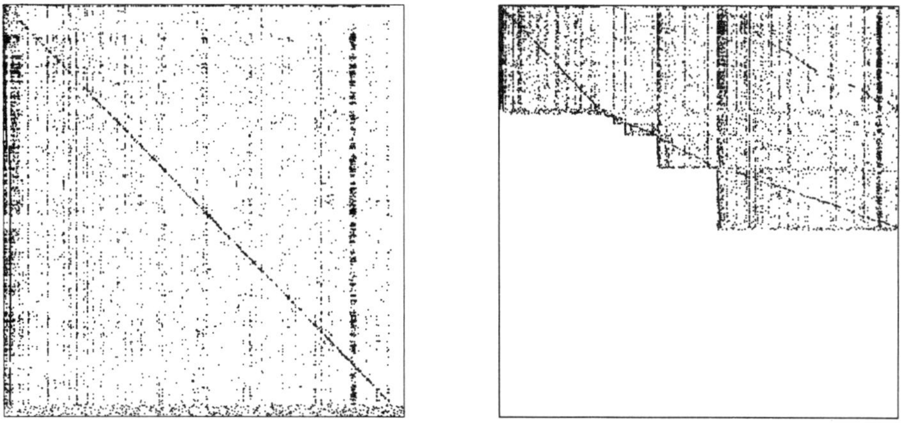

Figure 8.3 Original and reordered **H** for sample web hyperlink matrix

H, and the right pane is the nonzero pattern after the rows of **H** are reordered according to the recursive dangling node idea.

In general, after this symmetric reordering, the coefficient matrix of the linear system formulation of the PageRank problem of equation (7.2.1) has the following structure.

$$(\mathbf{I} - \alpha\mathbf{H}) = \begin{pmatrix} \mathbf{I} - \alpha\mathbf{H}_{11} & -\alpha\mathbf{H}_{12} & -\alpha\mathbf{H}_{13} & \cdots & -\alpha\mathbf{H}_{1b} \\ & \mathbf{I} & -\alpha\mathbf{H}_{23} & \cdots & -\alpha\mathbf{H}_{2b} \\ & & \mathbf{I} & \cdots & -\alpha\mathbf{H}_{3b} \\ & & & \ddots & \\ & & & & \mathbf{I} \end{pmatrix},$$

where b is the number of square diagonal blocks in the reordered matrix. Thus, the reordered system can be solved by forward substitution. The only system that must be solved directly is the first subsystem, $\mathbf{x}_1^T(\mathbf{I} - \alpha\mathbf{H}_{11}) = \mathbf{v}_1^T$, where $\boldsymbol{\pi}^T$ and $\mathbf{v}^T$ have also been partitioned accordingly. The remaining subvectors of $\mathbf{x}^T$ are computed quickly and efficiently by forward substitution.

DANGLING NODE PAGERANK ALGORITHM 2

1. Reorder the states of the original Markov chain, so that the reordered matrix has the structure given above.

2. Solve for $\mathbf{x}_1^T$ in $\mathbf{x}_1^T(\mathbf{I} - \alpha\mathbf{H}_{11}) = \mathbf{v}_1^T$.

3. For $i = 2$ to b, compute $\mathbf{x}_i^T = \alpha \sum_{j=1}^{i-1} \mathbf{x}_j^T \mathbf{H}_{ji} + \mathbf{v}_i^T$.

4. Normalize $\boldsymbol{\pi}^T = [\mathbf{x}_1^T \;\; \mathbf{x}_2^T \;\; \cdots \;\; \mathbf{x}_b^T] / \|[\mathbf{x}_1^T \;\; \mathbf{x}_2^T \;\; \cdots \;\; \mathbf{x}_b^T]\|_1$.

In the example from Figure 8.3, a $2,622 \times 2,622$ system can be solved instead of the full $9,664 \times 9,664$ system. The small subsystem $\mathbf{x}_1^T(\mathbf{I} - \alpha\mathbf{H}_{11}) = \mathbf{v}_1^T$ can be solved by a direct method (if small enough) or an iterative method (such as the Jacobi method). Reference [109] provides further details of the reordering method along with experimental results, suggested methods for solving the $\mathbf{x}_1^T(\mathbf{I} - \alpha\mathbf{H}_{11}) = \mathbf{v}_1^T$ system, and convergence properties. Fortunately, it turns out that this dangling node PageRank algorithm has the same asymptotic rate of convergence as the original PageRank algorithm of equation (5.3.1), which means that because it operates on a much smaller problem it can take much less time than the standard PageRank power method, provided the reordering can be efficiently implemented.

8.5 BACK BUTTON MODELING

Related to the topic of dangling nodes is the issue of the back button. Often times during a PageRank talk at a scientific conference, right after we've introduced dangling nodes and their problems and solutions, we are asked, "But what about the browser's back button? How does PageRank account for this button?" The short answer is that, as originally conceived, the PageRank model does not allow for a back button. Our questioner usually doesn't give in so easily, "Whenever I'm surfing and I enter a dangling node, I simply back my way out until I can proceed with forward links again." We concede—that's exactly what most surfers do. However, accounting for the back button complicates the mathematics of the PageRank model. In fact, the defining property of a Markov chain is that it's memoryless. That is, upon transitioning and arriving at a new webpage, the chain does not remember from whence it came. Therefore, one way to model the back button would be to add memory to the Markov chain. Unfortunately, this quickly obscures the elegant mathematical and computational beauty of the Markov chain. Nevertheless, several researchers have proceeded in this direction [67, 119, 157], hoping that the increase in complexity is offset by the back button's ability to more accurately capture true Web surfing behavior.

There are many ways to model the back button on a Web browser. We propose one very simplistic approach that incorporates limited back button usage into the PageRank model yet still stays in the Markov framework. In this model, once the random surfer arrives at a dangling node, he immediately returns to the page he came from. It's important to note that this bounce-back feature simulates the back button only for dangling nodes. Unfortunately, in order to achieve this bounce back, we need to add a new node for every inlink into each dangling node. However, the resulting, larger hyperlink matrix, which we call $\bar{\mathbf{H}}$, has some nice structure. To understand the bounce-back model, consider an example based on Figure 8.4. The hyperlink matrix $\mathbf{H}$ associated with Figure 8.4 is

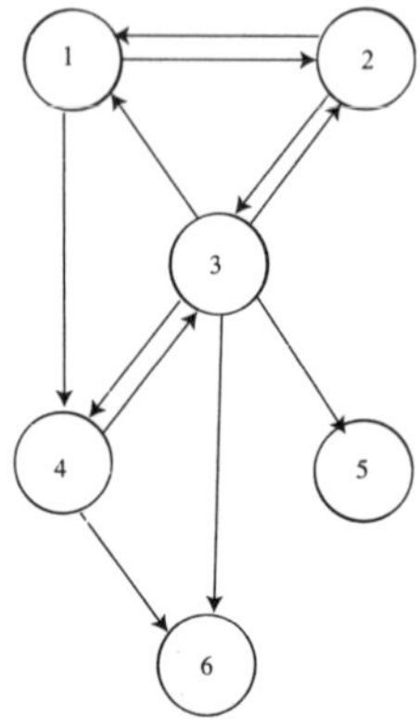

Figure 8.4 Original 6-node graph for back button model

$$\mathbf{H} = \begin{array}{c} \\ 1 \\ 2 \\ 3 \\ 4 \\ 5 \\ 6 \end{array} \begin{array}{c} \begin{array}{cccccc} 1 & 2 & 3 & 4 & 5 & 6 \end{array} \\ \begin{pmatrix} 0 & 1/2 & 0 & 1/2 & 0 & 0 \\ 1/2 & 0 & 1/2 & 0 & 0 & 0 \\ 1/5 & 1/5 & 0 & 1/5 & 1/5 & 1/5 \\ 0 & 0 & 1/2 & 0 & 0 & 1/2 \\ 0 & 0 & 0 & 0 & 0 & 0 \\ 0 & 0 & 0 & 0 & 0 & 0 \end{pmatrix} \end{array}.$$

The modified graph with bounce back capability appears in Figure 8.5. The modifications are shown with dashes. Thus, the bounce-back hyperlink matrix $\bar{\mathbf{H}}$ is

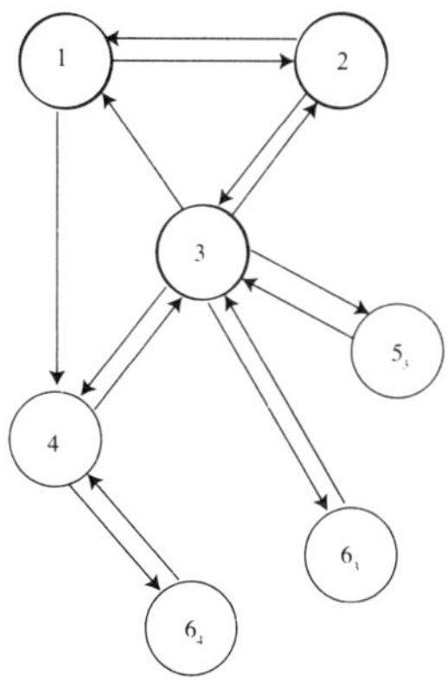

Figure 8.5 Bounce-back 6-node graph for back button model

$$\bar{\mathbf{H}} = \begin{array}{c} \\ 1 \\ 2 \\ 3 \\ 4 \\ 5_3 \\ 6_3 \\ 6_4 \end{array} \begin{array}{c} \begin{array}{ccccccc} 1 & 2 & 3 & 4 & 5_3 & 6_3 & 6_4 \end{array} \\ \begin{pmatrix} 0 & 1/2 & 0 & 1/2 & 0 & 0 & 0 \\ 1/2 & 0 & 1/2 & 0 & 0 & 0 & 0 \\ 1/5 & 1/5 & 0 & 1/5 & 1/5 & 1/5 & 0 \\ 0 & 0 & 1/2 & 0 & 0 & 0 & 1/2 \\ 0 & 0 & 1 & 0 & 0 & 0 & 0 \\ 0 & 0 & 1 & 0 & 0 & 0 & 0 \\ 0 & 0 & 0 & 1 & 0 & 0 & 0 \end{pmatrix} \end{array}.$$

$\bar{\mathbf{H}}$ is now stochastic, so no artificial stochastic fix is needed. However, eventually an irreducibility fix must still be applied. Execute the following steps to create $\bar{\mathbf{H}}$, the stochastic hyperlink matrix for the bounce back model. (Note that $\bar{\mathbf{H}}$ could be called $\bar{\mathbf{S}}$.)

- Reorder $\mathbf{H}$ so that $\mathbf{H} = \begin{array}{c} \\ \text{ND} \\ \text{D} \end{array} \begin{array}{c} \begin{array}{cc} \text{ND} & \text{D} \end{array} \\ \begin{pmatrix} \mathbf{H}_{11} & \mathbf{H}_{12} \\ \mathbf{0} & \mathbf{0} \end{pmatrix} \end{array}$. See section 8.4.
- For each inlink into a dangling node, create a bounce-back node. There will be $nnz(\mathbf{H}_{12})$ of these bounce-back nodes instead of the $|\text{D}|$ nodes in the dangling node set. If each dangling node has more than one inlink and there are many dangling nodes, this could drastically increase the size of the matrix. The bounce-back hyper-

link matrix has the following block form.

$$\bar{\mathbf{H}} = \begin{matrix} & \text{ND} & \text{BB} \\ \text{ND} & \bar{\mathbf{H}}_{11} & \bar{\mathbf{H}}_{12} \\ \text{BB} & \bar{\mathbf{H}}_{21} & \mathbf{0} \end{matrix}.$$

- Form the three nonzero blocks of $\bar{\mathbf{H}}$. First, $\bar{\mathbf{H}}_{11} = \mathbf{H}_{11}$. Second, there is structural symmetry between $\bar{\mathbf{H}}_{12}$ and $\bar{\mathbf{H}}_{21}$ that can be exploited. That is, if element (i, j) of $\bar{\mathbf{H}}_{12}$ is nonzero, then element (j, i) of $\bar{\mathbf{H}}_{21} = 1$. Further, while the size of $\bar{\mathbf{H}}$ can be much larger than the size of $\mathbf{H}$, $\bar{\mathbf{H}}$ only has $nnz(\mathbf{H}_{12})$ more nonzeros than $\mathbf{H}$ and all of these are the integer 1. As a result of this nice structure, the Matlab commands `find` and `sparse` can be used to create the $\bar{\mathbf{H}}_{12}$ and $\bar{\mathbf{H}}_{21}$ blocks.

```
[r,c,v]=find(H12);
H̄12 =sparse(r,1:nnz(H12),v);
H̄21 =(H̄12 > 0)';
```

To compute the bounce-back PageRank vector, simply run any PageRank algorithm such as the original algorithm of equation 4.6.1 on page 40 or the accelerated versions of Chapter 9 on $\bar{\mathbf{G}} = \alpha\bar{\mathbf{H}} + (1-\alpha)\mathbf{e}\mathbf{v}^T$. Of course, the algorithms are slightly modified due to the fact that $\bar{\mathbf{H}}$ is now also stochastic. Thus, the bounce-back PageRank power method is

$$\begin{aligned} \bar{\pi}^{(k+1)T} &= \bar{\pi}^{(k)T}\bar{\mathbf{G}} \\ &= \alpha\,\bar{\pi}^{(k)T}\bar{\mathbf{H}} + (1-\alpha)\mathbf{v}^T \end{aligned}$$

The bounce-back PageRank vector for $\bar{\mathbf{H}}$ is longer than the standard PageRank vector for $\mathbf{H}$. To compare the two vectors, simply collapse multiple bounce-back nodes for each dangling node back into one node. For the above example, with $\alpha = .85$ and $\mathbf{v}^T = \mathbf{e}^T/n$,

$$\begin{matrix} & 1 & 2 & 3 & 4 & 5 & 6 & \\ \pi^T(\mathbf{H}) = & (0.1726 & 0.1726 & 0.2102 & 0.1726 & 0.0993 & 0.1726) & \text{and} \\ & 1 & 2 & 3 & 4 & 5_3 & 6_3 & 6_4 \\ \bar{\pi}^T(\bar{\mathbf{H}}) = & (0.1214 & 0.1214 & 0.2846 & 0.2186 & 0.0698 & 0.0698 & 0.1143). \end{matrix}$$

The collapsed vector $\bar{\pi}^T = (\,0.1214 \quad 0.1214 \quad 0.2846 \quad 0.2186 \quad 0.0698 \quad .1841\,)$. The ranking of pages (from most to least important) associated with π^T is $(\,3 \quad 1/2/4/6 \quad 5\,)$, while the ranking associated with $\bar{\pi}^T$ is $(\,3 \quad 4 \quad 6 \quad 1/2 \quad 5\,)$, where the / symbol indicates a tie. Of course, on such a small example the difference in the two rankings is apparent. Much larger experiments are needed to determine the value of bounce-back PageRank as an alternative ranking.

ASIDE: Google's Initial Public Offering

Speculation and rumors about Google's initial public offering (IPO) of stock shares began in 2003. On August 1, 2004, Google issued a press release about their IPO. True to their founding principles, Google's IPO was original. Google used a Dutch auction to take bids from investors. For the auction, investors submitted a bid with the price and number of *shares they were willing to buy. Then Google and its underwriting bankers, Morgan Stanley and Credit Suisse Group First Boston determined the clearing price, which is the highest price at which there is a demand for all of the 24.6 million shares. The offer price was then set at or below the clearing price. Google believed the Dutch auction was the best way to level the playing field and allow small individual investors and large corporate investors equal access to shares. Google expected the offer price to fall somewhere between $108 and $135. On July 31, 2004, the IPO information website,* `www.ipo.google.com` *opened. This site contained a 100-plus page prospectus that informed prospective investors about the risk factors, auction process, company history and mission, search trends, and financial data. It also contained a Meet the Management presentation in which the company's leaders, founders Sergey Brin and Larry Page, CEO Eric Schmidt, and CFO George Reyes, summarize some of the main issues in the detailed prospectus. Google shares ended up selling on August 19, 2004 for $85 each, bringing in over $1.1 billion for the company and making it the biggest technology IPO in history and the 25th largest IPO overall. You can track the price of Google shares by watching the Nasdaq ticker symbol GOOG.*

Chapter Nine

Accelerating the Computation of PageRank

People have a natural fascination with speed. Look around; articles abound on Nascar and the world's fastest couple—Marion Jones and Tim Montgomery—speedboat racing and speed dating, fast food and the Concorde jet. So the interest in speeding up the computation of PageRank seems natural, but actually it's essential because the PageRank computation by the standard power method takes days to converge. And the Web is growing rapidly, so days could turn into weeks if new methods aren't discovered.

Because the classical power method is known for its slow convergence, researchers immediately looked to other solution methods. However, the size and sparsity of the web matrix create limitations on the solution methods and have caused the predominance of the power method. This restriction to the power method has forced new research on the often criticized power method and has resulted in numerous improvements to the vanilla-flavored power method that are tailored to the PageRank problem. Since 1998, the resurgence in work on the power method has brought exciting, innovative twists to the old, unadorned workhorse. As each iteration of the power method on a web-sized matrix is so expensive, reducing the number of iterations by a handful can save hours of computation. Some of the most valuable contributions have come from researchers at Stanford who have discovered several methods for accelerating the power method. There are really just two ways to reduce the work involved in any iterative method: either reduce the work per iteration or reduce the total number of iterations. These goals are often at odds with one another. That is, reducing the number of iterations usually comes at the expense of a slight increase in the work per iteration, and vice versa. As long as this overhead is minimal, the proposed acceleration is considered beneficial. In this chapter, we review three of the most successful methods for reducing the work associated with the PageRank vector.

9.1 AN ADAPTIVE POWER METHOD

The goal of the PageRank game is to compute π^T, the stationary vector of $\mathbf{G}$, or technically, the power iterates $\pi^{(k)T}$ such that $\|\pi^{(k)T} - \pi^{(k-1)T}\|_1 < \tau$, where τ is some acceptable convergence criterion. Suppose, for the moment, that we magically know π^T from the start. We'd, of course, be done, problem solved. But, out of curiosity, let's run the power method to see how far the iterates $\pi^{(k)T}$ are from the final answer π^T. We want to know what kind of progress the power method is making throughout the iteration history. There are several ways to do this. You can take a macroscopic view and look at how far $\pi^{(k)T}$, the current iterate, is from π^T, the magical final answer, by computing $\|\pi^{(k)T} - \pi^T\|_1$. By using the norm, the individual errors in each component are lumped into a single scalar which gives the aggregated error. The standard power method takes the macroscopic view at each iteration, using a convergence test that looks at an aggregated error, $\|\boldsymbol{\pi}^{(k)T} - \boldsymbol{\pi}^{(k-1)T}\|_1$. Another idea is to take a microscopic view and look at individual components in the two vectors, examining how far $\pi_i^{(k)}$ is from π_i at each iteration. This is exactly what Stanford researchers Sep Kamvar, Taher Haveliwala, Gene Golub, and Chris Manning did [102].

Kamvar et al. [102] noticed that some pages converge to their PageRank values faster than other pages. However, the standard power method with its macroscopic view doesn't notice this, and blindly charges on, making unnecessary calculations. In fact, the Stanford group found that most pages converge to their final PageRank values quickly. The power method is forced to drag on because a small proportion of obstinate pages take longer to settle down to their final PageRank values. As elements of the PageRank vector converge, the adaptive PageRank method "locks" them and does not compute them in subsequent iterations. But how do you know which elements to lock and when? In the case when we magically know $\boldsymbol{\pi}^T$, lock element i when $|\pi_i^{(k)} - \pi_i| < \epsilon$, where ϵ is the microscopic convergence tolerance. (Kamvar et al. used $\epsilon = 10^{-3}$.) In practice, lock element i when $|\pi_i^{(k)} - \pi_i^{(k-1)}| < \epsilon$, i.e., the difference in successive iterates is small enough.

This adaptive power method provides a modest speedup in the computation of the PageRank vector, i.e., 17% on Kamvar et al.'s experimental datasets. However, while this algorithm was shown to converge in practice on a handful of datasets, there are serious open theoretical issues with the algorithm. For instance, there is no proof regarding convergence of the algorithm; the algorithm may or may not converge. And even if it does converge, the final answer may not be right. Because only short-run dynamics are considered in the locking decision, it's not clear whether the algorithm converges to the true PageRank values or some gross approximation of them. In fact, nearly uncoupled chains are known to exhibit short-run stabilization in each cluster, which is then followed by a period of progress toward the global equilibrium. Further, the final global equilibrium often does not resemble properties of the short run equilibria, meaning the adaptive method could stop too soon with a grossly inaccurate answer for an uncoupled chain. Nevertheless, the adaptive algorithm makes a practical contribution to PageRank acceleration by attempting to reduce the work per iteration required by the power method.

9.2 EXTRAPOLATION

Another acceleration method proposed by the same group of Stanford researchers aims to reduce the number of power iterations. The expected number of power iterations is governed by the size of the subdominant eigenvalue λ_2. The idea of extrapolation goes something like this: "if the subdominant eigenvalue causes the power method to sputter, cut it out and throw it away." To understand what this means, let's look at the power iterates using special *spectral decomposition* goggles. Spectral decomposition goggles are a bit like x-ray vision in that they allow one to see deep into a matrix to examine its spectral components. For simplicity, assume that $\mathbf{G}$ is diagonalizable and $1 > |\lambda_2| > \cdots \geq |\lambda_n|$. Then, the power iterates look like

$$\begin{aligned}\boldsymbol{\pi}^{(k)T} &= \boldsymbol{\pi}^{(k-1)T}\mathbf{G} = \boldsymbol{\pi}^{(0)T}\mathbf{G}^k \\ &= \boldsymbol{\pi}^{(0)T}(\mathbf{e}\boldsymbol{\pi}^T + \lambda_2^k\mathbf{x}_2\mathbf{y}_2^T + \lambda_3^k\mathbf{x}_3\mathbf{y}_3^T + \cdots + \lambda_n^k\mathbf{x}_n\mathbf{y}_n^T) \\ &= \boldsymbol{\pi}^T + \lambda_2^k\gamma_2\mathbf{y}_2^T + \lambda_3^k\gamma_3\mathbf{y}_3^T + \cdots + \lambda_n^k\gamma_n\mathbf{y}_n^T, \qquad (9.2.1)\end{aligned}$$

where $\mathbf{x}_i$ and $\mathbf{y}_i$ are the right-hand and left-hand eigenvectors of $\mathbf{G}$ corresponding to λ_i and $\gamma_i = \boldsymbol{\pi}^{(0)T}\mathbf{x}_i$. It's frustrating—at each iteration the desired PageRank vector $\boldsymbol{\pi}^T$ is sitting right there, taunting us. In fact, equation (9.2.1) shows that $\lambda_2^k\gamma_2\mathbf{y}_2^T$ does the spoiling for the power method. $\boldsymbol{\pi}^T$ is hidden until $\lambda_2^k \to 0$, which takes a while when $|\lambda_2|$ is large. The technique of extrapolation removes the spoiler. Notice that

$$\boldsymbol{\pi}^{(k)T} - \lambda_2^k\gamma_2\mathbf{y}_2^T = \boldsymbol{\pi}^T + \lambda_3^k\gamma_3\mathbf{y}_3^T + \cdots + \lambda_n^k\gamma_n\mathbf{y}_n^T,$$

which is closer to the correct PageRank $\boldsymbol{\pi}^T$ when $|\lambda_2| > |\lambda_3|$. This means that if we could subtract $\lambda_2^k\gamma_2\mathbf{y}_2^T$ from the current iterate we could propel the power method forward. However, the problem is how to compute $\lambda_2^k\gamma_2\mathbf{y}_2^T$. When we take off the spectral decomposition goggles, the spectral components are lumped together and we see only one vector, $\boldsymbol{\pi}^{(k)T}$. Fortunately, we can estimate $\lambda_2^k\gamma_2\mathbf{y}_2^T$ by using things we do have, or can get, $\boldsymbol{\pi}^{(k+2)T}$, $\boldsymbol{\pi}^{(k+1)T}$, and $\boldsymbol{\pi}^{(k)T}$. Kamvar et al. have shown that

$$\lambda_2^k\gamma_2\mathbf{y}_2^T \approx \frac{(\boldsymbol{\pi}^{(k+1)T} - \boldsymbol{\pi}^{(k)T})^{.2}}{\boldsymbol{\pi}^{(k+2)T} - 2\boldsymbol{\pi}^{(k+1)T} - \boldsymbol{\pi}^{(k)T}},$$

where $(*)^{.2}$ indicates component-wise squaring of elements in the vector $(*)$. Since extrapolation requires additional computation (getting and storing the two subsequent iterates), it should only be applied periodically, say every 10 iterations. Unfortunately, this method, which is referred to as Aitken extrapolation because it is derived from the classic Aitken Δ^2 method for accelerating linearly convergent sequences, gives only modest speedups. One reason concerns the eigenvalue λ_3. If λ_2 and λ_3 are complex conjugates, then $|\lambda_2| = |\lambda_3|$ and Aitken extrapolation performs poorly.

Kamvar et al. developed an improved extrapolation method, called quadratic extrapolation, which while more complicated, is based on the same idea as Aitken extrapolation. That is, "if λ_2 and λ_3 cause you problems, cut them both out and throw them away." On the datasets tested, quadratic extrapolation reduces PageRank computation time by 50–300% with minimal overhead. Figure 9.1 compares the residuals when the standard power method and the power method with quadratic extrapolation are applied to a small web graph. In this example, quadratic extrapolation is applied every 20 iterations.

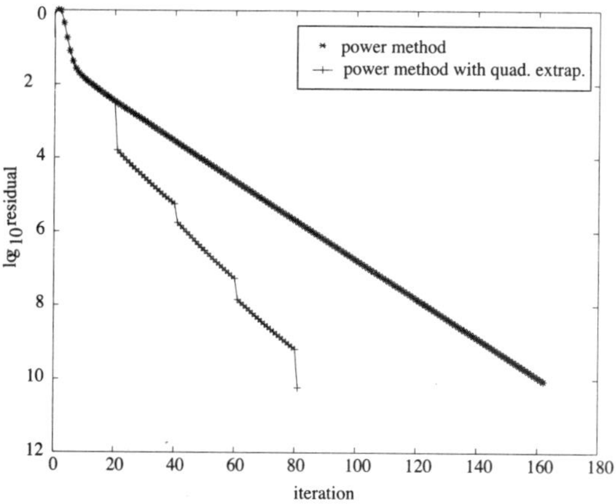

Figure 9.1 Residual plot for power method vs. power method with quadratic extrapolation

Notice how the iterate that results at each application of quadratic extrapolation makes dramatic progress toward the solution. Unfortunately, quadratic extrapolation is expensive and can be done only periodically. Researchers, such as extrapolation expert Claude Brezinski, have recently begun experimenting with other classic extrapolation methods, such as Chebyshev and ϵ-extrapolation.

Matlab m-file for PageRank Power Method with Aitken extrapolation

This m-file implements the PageRank power method applied to the Google matrix $\mathbf{G} = \alpha\mathbf{S} + (1-\alpha)\mathbf{e}\mathbf{v}^T$ with Aitken extrapolation applied every `'l'` iterations.

```
function [pi,time,numiter]=aitkenPageRank(pi0,H,v,n,alpha,epsilon,l);

% AITKENPageRank  computes the PageRank vector for an n-by-n Markov
%                 matrix H with starting vector pi0 (a row vector),
%                 scaling parameter alpha (scalar), and teleportation
%                 vector v (a row vector).  Uses power method with
%                 Aitken extrapolation applied every l iterations.
%
% EXAMPLE:  [pi,time,numiter]=aitkenPageRank(pi0,H,v,900,.9,1e-8,10);
%
% INPUT:  pi0 = starting vector at iteration 0 (a row vector)
%         H = row-normalized hyperlink matrix (n-by-n sparse matrix)
%         v = teleportation vector (1-by-n row vector)
%         n = size of P matrix (scalar)
%         alpha = scaling parameter in PageRank model (scalar)
%         epsilon = convergence tolerance (scalar, e.g. 1e-8)
%         l = Aitken extrapolation applied every l iterations (scalar)
%
% OUTPUT:   pi = PageRank vector
%           time = time required to compute PageRank vector
%           numiter = number of iterations until convergence
%
% The starting vector is usually set to the uniform vector,
% pi0=1/n*ones(1,n).
% NOTE: Matlab stores sparse matrices by columns, so it is faster
%       to do some operations on H', the transpose of H.


% get "a" vector, where a(i)=1, if row i is dangling node
%   and 0, o.w.

rowsumvector=ones(1,n)*H';
nonzerorows=find(rowsumvector);
zerorows=setdiff(1:n,nonzerorows); l=length(zerorows);
a=sparse(zerorows,ones(l,1),ones(l,1),n,1);


k=0;
residual=1;
pi=pi0;
tic;

while (residual >= epsilon)
```

```
  prevpi=pi;
  k=k+1;
  pi=alpha*pi*H + (alpha*(pi*a)+1-alpha)*v;
  residual=norm(pi-prevpi,1);
  if (mod(k,l))==0
    % 'Aitken extrapolation'
      nextpi=alpha*pi*H + (alpha*(pi*a)+1-alpha)*v;
      g=(pi-prevpi).^2;
      h=nextpi-2*pi+prevpi;
      nextpi=prevpi-(g./h);
      if (any(nextpi==-Inf)==1)
          pi=pi;
        else
            pi=nextpi;
      end
      %'end Aitken extrapolation'
  end
end
numiter=k;
time=toc;
```

Matlab m-file for PageRank Power Method with quadratic extrapolation

This m-file implements the PageRank power method applied to the Google matrix $\mathbf{G} = \alpha\mathbf{S} + (1-\alpha)\mathbf{e}\mathbf{v}^T$ with quadratic extrapolation applied every `'l'` iterations.

```
function [pi,time,numiter]=quadPageRank(pi0,H,v,n,alpha,epsilon,l);

% QUADPageRank  computes the PageRank vector for an n-by-n Markov
%               matrix H with starting vector pi0 (a row vector),
%               scaling parameter alpha (scalar), and teleportation
%               vector v (a row vector).  Uses power method with
%               quadratic extrapolation applied every l ("ell") iterations.
%
% EXAMPLE: [pi,time,numiter]=quadPageRank(pi0,H,v,900,.9,1e-8,10);
%
% INPUT:  pi0 = starting vector at iteration 0 (a row vector)
%         H = row-normalized hyperlink matrix (n-by-n sparse matrix)
%         v = teleportation vector (1-by-n row vector)
%         n = size of P matrix (scalar)
%         alpha = scaling parameter in PageRank model (scalar)
%         epsilon = convergence tolerance (scalar, e.g. 1e-8)
%         l ("ell") = quadratic extrapolation applied every l ("ell")
%                     iterations (scalar)
%
% OUTPUT:   pi = PageRank vector
%           time = time required to compute PageRank vector
%           numiter = number of iterations until convergence
%
% The starting vector is usually set to the uniform vector,
% pi0=1/n*ones(1,n).
% NOTE: Matlab stores sparse matrices by columns, so it is faster
%       to do some operations on H', the transpose of H.
```

```
% get "a" vector, where a(i)=1, if row i is dangling node
%   and 0, o.w.

rowsumvector=ones(1,n)*H';
nonzerorows=find(rowsumvector);
zerorows=setdiff(1:n,nonzerorows); l=length(zerorows);
a=sparse(zerorows,ones(l,1),ones(l,1),n,1);


k=0;
residual=1;
pi=pi0;
tic;

while (residual >= epsilon)
  prevpi=pi;
  k=k+1;
  pi=alpha*pi*H + (alpha*(pi*a)+1-alpha)*v;
  residual=norm(pi-prevpi,1);
  if (mod(k,l))==0
    % 'quadratic extrapolation'
      nextpi=alpha*pi*H + (alpha*(pi*a)+1-alpha)*v;
      nextnextpi=alpha*nextpi*H + (alpha*(nextpi*a)+1-alpha)*v;
      y=pi-prevpi;   nexty=nextpi-prevpi;   nextnexty=nextnextpi-prevpi;
      Y=[y' nexty'];
      gamma3=1;
      % do modified gram-schmidt QR instead of matlab's [Q,R]=qr(Y);
      [m, n] = size(Y);
      Q = zeros(m,n);
      R = zeros(n);
      for j=1:n
          R(j,j) = norm(Y(:,j));
          Q(:,j) = Y(:,j)/R(j,j);
          R(j,j+1:n) = Q(:,j)'*Y(:,j+1:n);
          Y(:,j+1:n) = Y(:,j+1:n) - Q(:,j)*R(j,j+1:n);
      end
      Qnextnexty=Q'*nextnexty';
      gamma2=-Qnextnexty(2)/R(2,2);
      gamma1=(-Qnextnexty(1)-gamma2*R(1,2))/R(1,1);
      gamma0=-(gamma1+gamma2+gamma3);
      beta0=gamma1+gamma2+gamma3;
      beta1=gamma2+gamma3;
      beta2=gamma3;
      nextnextpi=beta0*pi+beta1*nextpi+beta2*nextnextpi;
      nextnextpi=nextnextpi/sum(nextnextpi);
      pi=nextnextpi;
      %'end quadratic extrapolation'
  end
  pi=pi/sum(pi);
end
numiter=k;
time=toc;
```

9.3 AGGREGATION

The same group of Stanford researchers, Kamvar et al. [101] has produced one more contribution to the acceleration of PageRank. This method works on both acceleration goals simultaneously, trying to reduce both the number of iterations and the work per iteration. This very promising method, called BlockRank, is an aggregation method that lumps sections of the Web by hosts. BlockRank begins by taking the webgraph (where nodes represent webpages) and compresses this into a hostgraph (where the nodes represent hosts). Hosts are the high-level webpages like `www.ncsu.edu`, under which lots of other pages sit. Most pages within a host intralink to other pages within the host, but a few links are interhost links, meaning they link between hosts. In the global hostgraph, intralinks are ignored. When the PageRank model is applied to the small hostgraph, a HostRank vector is output. The HostRank for host i gives the relative importance of that host. While the HostRank problem is much smaller than the original PageRank problem, it doesn't give us what we want, which is the importance of individual pages, not individual hosts. In order to get one global PageRank vector, we first compute many local PageRank vectors—the PageRank vector for pages in each individual host. Now only the intralinks are used, and the interlinks are ignored. This is an easy computation since hosts generally have less than a few thousand pages. Thus, the PageRank model is applied to each host, `www.ncsu.edu`, `www.msmary.edu`, `www.cofc.edu`, and so on. At this point, there is one global $1 \times |H|$ HostRank vector, where $|H|$ is the number of hosts, as well as $|H|$ local PageRank vectors, each $1 \times |H_i|$ in size, where $|H_i|$ is the number of pages in host H_i. To approximate the global PageRank vector, simply multiply the local PageRank vector for host H_i by the probability of being in that host, given by the ith element of the HostRank vector. This is called the expansion step.

This method gives an approximation to the true PageRank vector that the power method computes. It's an approximation because at each step some links are ignored, which means that valuable information is lost in the compression or so-called aggregation step. Fortunately, this approximation can be improved if, in an accordion style, the collasping/expanding process is repeated until convergence. BlockRank is actually just classic aggregation [51, 56, 92, 151, 155] applied to the PageRank problem. (See sections 10.3–10.5 for more on aggregation.) This method often reduces both the number of iterations required and the work per iteration. It produced a speedup of a factor of 2 on some datasets used by Kamvar et al. More recent, but very related, algorithms [42, 116] use similar aggregation techniques to exploit the Web's structure to speed ranking computations.

EXAMPLE In order to understand the basic principles of aggregation used by the BlockRank algorithm, consider the nearly uncoupled chain of Example 2 from Chapter 6. The 7-node graph is reproduced below in Figure 9.2. Clearly, nodes 1, 2, 3, and 7 can be considered as one host (called Host 1), due to their strong interaction. Nodes 4, 5, and 6 then make up Host 2. The BlockRank algorithm aggregates the 7-node graph into a smaller 2-node graph of hosts. The transition matrix associated with this host graph is

$$\begin{array}{c} \\ H_1 \\ H_2 \end{array} \begin{array}{c} \begin{array}{cc} H_1 & H_2 \end{array} \\ \begin{pmatrix} .96 & .04 \\ 0 & 1 \end{pmatrix} \end{array}.$$

The HostRank vector associated with the host graph, the stationary vector of the Google matrix for the host graph, is $(\,.3676 \quad .6324\,)$ (here we used $\alpha = .9$ and $\mathbf{v}^T = (\,.5 \quad .5\,)$). This means that 36.76% of the time we expect the random surfer to visit the states of Host 1, i.e., webpages 1, 2, 3, and 7.

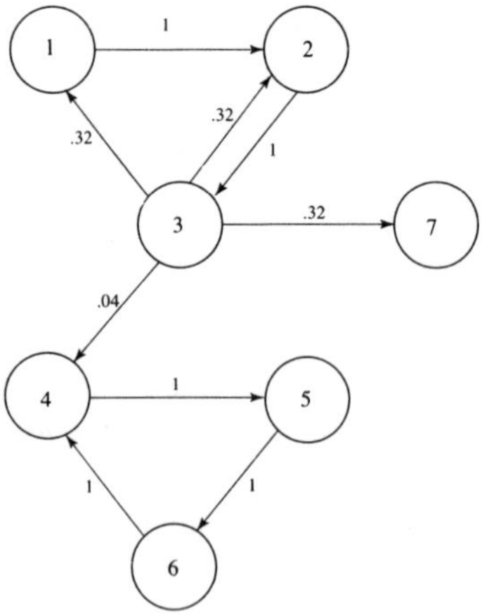

Figure 9.2 Nearly uncoupled graph for web of seven pages

Next, local PageRank vectors are computed for each host. For Host 1, the hyperlink matrix is

$$\mathbf{H}_1 = \begin{array}{c} \\ P_1 \\ P_2 \\ P_3 \\ P_7 \end{array} \begin{array}{c} \begin{array}{cccc} P_1 & P_2 & P_3 & P_7 \end{array} \\ \begin{pmatrix} 0 & 1 & 0 & 0 \\ 0 & 0 & 1 & 0 \\ 1/3 & 1/3 & 0 & 1/3 \\ 0 & 0 & 0 & 0 \end{pmatrix} \end{array}.$$

Only within-host links are used to create $\mathbf{H}_1$, all intrahost links are ignored, namely, the link $3 \rightarrow 4$. With $\alpha = .9$ and $\mathbf{v}^T = (\,.25 \quad .25 \quad .25 \quad .25\,)$ the local PageRank vector for Host 1 is $(\,.1671 \quad .3175 \quad .3483 \quad .1671\,)$. The interpretation of the second element of this vector is that, *given the random surfer is in the states of Host 1*, 31.75% of the time he visits webpage 2. Similarly, the local hyperlink matrix for Host 2 is

$$\mathbf{H}_2 = \begin{array}{c} \\ P_4 \\ P_5 \\ P_6 \end{array} \begin{array}{c} \begin{array}{ccc} P_4 & P_5 & P_6 \end{array} \\ \begin{pmatrix} 0 & 1 & 0 \\ 0 & 0 & 1 \\ 1 & 0 & 0 \end{pmatrix} \end{array}.$$

And the local PageRank vector for Host 2 is $(\,1/3 \quad 1/3 \quad 1/3\,)$.

The final step is the disaggregation step, which uses these three small vectors to create a 1×7 vector $\tilde{\boldsymbol{\pi}}^T$ that approximates the exact PageRank vector $\boldsymbol{\pi}^T$.

$$\begin{aligned} \tilde{\boldsymbol{\pi}}^T &= .3676 \; \big(\overset{1}{(.1671} \quad \overset{2}{.3175} \quad \overset{3}{.3483} \quad \overset{7}{.1671)} \quad .6324 \quad \overset{4}{(1/3} \quad \overset{5}{1/3} \quad \overset{6}{1/3)} \big) \\ &= \big(\overset{1}{.0614} \quad \overset{2}{.1167} \quad \overset{3}{.1280} \quad \overset{7}{.0614} \quad \overset{4}{.2108} \quad \overset{5}{.2108} \quad \overset{6}{.2108} \big). \end{aligned}$$

Compare this with the exact PageRank vector $\boldsymbol{\pi}^T$ computed by the power method.

$$\boldsymbol{\pi}^T = \big(\overset{1}{.0538} \quad \overset{2}{.1022} \quad \overset{3}{.1132} \quad \overset{7}{.0538} \quad \overset{4}{.2271} \quad \overset{5}{.2256} \quad \overset{6}{.2242} \big).$$

Classic aggregation methods are known to work well and reduce effort when computing the stationary vector for a nearly uncoupled Markov chain. The web chain is somewhat uncoupled so BlockRank works well so long as an appropriate level of host aggregation is done.

9.4 OTHER NUMERICAL METHODS

Yet another group of researchers from Stanford, joined by IBM scientists, dropped the restriction to the power method. In their short paper, Arasu et al. [10] provide one small experiment with the Gauss-Seidel method applied to the PageRank problem. Bianchini et al. [29] suggest using the Jacobi method to compute the PageRank vector. Golub and Greif also conduct some experiments with the Arnoldi method [81].

Another promising avenue for PageRank acceleration recently began receiving academic attention: parallel processing. Daniel Szyld and his colleagues have conducted experiments that execute the PageRank power method in parallel with very little overhead communication between processors. Others have corroborated the benefits and particular challenges of parallel processing for PageRank computation [80, 118].

Despite this progress, these are just beginnings. If the holy grail of real-time personalized search is ever to be realized, then drastic speed improvements must be made, perhaps by innovative new algorithms, or the simple combination of many of the current acceleration methods into one algorithm.

ASIDE: Google API

In April 2002, Google released its Web Application Programming Interface (API), which provides fans a free (for now) and legal way to access their search results with automated queries. (Without the API, automated querying is against Google's Terms of Service.) By doing this, Google let the world's programmers virtually run free in Google labs. Google suddenly had thousands of free employees, some more productive and generous than others, creating new services and applications of Google and offering to give them back to the public. For example, four products from API programmers are available at `http://www.tele-pro.co.uk/scripts/google/`. *Developers are free to publish their results as long as they are for noncommercial purposes. Software developers interested in the API download the free developer's kit, create an account, and get a license key. The license key allows a developer 1,000 queries a day (which explains why the API-generated application, RankPulse of the aside on page 65, tracks exactly 1,000 terms). With the key, developers are free to experiment with ways of accessing the standard Google index (which does not include the image, news, shopping, or other special-purpose indexes). For example, the book* Google Hacks *(see box on page 73) provides API code for adding to any webpage a small box of Google results for your chosen query that are refreshed daily. Other developers anticipate using the API to create applications that search both traditional library catalogs as well as the entire Web from a single command. Of course, with access to one of the world's largest indexes, the API is an excellent way for web ranking researchers to test their new algorithms.*

Chapter Ten

Updating the PageRank Vector

Every month a famous dance takes place on the Web. While there have been famous dances throughout modern history—the Macarena, the Mambo #5, the Chicken Dance—this dance is the first to have a profound impact on the search community. Every month search engine optimizers (SEOs) watch the **Google Dance** carefully, anxious to see if any steps have changed. Sometimes the modifications are easy to roll with, other times they cause a stir.

The Google Dance is the nickname given to Google's monthly updating of its rankings. We begin with some statistics that emphasize the need for updating rankings frequently. A study by web researchers Junghoo Cho and Hector Garcia-Molina [52] in 2000 reported that 40% of all webpages in their dataset changed within a week, and 23% of the .com pages changed daily. In a much more extensive and recent study, the results of Dennis Fetterly and his colleagues [74] concur. About 35% of all webpages changed over the course of their study, and also pages that were larger in size changed more often and more extensively than their smaller counterparts. In the above studies, change was defined as either a change in page content or a change in page outlinks or both. Now consider news webpages, where updates to both content and links might occur on an hourly basis. Both the content score, which incorporates page content, and the PageRank score, which incorporates the Web's graph structure, must be updated frequently to stay fresh. Ideally, the ranking scores would be as dynamic as the Web. Currently, it is believed that Google updates its PageRank vector monthly and possibly its content scores more often [7]. Consequently, researchers have been working to make updating easier, taking advantage of old computations to speed updated computations, and thereby making more frequent updating possible.

In this chapter we focus on the mathematical problem associated with the Google Dance, specifically the issue of updating the PageRank vector. The phrase "updating PageRank" refers to the process of computing the new PageRank vector after monthly changes have been made to the Web's graph structure. Between updates, thousands of links are added and removed, and thousands of pages are added and removed. The simplest, most naive updating strategy starts from scratch, that is, it recomputes the new PageRank vector making no use of the previous PageRank vector. To our knowledge, the PageRank vector for Google's entire index is recomputed each month from scratch or nearly from scratch. (Popular sites may have their PageRank updated more frequently.) That is, last month's vector is not used to create this month's vector. A Google spokesperson at the annual SIAM meeting in 2002 reported that restarting this month's power method with last month's vector seemed to provide no improvement. The goal of updating is to beat this naive method. Surely, all that effort spent last month to compute PageRank has some value toward computing this month's PageRank with less work.

The setup for the updating problem follows. Suppose that the PageRank vector $\boldsymbol{\phi}^T = (\phi_1, \phi_2, \ldots, \phi_m)$ for last month's Google matrix $\mathbf{Q}_{m\times m}$ is known (by prior computation), but the web graph requires updating because some hyperlinks have been altered or some webpages have been added or deleted. The updated Google matrix $\mathbf{G}_{n\times n}$ may have a different size than $\mathbf{Q}$, i.e., $m \neq n$. The updating problem is to compute the updated PageRank $\boldsymbol{\pi}^T = (\pi_1, \pi_2, \ldots, \pi_n)$ for $\mathbf{G}$ by somehow using the components in $\boldsymbol{\phi}^T$ to produce $\boldsymbol{\pi}^T$ with less effort than that required by working blind (i.e., by computing $\boldsymbol{\pi}^T$ without knowledge of $\boldsymbol{\phi}^T$).

10.1 THE TWO UPDATING PROBLEMS AND THEIR HISTORY

One fact that makes updating PageRank so challenging is that there are really two types of updates that are possible. First, when hyperlinks are added to or removed from the Web (or their weights are changed), the elements of the hyperlink matrix $\mathbf{H}$ change but the size of the matrix does not. If these are the only type of updates allowed, then the problem is called a link-updating problem. However, webpages themselves may be added to or removed from the Web. With this page-updating problem, states are added to or removed from the Google Markov chain, and the size of the Google matrix changes. Of the two updating problems, the page-updating problem is more difficult, and it generally includes the link-updating problem as a special case. (In section 10.6, we present a general-purpose algorithm that simultaneously handles both kinds of updating problems.)

Since Markov chains and their stationary vectors have been around for nearly a century, the updating problem is not new. Researchers have been studying the problem for decades. History has followed theory; the easier link-updating problem has been studied much more extensively than the tougher page-updating problem. In fact, several solutions for link-updating already exist. In 1980, a theoretical formula for exact link-updating was derived in [129]. Unfortunately, the formula restricts updates so that only a single row of link-updates can be made to the Markov transition matrix. Thus, more general updates must be handled with a sequential one-row-at-a-time procedure. The idea is similar to the well-known Sherman–Morrison formula [127, p. 124] for updating a solution to a nonsingular linear system, but the techniques must be adapted to the singular matrix $\mathbf{A} = \mathbf{I} - \mathbf{Q}$. The mechanism for doing this is by means of the group inverse $\mathbf{A}^{\#}$ for $\mathbf{A}$, which is the unique matrix satisfying the three equations: $\mathbf{A}\mathbf{A}^{\#}\mathbf{A} = \mathbf{A}$, $\mathbf{A}^{\#}\mathbf{A}\mathbf{A}^{\#} = \mathbf{A}^{\#}$ and $\mathbf{A}\mathbf{A}^{\#} = \mathbf{A}^{\#}\mathbf{A}$. This matrix is often involved in questions concerning Markov chains—see [46, 122, 127] for some general background and [46, 49, 50, 76, 83, 130, 122, 124, 121, 126, 129] for Markov chain applications.

The primary exact updating results from [129], as they apply to the PageRank problem, are summarized below.

Theorem 10.1.1. *Let $\mathbf{Q}$ be the transition probability matrix of a Google Markov matrix and suppose that the i-th row $\mathbf{q}^T$ of $\mathbf{Q}$ is updated to produce $\mathbf{g}^T = \mathbf{q}^T - \boldsymbol{\delta}^T$, the i-th row of $\mathbf{G}$, which is the Google matrix of an updated Markov chain. If $\boldsymbol{\phi}^T$ and $\boldsymbol{\pi}^T$ denote the stationary probability distributions of $\mathbf{Q}$ and $\mathbf{G}$ respectively, and if $\mathbf{A} = \mathbf{I} - \mathbf{Q}$, then*

$\pi^T = \phi^T - \epsilon^T$, *where*

$$\epsilon^T = \left[\frac{\phi_i}{1 + \delta^T \mathbf{A}^{\#}_{*i}}\right] \delta^T \mathbf{A}^{\#} \qquad (\mathbf{A}^{\#}_{*i} = \textit{the i-th column of } \mathbf{A}^{\#}). \tag{10.1.1}$$

To handle multiple row updates to $\mathbf{Q}$*, this formula must be sequentially applied one row at a time, which means that the group inverse must be sequentially updated. The formula for updating* $(\mathbf{I} - \mathbf{Q})^{\#}$ *to* $(\mathbf{I} - \mathbf{G})^{\#}$ *is as follows.*

$$(\mathbf{I} - \mathbf{G})^{\#} = \mathbf{A}^{\#} + \mathbf{e}\epsilon^T \left[\mathbf{A}^{\#} - \gamma \mathbf{I}\right] - \frac{\mathbf{A}^{\#}_{*i}\epsilon^T}{\phi_i}, \tag{10.1.2}$$

$$\textit{where} \quad \gamma = \frac{\epsilon^T \mathbf{A}^{\#}_{*i}}{\phi_i} \quad \textit{and } \mathbf{e} \textit{ is a column of ones.}$$

While these results provide theoretical answers to the link-updating problem, they are not computationally satisfying, especially if more than just one or two rows are involved. If every row is changed, then the formulas require $O(n^3)$ floating point operations.

Other updating formulas exist [50, 77, 96, 104, 148], but all are variations of the same rank-one updating idea involving a Sherman–Morrison [127, p. 124] type of formula, and all are $O(n^3)$ algorithms for a general update. Moreover, all of these rank-one updating techniques apply only to the simpler link-updating problem, and they are not easily adapted to handle the more complicated page-updating problem. Consequently, the conclusion is that while the known exact link-updating formulas might be useful when only a row or two is changed and no pages are added or deleted, they are not computationally practical for making more general updates, and thus, because of the dynamics of the Web, are virtually useless for updating PageRank. The survey of the available solutions for the page-updating problem is even bleaker. No theoretical or practical solutions for the page-updating problem for a Markov chain exist. In light of the dynamics of the Web, updating PageRank is quite an important and open challenge.

10.2 RESTARTING THE POWER METHOD

It appears then that starting from scratch is perhaps the only alternative for the PageRank updating problem. Let's begin our discussion with the simpler type of problem, the link-updating problem. Therefore, assume $\mathbf{Q}$ undergoes only link updates to create $\mathbf{G}$. Suppose that the power method is applied to the new, updated Google matrix $\mathbf{G}$, but the old PageRank vector ϕ^T is used as the starting vector for the iterative process (as opposed to a random or uniform starting vector). Suppose that it is known that the updated stationary distribution π^T for $\mathbf{G}$ is in some sense close to the original stationary distribution ϕ^T for $\mathbf{Q}$. For example, this might occur if the perturbations to $\mathbf{Q}$ are small. It's intuitive that if ϕ^T and π^T are close, then applying

$$\pi^{(k+1)T} = \pi^{(k)T}\mathbf{G} \quad \text{with} \quad \pi^{(0)T} = \phi^T \tag{10.2.1}$$

should produce an accurate approximation to π^T in fewer iterations than that required when an arbitrary initial vector is used. To some extent this is true, but intuition generally overestimates the impact, as explained below.

It's well known that if λ_2 is the subdominant eigenvalue of $\mathbf{G}$, and if λ_2 has *index* one (linear elementary divisors), then the *asymptotic rate of convergence* [127, p. 621] of

(10.2.1) is

$$R = -\log_{10}|\lambda_2|. \tag{10.2.2}$$

For *linear stationary iterative procedures* the asymptotic rate of convergence R is an indication of the number of digits of accuracy that can be expected to be eventually gained on each iteration, and this is independent of the initial vector. For example, suppose that the entries of $\mathbf{G} - \mathbf{Q}$ are small enough to ensure that each component π_i agrees with ϕ_i in the first significant digit, and suppose that the goal is to compute the update $\boldsymbol{\pi}^T$ to twelve significant places by using (10.2.1). Since $\boldsymbol{\pi}^{(0)T} = \boldsymbol{\phi}^T$ already has one correct significant digit, and since about $1/R$ iterations are required to gain each additional significant digit of accuracy, (10.2.1) requires about $11/R$ iterations, whereas starting from scratch with an initial vector containing no significant digits of accuracy requires about $12/R$ iterations. In other words, the effort is reduced by about 8% for each correct significant digit that can be built into $\boldsymbol{\pi}^{(0)T}$. This dictates how much effort should be invested in determining a "good" initial vector.

To appreciate what this means concerning the effectiveness of using (10.2.1) as an updating technique, suppose, for example, that $|\lambda_2| = .85$ (as is common for PageRank), and suppose that the perturbations resulting from updating $\mathbf{Q}$ to $\mathbf{G}$ are such that each component π_i agrees with ϕ_i in the first significant digit. If (10.2.1) is used to produce twelve significant digits of accuracy, then it follows from (10.2.2) that about 156 iterations are required. This is only about 16 fewer than needed when starting blind with a random initial vector. Consequently, restarting the power method with the old PageRank vector is not an overly attractive approach to the link-updating problem even when changes are relatively small. Because the power method is not easily adapted to handle more complicated page-updating problems, it's clear that, by itself, restarting the power method with the old PageRank vector is not a viable updating technique.

At this point, it seems that efficiently updating the stationary vector $\boldsymbol{\pi}^T$ of a Markov chain $\mathbf{G}$ with knowledge of $\mathbf{Q}$ and $\boldsymbol{\phi}^T$ may be too lofty a goal. The only available method for both link-updating and page-updating, restarting the power method with $\boldsymbol{\phi}^T$, has little benefit over starting completely from scratch, i.e., restarting the power method with a random or uniform vector.

10.3 APPROXIMATE UPDATING USING APPROXIMATE AGGREGATION

If, instead of aiming for the exact value of the updated stationary distribution, you are willing to settle for an approximation, then the door opens wider. For example, Steve Chien and his coworkers [48] estimate Google's PageRank with an approximation approach that is based on state aggregation. State aggregation is part of a well-known class of methods known as *approximate aggregation techniques* [151] that have been used in the past to estimate stationary distributions of nearly uncoupled chains. The BlockRank algorithm of Chapter 9 used aggregation to accelerate the computation of PageRank.

Even though it produces only estimates of $\boldsymbol{\pi}^T$, approximate aggregation can handle both link-updating as well as page-updating, and it is computationally cheap.

The underlying idea of approximate aggregation is to use the previously known distribution

$$\boldsymbol{\phi}^T = (\phi_1, \phi_2, \ldots, \phi_m)$$

together with the updated transition probabilities in $\mathbf{G}$ to build an aggregated Markov chain having a transition probability matrix $\mathbf{C}$ that is smaller in size than $\mathbf{G}$. The stationary distribution $\boldsymbol{\xi}^T$ of $\mathbf{C}$ is used to generate an estimate of the true updated distribution $\boldsymbol{\pi}^T$ as outlined below.

The state space $\mathcal{S}$ of the updated Markov chain is first partitioned into two groups as $\mathcal{S} = L \cup \overline{L}$, where L is the subset of states whose stationary probabilities are likely to be most affected by the updates (newly added states are automatically included in L, and deleted states are accounted for by changing affected transition probabilities to zero). The complement $\overline{L}$ naturally contains all other states. The intuition is that the effect on the stationary vector of perturbations involving only a few states in large sparse chains (such as those in Google's PageRank application) is primarily local, and as a result, most stationary probabilities are not significantly affected. Deriving good methods for determining L is a pivotal issue, and this is discussed in more detail in section 10.7.

Partitioning the states of the updated chain as $\mathcal{S} = L \cup \overline{L}$ induces a partition (and reordering) of the updated transition matrix and its respective stationary distribution

$$\mathbf{G}_{n\times n} = \begin{array}{c} \\ L \\ \overline{L} \end{array} \!\!\begin{array}{c} \begin{array}{cc} L & \overline{L} \end{array} \\ \begin{pmatrix} \mathbf{G}_{11} & \mathbf{G}_{12} \\ \mathbf{G}_{21} & \mathbf{G}_{22} \end{pmatrix} \end{array} \quad \text{and} \quad \boldsymbol{\pi}^T = (\pi_1, \dots \pi_l \,|\, \pi_{l+1}, \dots, \pi_n), \tag{10.3.1}$$

where $\mathbf{G}_{11}$ is $l \times l$ with $l = |L|$ being the cardinality of L and and $\mathbf{G}_{22}$ is $(n-l)\times(n-l)$. The stationary probabilities from the original distribution $\boldsymbol{\phi}^T$ that correspond to the states in $\overline{L}$ are placed in a row vector $\boldsymbol{\omega}^T$, and the states in $\overline{L}$ are lumped into one superstate to create a smaller aggregated Markov chain whose transition matrix is the $(l+1)\times(l+1)$ matrix given by

$$\widetilde{\mathbf{C}} = \begin{pmatrix} \mathbf{G}_{11} & \mathbf{G}_{12}\mathbf{e} \\ \tilde{\mathbf{s}}^T\mathbf{G}_{21} & 1 - \tilde{\mathbf{s}}^T\mathbf{G}_{21}\mathbf{e} \end{pmatrix}, \qquad \text{where} \quad \tilde{\mathbf{s}}^T = \frac{\boldsymbol{\omega}^T}{\boldsymbol{\omega}^T\mathbf{e}} \qquad (\mathbf{e} \text{ is a column of ones}). \tag{10.3.2}$$

The approximation procedure in [48] computes the stationary distribution

$$\widetilde{\boldsymbol{\xi}}^T = \left(\tilde{\xi}_1, \tilde{\xi}_2, \dots, \tilde{\xi}_l, \tilde{\xi}_{l+1}\right),$$

for $\widetilde{\mathbf{C}}$ and uses the first l components in $\widetilde{\boldsymbol{\xi}}^T$ along with those in $\boldsymbol{\omega}^T$ to create an approximation $\widetilde{\boldsymbol{\pi}}^T$ to the exact updated distribution $\boldsymbol{\pi}^T$ by setting

$$\widetilde{\boldsymbol{\pi}}^T = \left(\tilde{\xi}_1, \tilde{\xi}_2, \dots, \tilde{\xi}_l \,|\, \boldsymbol{\omega}^T\right). \tag{10.3.3}$$

In other words,

$$\tilde{\pi}_i = \begin{cases} \tilde{\xi}_i, & \text{if state } i \text{ belongs to } L, \\ \phi_i, & \text{if state } i \text{ belongs to } \overline{L}. \end{cases}$$

The theoretical justification for this approximation scheme along with its accuracy is discussed in section 10.4. For now, it's important to recognize the reduction in work that is possible with approximate aggregation. Rather than finding the full updated PageRank vector $\boldsymbol{\pi}^T$, a much much smaller stationary vector $\widetilde{\boldsymbol{\xi}}^T$ is used to build an approximation $\widetilde{\boldsymbol{\pi}}^T$ to $\boldsymbol{\pi}^T$.

It's reported in [48] that numerical experiments on chains with millions of states provide estimates such that

$$\|\boldsymbol{\pi}^T - \tilde{\boldsymbol{\pi}}^T\|_1 = O(10^{-5}).$$

However, it's not clear that this is a good result because it is an *absolute* error, and absolute errors can be deceptive indicators of accuracy in large chains. If a chain has millions of states, and if, as is reasonable to expect, some stationary probability π_i is on the order of 10^{-5}, then an approximation $\tilde{\pi}_i$ can be as much as 100% different from the exact π_i in a relative sense yet yield a deceptively small absolute difference. Making the complete case should involve a relative measure.

10.4 EXACT AGGREGATION

The technique described in section 10.3 is simply one particular way to approximate the results of *exact* aggregation, which was developed in [125] and is briefly outlined below. For an irreducible n-state Markov chain whose state space has been partitioned into k disjoint groups $\mathcal{S} = L_1 \cup L_2 \cup \cdots \cup L_k$, the associated transition probability matrix assumes the block-partitioned form

$$\mathbf{G}_{n\times n} = \begin{array}{c} \\ L_1 \\ L_2 \\ \vdots \\ L_k \end{array} \begin{array}{c} \begin{array}{cccc} L_1 & L_2 & \cdots & L_k \end{array} \\ \begin{pmatrix} \mathbf{G}_{11} & \mathbf{G}_{12} & \cdots & \mathbf{G}_{1k} \\ \mathbf{G}_{21} & \mathbf{G}_{22} & \cdots & \mathbf{G}_{2k} \\ \vdots & \vdots & \ddots & \vdots \\ \mathbf{G}_{k1} & \mathbf{G}_{k2} & \cdots & \mathbf{G}_{kk} \end{pmatrix} \end{array} \quad \text{(with square diagonal blocks).} \quad (10.4.1)$$

This *parent* Markov chain defined by $\mathbf{G}$ induces k smaller Markov chains, called *censored chains*, as follows. The *censored Markov chain* associated with a group of states L_i is defined to be the Markov process that records the location of the parent chain only when the parent chain visits states in L_i. Visits to states outside of L_i are ignored. The transition probability matrix for the i-th censored chain is known to be *the i-th stochastic complement* [125] given by the formula

$$\mathbf{S}_i = \mathbf{G}_{ii} + \mathbf{G}_{i\star}(\mathbf{I} - \mathbf{G}_i^\star)^{-1}\mathbf{G}_{\star i}, \quad (10.4.2)$$

where $\mathbf{G}_{i\star}$ and $\mathbf{G}_{\star i}$ are, respectively, the i-th row and the i-th column of blocks with $\mathbf{G}_{ii}$ removed, and $\mathbf{G}_i^\star$ is the principal submatrix of $\mathbf{G}$ obtained by deleting the i-th row and i-th column of blocks. For example, if the partition consists of just two groups $\mathcal{S} = L_1 \cup L_2$, then there are only two censored chains, and their respective transition matrices are the two stochastic complements

$$\mathbf{S}_1 = \mathbf{G}_{11} + \mathbf{G}_{12}(\mathbf{I} - \mathbf{G}_{22})^{-1}\mathbf{G}_{21} \quad \text{and} \quad \mathbf{S}_2 = \mathbf{G}_{22} + \mathbf{G}_{21}(\mathbf{I} - \mathbf{G}_{11})^{-1}\mathbf{G}_{12}.$$

If the stationary distribution for $\mathbf{G}$ is $\boldsymbol{\pi}^T = (\,\boldsymbol{\pi}_1^T \mid \boldsymbol{\pi}_2^T \mid \cdots \mid \boldsymbol{\pi}_k^T\,)$ (partitioned conformably with $\mathbf{G}$), then the *i-th censored distribution* (the stationary distribution for $\mathbf{S}_i$) is known to be equal to

$$\mathbf{s}_i^T = \frac{\boldsymbol{\pi}_i^T}{\boldsymbol{\pi}_i^T\mathbf{e}} \quad \text{(e is an appropriately sized column of ones).} \quad (10.4.3)$$

For *regular* chains [104], the j-th component of $\mathbf{s}_i^T$ is the limiting conditional probability of being in the j-th state of group L_i given that the process is somewhere in L_i.

To compress each group L_i into a single state in order to create a small k-state aggregated chain, squeeze the parent transition matrix $\mathbf{G}$ down to the *aggregated transition matrix* (also known as the *coupling matrix*) by setting

$$\mathbf{C}_{k\times k} = \begin{pmatrix} \mathbf{s}_1^T\mathbf{G}_{11}\mathbf{e} & \cdots & \mathbf{s}_1^T\mathbf{G}_{1k}\mathbf{e} \\ \vdots & \ddots & \vdots \\ \mathbf{s}_k^T\mathbf{G}_{k1}\mathbf{e} & \cdots & \mathbf{s}_k^T\mathbf{G}_{kk}\mathbf{e} \end{pmatrix} \quad \text{(known to be stochastic and irreducible).} \tag{10.4.4}$$

For regular chains, transitions between states in the aggregated chain defined by $\mathbf{C}$ correspond to transitions between groups L_i in the unaggregated parent chain when the parent chain is in equilibrium.

The remarkable feature surrounding this aggregation idea is that it allows a parent chain to be decomposed into k small censored chains that can be independently solved, and the resulting censored distributions $\mathbf{s}_i^T$ can be combined through the stationary distribution of $\mathbf{C}$ to construct the parent stationary distribution $\boldsymbol{\pi}^T$. This is the exact aggregation theorem.

Theorem 10.4.1. (The Exact Aggregation Theorem [125]). *If* $\mathbf{G}$ *is the block-partitioned transition probability matrix* (10.4.1) *for an irreducible* n*-state Markov chain whose stationary probability distribution is*

$$\boldsymbol{\pi}^T = (\,\boldsymbol{\pi}_1^T \mid \boldsymbol{\pi}_2^T \mid \cdots \mid \boldsymbol{\pi}_k^T\,) \quad \textit{(partitioned conformably with } \mathbf{G}\textit{)},$$

and if $\boldsymbol{\xi}^T = (\xi_1, \xi_2, \ldots, \xi_k)$ *is the stationary distribution for the aggregated chain defined by the matrix* $\mathbf{C}_{k\times k}$ *in* (10.4.4), *then the stationary distribution for* $\mathbf{G}$ *is*

$$\boldsymbol{\pi}^T = \left(\xi_1\mathbf{s}_1^T \mid \xi_2\mathbf{s}_2^T \mid \cdots \mid \xi_k\mathbf{s}_k^T\right),$$

where $\mathbf{s}_i^T$ *is the censored distribution associated with the stochastic complement* $\mathbf{S}_i$ *in* (10.4.2).

10.5 EXACT VS. APPROXIMATE AGGREGATION

While exact aggregation as presented in Theorem 10.4.1 is elegant and appealing with its divide and conquer philosophy, it's an inefficient numerical procedure for computing $\boldsymbol{\pi}^T$ because costly inversions are embedded in the stochastic complements (10.4.2) that are required to produce the censored distributions $\mathbf{s}_i^T$. Consequently, it's common to attempt to somehow approximate the censored distributions, and there are at least two methods for doing so. Sometimes the stochastic complements $\mathbf{S}_i$ are first estimated (e.g., approximating $\mathbf{S}_i$ with $\mathbf{G}_{ii}$ works well for nearly uncoupled chains). Then the distributions of these estimates are computed to provide approximate censored distributions, which in turn lead to an approximate aggregated transition matrix that is used by the exact aggregation theorem to produce an approximation to $\boldsymbol{\pi}^T$. The other approach is to bypass the stochastic complements altogether and somehow estimate the censored distributions $\mathbf{s}_i^T$ directly, and this is the essence of the PageRank approximation scheme that was described in section 10.3.

To see this, consider the updated transition matrix $\mathbf{G}$ given in (10.3.1) to be partitioned into $l+1$ levels in which the first l diagonal blocks are just 1×1, and the lower right-hand block is the $(n-l)\times(n-l)$ matrix $\mathbf{G}_{22}$ associated with the states in $\overline{L}$. In other words, to fit the context of Theorem 10.4.1, the partition in (10.3.1) is viewed as

$$\mathbf{G} = \begin{array}{c} \\ L \\ \overline{L} \end{array}\!\!\begin{array}{c} \begin{array}{cc} L & \overline{L} \end{array} \\ \begin{pmatrix} \mathbf{G}_{11} & \mathbf{G}_{12} \\ \mathbf{G}_{21} & \mathbf{G}_{22} \end{pmatrix} \end{array} = \left(\begin{array}{c|c|c|c} g_{11} & \cdots & g_{1l} & \mathbf{G}_{1\star} \\ \hline \vdots & \ddots & \vdots & \vdots \\ \hline g_{l1} & \cdots & g_{ll} & \mathbf{G}_{l\star} \\ \hline \mathbf{G}_{\star 1} & \cdots & \mathbf{G}_{\star l} & \mathbf{G}_{22} \end{array}\right), \tag{10.5.1}$$

where

$$\mathbf{G}_{11} = \begin{pmatrix} g_{11} & \cdots & g_{1l} \\ \vdots & \ddots & \vdots \\ g_{l1} & \cdots & g_{ll} \end{pmatrix}, \quad \mathbf{G}_{12} = \begin{pmatrix} \mathbf{G}_{1\star} \\ \vdots \\ \mathbf{G}_{l\star} \end{pmatrix}, \quad \text{and} \quad \mathbf{G}_{21} = \left(\mathbf{G}_{\star 1} \cdots \mathbf{G}_{\star l}\right).$$

Since the first l diagonal blocks in the partition (10.5.1) are 1×1 (i.e., scalars), it's evident that the corresponding stochastic complements are $\mathbf{S}_i = 1$ (they are 1×1 stochastic matrices), so the censored distributions are $\mathbf{s}_i{}^T = 1$ for $i = 1, \ldots, l$. This means that the *exact* aggregated transition matrix (10.4.4) associated with the partition (10.5.1) is

$$\mathbf{C} = \left(\begin{array}{c|c|c|c} g_{11} & \cdots & g_{1l} & \mathbf{G}_{1\star}\mathbf{e} \\ \hline \vdots & \ddots & \vdots & \vdots \\ \hline g_{l1} & \cdots & g_{ll} & \mathbf{G}_{l\star}\mathbf{e} \\ \hline \mathbf{s}^T\mathbf{G}_{\star 1} & \cdots & \mathbf{s}^T\mathbf{G}_{\star l} & \mathbf{s}^T\mathbf{G}_{22}\mathbf{e} \end{array}\right)_{(l+1)\times(l+1)} \tag{10.5.2}$$

$$= \begin{pmatrix} \mathbf{G}_{11} & \mathbf{G}_{12}\mathbf{e} \\ \mathbf{s}^T\mathbf{G}_{21} & \mathbf{s}^T\mathbf{G}_{22}\mathbf{e} \end{pmatrix} = \begin{pmatrix} \mathbf{G}_{11} & \mathbf{G}_{12}\mathbf{e} \\ \mathbf{s}^T\mathbf{G}_{21} & 1 - \mathbf{s}^T\mathbf{G}_{21}\mathbf{e} \end{pmatrix},$$

where $\mathbf{s}^T$ is the censored distribution derived from the only significant stochastic complement

$$\mathbf{S} = \mathbf{G}_{22} + \mathbf{G}_{21}\left(\mathbf{I} - \mathbf{G}_{11}\right)^{-1}\mathbf{G}_{12}.$$

Compare the exact coupling matrix $\mathbf{C}$ above with the approximate $\widetilde{\mathbf{C}}$ suggested by Chien et al. in equation (10.3.2). If the stationary distribution for $\mathbf{C}$ is

$$\boldsymbol{\xi}^T = \left(\xi_1, \ldots, \xi_l, \xi_{l+1}\right),$$

then exact aggregation (Theorem 10.4.1) ensures that the *exact* stationary distribution for $\mathbf{G}$ is

$$\boldsymbol{\pi}^T = \left(\xi_1, \ldots, \xi_l \mid \xi_{l+1}\mathbf{s}^T\right) = \left(\pi_1, \ldots, \pi_l \mid \boldsymbol{\pi}_2^T\right). \tag{10.5.3}$$

It's a fundamental issue to describe just how well the estimate $\widetilde{\boldsymbol{\pi}}^T$ given in equation (10.3.3) approximates the exact distribution $\boldsymbol{\pi}^T$ given in (10.5.3). Obviously, the degree to which $\widetilde{\pi}_i \approx \pi_i$ for $i > l$ (i.e., the degree to which $\boldsymbol{\omega}^T \approx \boldsymbol{\pi}_2^T$) depends on the degree to which the partition $\mathcal{S} = L \cup \overline{L}$ can be adequately constructed. While it's somewhat intuitive that this should also affect the degree to which $\widetilde{\pi}_i$ approximates π_i for $i \leq l$, it's not clear, at least on the surface, just how good this latter approximation is expected to be. The analysis is as follows.

Instead of using the exact censored distribution $\mathbf{s}^T$ to build the exact aggregated matrix $\mathbf{C}$ in (10.5.2), the vector $\tilde{\mathbf{s}}^T = \boldsymbol{\omega}^T/\boldsymbol{\omega}^T\mathbf{e}$ is used to approximate $\mathbf{s}^T$ in order to construct $\widetilde{\mathbf{C}}$ in (10.3.2). The magnitude of

$$\boldsymbol{\delta}^T = \mathbf{s}^T - \tilde{\mathbf{s}}^T = \frac{\boldsymbol{\pi}_2^T}{\boldsymbol{\pi}_2^T\mathbf{e}} - \frac{\boldsymbol{\omega}^T}{\boldsymbol{\omega}^T\mathbf{e}}$$

and the magnitude of

$$\mathbf{E} = \mathbf{C} - \widetilde{\mathbf{C}} = \begin{pmatrix} \mathbf{0} & \mathbf{0} \\ \boldsymbol{\delta}^T\mathbf{G}_{21} & -\boldsymbol{\delta}^T\mathbf{G}_{21}\mathbf{e} \end{pmatrix} = \begin{pmatrix} \mathbf{0} \\ \boldsymbol{\delta}^T \end{pmatrix} \mathbf{G}_{21}(\mathbf{I} \mid -\mathbf{e}) \tag{10.5.4}$$

are clearly of the same order. This suggests that if the partition $\mathcal{S} = L \cup \overline{L}$ can be adequately constructed so as to insure that the magnitude of $\boldsymbol{\delta}^T$ is small, then $\widetilde{\mathbf{C}}$ is close to $\mathbf{C}$, so their respective stationary distributions $\widetilde{\boldsymbol{\xi}}^T$ and $\boldsymbol{\xi}^T$ should be close, thus ensuring that $\widetilde{\pi}_i$ and π_i are close for $i \leq l$. However, some care must be exercised before jumping to this conclusion because Markov chains can sometimes exhibit sensitivities to small perturbations.

The effects of perturbations in Markov chains are well documented, and there are a variety of ways to measure the degree to which the stationary probabilities are sensitive to changes in the transition probabilities. These measures include the extent to which magnitude of the subdominant eigenvalue of the transition matrix is close to one [126, 128], the degree to which various "condition numbers" are small [50, 76, 83, 98, 123], and the degree to which the mean first passage times are small [49]. Any of these measures can be used to produce a detailed perturbation analysis that revolves around the perturbation term in (10.5.4), but, for the purposes at hand, it's sufficient to note that it's certainly possible for $\widetilde{\xi}_i$ and ξ_i (and hence $\widetilde{\pi}_i$ and π_i) to be relatively far apart for $i \leq l$ even when $\boldsymbol{\delta}^T$ (and hence $\mathbf{E}$) have small components. For example, this badly conditioned behavior can occur if the magnitude of $\mathbf{G}_{12}$ is small because this ensures that the subdominant eigenvalue of $\mathbf{C}$ is close to 1 (and some mean first passage times are large), and this is known [49, 126, 128] to make the stationary probabilities sensitive to perturbations. Other aberrations in $\mathbf{C}$ can also cause similar problems. Of course, if the chain defined by $\mathbf{C}$ is well conditioned by any of the measures referenced above, then $\boldsymbol{\xi}^T$ will be relatively insensitive to small perturbations, and the degree to which $\boldsymbol{\omega}^T \approx \boldsymbol{\pi}_2^T$ (i.e., the degree to which $\mathcal{S} = L \cup \overline{L}$ can be adequately constructed) will more directly reflect the degree to which $\widetilde{\pi}_i \approx \pi_i$ for $i \leq l$. The point being made here is that unless the degree to which $\mathbf{C}$ is well conditioned is established, the degree of the approximation in (10.3.3) is in doubt regardless of how well $\boldsymbol{\omega}^T$ approximates $\boldsymbol{\pi}_2^T$.

This may seem to be a criticism of the idea behind the approximation (10.3.3), but, to the contrary, the purpose of this chapter is to argue that this is in fact a good idea because it can be viewed as the first step in an *iterative* aggregation scheme that performs remarkably well. The following section is dedicated to developing an iterative aggregation approach to updating stationary probabilities.

10.6 UPDATING WITH ITERATIVE AGGREGATION

Iterative aggregation is an algorithm for solving nearly uncoupled (sometimes called nearly completely decomposable) Markov chains, and it is discussed in detail in [154]. Iterative aggregation is not a general-purpose technique, and it usually doesn't work for chains that are not nearly uncoupled. However, the ideas can be adapted to the updating problem, and these variations work extremely well, even when applied to Markov chains that are not nearly uncoupled. This is in part due to the fact that the approximate aggregation matrix (10.3.2) differs from the exact aggregation matrix (10.5.2) in only one row, namely, the last row. The iterative aggregation updating algorithm is described below.

Assume that the stationary distribution

$$\boldsymbol{\phi}^T = (\phi_1, \phi_2, \ldots, \phi_m)$$

for some irreducible Markov chain $\mathcal{C}$ is already known, perhaps from prior computations, and suppose that $\mathcal{C}$ needs to be updated. As in earlier sections, let the transition probability matrix and stationary distribution for the updated chain be denoted by $\mathbf{G}$ and

$$\boldsymbol{\pi}^T = (\pi_1, \pi_2, \ldots, \pi_n),$$

respectively. The updated matrix $\mathbf{G}$ is assumed to be irreducible. Of course, the specific application we have in mind is Google's PageRank (in which case the matrix is guaranteed to be irreducible), but this method can be used to update other general irreducible Markov chains. Notice that m is not necessarily equal to n because the updating process may add or delete states as well as alter transition probabilities.

THE ITERATIVE AGGREGATION UPDATING ALGORITHM

Initialization

- Partition the states of the updated chain as $\mathcal{S} = L \cup \overline{L}$ and reorder $\mathbf{G}$ as described in (10.3.1)
- $\boldsymbol{\omega}^T \longleftarrow$ the components from $\boldsymbol{\phi}^T$ that correspond to the states in $\overline{L}$
- $\mathbf{s}^T \longleftarrow \boldsymbol{\omega}^T/(\boldsymbol{\omega}^T\mathbf{e})$ (an initial approximate censored distribution)

Iterate until convergence

1. $\mathbf{C} \longleftarrow \begin{pmatrix} \mathbf{G}_{11} & \mathbf{G}_{12}\mathbf{e} \\ \mathbf{s}^T\mathbf{G}_{21} & 1 - \mathbf{s}^T\mathbf{G}_{21}\mathbf{e} \end{pmatrix}_{(l+1)\times(l+1)}$ $\quad (l = |L|)$

2. $\boldsymbol{\xi}^T \longleftarrow (\xi_1, \xi_2, \ldots, \xi_l, \xi_{l+1})$, the stationary distribution of $\mathbf{C}$

3. $\boldsymbol{\chi}^T \longleftarrow (\xi_1, \xi_2, \ldots, \xi_l \mid \xi_{l+1}\mathbf{s}^T)$

4. $\boldsymbol{\psi}^T \longleftarrow \boldsymbol{\chi}^T\mathbf{G} = (\boldsymbol{\psi}_1^T \mid \boldsymbol{\psi}_2^T)$ (see note following the algorithm)

5. If $\|\boldsymbol{\psi}^T - \boldsymbol{\chi}^T\| < \tau$ for a given tolerance τ, then quit—else $\mathbf{s}^T \longleftarrow \boldsymbol{\psi}_2^T/\boldsymbol{\psi}_2^T\mathbf{e}$ and go to step 1

Note concerning step 4. Step 4 is necessary because the vector $\boldsymbol{\chi}^T$ generated in step 3 is a fixed point in the sense that if step 4 is omitted and the algorithm is restarted with $\boldsymbol{\chi}^T$ instead of $\boldsymbol{\psi}^T$, then the same $\boldsymbol{\chi}^T$ is simply reproduced at step 3 on each subsequent iteration. Step 4 has two purposes—it moves the iterate off the fixed point while simultaneously contributing to the convergence process. Step 4 is the analog of the smoothing operation in algebraic multigrid algorithms, and it can be replaced by a step from almost any iterative procedure used to solve linear systems—e.g., a Gauss-Seidel step [154] is sometimes used.

While precise rates of convergence for general iterative aggregation algorithms are difficult to articulate, the specialized nature of our iterative aggregation updating algorithm allows us to easily establish its rate of convergence. The following theorem shows that this rate is directly dependent on how fast the powers of the one significant stochastic complement $\mathbf{S} = \mathbf{G}_{22} + \mathbf{G}_{21}(\mathbf{I} - \mathbf{G}_{11})^{-1}\mathbf{G}_{12}$ converge. In other words, since $\mathbf{S}$ is an irreducible stochastic matrix, the rate of convergence is completely dictated by the largest subdominant eigenvalue (and Jordan structure) of $\mathbf{S}$.

Theorem 10.6.1. (Convergence Theorem for the Iterative Aggregation Updating Algorithm [111]). *The iterative aggregation updating algorithm defined above converges to the stationary distribution $\boldsymbol{\pi}^T$ of $\mathbf{G}$ for all partitions $\mathcal{S} = L \cup \overline{L}$. The rate at which the iterates converge to $\boldsymbol{\pi}^T$ is exactly the rate at which the powers $\mathbf{S}^n$ converge, which is dictated by the largest subdominant eigenvalue λ_2 (and Jordan structure) of $\mathbf{S}$. In the common case when λ_2 is real and simple, the iterates converge to $\boldsymbol{\pi}^T$ at the rate at which $\lambda_2^n \to 0$.*

Further, Ilse Ipsen and Steve Kirkland have proven that, under a few assumptions (that are easily satisfied for the PageRank case), the rate of convergence of this iterative aggregation updating algorithm is always less than or equal to the rate of convergence of the standard power method [97].

10.7 DETERMINING THE PARTITION

The iterative aggregation updating algorithm always converges, and it never requires more iterations than the power method to attain a given level of convergence. However, iterative aggregation requires more work per iteration than the power method. The key to realizing an improvement in iterative aggregation over the power method rests in properly choosing the partition $\mathcal{S} = L \cup \overline{L}$. As Theorem 10.6.1 shows, good partitions are precisely those that yield a stochastic complement $\mathbf{S} = \mathbf{G}_{22} + \mathbf{G}_{21}(\mathbf{I} - \mathbf{G}_{11})^{-1}\mathbf{G}_{12}$ whose subdominant eigenvalue λ_2 is small in magnitude.

While it's not a theorem, experience indicates that as $|L| = l$ (the size of $\mathbf{G}_{11}$) becomes larger, iterative aggregation tends to converge in fewer iterations. But as l becomes larger, each iteration requires more work, so the trick is to strike an acceptable balance. A small l that significantly reduces $|\lambda_2|$ is the ideal situation.

Even for moderately sized problems there is an extremely large number of possible partitions, but there are some useful heuristics that can help guide the choice of L so that reasonably good results are produced. For example, a relatively simple approach is to take L to be the set of all states "near" the updates, where "near" might be measured in a graph theoretic sense or else by the magnitude of transient flow. In the absence of any other information, this is not a completely bad strategy, and it is at least a good place to start. However, there are usually additional options that lead to even better "L-sets," and some of these are described below.

10.7.1 Partitioning by Differing Time Scales

In most applications involving irreducible aperiodic Markov chains the components of the n-th step distribution vector do not converge at a uniform rate, and consequently iterative techniques, including the power method, often spend the majority of the time resolving a minority of slow converging components. The slow converging components can be isolated either by monitoring the process for a few iterations or by theoretical means such as those described in [111]. (Section 9.1 already introduced the idea and detection of slow vs. fast converging states for the PageRank problem.) If the states corresponding to the slower converging components are placed in L while the faster converging states are lumped into $\overline{L}$, then the iterative aggregation algorithm concentrates its effort on resolving the smaller number of slow converging states.

In loose terms, the effect of steps 1–3 in the iterative aggregation algorithm is essentially to make progress toward achieving an equilibrium (or steady state) for a smaller chain consisting of just the "slow states" in L together with one additional aggregated state that accounts for all "fast states" in $\overline{L}$. The power iteration in step 4 moves the entire process ahead on a global basis, so if the slow states in L are substantially resolved by steps 1–3, then not many global power steps are required to push the entire chain toward its global equilibrium. This is the essence of the original Simon–Ando idea as explained and analyzed in [151] and [125]. If $l = |L|$ is small relative to n, then steps 1–3 are relatively cheap to execute, so the process can converge rapidly (in both iteration count and wall-clock time). Examples are given in [111].

In some applications the slow states are particularly easy to identify because they are the ones having the larger stationary probabilities. This is a particularly nice state of affairs for the updating problem because we have the stationary probabilities from the prior period at our disposal, so all we have to do to construct a good L-set is to include the states with large prior stationary probabilities and throw in the states that were added or updated along with a few of their nearest neighbors. Clearly, this is an advantage only when there are just a few "large" states. Fortunately, it turns out that this is a characteristic feature of Google's PageRank application and other scale-free networks with power law distributions.

10.7.2 Scale-Free Networks and Google's PageRank

As discussed in [16, 17, 41, 63], the link structure of the Web constitutes a "scale-free" network. This means that the number of nodes $n(j)$ having j edges (possibly directed) is proportional to j^{-k} where k is a constant that doesn't change as the network expands (hence the term "scale-free"). In other words, the distribution of nodal degrees seems to follow a "power law distribution" in the sense that

$$Prob[deg(N) = d] \propto \frac{1}{d^k}, \qquad \text{for some } k > 1.$$

(The symbol $\propto$ is read "is proportional to.") For example, studies [16, 17, 41, 63] have shown that for the Web the parameter for the indegree power-law distribution is $k \approx 2.1$, while the outdegree distribution has $k \approx 2.7$.

The scale-free nature of the Web translates into a power law for PageRanks. In fact, experiments described in [63, 136] indicate that PageRank has a power law distribution with a parameter $k \approx 2.1$. In other words, there are relatively very few pages that have a significant PageRank while the overwhelming majority of pages have a nearly negligible PageRank. Consequently, when PageRanks are plotted in order of decreasing magnitude, the resulting graph has a pronounced "L" shape with an extremely sharp bend. Figure 10.1 shows the PageRanks sorted in decreasing order of magnitude for a sample web graph containing over 6,000 pages collected from the `hollins.edu` domain. It's this characteristic

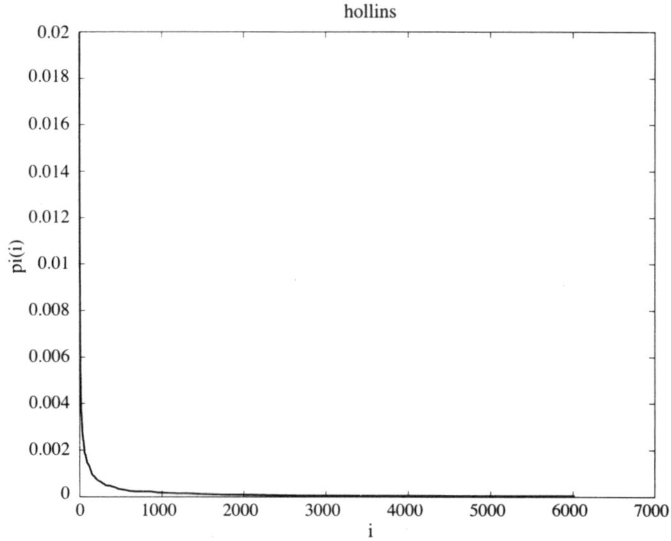

Figure 10.1 Power law distribution of PageRanks

"L-shape" of PageRank distributions that reveals a near optimal partition $\mathcal{S} = L \cup \overline{L}$, as described in the next section and shown experimentally in [111].

10.8 CONCLUSIONS

Reference [111] contains the results of numerous experiments that apply the iterative aggregation algorithm to update the PageRank for small subsets of the Web. The experiments lead to several conclusions.

1. The iterative aggregation technique provides a significant improvement over the power method when a good L-set is used. In some cases, it requires less than 1/7 of the time required by the power method.

2. The improvements become more pronounced as the size of the datasets increases.

3. The iterative aggregation approach offers room for even greater improvements. For example, the extrapolation technique introduced in section 9.1 can be employed in conjunction with the iterative aggregation algorithm to further accelerate the updating process.

4. Good L-sets can be constructed by:

    - first putting all new states and states with altered links (perhaps along with some nearest neighbors) into L,
    - then adding other states that remain after the update in order of the magnitude of their prior stationary probabilities up to the point where these stationary probabilities level off (i.e., include states to the left of the bend in the PageRank L-curve).

Of course, there is some subjectiveness in this strategy for choosing the L-set. However, the leveling-off point is relatively easy to discern in distributions having a very sharply defined bend in the L-curve, and only distributions that gradually die away or do not conform to a power distribution are problematic.

5. Finally (but very important), when iterative aggregation is used as an updating technique, the fact that updates change the problem size is of little or no consequence. Thus, the algorithm is the first to handle both types of updates, link and page updates.

ASIDE: The Google Dance

It's believed that Google updates their PageRank vector on a monthly basis. The process of updating is known as the **Google Dance** *because pages dance up and down the rankings during the three days of updating computation. There's a nifty tool called the Google Dance Tool (`http://www.seochat.com/googledance/`) for watching this dance. The tool sends the query off to Google's three primary servers. First, it goes to the main Google server, `www.google.com`, then the two auxiliary servers `www2.google.com` and `www3.google.com`, which are believed to be test servers. The tool reports the three sets of top ten rankings side by side in a chart.*

Most times of the month, the three lists show little or no variation. But it's clear when Google is in the process of updating, the lists vary substantially. It's possible that during the updating time of the month, the main server uses last month's PageRank vector, then the test servers show rankings that use iterates of the updated PageRank vector as it is being computed. After a few days, when the dancing is done, all servers show the same lists again as they all use the completely updated PageRank vector.

Many webmasters have come to fear the Google Dance. After working so hard to improve their rankings (by hook or by crook or by good content), just a slight tweak by Google in their PageRank or content score algorithms can ruin a webmaster's traffic and business. In fact, the famous ethical SEO guru Danny Sullivan (see the aside on page 43) created the term Google Dance Syndrome (GDS) to describe the ailment that some webmasters suffer each month. In May 2003, there was a huge outbreak of GDS when Google made some substantial modifications to its algorithms, adding spam filters, quick fresh updates for popular pages, and more mirror sites. In September 2002 with their usual playful style, Google hosted an actual Google Dance (see photos at `http://www.google.com/googledance2002/`), inviting attendees of the nearby Search Engine Strategies Conference to the Googleplex to dance the night away.

ASIDE: Googleopoly

Reporters use the term Googleopoly to refer to Google's dominance of web search. In May 2004, Google claimed 36.8% of the market. The Yahoo conglomerate, which includes Yahoo, AllTheWeb, AltaVista, and Overture, took second place with 26.6%, MSN followed with 14.5%. Google has steadily added more handy features like an online calculator, dictionary, and spelling correction. Their recent rollout of Gmail, their email service that allows for 1KB of storage and search within messages and message threads, has convinced many that Google is poised to completely take over the market. BBC technology journalist Bill Thompson has gone as far as to claim that government intervention is needed to break up the Googleopoly. Thompson says that Google is a public utility that must be regulated in the public interest. Googlites personally defend Google, citing the company's history of making morally good decisions and referring to the monopoly-busting cries as alarmist chatter. Besides, they argue, Brin and Page made the company motto, "Don't be evil," which clearly reveals their earnest intentions.

Librarians deal with the Googleopoly everyday. They have to beg students to use search services other than Google. Students are often surprised when a librarian finds a piece of information that they couldn't find on Google. It's as if the information doesn't exist if it's not on Google. Other diversified, specialized search tools have great value that a general purpose engine like Google can't supply. As the librarians preach, learn to use several search engines, general and specialized, and watch your search skills multiply. Incidentally, number 8 on the top 10 list of signs that you're addicted to Google is: shouting at the librarian if he takes longer than .1 seconds to find your information. A related bit of humor appears in the form of a cartoon that is floating around the Web. The cartoon pictures Bart Simpson learning his lesson by writing "I will use Google before asking dumb questions" over and over again on the chalkboard.

Chapter Eleven

The HITS Method for Ranking Webpages

If you're a sports fan, you've seen those "—— is Life" t-shirts, where the blank is filled in by a sport like football, soccer, cheerleading, fishing, etc. After reading the first ten chapters of this book, you might be ready to declare "Google is Life." But your mom probably told you long ago that "there's more to life than sports." And there's more to search than Google. In fact, there's Teoma, and Alexa, and A9, to name a few. The next few chapters are devoted to search beyond Google. This chapter focuses specifically on one algorithm, HITS, the algorithm that forms the basis of Teoma's popularity ranking.

11.1 THE HITS ALGORITHM

We first introduced HITS, the other system for ranking webpages by popularity back in Chapter 3. Since that was many pages ago, we review the major points regarding HITS. HITS, which is an acronym for Hypertext Induced Topic Search, was invented by Jon Kleinberg in 1998—around the same time that Brin and Page were working on their PageRank algorithm. HITS, like PageRank, uses the Web's hyperlink structure to create popularity scores associated with webpages. However, HITS has some important differences. Whereas the PageRank method produces one popularity score for each page, HITS produces two. Whereas PageRank is query-independent, HITS is query-dependent. HITS thinks of webpages as authorities and hubs. An authority is a page with many inlinks, and a hub is a page with many outlinks. Authorities and hubs deserve the adjective *good* when the following circular statement holds: *Good authorities are pointed to by good hubs and good hubs point to good authorities.* And so every page is some measure of an authority and some measure of a hub. The authority and hub measures of HITS have been incorporated into the CLEVER project at IBM Almaden Research Center [2]. HITS is also part of the ranking technology used by the new search engine Teoma [150].

After this recap, we are ready to translate these words about what HITS does into mathematics. Every page i has both an **authority score** x_i and a **hub score** y_i. Let E be the set of all directed edges in the web graph and let e_{ij} represent the directed edge from node i to node j. Given that each page has somehow been assigned an initial authority score $x_i^{(0)}$ and hub score $y_i^{(0)}$, HITS successively refines these scores by computing

$$x_i^{(k)} = \sum_{j:e_{ji}\in E} y_j^{(k-1)} \quad \text{and} \quad y_i^{(k)} = \sum_{j:e_{ij}\in E} x_j^{(k)} \quad \text{for } k = 1, 2, 3, \ldots \qquad (11.1.1)$$

These equations, which were Kleinberg's original equations, can be written in matrix form with the help of the adjacency matrix $\mathbf{L}$ of the directed web graph.

$$\mathbf{L}_{ij} = \begin{cases} 1, & \text{if there exists an edge from node } i \text{ to node } j, \\ 0, & \text{otherwise.} \end{cases}$$

For example, the adjacency matrix $\mathbf{L}$ for the small graph in Figure 11.1 is

$$\mathbf{L} = \begin{array}{c} \\ P_1 \\ P_2 \\ P_3 \\ P_4 \end{array} \begin{array}{c} \begin{array}{cccc} P_1 & P_2 & P_3 & P_4 \end{array} \\ \begin{pmatrix} 0 & 1 & 1 & 0 \\ 1 & 0 & 1 & 0 \\ 0 & 1 & 0 & 1 \\ 0 & 1 & 0 & 0 \end{pmatrix} \end{array}.$$

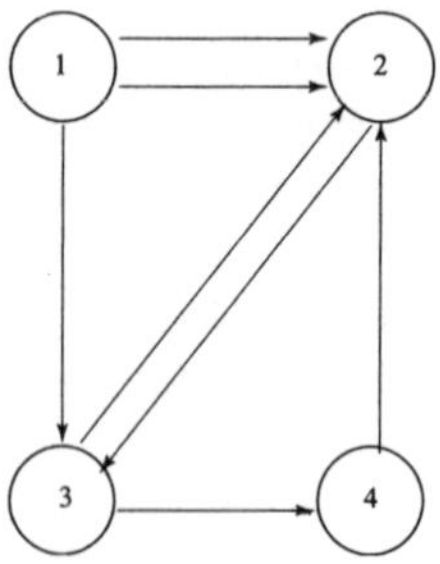

Figure 11.1 Graph for 4-page web

In matrix notation, the equations in (11.1.1) assume the form

$$\mathbf{x}^{(k)} = \mathbf{L}^T\mathbf{y}^{(k-1)} \quad \text{and} \quad \mathbf{y}^{(k)} = \mathbf{L}\mathbf{x}^{(k)},$$

where $\mathbf{x}^{(k)}$ and $\mathbf{y}^{(k)}$ are $n \times 1$ vectors holding the approximate authority and hub scores at each iteration.

This leads to the following iterative algorithm for computing the ultimate authority scores $\mathbf{x}$ and hub scores $\mathbf{y}$.

THE ORIGINAL HITS ALGORITHM

1. Initialize: $\mathbf{y}^{(0)} = \mathbf{e}$, where $\mathbf{e}$ is a column vector of all ones. Other positive starting vectors may be used. (See section 11.3.)

2. Until convergence, do

$$\begin{aligned} \mathbf{x}^{(k)} &= \mathbf{L}^T\mathbf{y}^{(k-1)} \\ \mathbf{y}^{(k)} &= \mathbf{L}\mathbf{x}^{(k)} \\ k &= k+1 \end{aligned}$$

Normalize $\mathbf{x}^{(k)}$ and $\mathbf{y}^{(k)}$. (See section 11.3.)

Note that in step 2 of this algorithm, the two equations

$$\mathbf{x}^{(k)} = \mathbf{L}^T\mathbf{y}^{(k-1)}$$
$$\mathbf{y}^{(k)} = \mathbf{L}\mathbf{x}^{(k)}$$

can be simplified by substitution to

$$\mathbf{x}^{(k)} = \mathbf{L}^T\mathbf{L}\mathbf{x}^{(k-1)}$$
$$\mathbf{y}^{(k)} = \mathbf{L}\mathbf{L}^T\mathbf{y}^{(k-1)}.$$

These two new equations define the *iterative power method* for computing the *dominant eigenvector* for the matrices $\mathbf{L}^T\mathbf{L}$ and $\mathbf{L}\mathbf{L}^T$. This is very similar to the PageRank power method of Chapter 4, except a different coefficient matrix is used ($\mathbf{L}^T\mathbf{L}$ or $\mathbf{L}\mathbf{L}^T$) instead of the Google matrix $\mathbf{G}$. Since the matrix $\mathbf{L}^T\mathbf{L}$ determines the authority scores, it is called the **authority matrix**, and $\mathbf{L}\mathbf{L}^T$ is known as the **hub matrix**. $\mathbf{L}^T\mathbf{L}$ and $\mathbf{L}\mathbf{L}^T$ are *symmetric positive semidefinite* matrices. Computing the authority vector $\mathbf{x}$ and the hub vector $\mathbf{y}$ can be viewed as finding dominant right-hand eigenvectors of $\mathbf{L}^T\mathbf{L}$ and $\mathbf{L}\mathbf{L}^T$, respectively.

11.2 HITS IMPLEMENTATION

The implementation of HITS involves two main steps. First, a **neighborhood graph** N related to the query terms is built. Second, the authority and hub scores ($\mathbf{x}$ and $\mathbf{y}$) for each page in N are computed, and two ranked lists of the most authoritative pages and most "hubby" pages are presented to the user. Since the second step was described in the previous section, we focus on the first step. All pages containing references to the query terms are put into the neighborhood graph N. There are various ways to determine these pages. One simple method consults the **inverted file index** (see Chapter 2), which might look like:

- term 1 (aardvark) - 3, 117, 3961

  ⋮

- term 10 (aztec) - 3, 15, 19, 101, 673, 1199
- term 11 (baby) - 3, 31, 56, 94, 673, 909, 11114, 253791

  ⋮

- term m (zymurgy) - 1159223

For each term, the pages mentioning that term are stored in list form. Thus, a query on terms 1 and 10 would pull pages 3, 15, 19, 101, 117, 673, 1199, and 3961 into N. Next, the graph around the subset of nodes in N is expanded by adding nodes that point either to or from nodes in N. This expansion allows some semantic associations to be made. That is, for the query term `car`, with the expansion about pages containing `car`, some pages containing `automobile` may now be added to N (presuming some pages about cars point to pages about automobiles and vice versa). This usually resolves the problem of synonyms. However, the set N can become very large due to the expansion process; a page containing the query terms may possess a huge indegree or outdegree. Thus, in practice, the maximum number of inlinking nodes and outlinking nodes to add for a particular node in N is fixed, at say 100, in which case only the first 100 outlinking nodes of a page containing a query term are added to N. (The process of building the neighborhood graph is strongly related to building level sets in information filtering, which reduces a sparse matrix to a much smaller more query-relevant matrix [165].)

Once the set N is built, the adjacency matrix $\mathbf{L}$ corresponding to the nodes in N is formed. The order of $\mathbf{L}$ is much smaller than the total number of pages on the Web. Therefore, computing authority and hub scores using the dominant eigenvectors of $\mathbf{L}^T\mathbf{L}$ and $\mathbf{L}\mathbf{L}^T$ incurs a small cost, small in comparison to computing authority and hub scores when all documents on the Web are placed in N (as is done by the PageRank method).

An additional cost reduction exists. Only one dominant eigenvector needs to be computed, that of either $\mathbf{L}^T\mathbf{L}$ or $\mathbf{L}\mathbf{L}^T$, but not both. For example, the authority vector $\mathbf{x}$ can be obtained by computing the dominant eigenvector of $\mathbf{L}^T\mathbf{L}$, then the hub vector $\mathbf{y}$ can be obtained from the equation $\mathbf{y} = \mathbf{L}\mathbf{x}$. A similar statement applies if the hub vector is computed first from the eigenvector problem.

Notation for the HITS Problem

N	neighborhood graph
$\mathbf{L}$	sparse binary adjacency matrix for N
$\mathbf{L}^T\mathbf{L}$	sparse authority matrix
$\mathbf{L}\mathbf{L}^T$	sparse hub matrix
n	number of pages in N = order of $\mathbf{L}$
$\mathbf{x}$	authority vector
$\mathbf{y}$	hub vector

Matlab m-file for the HITS algorithm

This m-file is a Matlab implementation of the HITS power method given in section 11.1.

```
function [x,y,time,numiter]=hits(L,x0,n,epsilon);

% HITS computes the HITS authority vector x and hub vector y
%      for an n-by-n adjacency matrix L with starting vector
%      x0 (a row vector). Uses power method on L'*L.
%
% EXAMPLE: [x,y,time,numiter]=hits(L,x0,100,1e-8);
%
% INPUT:  L = adjacency matrix (n-by-n sparse matrix)
%         x0 = starting vector (row vector)
%         n = size of L matrix (integer)
%         epsilon = convergence tolerance (scalar, e.g. 1e-8)
%
% OUTPUT:   x = HITS authority vector
```

```
%            y = HITS hub vector
%            time = time until convergence
%            numiter = number of iterations until convergence
%
% The starting vector is usually set to the uniform vector,
% x0=1/n*ones(1,n).

k=0;
residual=1;
x=x0;
tic;

while (residual >= epsilon)
  prevx=x;
  k=k+1;
  x=x*L';
  x=x*L;
  x=x/sum(x);
  residual=norm(x-prevx,1);
end
y=x*L';
y=y/sum(y);
numiter=k;
time=toc;
```

11.3 HITS CONVERGENCE

The iterative algorithm for computing HITS vectors is actually the *power method* (our friend from Chapter 4) applied to $\mathbf{L}^T\mathbf{L}$ and $\mathbf{L}\mathbf{L}^T$. For a *diagonalizable* matrix $\mathbf{B}_{n\times n}$ whose distinct eigenvalues are $\{\lambda_1, \lambda_2, \ldots, \lambda_k\}$ such that $|\lambda_1| > |\lambda_2| \geq |\lambda_3| \cdots \geq |\lambda_k|$, the power method takes an initial vector $\mathbf{x}^{(0)}$ and iteratively computes

$$\mathbf{x}^{(k)} = \mathbf{B}\,\mathbf{x}^{(k-1)}, \quad \mathbf{x}^{(k)} \longleftarrow \frac{\mathbf{x}^{(k)}}{m(\mathbf{x}^{(k)})},$$

where $m(\mathbf{x}^{(k)})$ is a normalizing scalar derived from $\mathbf{x}^{(k)}$. For example, it is common to take $m(\mathbf{x}^{(k)})$ to be the (signed) component of maximal magnitude (use the first if there are more than one), in which case $m(\mathbf{x}^{(k)})$ converges to the dominant eigenvalue λ_1, and $\mathbf{x}^{(k)}$ converges to an associated normalized eigenvector [127]. If only a dominant eigenvector is needed (and not the eigenvalue λ_1), then a normalization such as $m(\mathbf{x}^{(k)}) = \|\mathbf{x}^{(k)}\|$ can be used. (If $\lambda_1 < 0$, then $m(\mathbf{x}^{(k)}) = \|\mathbf{x}^{(k)}\|$ can't converge to λ_1, but $\mathbf{x}^{(k)}$ still converges to a normalized eigenvector associated with λ_1.) The asymptotic rate of convergence of the power method is the rate at which $(|\lambda_2(\mathbf{B})|/|\lambda_1(\mathbf{B})|)^k \to 0$.

The matrices $\mathbf{L}^T\mathbf{L}$ and $\mathbf{L}\mathbf{L}^T$ are *symmetric*, *positive semidefinite*, and *nonnegative*, so their distinct *eigenvalues* $\{\lambda_1, \lambda_2, \ldots, \lambda_k\}$ are necessarily real and nonnegative with $\lambda_1 > \lambda_2 > \cdots > \lambda_k \geq 0$. In other words, it is not possible to have multiple eigenvalues on the *spectral circle*. Consequently, the HITS specialization of the power method avoids most problematic convergence issues—HITS with normalization always converges. And the rate of convergence is given by the rate at which $[\lambda_2(\mathbf{L}^T\mathbf{L})/\lambda_1(\mathbf{L}^T\mathbf{L})]^k \to 0$. Unlike PageRank, we cannot give a good approximation to the asymptotic rate of convergence for HITS. (Recall that the asymptotic rate of convergence for the PageRank problem is the rate at which $\alpha^k \to 0$.) Many experiments show the eigengap $(\lambda_1 - \lambda_2)$ for HITS problems to be large, and researchers suggest that only 10-15 iterations are required for convergence

[59, 60, 106, 134, 133]. However, despite the quick convergence, there can be a problem with the uniqueness of the limiting authority and hub vectors. While $\lambda_1 > \lambda_2$, the structure of $\mathbf{L}$ might allow λ_1 to be a repeated root of the *characteristic polynomial*, in which case the associated *eigenspace* is multidimensional. This means that different limiting authority (and hub) vectors can be produced by different choices of the initial vector.

A simple example from [72] demonstrates this problem. In this example,

$$\mathbf{L} = \begin{pmatrix} 0 & 0 & 0 & 0 \\ 1 & 0 & 0 & 0 \\ 1 & 0 & 0 & 0 \\ 0 & 1 & 1 & 0 \end{pmatrix} \quad \text{and} \quad \mathbf{L}^T\mathbf{L} = \begin{pmatrix} 2 & 0 & 0 & 0 \\ 0 & 1 & 1 & 0 \\ 0 & 1 & 1 & 0 \\ 0 & 0 & 0 & 0 \end{pmatrix}.$$

The authority matrix $\mathbf{L}^T\mathbf{L}$ (and also the hub matrix $\mathbf{L}\mathbf{L}^T$) has two distinct eigenvalues, $\lambda_1 = 2$ and $\lambda_2 = 0$, which are each repeated twice. For the initial vector $\mathbf{x}^{(0)} = 1/4\,\mathbf{e}^T$, the power method applied to $\mathbf{L}^T\mathbf{L}$ (with normalization by the 1-norm) converges to the vector $\mathbf{x}^{(\infty)} = (\,1/3 \quad 1/3 \quad 1/3 \quad 0\,)^T$. Yet for $\mathbf{x}^{(0)} = (\,1/4 \quad 1/8 \quad 1/8 \quad 1/2\,)^T$, the power method converges to $\mathbf{x}^{(\infty)} = (\,1/2 \quad 1/4 \quad 1/4 \quad 0\,)^T$. At the heart of this uniqueness problem is the issue of reducibility.

A square matrix $\mathbf{B}$ is said to be *reducible* if there exists a *permutation matrix* $\mathbf{Q}$ such that

$$\mathbf{Q}^T\mathbf{B}\mathbf{Q} = \begin{pmatrix} \mathbf{X} & \mathbf{Y} \\ \mathbf{0} & \mathbf{Z} \end{pmatrix}, \qquad \text{where } \mathbf{X} \text{ and } \mathbf{Z} \text{ are both square.}$$

Otherwise, the matrix is *irreducible*. The reducibility of a matrix means that there's a set of states that it's possible to enter, but once entered, it's impossible to exit. On the other hand, a matrix is irreducible if every state is reachable from every other state. The *Perron-Frobenius theorem* [127] ensures that an irreducible nonnegative matrix possesses a unique normalized positive dominant eigenvector, called the *Perron vector*. Consequently, it's the reducibility of $\mathbf{L}^T\mathbf{L}$ that causes the HITS algorithm to converge to nonunique solutions. PageRank actually encounters the same uniqueness problem, but the Google founders suggested a way to cheat and alter the matrix, forcing irreducibility (actually primitivity as well) and hence guaranteeing existence and uniqueness of the ranking vector—see section 4.5. A modification similar to the Google primitivity trick can also be applied to HITS. That is, a modified authority matrix $\xi\mathbf{L}^T\mathbf{L} + (1-\xi)/n\,\mathbf{e}\mathbf{e}^T$ can be created, where $0 < \xi < 1$ [134]. The modified hub matrix is similar. Miller et al. [72] and Ng et al. [134] have developed similar modifications to HITS, called Exponentiated HITS and Randomized HITS.

One final caveat regarding the power method concerns the starting vector $\mathbf{x}^{(0)}$. In general, regardless of whether the dominant eigenvalue λ_1 of the iteration matrix $\mathbf{B}$ is simple or repeated, convergence to a nonzero vector depends on the initial vector $\mathbf{x}^{(0)}$ not being in the range of $(\mathbf{B} - \lambda_1\mathbf{I})$. If $\mathbf{x}^{(0)}$ is randomly generated, almost certainly this condition will hold, so in practice this is rarely an issue.

11.4 HITS EXAMPLE

We present a very small example to demonstrate the implementation of the HITS algorithm. First, a user presents query terms to the HITS system. There are several schemes that can be used to determine which nodes "contain" query terms. For instance, one could take nodes using at least one query term. Or to create a smaller sparse graph, one could take only nodes using all query terms. For our example, suppose the subset of nodes containing the query terms is $\{1, 6\}$. Next, we build the neighborhood graph about nodes 1 and 6. Suppose this produces the following graph N, shown in Figure 11.2. From this neighborhood graph N,

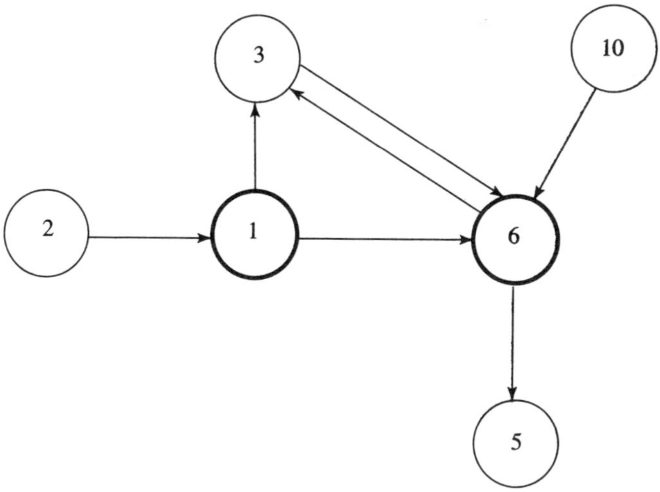

Figure 11.2 Neighborhood graph N for pages 1 and 6

the adjacency matrix $\mathbf{L}$ is formed.

$$\mathbf{L} = \begin{array}{c} \\ 1 \\ 2 \\ 3 \\ 5 \\ 6 \\ 10 \end{array} \begin{array}{c} \begin{array}{cccccc} 1 & 2 & 3 & 5 & 6 & 10 \end{array} \\ \begin{pmatrix} 0 & 0 & 1 & 0 & 1 & 0 \\ 1 & 0 & 0 & 0 & 0 & 0 \\ 0 & 0 & 0 & 0 & 1 & 0 \\ 0 & 0 & 0 & 0 & 0 & 0 \\ 0 & 0 & 1 & 1 & 0 & 0 \\ 0 & 0 & 0 & 0 & 1 & 0 \end{pmatrix} \end{array}.$$

The respective authority and hub matrices are:

$$\mathbf{L}^T\mathbf{L} = \begin{array}{c} \\ 1 \\ 2 \\ 3 \\ 5 \\ 6 \\ 10 \end{array} \begin{array}{c} \begin{array}{cccccc} 1 & 2 & 3 & 5 & 6 & 10 \end{array} \\ \begin{pmatrix} 1 & 0 & 0 & 0 & 0 & 0 \\ 0 & 0 & 0 & 0 & 0 & 0 \\ 0 & 0 & 2 & 1 & 1 & 0 \\ 0 & 0 & 1 & 1 & 0 & 0 \\ 0 & 0 & 1 & 0 & 3 & 0 \\ 0 & 0 & 0 & 0 & 0 & 0 \end{pmatrix} \end{array} \quad \text{and} \quad \mathbf{L}\mathbf{L}^T = \begin{array}{c} \\ 1 \\ 2 \\ 3 \\ 5 \\ 6 \\ 10 \end{array} \begin{array}{c} \begin{array}{cccccc} 1 & 2 & 3 & 5 & 6 & 10 \end{array} \\ \begin{pmatrix} 2 & 0 & 1 & 0 & 1 & 1 \\ 0 & 1 & 0 & 0 & 0 & 0 \\ 1 & 0 & 1 & 0 & 0 & 1 \\ 0 & 0 & 0 & 0 & 0 & 0 \\ 1 & 0 & 0 & 0 & 2 & 0 \\ 1 & 0 & 1 & 0 & 0 & 1 \end{pmatrix} \end{array}.$$

The normalized principal eigenvectors with the authority scores $\mathbf{x}$ and hub scores $\mathbf{y}$ are:

$$\mathbf{x}^T = (0 \quad 0 \quad .3660 \quad .1340 \quad .5 \quad 0) \qquad \text{and}$$
$$\mathbf{y}^T = (.3660 \quad 0 \quad .2113 \quad 0 \quad .2113 \quad .2113).$$

This example shows that there are two types of ties that can occur: ties at 0 and ties at positive values. Ties at 0 can be avoided with the primitivity modification suggested at the end of section 11.3. For the much larger matrices that occur in practice, the existence of identical positive values in a dominant eigenvector is unlikely. Nevertheless, ties may occur and can be broken by any tie-breaking strategy. Using a "first-come, first-served" tie-breaking strategy, the authority and hub scores are sorted in decreasing order and the page numbers are presented.

$$\text{Authority ranking} = (\,6 \quad 3 \quad 5 \quad 1 \quad 2 \quad 10\,),$$
$$\text{Hub ranking} = (\,1 \quad 3 \quad 6 \quad 10 \quad 2 \quad 5\,).$$

This means that page 6 is the most authoritative page for the query while page 1 is the best hub for this query.

For comparison purposes, we now recompute the authority and hub vectors for the modified HITS method, using the irreducible matrix $\xi \mathbf{L}^T\mathbf{L} + (1-\xi)/n\,\mathbf{e}\mathbf{e}^T$ as the authority matrix and $\xi \mathbf{L}\mathbf{L}^T + (1-\xi)/n\,\mathbf{e}\mathbf{e}^T$ as the hub matrix. With this modification, the matrices are irreducible, and by the Perron-Frobenius theorem, they each possess a unique, normalized, positive dominant eigenvector (called the Perron vector). For the case when $\xi = .95$,

$$\mathbf{x}^T = (\,0.0032 \quad 0.0023 \quad 0.3634 \quad 0.1351 \quad 0.4936 \quad 0.0023\,) \text{ and}$$
$$\mathbf{y}^T = (\,0.3628 \quad 0.0032 \quad 0.2106 \quad 0.0023 \quad 0.2106 \quad 0.2106\,).$$

Notice that, for this example, this irreducible modification does not change the authority and hub rankings. Yet these modified scores are more appealing because they are unique and positive (and thus, avoid ties at 0), and the power method is guaranteed to converge to them in a finite number of steps.

11.5 STRENGTHS AND WEAKNESSES OF HITS

One advantage of the HITS algorithm is its dual rankings. HITS presents two ranked lists to the user: one with the most authoritative documents related to the query and the other with the most "hubby" documents. As a user, it's nice to have this option. Sometimes you want authoritative pages because you are searching deeply on a research query. Other times you want hub (or portal) pages because you're doing a broad search. Another advantage of HITS is the size of the problem. HITS casts the ranking problem as a small problem, finding the dominant eigenvectors of small matrices. The size of these matrices is very small relative to the total number of pages on the Web.

However, there are some clear disadvantages to the HITS ranking system. Most troublesome is HITS's query-dependence. At query time, a neighborhood graph must be built and at least one matrix eigenvector problem solved. And this must be done for each query. Of course, it's easy to make HITS query-independent. Simply, drop the neighborhood graph step and compute the authority and hub vectors, $\mathbf{x}$ and $\mathbf{y}$, using the adjacency matrix of the entire web graph. For more on the query-independent version of HITS, see section 11.7.

HITS's susceptibility to spamming creates a second strong disadvantage. By adding links to and from your webpage, you can slightly influence the authority and hub scores of your page. A slight change in these scores might be enough to move your webpage a few notches up the ranked lists returned to users. We've already mentioned how important it is to get into the first few pages of a search engine's results since users generally view only the top 20 pages returned in a ranked list. Of course, adding outlinks from your page is much easier than adding inlinks. So influencing your hub score is not difficult.

Yet since hub scores and authority scores share a mutual dependence and are computed interdependently, an authority score will increase as a hub score increases. Further, since the neighborhood graph is small in comparison to the entire Web, local changes to the link structure appear more drastic. Fortunately, Monika Henzinger and Krishna Bharat have proposed a modification to HITS that mitigates the problem of link spamming by using something called an L1 normalization step [26].

A final disadvantage of HITS is the problem of topic drift. In building the neighborhood graph N for a query it is possible that a very authoritative yet off-topic page be linked to a page containing the query terms. This very authoritative page can carry so much weight that it and its neighboring documents dominate the relevant ranked list returned to the user, skewing the results toward off-topic documents. Henzinger and Bharat suggest a solution to the problem of topic drift, weighting the authority and hub scores of the nodes in N by a measure of relevancy to the query [26]. In fact, to measure relevance of a node in N to the query, they use the same cosine similarity measure that is often used by vector space methods such as LSI [24, 64]. This solution to the topic drift problem is similar to the intelligent surfer modification to the basic PageRank model (see section 5.2). The binary elements in $\mathbf{L}$ (rather than $\mathbf{H}$ for the PageRank model) are given weights, which in effect improves the IQ of the HITS system.

11.6 HITS'S RELATIONSHIP TO BIBLIOMETRICS

The HITS algorithm has strong connections to bibliometrics research. Bibliometrics is the study of written documents and their citation structure. Such research uses the citation structure of a body of documents to produce numerical measures of the importance and impact of papers. Chris Ding and his colleagues at the Lawrence Berkeley National Laboratory have noted the underlying connection between HITS and two common bibliometrics concepts, **co-citation** and **co-reference** [59, 60].

In bibliometrics, co-citation occurs when two documents are both cited by the same third document. Co-reference occurs when two documents both refer to the same third document. On the Web, co-citation occurs when two nodes share a common inlinking node, while co-reference means two nodes share a common outlinking node. Ding et al. have shown that the authority matrix $\mathbf{L}^T\mathbf{L}$ of HITS has a direct relationship to the concept of co-citation, while the hub matrix $\mathbf{L}\mathbf{L}^T$ is related to co-reference [59, 60]. Suppose the small hyperlink graph of Figure 11.1 is studied again. The adjacency matrix is

$$\mathbf{L} = \begin{array}{c} \\ P_1 \\ P_2 \\ P_3 \\ P_4 \end{array} \begin{array}{c} \begin{array}{cccc} P_1 & P_2 & P_3 & P_4 \end{array} \\ \begin{pmatrix} 0 & 1 & 1 & 0 \\ 1 & 0 & 1 & 0 \\ 0 & 1 & 0 & 1 \\ 0 & 1 & 0 & 0 \end{pmatrix} \end{array}.$$

So the authority and hub matrices are:

$$\mathbf{L}^T\mathbf{L} = \begin{pmatrix} 1 & 0 & 1 & 0 \\ 0 & 3 & 1 & 1 \\ 1 & 1 & 2 & 0 \\ 0 & 1 & 0 & 1 \end{pmatrix} = \mathbf{D}_{in} + \mathbf{C}_{cit}, \quad \text{and}$$

$$\mathbf{L}\mathbf{L}^T = \begin{pmatrix} 2 & 1 & 1 & 1 \\ 1 & 2 & 0 & 0 \\ 1 & 0 & 2 & 1 \\ 1 & 0 & 1 & 1 \end{pmatrix} = \mathbf{D}_{out} + \mathbf{C}_{ref}.$$

In general, Ding et al. [59, 60] show that $\mathbf{L}^T\mathbf{L} = \mathbf{D}_{in} + \mathbf{C}_{cit}$, where $\mathbf{D}_{in}$ is a diagonal matrix with the indegree of each node along the diagonal and $\mathbf{C}_{cit}$ is the co-citation matrix. For example, the $(3, 3)$-element of $\mathbf{L}^T\mathbf{L}$ means that node 3 has an indegree of 2. The $(1, 3)$-element of $\mathbf{L}^T\mathbf{L}$ means that nodes 1 and 3 share only one common inlinking node, node 2, as is apparent from Figure 11.1. The $(4, 3)$-element of $\mathbf{L}^T\mathbf{L}$ implies that nodes 3 and 4 do not share a common inlinking node, again, as is apparent from Figure 11.1. Similarly, the hub matrix is actually $\mathbf{D}_{out} + \mathbf{C}_{ref}$, where $\mathbf{D}_{out}$ is the diagonal matrix of outdegrees and $\mathbf{C}_{ref}$ is the co-reference matrix. The $(1, 2)$-element of $\mathbf{L}\mathbf{L}^T$ means that nodes 1 and 2 share a common outlinking node, node 3. The $(4, 2)$-element implies that nodes 4 and 2 do not share a common outlinking node. Ding et al. use these relationships between authority and co-citation and hubs and co-reference to claim that simple inlink ranking provides a decent approximation to the HITS authority score and simple outlink ranking provides a decent approximation to hub ranking [59, 60, 61].

11.7 QUERY-INDEPENDENT HITS

HITS can be forced to be query-independent by computing a global authority and a global hub vector, which consequently slightly reduces the influence of link spamming. An efficient, foolproof way to do this is with the algorithm below, which is guaranteed to converge to the unique positive hub and authority vectors, regardless of the reducibility of the web graph (because the modified HITS matrices are used). We recommend automatically using the modified HITS matrices because the web graph associated with an engine's entire index will almost certainly be reducible, and therefore cause convergence and uniqueness problems for HITS.

A QUERY-INDEPENDENT MODIFIED HITS ALGORITHM

1. Initialize: $\mathbf{x}^{(0)} = \mathbf{e}/n$, where $\mathbf{e}$ is a column vector of all ones. (Other positive normalized starting vectors may be used.)

2. Until convergence, do

$$\begin{aligned} \mathbf{x}^{(k)} &= \xi\mathbf{L}^T\mathbf{L}\mathbf{x}^{(k-1)} + (1-\xi)/n\,\mathbf{e} \\ \mathbf{x}^{(k)} &= \mathbf{x}^{(k)}/\|\mathbf{x}^{(k)}\|_1 \\ \mathbf{y}^{(k)} &= \xi\mathbf{L}\mathbf{L}^T\mathbf{y}^{(k-1)} + (1-\xi)/n\,\mathbf{e} \\ \mathbf{y}^{(k)} &= \mathbf{y}^{(k)}/\|\mathbf{y}^{(k)}\|_1 \\ k &= k+1 \end{aligned}$$

3. Set the authority vector $\mathbf{x} = \mathbf{x}^{(k)}$ and the hub vector $\mathbf{y} = \mathbf{y}^{(k)}$.

When the query-independent HITS algorithm is used, $\mathbf{L}$ is the adjacency matrix for the search engine's entire web graph, because the neighborhood graph N is no longer formed. If Teoma used query-independent HITS, $\mathbf{L}$ would be about 1.5 billion in size.

It's worthwhile to compare the query-independent HITS algorithm above with the other query-independent ranking method, PageRank. The work in each step boils down to the matrix-vector multiplications: $\mathbf{L}^T\mathbf{L}\mathbf{x}^{(k-1)}$ for HITS, $\mathbf{L}^T\mathbf{D}^{-1}\mathbf{x}^{(k-1)}$ for random surfer PageRank, and $\mathbf{H}^T\mathbf{x}^{(k-1)}$ for intelligent surfer PageRank. The approximate work required by one iteration of each method is given in Table 11.1. Here $nnz(\mathbf{L})$ is the number of nonzeros in $\mathbf{L}$ and n is the size of the matrix.

Table 11.1 Work per iteration required by the query-independent ranking methods

Method	Multiplications	Additions
HITS	0	$2nnz(\mathbf{L})$
Modified HITS	0	$4nnz(\mathbf{L}) + 2n$
Random surfer PageRank	n	$nnz(\mathbf{L}) + n$
Intelligent Surfer PageRank	$nnz(\mathbf{H})$	$nnz(\mathbf{H}) + n$

For query-independent HITS, $nnz(\mathbf{L}) = nnz(\mathbf{H})$, but for query-dependent HITS $nnz(\mathbf{L}) \ll nnz(\mathbf{H})$, where $\mathbf{H}$ is PageRank's raw hyperlink matrix. Query-independent HITS requires about twice (and as much as four times) as much work per iteration as PageRank. (There are other ways to implement modified HITS so that only one power method is required, not two. For example, form the modified authority matrix $\mathbf{M} = \tilde{\mathbf{L}}^T\tilde{\mathbf{L}}$, where $\tilde{\mathbf{L}} = \mathbf{L} + \xi\mathbf{e}\mathbf{e}^T$. However, these methods do not come with the cute mathematical properties of our proposed modification. See theorem 11.7.1.) Now to make the comparison complete, let's discuss the number of iterations required by the four methods.

There's one very nice consequence of the modification to HITS that we've suggested in this chapter. Unlike other modifications [72, 134], ours allows us to say a great deal about the spectrum of our modified HITS matrix. Adapting a statement from [82] to our particular situation gives the following theorem for the modified authority matrix. Similar statements hold for the hub matrix.

Theorem 11.7.1. *Let* $\mathbf{M} = \xi\mathbf{L}^T\mathbf{L} + (1-\xi)/n\,\mathbf{e}\mathbf{e}^T$ *be the modified authority matrix. Let* $\lambda_1 \geq \lambda_2 \geq \cdots \geq \lambda_n$ *be the eigenvalues of* $\mathbf{L}^T\mathbf{L}$ *and* $\gamma_1 \geq \gamma_2 \geq \cdots \geq \gamma_n$ *be the eigenvalues of* $\mathbf{M}$. *Then, the following interlacing property holds,*

$$\gamma_1 \geq \alpha\lambda_1 \geq \gamma_2 \geq \alpha\lambda_2 \geq \cdots \geq \gamma_n \geq \alpha\lambda_n.$$

And further, there exist scalars $\beta_i \geq 0$, $\sum_{i=1}^{n} \beta_i = 1$ *such that* $\gamma_i = \xi\lambda_i + (1-\xi)\beta_i$.

With this theorem we can now compare the asymptotic rate of convergence of the four query-independent methods. See Table 11.2. The bounds for γ_2/γ_1 are derived by examining extreme behavior. In the best case scenario, the modification to $\mathbf{L}^T\mathbf{L}$ increases only λ_2 by the maximal amount to $\lambda_2 + 1 - \xi$ (i.e., $\beta_2 = 1, \beta_i = 0$ for all $i \neq 2$). In the worst case scenario, only λ_1 increases to $\lambda_1 + 1 - \xi$ (i.e., $\beta_1 = 1, \beta_i = 0$ for all $i \neq 1$). In practice, many β_i's change at once (but $\sum_i \beta_i = 1$), making the effect less pronounced than the two extreme cases. Regardless of the exact values for the β_i's, for modified HITS, ξ is usually chosen to be close to 1, so therefore, $\gamma_2/\gamma_1 \approx \lambda_2/\lambda_1$. Thus, the asymptotic rates of convergence of HITS and modified HITS are nearly the same. Many HITS experiments have shown $\lambda_2/\lambda_1 < .5$ [59, 60, 106, 133, 134], which is much less than $\alpha = .85$ (the typical PageRank factor), so we can conclude that HITS and modified HITS

Table 11.2 Asymptotic rate of convergence of the query-independent ranking methods

	General
HITS	$\frac{\lambda_2}{\lambda_1}$
Modified HITS	$\frac{\xi\lambda_2}{\xi\lambda_1+1-\xi} \leq \frac{\gamma_2}{\gamma_1} \leq \frac{\lambda_2}{\lambda_1} + \frac{(1-\xi)}{\xi\lambda_1}$
Random surfer PageRank	α
Intelligent Surfer PageRank	α

require many fewer iterations than PageRank.

So the query-independent HITS takes about twice as long per iteration as query-independent PageRank, but takes less than a quarter the number of iterations to reach the same tolerance level. Query-independent HITS (even with our theoretically pretty but practically slow version of modified HITS, which requires two power methods) is faster than the query-independent PageRank. And further, you get two HITS ranking vectors for the cost of one PageRank vector.

11.8 ACCELERATING HITS

Kleinberg used the power method in his original HITS paper [106] to compute the hub and authority vectors, which are the dominant right-hand eigenvectors of $\mathbf{L}^T\mathbf{L}$ and $\mathbf{L}\mathbf{L}^T$, respectively. Computing dominant eigenvectors is an old problem, for which there are several available numerical methods, especially for sparse symmetric systems [18, 57, 137, 145, 162].

The problem of computing the original, query-dependent HITS vectors is different from that of the PageRank vector because the sizes of the matrices involved are so different. The HITS matrices are small, just the size of the neighborhood graph, whereas the PageRank matrix is huge, the size of the search engine's entire index. PageRank methods are limited to memory-efficient methods that are matrix-free and don't require the storage of extra intermediate information, which explains the prevalence of the power method in the PageRank literature. On the other hand, faster, more memory-intensive methods can be used on the much smaller HITS problem. We don't know what method a HITS-based commercial engine like Teoma uses, but we expect it'd be a faster iterative method like Lanczos [57, 82], for instance, not the slow power method. The small size of the matrices involved in the HITS problem is also one reason why no research has been done on accelerating the computation of the HITS vectors—it's already fast enough. On the other hand, because of the enormous size of the PageRank matrix, we spent an entire chapter (Chapter 9) on methods for accelerating the computation of PageRank. Of course, if query-independent HITS is done, then a large-scale implementation of HITS must handle the same issues that PageRank does. And acceleration techniques similar to those of PageRank, for instance the extrapolation techniques of Chapter 9, can be adapted to the HITS problem.

11.9 HITS SENSITIVITY

Suppose $\mathbf{L}$, the adjacency matrix for the HITS neighborhood graph, changes, creating a new matrix $\tilde{\mathbf{L}}$. The question we pose in this section is: how sensitive are the authority and hub vectors to these changes in the structure of the web graph? Regardless of the nature of the changes, the authority and hub matrices, $\tilde{\mathbf{L}}^T\tilde{\mathbf{L}}$ and $\tilde{\mathbf{L}}\tilde{\mathbf{L}}^T$, are still symmetric, positive definite matrices, which makes the perturbation analysis easier.

We adapt a theorem from Pete Stewart's book [152, p. 51] for our specific situation.

Theorem 11.9.1. *Let* $\mathbf{E}$ *be a perturbation matrix, so that* $\tilde{\mathbf{L}}^T\tilde{\mathbf{L}} = \mathbf{L}^T\mathbf{L} + \mathbf{E}$. *When* λ_1 *is simple,*

$$\sin \angle(\mathbf{x}, \tilde{\mathbf{x}}) \le \frac{\|\mathbf{E}\|_2}{\lambda_1 - \lambda_2}.$$

It is more appropriate to examine the angle between the old authority vector $\mathbf{x}$ and the new one $\tilde{\mathbf{x}}$ ($\angle(\mathbf{x}, \tilde{\mathbf{x}})$) than the difference in length ($\|\mathbf{x} - \tilde{\mathbf{x}}\|$) for two reasons: (1) the authority vectors are normalized in the HITS procedure, and (2) the ranking of elements is important. Theorem 11.9.1 tells us that the separation between the two dominant eigenvalues governs the sensitivity of the HITS vectors. If the *eigengap* $\delta = \lambda_1 - \lambda_2$ is large, then the authority vector is insensitive to small changes in the web graph. On the other hand, if the eigengap is small, the vector may be very sensitive. A similar theorem and interpretation exist for the hub vector.

This theorem only applies when λ_1 is a simple root, which is guaranteed by a modified HITS procedure (where an irreducible $\xi\mathbf{L}^T\mathbf{L} + (1-\xi)/n\mathbf{e}\mathbf{e}^T$, or another modified matrix [72, 134], replaces $\mathbf{L}^T\mathbf{L}$ as the authority matrix). If modified HITS is not done and λ_1 is a repeated root, then we can examine the sensitivity of the eigenspace associated with λ_1. A result from [153] gives the same conclusion: the sensitivity of the invariant subspace associated with the repeated root λ_1 of the symmetric matrix depends primarily on the eigengap.

Let's consider an extreme (but not uncommon) example that makes it clear why the HITS vectors can be sensitive when the eigengap is small. Suppose the neighborhood graph contains two separate *connected components*, so $\mathbf{L}$ is completely uncoupled. That is, $\mathbf{L}$ can be permuted to have the form

$$\begin{pmatrix} \mathbf{X} & \mathbf{0} \\ \mathbf{0} & \mathbf{Z} \end{pmatrix}.$$

First, we consider the case when the original unmodified HITS procedure is used. The spectrum of the authority matrix is related to the spectrums of the connected components; $\sigma(\mathbf{L}^T\mathbf{L}) = \sigma(\mathbf{X}^T\mathbf{X}) \cup \sigma(\mathbf{Z}^T\mathbf{Z})$. The component containing the largest eigenvalue is called the *largest connected component*. The dominant eigenvector of $\mathbf{L}^T\mathbf{L}$ (thus, the authority vector) has nonzero entries only in the positions corresponding to nodes in the largest connected component because $\mathbf{L}^T\mathbf{L}$ has an eigendecomposition of the form

$$\mathbf{L}^T\mathbf{L} = \begin{pmatrix} \mathbf{U}_1 & \mathbf{0} \\ \mathbf{0} & \mathbf{U}_2 \end{pmatrix} \begin{pmatrix} \mathbf{\Lambda}_1 & \mathbf{0} \\ \mathbf{0} & \mathbf{\Lambda}_2 \end{pmatrix} \begin{pmatrix} \mathbf{U}_1^T & \mathbf{0} \\ \mathbf{0} & \mathbf{U}_2^T \end{pmatrix}.$$

That is, the authority vector has the form $\mathbf{x} = \begin{pmatrix} \mathbf{x}_1 & \mathbf{0} \end{pmatrix}^T$. The addition of just one link that connects the two components can make the authority vector positive, which can significantly change the authority ranking.

A different perturbation, one that maintains the two separate connected components, can more drastically change the authority vector and its ranking. Assume the largest and second largest eigenvalues are in different components, and are not well separated. Suppose enough links are added to the component with the second largest eigenvalue, component 2, so that this component and its eigenvalue overtake the largest eigenvalue of the other component, component 1. The title of largest component is transferred from component 1 to component 2 and the authority vector now has nonzero entries only for nodes in component 2, rather than component 1.

In this example we began with a completely uncoupled matrix. However, even when the modified HITS procedure is used, so that $\mathbf{L}^T\mathbf{L}$ is irreducible, the authority matrix may be *nearly uncoupled.* Although somewhat disguised by the irreducibility modification, sensitivity to small perturbations can exist for the same reasons as in the completely uncoupled case. While the modification causes the zero entries in the authority vector to be positive, they are close to 0. See the effect of the modification on the numerical example of section 11.4. If a perturbation causes the two components to swap the title of largest component, then the large entries in the authority vector are swapped from one component to the other. (Ng et al. [134] propose a method called Subspace HITS that reduces the dominance of the largest connected component in the HITS rankings and tries to spread the scores across several connected components.)

Since we know a good bit about the spectrum of $\mathbf{M}$, the modified authority matrix, we might try to say something more specific about how the modification affects the sensitivity of the system. The eigengap of the unmodified method is given by $\delta = \lambda_1 - \lambda_2$, whereas the modified method has an eigengap denoted by $\rho = \gamma_1 - \gamma_2$. Using Theorem 11.7.1, we have

$$\xi\delta - (1-\xi) \leq \rho \leq \xi\delta + (1-\xi).$$

As $\xi \to 0$, the fudge factor matrix $1/n\,\mathbf{e}\mathbf{e}^T$ takes over, creating the uninteresting case with an eigengap of 1 and stable uniform authority and hub vectors. The more interesting case occurs when $\xi \to 1$. As expected, as $\xi \to 1$, the eigengap of the modified method ρ approaches the original eigengap δ. We can conclude that the modified HITS system is about as sensitive as the original HITS system. In summary, modified HITS does not significantly affect the rate of convergence or the sensitivity of the system; its only effect is on the existence and uniqueness of the HITS vectors. That is, modified HITS is guaranteed to converge to unique positive HITS vectors.

ASIDE: Ranking by Eigenvectors

PageRank and HITS both use the dominant eigenvector as a ranking tool. But this is not a new idea, the idea, although much less publicized, has been around for decades. In 1939, Maurice Kendall and Babington Smith wrote one of the first ranking papers to use linear algebra [105]. In order to create a ranking from voter preferences, Kendall and Smith built a preference matrix $\mathbf{A}$, *where* a_{ij} *is the number of voters who prefer player* i *to player* j. *Here a player could be a candidate, team, participant, webpage, etc. The normalized row sums* $\mathbf{r}$ *of the preference matrix are a measure of the "winning percentage" of player* i. *That is,* $\mathbf{r} = \mathbf{Ae}/\|\mathbf{Ae}\|$. *(Kendall and Smith also created a coefficient of agreement among voter preferences that can be used to locate voters who are inconsistent, and thus should have their scores tossed. This coefficient of agreement can also be used to determine whether the data warrant a global ranking—it may be that all voters appear inconsistent, which implies that voters have been challenged with the impossible task of ranking indistinguishable objects.)*

T. H. Wei extended the row sum ranking method to include powers of the preference matrix $\mathbf{A}$. *In his 1952 Cambridge University thesis [161], Wei suggested that the ranking vector* $\mathbf{r}^{(k)} = \mathbf{A}^k\mathbf{e}/\|\mathbf{A}^k\mathbf{e}\|$, *for some integer* k. *For* $k = 2$, *the ranking vector* $\mathbf{r}^{(2)}$ *gives some information about the strength of schedule. Using the sports ranking problem,* $r_i^{(2)}$ *is the winning percentage of teams defeated by team* i. *For* $k = 3$, $r_i^{(3)}$ *is the winning percentage of teams defeated by teams defeated by team* i. *And so on. More recently, in his 1993 paper [103], James P. Keener showed that many of the early ranking methods fall under the* Perron-Frobenius theorem. *In fact, Wei's powering idea can be extended so that* $\mathbf{r} = \lim_{k\to\infty} \mathbf{A}^k\mathbf{e}/\|\mathbf{A}^k\mathbf{e}\|$, *which can be arrived at by using the power method applied to* $\mathbf{A}$ *with the starting vector* $\mathbf{e}$. *The power method converges to the dominant eigenvector of* $\mathbf{A}$ *provided* $\mathbf{A}$ *is nonnegative and irreducible.*

Much of the art of the ranking problem is in how $\mathbf{A}$ *is defined. For the problem of ranking U.S. collegiate football teams, Keener provides the following possible definitions:*

- $a_{ij} = 1$, *if team* i *beats team* j, *0, otherwise,*
- $a_{ij} =$ *the proportion of times* i *beats* j,
- $a_{ij} =$ *the proportion of football ranking polls that have* i *outranking* j,
- $a_{ij} = s_{ij}/(s_{ij} + s_{ji})$, where s_{ij} *is the number of points* i *scored in encounter with* j.

Keener also extends this to other more complicated scoring schemes, but the common connection among all is the Perron-Frobenius theorem and the computation of a dominant eigenvector.

Using the dominant eigenvector for ranking problems has many applications besides webpage scoring and the ranking of sports teams. For example, other applications include tournament seeding (e.g., for tennis or golf) and handicapping assignments for betting purposes. The ranking problem has recently been explored for other networks, such as email networks among coworkers and networks of connection and communication among suspected terrorists. The dominant eigenvector also plays a prominent role in market share statistics and models of population dynamics.

Chapter Twelve

Other Link Methods for Ranking Webpages

The previous chapters dealt with the major ranking algorithms of PageRank and HITS in depth, but there are other minor players in the ranking game. This chapter provides a brief introduction to the ranking alternatives.

12.1 SALSA

In 1998, one could rank the popularity of webpages using either the PageRank or the HITS algorithm. In 2000, SALSA [114] sashayed into the game. SALSA, an acronym for Stochastic Approach to Link Structure Analysis, was developed by Ronny Lempel and Shlomo Moran and incorporated ideas from both HITS and PageRank to create yet another ranking of webpages. Like HITS, SALSA creates both hub and authority scores for webpages, and like PageRank, they are derived from Markov chains. In this section, we teach you the steps of SALSA with an example.

12.1.1 SALSA Example

In a manner similar to the original, query-dependent HITS, the neighborhood graph N associated with a particular query is formed. We use the same neighborhood graph N from the previous chapter, which is reproduced below in Figure 12.1.

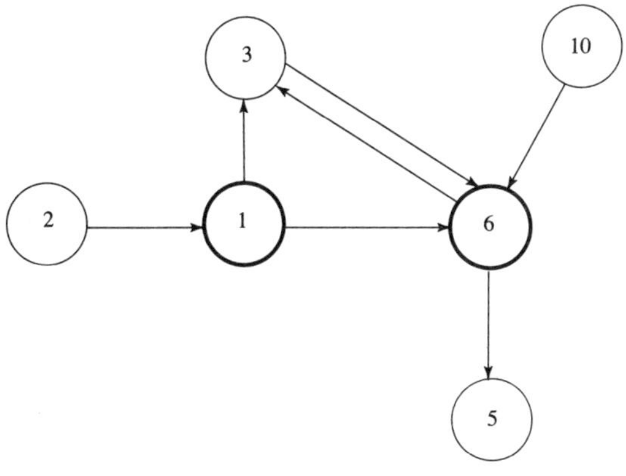

Figure 12.1 Neighborhood graph N for pages 1 and 6

SALSA differs from HITS in the next step. Rather than forming an adjacency matrix $\mathbf{L}$ for the neighborhood graph N, a *bipartite undirected graph*, denoted G, is built. G is defined by three sets: V_h, V_a, E, where V_h is the set of hub nodes (all nodes in N with outdegree > 0), V_a is the set of authority nodes (all nodes in N with indegree > 0), and E is the set of directed edges in N. Note that a node in N may be in both V_h and V_a. For the above neighborhood graph,

$$V_h = \{1, 2, 3, 6, 10\},$$
$$V_a = \{1, 3, 5, 6\}.$$

The bipartite undirected graph G, shown in Figure 12.2, has a "hub side" and an "authority side". Nodes in V_h are listed on the hub side and nodes in V_a are on the authority side. Every directed edge in E is represented by an undirected edge in G. Next, two Markov chains

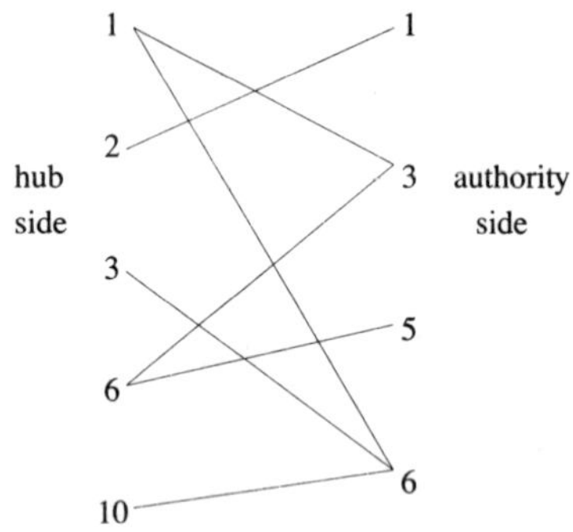

Figure 12.2 G: bipartite graph for SALSA

are formed from G, a hub Markov chain with transition probability matrix $\mathbf{H}$, and an authority Markov chain with matrix $\mathbf{A}$. Notice that in this chapter the $\mathbf{H}$ matrix is SALSA's hub matrix, not to be confused with PageRank's raw hyperlink matrix from several chapters prior. Reference [114] contains a formula for computing the elements of $\mathbf{H}$ and $\mathbf{A}$, but we feel a more instructive approach to building $\mathbf{H}$ and $\mathbf{A}$ clearly reveals SALSA's connection to both HITS and PageRank. Recall that HITS uses the adjacency matrix $\mathbf{L}$ of N to compute authority and hub scores using the unweighted matrix $\mathbf{L}$. On the other hand, PageRank computes a measure analogous to an authority score using a row-normalized weighted matrix $\mathbf{G}$. SALSA uses both row and column weighting to compute its hub and authority scores. Let $\mathbf{L}_r$ be $\mathbf{L}$ with each nonzero row divided by its row sum and $\mathbf{L}_c$ be $\mathbf{L}$ with each nonzero column divided by its column sum. For our example,

$$\mathbf{L} = \begin{array}{c} \\ 1 \\ 2 \\ 3 \\ 5 \\ 6 \\ 10 \end{array} \begin{array}{c} \begin{array}{cccccc} 1 & 2 & 3 & 5 & 6 & 10 \end{array} \\ \begin{pmatrix} 0 & 0 & 1 & 0 & 1 & 0 \\ 1 & 0 & 0 & 0 & 0 & 0 \\ 0 & 0 & 0 & 0 & 1 & 0 \\ 0 & 0 & 0 & 0 & 0 & 0 \\ 0 & 0 & 1 & 1 & 0 & 0 \\ 0 & 0 & 0 & 0 & 1 & 0 \end{pmatrix} \end{array},$$

$$\mathbf{L}_r = \begin{array}{c} \\ 1 \\ 2 \\ 3 \\ 5 \\ 6 \\ 10 \end{array} \begin{array}{c} \begin{array}{cccccc} 1 & 2 & 3 & 5 & 6 & 10 \end{array} \\ \begin{pmatrix} 0 & 0 & \frac{1}{2} & 0 & \frac{1}{2} & 0 \\ 1 & 0 & 0 & 0 & 0 & 0 \\ 0 & 0 & 0 & 0 & 1 & 0 \\ 0 & 0 & 0 & 0 & 0 & 0 \\ 0 & 0 & \frac{1}{2} & \frac{1}{2} & 0 & 0 \\ 0 & 0 & 0 & 0 & 1 & 0 \end{pmatrix} \end{array}, \quad \text{and} \quad \mathbf{L}_c = \begin{array}{c} \\ 1 \\ 2 \\ 3 \\ 5 \\ 6 \\ 10 \end{array} \begin{array}{c} \begin{array}{cccccc} 1 & 2 & 3 & 5 & 6 & 10 \end{array} \\ \begin{pmatrix} 0 & 0 & \frac{1}{2} & 0 & \frac{1}{3} & 0 \\ 1 & 0 & 0 & 0 & 0 & 0 \\ 0 & 0 & 0 & 0 & \frac{1}{3} & 0 \\ 0 & 0 & 0 & 0 & 0 & 0 \\ 0 & 0 & \frac{1}{2} & 1 & 0 & 0 \\ 0 & 0 & 0 & 0 & \frac{1}{3} & 0 \end{pmatrix} \end{array}.$$

Then $\mathbf{H}$, SALSA's hub matrix, consists of the nonzero rows and columns of $\mathbf{L}_r\mathbf{L}_c^T$ and $\mathbf{A}$ is the nonzero rows and columns of $\mathbf{L}_c^T\mathbf{L}_r$.

$$\mathbf{L}_r\mathbf{L}_c^T = \begin{array}{c} \\ 1 \\ 2 \\ 3 \\ 5 \\ 6 \\ 10 \end{array}\!\!\begin{array}{c} \begin{array}{cccccc} 1 & 2 & 3 & 5 & 6 & 10 \end{array} \\ \begin{pmatrix} \frac{5}{12} & 0 & \frac{2}{12} & 0 & \frac{3}{12} & \frac{2}{12} \\ 0 & 1 & 0 & 0 & 0 & 0 \\ \frac{1}{3} & 0 & \frac{1}{3} & 0 & 0 & \frac{1}{3} \\ 0 & 0 & 0 & 0 & 0 & 0 \\ \frac{1}{4} & 0 & 0 & 0 & \frac{3}{4} & 0 \\ \frac{1}{3} & 0 & \frac{1}{3} & 0 & 0 & \frac{1}{3} \end{pmatrix} \end{array}, \text{ and } \mathbf{L}_c^T\mathbf{L}_r = \begin{array}{c} \\ 1 \\ 2 \\ 3 \\ 5 \\ 6 \\ 10 \end{array}\!\!\begin{array}{c} \begin{array}{cccccc} 1 & 2 & 3 & 5 & 6 & 10 \end{array} \\ \begin{pmatrix} 1 & 0 & 0 & 0 & 0 & 0 \\ 0 & 0 & 0 & 0 & 0 & 0 \\ 0 & 0 & \frac{1}{2} & \frac{1}{4} & \frac{1}{4} & 0 \\ 0 & 0 & \frac{1}{2} & \frac{1}{2} & 0 & 0 \\ 0 & 0 & \frac{1}{6} & 0 & \frac{5}{6} & 0 \\ 0 & 0 & 0 & 0 & 0 & 0 \end{pmatrix} \end{array}.$$

As a result, the SALSA hub and authority matrices are

$$\mathbf{H} = \begin{array}{c} \\ 1 \\ 2 \\ 3 \\ 6 \\ 10 \end{array}\!\!\begin{array}{c} \begin{array}{ccccc} 1 & 2 & 3 & 6 & 10 \end{array} \\ \begin{pmatrix} \frac{5}{12} & 0 & \frac{2}{12} & \frac{3}{12} & \frac{2}{12} \\ 0 & 1 & 0 & 0 & 0 \\ \frac{1}{3} & 0 & \frac{1}{3} & 0 & \frac{1}{3} \\ \frac{1}{4} & 0 & 0 & \frac{3}{4} & 0 \\ \frac{1}{3} & \frac{1}{3} & 0 & 0 & \frac{1}{3} \end{pmatrix} \end{array} \quad \text{and} \quad \mathbf{A} = \begin{array}{c} \\ 1 \\ 3 \\ 5 \\ 6 \end{array}\!\!\begin{array}{c} \begin{array}{cccc} 1 & 3 & 5 & 6 \end{array} \\ \begin{pmatrix} 1 & 0 & 0 & 0 \\ 0 & \frac{1}{2} & \frac{1}{4} & \frac{1}{4} \\ 0 & \frac{1}{2} & \frac{1}{2} & 0 \\ 0 & \frac{1}{6} & 0 & \frac{5}{6} \end{pmatrix} \end{array}.$$

If the bipartite graph G is *connected*, then $\mathbf{H}$ and $\mathbf{A}$ are both irreducible Markov chains and $\boldsymbol{\pi}_h^T$, the stationary vector of $\mathbf{H}$, gives the hub scores for the query with neighborhood graph N, and $\boldsymbol{\pi}_a^T$ gives the authority scores. If G is not connected, then $\mathbf{H}$ and $\mathbf{A}$ contain multiple irreducible components. In this case, the global hub and authority scores must be pasted together from the stationary vectors for each individual irreducible component. (Reference [114] contains the justification for the two if-then statements above.)

Since an undirected graph G is connected if every node is reachable from every other node, our graph G from Figure 12.2 is not connected because, for instance, node 2 is not reachable from every other node. For bigger graphs, where connectedness cannot be determined by inspection, graph traversal algorithms exist that identify both the connectedness and the *connected components* of the graph [54]. Because G is not connected, $\mathbf{H}$ and $\mathbf{A}$ contain multiple connected components. $\mathbf{H}$ contains two connected components, $C = \{2\}$ and $D = \{1, 3, 6, 10\}$, while $\mathbf{A}$'s connected components are $E = \{1\}$ and $F = \{3, 5, 6\}$. Also clear from the structure of $\mathbf{H}$ and $\mathbf{A}$ is the *periodicity* of the Markov chains. All irreducible components of $\mathbf{H}$ and $\mathbf{A}$ contain self-loops, implying that the chains are aperiodic. The stationary vectors for the two irreducible components of $\mathbf{H}$ are

$$\boldsymbol{\pi}_h^T(C) = \begin{array}{c} 2 \\ \begin{pmatrix} 1 \end{pmatrix} \end{array}, \quad \boldsymbol{\pi}_h^T(D) = \begin{array}{c} \begin{array}{cccc} 1 & 3 & 6 & 10 \end{array} \\ \begin{pmatrix} \frac{1}{3} & \frac{1}{6} & \frac{1}{3} & \frac{1}{6} \end{pmatrix} \end{array},$$

while the stationary vectors for the two irreducible components of $\mathbf{A}$ are

$$\boldsymbol{\pi}_a^T(E) = \begin{array}{c} 1 \\ \begin{pmatrix} 1 \end{pmatrix} \end{array}, \quad \boldsymbol{\pi}_a^T(F) = \begin{array}{c} \begin{array}{ccc} 3 & 5 & 6 \end{array} \\ \begin{pmatrix} \frac{1}{3} & \frac{1}{6} & \frac{1}{2} \end{pmatrix} \end{array}.$$

Proposition 6 of the original SALSA paper [114] contains the method for pasting the hub and authority scores for the individual components into global popularity vectors. The suggestion there is simple and intuitive. Since the hub component C only contains 1 of the 5 total hub nodes, its stationary hub vector should be weighted by $1/5$, while D, containing 4 of the 5 hub nodes, has its stationary vector weighted by $4/5$. Thus the global hub vector is

$$\begin{aligned}
\pi_h^T &= \begin{array}{c} \begin{array}{ccccc} 1 & 2 & 3 & 6 & 10 \end{array} \\ \left(\begin{array}{ccccc} \frac{4}{5}\cdot\frac{1}{3} & \frac{1}{5}\cdot 1 & \frac{4}{5}\cdot\frac{1}{6} & \frac{4}{5}\cdot\frac{1}{3} & \frac{4}{5}\cdot\frac{1}{6} \end{array} \right) \end{array} \\
&= \begin{array}{c} \begin{array}{ccccc} 1 & 2 & 3 & 6 & 10 \end{array} \\ \left(\begin{array}{ccccc} .2667 & .2 & .1333 & .2667 & .1333 \end{array} \right). \end{array}
\end{aligned}$$

With similar weighting for authority nodes, the global authority vector can be constructed from the individual authority vectors as

$$\begin{aligned}
\pi_a^T &= \begin{array}{c} \begin{array}{cccc} 1 & 3 & 5 & 6 \end{array} \\ \left(\begin{array}{cccc} \frac{1}{4}\cdot 1 & \frac{3}{4}\cdot\frac{1}{3} & \frac{3}{4}\cdot\frac{1}{6} & \frac{3}{4}\cdot\frac{1}{2} \end{array} \right) \end{array} \\
&= \begin{array}{c} \begin{array}{cccc} 1 & 3 & 5 & 6 \end{array} \\ \left(\begin{array}{cccc} .25 & .25 & .125 & .375 \end{array} \right). \end{array}
\end{aligned}$$

Compare the SALSA hub and authority vectors with those of HITS in section 11.4. They are quite different. They're not even the same length and they give significantly different rankings for this example. Ranking the pages from most important to least important gives

$$\begin{aligned}
\text{SALSA hub ranking} &= (\,1/6 \quad 2 \quad 3/10\,) \\
\text{HITS hub ranking} &= (\,1 \quad 3/6/10 \quad 2 \quad 5\,) \\
\text{SALSA authority ranking} &= (\,6 \quad 1/3 \quad 5\,) \\
\text{HITS authority ranking} &= (\,6 \quad 3 \quad 5 \quad 1 \quad 2/10\,)
\end{aligned}$$

where the / symbol indicates a tie.

Our little example is instructive for two additional reasons. First, it shows one way to paste the individual component scores together to create global scores. There are, of course, other weighting schemes for the pasting process. Second, the presence of multiple connected components (which occurs when G is not connected, and is commonplace in practice) is computationally welcome because the Markov chains to be solved are much smaller. Contrast this with PageRank's artificial correction for a disconnected web graph, whereby connectedness is forced by adding direct links between all webpages. PageRank researchers Konstantin Avrachenkov and Nelly Litvak have suggested that, similar to SALSA, PageRank be computed on smaller connected components, then pasted together to get the global PageRank vector [11]. Of course, in order to implement their suggestion, the multiple connected components of the entire web graph must be found first. But that's not so hard—there's Tarjan's $O(V + E)$ linear time algorithm [54], where V and E are the number of vertices and edges in the graph. Unfortunately, it appears that the connected component decomposition for the PageRank problem can have only limited potential because researchers have discovered a bow-tie structure to the Web [41], which shows that the largest connected component of the Web is over a quarter of the size of the entire Web, meaning, at best, the decomposition can reduce the size of the problem by a factor of 4.

12.1.2 Strengths and Weaknesses of SALSA

Because SALSA combines some of the best features of HITS and PageRank, it has many strengths. For example, unlike HITS, SALSA is not victimized by the topic drift problem [26, 114], whereby off-topic but important pages sneak into the neighborhood set and dominate the scores. Recall that another problem with HITS was its susceptibility to spamming due to the interdependence of hub and authority scores. SALSA is less susceptible to spamming since the coupling between hub and authority scores is much less strict. However, both HITS and SALSA are a little easier to spam than PageRank. SALSA, like HITS, also has the benefit of dual rankings, something that PageRank does not supply. Lastly, the presence of multiple connected components in SALSA's bipartite graph G, a common occurrence in practice, is a computational blessing.

However, one serious drawback to the widespread use of the SALSA algorithm is its query-dependence. At query time, the neighborhood graph N for the query must be formed and the stationary vectors for two Markov chains must be computed. Another problematic issue for SALSA is convergence. The convergence of SALSA is similar to that of HITS. Because both HITS and SALSA in their original unmodified versions do not force irreducibility onto the graph, the resulting vectors produced by their algorithms may not be unique (and may depend on the starting vector) if the neighborhood graph is reducible [72]. Nevertheless, a simple solution is to adopt the PageRank fix and force irreducibility by altering the graph in some small way.

12.2 HYBRID RANKING METHODS

Due to the effectiveness of ranking algorithms in aiding web information retrieval, researchers have proposed many new algorithms for ranking webpages. Most are modifications to and combinations of the original three methods of PageRank, HITS, and SALSA [26, 36, 53, 60, 71, 88, 120, 134, 142]. In the next section, we discuss one of the most original new ranking algorithms, TrafficRank.

Some recent work attempts to merge the results from several independent ranking algorithms. This seems promising because experiments show that often the top-k lists of the ranking scores created by different algorithms are very different. This surprising lack of overlap is exciting—it suggests that in the future, perhaps medleys of information retrieval algorithms (realized through **meta-search engines**) will provide the most relevant and precise documents for user queries [120]. Cynthia Dwork, now of Microsoft, is one of the leaders of the field of rank aggregation, the field that studies how to best combine the top-k lists from several search engines into one unified ranked list.

ASIDE: Rank Aggregation and Voting Methods

The rank aggregation done by meta-search engines is very similar to the aggregation of voter preferences. In the case of web search, the political candidates are replaced by webpages and each ranked list of pages produced by a particular algorithm takes the place of the ranked list of candidates that a voter submits for an election. Given a stack of rank ordered lists, the goal in an election is usually to find one overall winner (and possibly a few runner-ups). For meta-search, the goal is to find not just the overall winner but the entire combined ranking, i.e., one ranking of all the candidates. Because of its influence on government, voting research, also known as social choice theory, has a long history. In 1785, Marie Jean Antoine Nicolas Caritat, the Marquis de Condorcet, a French philosopher, mathematician, economist, and social scientist, wrote an Essay on the Application of Analysis to the Probability of Majority Decisions, *in which he revealed the Condorcet voting paradox. In a voting system that studies pairwise comparisons, the Condorcet winner, if it exists, is the candidate that beats or ties all others in the pairwise comparisons of candidates. Consider an example. Three voters rank their preferences for three candidates A, B, and C as follows: voter 1 ranks the candidates A B C, voter 2, B C A, and voter 3, C A B. The majority of the voters have A beating B, B beating C, and C beating A, which creates a cycle, and thus, a Condorcet paradox because the majority rule is in conflict with itself. Many methods have been proposed for resolving the problem of cycles in order to declare a Condorcet winner.*

Related to the voting paradox is Kenneth Arrow's Impossibility Theorem. Arrow, an American economist, won the 1972 Nobel Prize in Economics for his work on social choice theory. His 1951 doctoral thesis, Social Choice and Individual Values, *described five properties that every fair voting system should have. He then proved that no voting system could satisfy all five properties. Scholars debate Arrow's conditions, arguing over which are truly necessary, which are less important, etc. Nevertheless, his theorem shows that in many situations there is no fair, logical way of aggregating individual preferences to accurately determine the collective preferences of the voters. Many voting systems now exist for a variety of voting situations, and voting systems are judged by various criteria, such as resistance to manipulation, Condorcet efficiency (the percentage of elections in which the Condorcet winner is selected), neutrality, and consistency.*

Understanding the problems with determining a fair voting system that declares one overall winner gives an appreciation for how much harder it is to determine a complete ranking of all candidates, and thus, how much harder the rank aggregation problem is for web search.

12.3 RANKINGS BASED ON TRAFFIC FLOW

The Internet is often called the Information SuperHighway. That image helps describe our final ranking method, TrafficRank. Rather than thinking about a lone surfer bouncing around the Web (as Google does), imagine millions, or billions, as actually happens in real life. Now the Web's links become highways between pages, which means there's congestion and traffic. While these things are unpleasant on the auto highway, they're useful for ranking webpages on the information superhighway. In the auto analogy, if we knew the total number of cars on the highways leading into the North Carolina Outer Banks, we'd have a measure of how popular the Outer Banks are as a destination. (If you've ever waited in the backup on Route 12 heading into Nags Head on a Saturday during the summer, you'd agree this gives a pretty good approximation to destination popularity.) Actually, the total number of cars entering the Outer Banks divided by the total number on all highways gives a relative measure of the Outer Banks' popularity compared to that of other destinations. Unfortunately, counting the number of surfers on links on the Web is impossible. (A related effort counts the number of surfers on pages, a much more manageable number. See the Alexa aside on page 138.) But all is not lost; there is a way to approximate the number of surfers on each link using the available graph information.

Let p_{ij} be the proportion of all web traffic on the link from page i to page j. Then $p_{ij} = 0$ if there is no hyperlink from i to j. This definition for p_{ij} means there's a variable for every hyperlink on the Web. The goal is to estimate these p_{ij}'s, then set $\sum_i p_{ij}$, which is the proportion of traffic entering page j, as the TrafficRank of page j. The variables p_{ij} must satisfy some constraints. First, of course, $\sum_{i,j} p_{ij} = 1$. Second, assuming traffic flow into a page equals traffic flow out of a page, $\sum_i p_{ij} - \sum_i p_{ji} = 0$ for every page j. Otherwise, the p_{ij}'s are free to take on any values. IBM researcher John Tomlin devised the following optimization problem to find the p_{ij}'s for his TrafficRank model [159].

$$\begin{aligned} \max \quad & -\sum_{i,j} p_{ij} log\, p_{ij} \quad \text{subject to} \\ & \sum_{i,j} p_{ij} = 1, \\ & \sum_i p_{ij} - \sum_i p_{ji} = 0, \quad \text{for every } j, \\ & p_{ij} \geq 0. \end{aligned}$$

The objective function is the famous entropy function from Claude Shannon's work on information theory [149]. The entropy function maximizes the freedom in choosing the p_{ij}'s. The theory says that the entropy function gives the best unbiased probability assignment to the variables given the constraints. It uses only the given information from the constraints and is maximally noncommittal with respect to the missing information.

OK, so just solve the optimization problem to get the p_{ij}'s and form the TrafficRank for each page. Problem solved. But wait, you protest, that optimization problem is huge; it has $|E|$ variables where $|E|$ is the number of edges in the web graph. True, but Tomlin provides a fast iterative algorithm for computing the variables. The algorithm uses Lagrange multipliers and impressively exploits the problem's structure so that solving the optimization problem only takes about 2.5 times longer than solving a PageRank problem for the same graph. Tomlin's results showed that TrafficRank was similar to HITS hub scores in the sense that high TrafficRank pages tended to have many outlinks. This similarity to hubs makes sense because TrafficRank measures flow through a page, and heavy flow requires a large number of both inlinks and outlinks.

The TrafficRank model has two interesting extensions. First, as more traffic information becomes available, it can easily be added to the model in the form of constraints. For instance, if actual data is collected on traffic at popular sites, then constraints of the form

$$\beta_j \leq \sum_i p_{ij} \leq \omega_j, \text{for } j \in J,$$

give an allowable range on the computed TrafficRank values of pages in the set J of popular sites. Second, the dual solution of the optimization problem has an interesting interpretation.[1] Inverting the Lagrange multipliers (there's one for each constraint) of the primal solution gives a "temperature" for each webpage. (This interpretation comes from the thermodynamics relationship between entropy and heat.) As a result, Tomlin used the dual measure to form a HotRank for each page. This HotRank was similar to, but generally outperformed, PageRank as a measure of authoritativeness.

[1] Many optimization problems have both primal and dual formulations whose solutions are related by the famous Duality Theorem.

Finally, we mention TrafficRank's connections to our two well-studied ranking algorithms, PageRank and HITS. The matrix $\mathbf{P}_{n\times n} = [p_{ij}]$ (where n is the number of pages in the index) formed from the solutions to the TrafficRank optimization problem is sparse, nonnegative, and substochastic. Of course, the Perron vector (the dominant eigenvector) could be computed for this matrix and compared with the query-independent HITS vector. Similarly, the Traffic Rank matrix $\mathbf{P}$ could be row-normalized so that it is stochastic. Then the dominant left-hand eigenvector is computed, which, in this case, is actually the PageRank vector for an intelligent surfer model.

ASIDE: Alexa Traffic Ranking

Alexa, an amazon.com search company, uses its Toolbar to gather information about web usage, which in turn produces popularity rankings based on site traffic. As the Alexa website says, "the more people [that] use Alexa [specifically its Toolbar], the more useful it will be." Alexa makes other use of their collected data. For example, there's a list of Movers and Shakers, the top ten websites with the most dramatic increase or decrease in their traffic ranking during the past week. There's also a list of the 500 most popular sites according to Alexa. And, there's the traffic ranking plot of popular webpages over time. Figure 12.3 shows the traffic rank trends for Yahoo!, Google, AltaVista, and Teoma from February to August 2004.

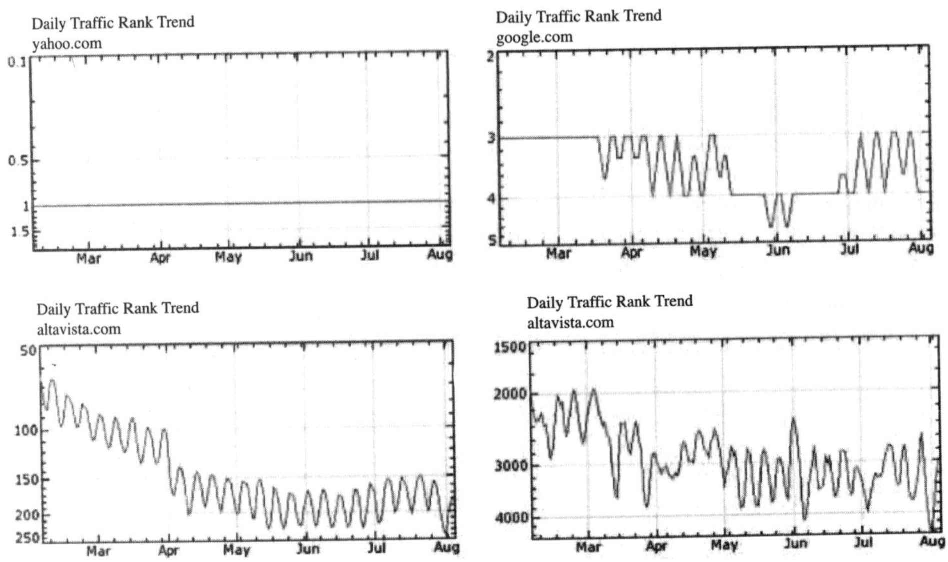

Figure 12.3 Alexa Traffic Rank Trends for 4 Search Engines

According to Alexa users, Yahoo! and Google clearly see more traffic than AltaVista and Teoma. Alexa is also the company that supplies the Internet Archive (see the box on page 21) with its regular donation of pages.

Chapter Thirteen

The Future of Web Information Retrieval

Web search is a young research field with great room for growth. In this chapter, we survey possible directions for future research, pausing along the way for some storytelling.

13.1 SPAM

ASIDE: The Ghosts of Search

Sammy the Spammer had been pecking away at his computer continuously for over 27 hours. Sammy was used to the sustained bursts of work—he'd been hacking, coding, programming, and spamming since he could type at the age of four. He came from a proud line of spammers. His older brother was a hacker, the brother before him, a hacker, and so Sammy naturally displayed the talent early on. The family was well known in the search engine optimization (SEO) community, with a reputation not too far from that of a leading mafia family. His family had worked hard (unethically some said) to rule the world of underground search rankings. If you needed to knock off a few competitors in the rankings, you came to Sammy. The family was well rewarded for their computer skills. Sammy himself had three houses—one in the Valley, Silicon, of course, one in Maui, and one in London.

Sammy had fallen asleep at the keyboard many nights after 20-plus hour days. But this time when he woke up, something was different. His vision was blurry, his thoughts muddled. He thought he saw a thin, white-haired man dressed in a red gown, a glow about his head, standing ten feet in front of him. Sammy blinked twice; the man remained. He'd never seen the man before, yet somehow felt as if he might have. He felt strangely unalarmed by the apparition. Convinced he was dreaming, Sammy decided to play along with the scene, and asked the man, "Are you a spirit?" "I am," came a gentle reply. "Who and what are you?" Sammy pried. "I am the Ghost of Search Past." "Long past?" Sammy asked. "No, your past," the spirit said.

The ghost held Sammy's arm as they whisked by the scenes of his past. Sammy saw a young boy getting an award at a science fair. Sammy remembered the project—he'd built a web crawler to find and connect the webpages of other young inventors on the Web. Next, Sammy saw his 13-year-old self sitting at a table in a pizzeria talking with his older brothers. They'd just taken little Sammy to his first SEO conference. The trio was buzzing about the financial potential of the Web. They sat making plans for making money on the Web. Witnessing that conversation now, Sammy felt the same excitement he'd felt years before. He was jolted back to the present. The Ghost of Search Past said, "My time grows short. Quick." Sammy witnessed one last scene. Sammy and his brother sat in an office listening intently as their older brother took a phone call from their friend Paul. That was the conversation where Paul warned them to learn from his mistakes; he'd just lost a legal battle with the search engine Anetta, and, consequently, his business.

Suddenly Sammy found himself back in his room. The Ghost of Search Past was gone but another one had arrived. "You must be the Ghost of Search Present," Sammy said. "Yes, but we haven't any time for me; we need to move this story along," the spirit said. There was a flash, darkness, then when Sammy could see again, he found himself standing in a cemetery next to a shrouded, dark spirit, the Ghost of Search Future. The ghost pointed at a headstone—PageRank 1998–2006. "What happened?" Sammy asked. "PageRank ruled search. Before PageRank, web search was elementary. That algorithm changed everything. I did all my projects from my keyboard, I hardly had to leave my room, thanks to PageRank. What happened?" Sammy asked again. The spirit handed him a PDA. On it was an obituary.

> *Obituary: Born in 1998, PageRank is succeeded by parents Larry Page and Sergey Brin. Died on November 27, 2006. After a long, hard-fought battle with link spammers, PageRank finally succumbed to ...*

The PDA slipped from Sammy's hand as he blankly turned to the spirit. "Tell me truly, Spirit, did I do this? Could I have changed the course of this algorithm's life?" There was no reply. Of course not. Sammy knew future spirits never spoke. Sammy slowly scanned the graveyard. He saw headstones for other algorithms he'd known; HITS, SALSA, TrafficRank. It was too much at once. Sammy begged to go back; he pleaded with the silent spirit. And snap, back to reality. Sammy awoke in his room in front of his keyboard.

The story, the Ghosts of Search, might not be too outlandish. In fact, it was inspired by a recent weblog posting. On May 24, 2003, Jeremy Zawodny declared PageRank dead. He claimed the algorithm was no longer useful because bloggers and SEOs had learned too much about it and had, in effect, changed the nature of the Web. Since PageRank is based on an optimistic assumption that all links are conceived in good faith with no ulterior motives, an assumption that no longer holds, then PageRank is no longer useful. The blog article "PageRank is Dead" inspired many interesting rebuttals. We are certain (private communication) that PageRank is not dead. It's still a major part of the Google technology, but just one part—new additions and refinements are constantly made. Nevertheless, while spam may not have killed PageRank completely, it has initiated a lot of damage control. In fact, spam is a major area of research for all search engines. New search engines turn heads when they back up claims that their algorithms are impervious to spam.

Creating spam-resistant ranking algorithms is a current goal. But in the meantime, many engines settle for simply identifying spam pages, which they can then devalue significantly after the ranking computation. Spam identification probably isn't any easier than starting from scratch, trying to create a new, spam-resistant algorithm. But it's a route many engines are taking due to the personal attachment and resources they've already invested in their existing ranking algorithms.

One algorithm for identifying link spam uses the structure of link farms and link exchanges, the primary means for boosting rankings, to identify pages participating in link spam. Specifically, the algorithm considers each page one at a time, and asks, "What proportion of this page's outlinking pages point back to it?" (In other words, what percentage of a page's links are reciprocal?) If the answer is greater than some threshold (say 80%), then that page is identified as a page likely to be participating in link spam. The identified page is then sent an email similar to the following message.

> You've been identified as a link spammer. Your pages will be removed from

> our index unless you immediately remove all links to fellow spammers participating in an exchange or farm program.

Search engine professionals cite an added bonus to the method: a spammer who has been caught often rats on his fellow spammers participating in the same exchange program to make sure they don't reap the benefits of his lost business. Noticing which links the identified spammer then removes also helps identify other potential spammers. However, this simple algorithm has a few drawbacks. First, it's a tedious computation that must be done for each page in the index. Second, it's not foolproof. Consider the following email invitation that we received from a smarter link spammer (or perhaps one who'd been caught once before).

> Hello,
>
> We offer accommodation services and I thought you might be interested in link exchange. We provide several travel-related sites. All of them are PageRank 6.
>
> Due to the possible harming nature of too many reciprocal links we suggest non reciprocal links. You can link to us from your site and we will link back from another of our sites.
>
> If you got this message in error please forward this mail to your webmaster.
>
> I look forward to hearing from you.
>
> Best Regards, Mark

Another idea for deterring link spam is to build a score that is the "opposite" of PageRank. It's called BadRank (`http://pr.efactory.de/`). PageRank is a measure of how good a page is, as measured by the quality of pages that point to it. Since goodness does not mean the absence of badness, we can also give every page a BadRank score that measures how bad the page is. The BadRank thesis is: a page is bad if it points to other bad pages. BadRank is an outlink propagation whereas PageRank propagates along inlinks. PageRank and BadRank can be combined to give an overall fitness score to each page. Andrei Broder and his IBM colleagues presented a similar idea [15] at the 2004 World Wide Web conference in New York City. Their method creates a PageRank-like algorithm for penalizing pages that point to dead pages, which are abandoned sites.

Some claim that, in the long run, the best spam deterrent may be the most obvious—simply offer search engine optimizers an alternative way to boost their rank. Rather than crawling their way up the rankings by haggling with competitors over link reciprocation, let them buy their way to the top. The price of cost-per-click advertising, which is cheap for more specific, less popular queries, often outweighs the effort and stress associated with link spamming. However, since **sponsored links** don't carry the authority that **pure links** do in the list of results (and many users ignore them), some SEOs are willing to invest the time to link spam their way into the list of pure results.

> *Well, there's egg and bacon; egg sausage and bacon; egg and spam; egg bacon and spam; egg bacon sausage and spam; spam bacon sausage and spam; spam egg spam spam bacon and spam; spam sausage spam spam bacon spam tomato and spam.*–Monty Python Spam Skit

Like the Monty Python skit, it seems we just can't escape spam on the Web. Spam has clearly become an increasingly challenging problem. In the future, we predict the best search engines will be the ones with entirely new ranking algorithms that were devised from the start to handle the issues of spam.

13.2 PERSONALIZATION

In section 5.3, we talked about personalized search where the motto is to let you "have it your way" with regard to the rankings of search results. Google's Personalized Search (in beta in Google Labs) lets you do this, up to the granularity provided by their check box categories of user interests. (See Section 5.3 and the box on page 51.) However, there's a newer company that offers much more personalization. A9 (`www.a9.com`), an Amazon company, bases its search results on a simple idea. Whenever you are trying to find something, especially something you've lost, try retracing your steps. A9 keeps track of your steps for you. The search engine automatically records a detailed history of your search life: pages you've visited, when you visited them, how often, and what queries you've attempted in the past. A9 results pages also come with a "site info" button, which contains statistics such as Amazon's average traffic rank for that page, lists of customer reviews, online birth date, number of inlinks, plus Amazon's famous recommendation system: "people who visited this webpage also visited ..." It seems A9 is part of a growing trend—there will be even more personalization for web users in the future.

13.3 CLUSTERING

The major search engines spend a lot of energy improving their ranking algorithms. They are constantly tweaking their rankings because they know that users look only at the first 20 results. It's important, in order to maintain user loyalty, that these be the best, most relevant pages. However, some newer search companies believe that only modest gains are to be had by these ranking refinements. No matter how hard you try, you just can't pack more than 20 highly relevant pages into the top 20 results. Instead, these companies abandon the fixation with ranking one list and work on creating hierarchical clusterings of results. These clusters help users drill down and quickly find the most appropriate category. This, in turn, helps with query refinement, the process of submitting a slightly revised query based on the prior search results. Teoma, which uses the HITS-based algorithm, actually has a third set of results, in addition to the hub and authority lists we mentioned in Chapter 11, called the Refine List, which contains categories associated with the query.

Along these lines, the rising meta-search engine Viv´isimo is trying to set "a new standard for the way document collections are organized." Viv´isimo was founded in 2000 by computer scientists at Carnegie Mellon University. On the left-hand side of the results page are hierarchical category folders. For example, try a query on "Kerri Walsh," the taller half of the May/Walsh pro beach volleyball pair, which recently won the gold medal in the Athens Olympic games. Viv´isimo finds 153 results: 47 are grouped under the Gold category, 20 under AVP (Association of Volleyball Professionals), 8 under Youngs/McPeak (May/Walsh's toughest competitor), 5 under Misty (Walsh's doubles partner, Misty May), and so on. The right-hand side looks like the results from a standard search engine like Google or AltaVista. That is, the 153 results are listed from most relevant to least relevant regardless of category. Viv´isimo technology is not limited to the Web; they recently created a special tool to help the media and public find information quickly in the 570+ page report of the 9/11 Commission. (You can give it a try at `http://vivisimo.com/911`.)

ASIDE: Kartoo Clustering

The French meta-search engine KartOO (`http://www.kartoo.com/`) is a really fun tool. It's like an artist's rendition of the Vivísimo results. KartOO displays clustered search results both on the left-hand side in a list as well as visually on an interactive map. Notice in Figure 13.1 how the results of the example query of "Kerri Walsh" brighten up.

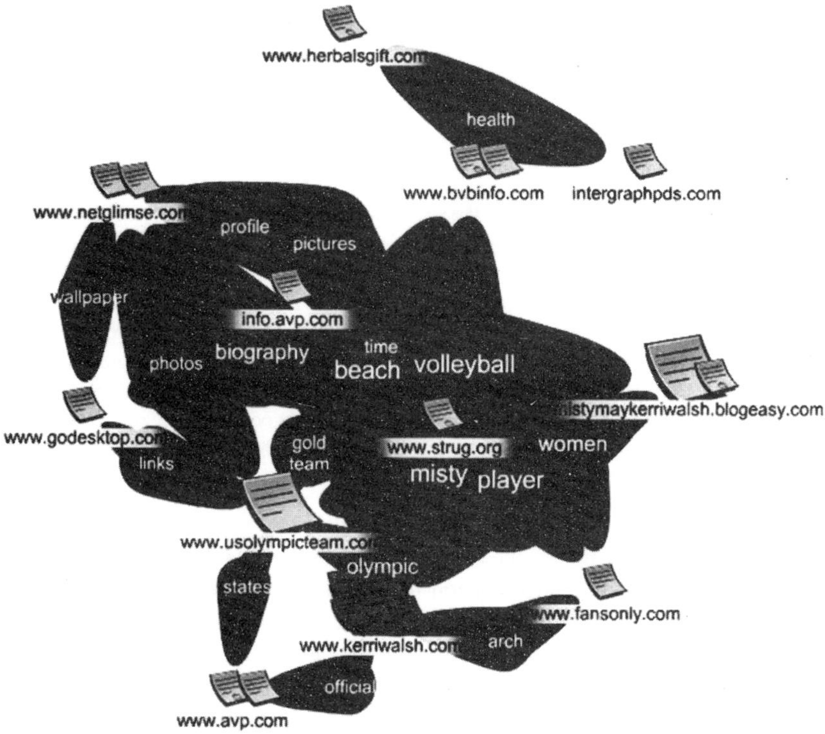

Figure 13.1 Sample map of KartOO results

Unfortunately, this screen shot does not allow interactivity, so you can't see the links between topics and webpages that would appear as your mouse scrolls over the map. Clicking on any topic in the map automatically refines the query, biasing the revised results toward that topic. KartOO is at the other end of the spectrum of search engines. Most search engines give users a simple clean list of ranked results, assuming users lack time, effort, and discrimination. KartOO instead fills the page with as much information as possible and allows users to sort through the pages creating new connections as they proceed. Which type of display do users prefer? Depends on who you ask and when you ask them. Sometimes you're in a hurry and want the search engine to do all the work, and sometimes you have the time to play around and discover things for yourself.

13.4 INTELLIGENT AGENTS

ASIDE: The First Brain Implant

NY Times–June 30, 2009. Yesterday 36-year old Larry Page woke up from surgery still feeling a little groggy. His first post-surgery words were "I'm hungry." The reporters were hoping for something a little more prophetic, but the event itself is news enough. Just 12 hours prior, the Google cofounder and owner, in a bold public relations move, became the first person to undergo a radical new surgery—the Google brain implant.

It was only six years ago when Page, speaking of the future of search, said, "On the more exciting front, you can imagine your brain being augmented by Google" [135]. What progress for mankind in such short time. Marjorie States already knows how she'd use a Google implant. States loved using the GPS system in her Acura to find restaurants and directions around town when she lived in Poughkeepsie. Since she moved to New York City three months ago, she's been walking around town or using the subway instead of the car. She can't wait for a Google brain implant to replace her current on-the-go restaurant locator method of dialing 411. "Using 411 on the cell is so 1990s. With the Google implant I'll save like 5 blocks of walking and 15 minutes everyday." You can't put a value on time lost.

But not all citizens are thrilled by the scientific achievement. In fact, for months a small but passionate group has been lobbying in D.C. for a constitutional amendment to ban brain implants of any sort—informational, memory, sensory, audio/visual, etc. While this group describes doomsday predictions of mind control, regression of analytical skills, and long-term memory damage, others have literally sold the family farm to secure their $200,000 spot on the recipient list. These implant hopefuls believe the benefits of improved test scores, increased job performance, and general convenience far outweigh the risks. And Dr. Jonas Smith, a neurosurgeon from Johns Hopkins University, puts the risks in perspective, "my feeling about brain implantation is that only time will tell who is right and who is dead." Indeed, it's a very scary but exciting time for science.

While Larry Page's vision of the future of web search is a bit far-fetched, the story is a good introduction to a more realistic vision—one that includes search pets and intelligent agents. An **intelligent agent** is a software robot designed to retrieve specific information automatically. The adjective *intelligent* describes the agent's ability to run without supervision and learn about your preferences based on your search history, browser cookies, etc. Intelligent agents exist already. Many go hunting for new postings on topics you preselect like the Google Web Alert (available at Google Labs). Some find the best price for an item you want to buy. Others collect and organize your e-mail.

There's a futuristic agent that Google's Director of Technology Craig Silverstein calls a search pet. Most searches today are limited to facts. However, according to Silverstein, that won't be the case in the future. Because these search pets will be able to understand emotions and the way humans interact, people will be able to search for things that aren't necessarily facts. That's a tall order for a search pet, since most humans have trouble understanding how other humans work. Nevertheless, we'll be seeing much more from intelligent agents in the future.

13.5 TRENDS AND TIME-SENSITIVE SEARCH

ASIDE: Blogs and Trends

In May 2004 I attended my first WWW conference, the Thirteenth International World Wide Web Conference, held in New York City. Not being a computer scientist, I felt a bit out of place as I was outnumbered at least 20 to 1 by computer scientists. During the first presentation, I noticed how different the WWW conference was from the SIAM (Society for Industrial and Applied Mathematicians) conferences I normally attend. How rude of my new colleagues to check their email and surf the Web on their laptops while the speaker covered his material, I thought. I mentioned this fact, that over 80% of the audience (including those in the front row) were pecking on their keyboards during the talks, to a friend. At least inattentive SIAM attendees sat in the back. He explained that most of the audience members were not being rude, but rather very attentive. They were following along, hosting chat rooms about the ongoing talk, and surfing for definitions of acronyms. I was impressed with their use of technology.

Here's how one conversation with a new computer science friend went. "How much of a computer geek are you, Amy?" asked Urban. "Not much of one," I said. "So you don't have a **blog***!" "No." "But you have read Slashdot, right?" "Never heard of it," I said. Urban gasped. "The blog Slashdot–News for Nerds. Stuff that matters. Just last week they had this article on ..."*

Throughout the conference, my new computer science friends gladly filled my tabula rasa. I soon learned much to amend for my blogging deficits. I learned that blog (rhymes with flog) was short for weblog, which is an interactive online diary of time-stamped entries. Soon I was curious to surf Salon and Slashdot, blogs with supposedly entertaining stories, witty political commentary, and geeky must-read news. I also learned that blogs are easy to start and maintain. (Anybody's brother, with the help of software such as Blogger, Radio Userland, or Live Journal, can host his own blog.) I learned that most blogs have a blog roll, which is a list of other blogs the author recommends. Blogs contain lots of links so readers can follow conversations across different blogs. Blogs are often organized by threads, which are strings of comments on the same topic. I learned that some blogs have daily devotees, while most others are read by a handful of fans. I also learned that, for the most part, I could care less about the information contained in blogs. Most blogs serve as a creative outlet for wannabe artists, writers, poets, political commentators, and the like. Every day Uncle Pete in Franklin, Michigan can tell his family (and the world) what he thinks about his 1980 Ford truck. Despite this, a precious few blogs do contain information that serves a community's needs and provides useful archival potential. That observation led me to the most important thing I learned about blogs all week: searching blogs is an interesting new research area.

There are several issues when it comes to searching blogs. For example, should blog results be listed in the search engine's list of results or are blogs really a different beast? Since most blogs contain little or no information, most people think they should not be mixed in with the standard search results. But blogs aren't completely useless, either. For example, if you need to know how to install replacement bulbs for the headlights on your 1980 truck, then you'd be interested in searching the pictures and postings by Uncle Pete of Franklin, Michigan. Perhaps, instead, blogs should be searched in a separate domain, similar to the way Google News searches just within news sites. That's the prevailing feeling because blogs really are different from most webpages. Blogs are updated even more frequently than ordinary webpages, and blogs contain a time stamp that can be very helpful in searching for time-sensitive information. Blogs are also link-rich and content-poor. Blogs are full of links like "check out this cool page" or "here's a great article" interspersed with a sentence or two of commentary. This means traditional information retrieval scores have trouble identifying topics when pages contain so little content. But it also highlights the editorial nature of blogs. Blogs contain short snippets of personal opinions, shared and conflicting, whereas news sites contain one aggregate opinion presented by the author. These personal opinions may be very helpful when you're deciding whether to buy the 10 GB iPod or the 20 GB iPod. Technorati, `www.technorati.com`*, is one search engine that keeps track of the* **blogspace***, the world of blogs, by watching over 3 million blogs and 470 million links. For example, Technorati* *tracks interesting opinions on the top books and news stories.*

Eytan Adar and his colleagues at the Hewlett-Packard Information Dynamics Lab have created an algorithm for ranking pages in the blogspace [8]. They rank blogs by their so-called epidemic importance, that is, their ability to spread information quickly. Their algorithm, called iRank, is very similar to PageRank. But there are two essential differences. First, the original link graph for the blogspace, called the explicit graph, is augmented by what they call implicit links. An implicit link between two blogs that are not explicitly connected by a hyperlink is made if an implicit reference between the two blogs is found in the text of one of the blogs or if the text and link similarity between the two is high. For instance, Andy's blog might say "Brian's blog has an interesting post about the new Elmo stuffed toy. You can buy the toys at `website1` or `website2`." Explicit links from Andy's blog are made to the two online stores, but no explicit link is made to Brian's blog. However, there's a clear connection between the two blogs, and readers of one probably read the other. Adar's algorithm uses text analysis to find and add these implicit links to the blog graph. The second distinguishing feature of iRank is its temporal factor. All links are weighted by their freshness. A link's weight is inversely proportional to the difference in dates between the two blogs. Thus, a blog is rewarded for citing recent postings on another blog. At this point, ordinary PageRank is run on this augmented, time-weighted graph, giving an iRank vector that contains the ranking for the blogs. Adar et al. found that iRank results differ substantially from PageRank results. Blogs with high iRank tend to be portal pages or pages aimed at finding the most current information, whereas blogs with high PageRank usually contained original authoritative material. Depending on the search goal, one ranking may be more valuable than the other.

The use of time as a discriminating factor in search is relatively new. Some information on the Web such as blog postings and news articles does come with an explicit time stamp. In other cases, time-sensitive information can be extracted implicitly. For example, the Internet Archive gets an approximation of dates for revisions to webpages with its periodic crawls. The Recall Machine from the Internet Archive as well as Google Groups allow search for information posted within specific time frames. This feature allows for very focused queries. For example, with the time-sensitive search capability, it's easy to compare the tone and content of articles written within a month of the September 11, 2001 tragedy with those written three years later.

13.6 PRIVACY AND CENSORSHIP

Deciding which pages to index is not as simple as it once was. In the Web's early days, the goal was simply to index as many pages as possible. Now search companies must be more judicious. They must also consider the privacy of users. For example, spiders must carefully obey all robots.txt files. Similarly, deciding which pages to retrieve for user queries is complicated by issues like user safety. Because children have easy access to search engines, most companies have added safe search filters to their offerings. These issues and the two asides below demonstrate that the leaders of search companies must be critical thinkers and students of the liberal arts. They routinely face philosophical, ethical, political, business, and legal issues far afield from their graduate studies in computer science, engineering, or mathematics.

ASIDE: Google's Cookie

Privacy advocates think Google's toolbar and Gmail are a nightmare. These privacy hounds despise Google's "immortal" cookie, which collects the IP address, time, date, and search terms of Toolbar users and does not expire until 2038. The lengthy expiration date is evidence enough for privacy hounds that Google cannot be trusted. However, Google could make good use of some of the collected information. For example, they could use the IP address to augment their new local search service, by sorting results for some queries (such as those for businesses, addresses, phone numbers, etc.) by proximity to the location of the user's computer. Many Toolbar users are calmed by the fact that the amount of aggregated data that Google collects makes individuals nearly anonymous. Especially cautious users can turn off some features of the Toolbar to restrict Google's data collection if they desire.

ASIDE: Search in China

In early September 2002, the Google homepage was inaccessible in China. A user entering the Google URL was rerouted to Tianwang Search, a search engine operated by Peking University. Google was blocked because its searches could return links to pornography, democratic forums, content associated with the banned spiritual movement Falun Gong, and information endangering national security. The Great Firewall of China, a reference to the government's open attempts to control web content by blocking foreign news sites and forcing domestic sites to remove unwholesome content, has been in place since the birth of the Internet. However, this was the first time censors had hijacked a search engine domain name and rerouted traffic to another site. One week later, AltaVista was blocked as well. Apparently, the volume of complaints by Chinese surfers was enough to lift the block. Within a few weeks, access to Google and AltaVista was restored. Human rights groups have written letters to the CEOs of Google and AltaVista requesting that they fight the Chinese censorship. Often the search engines, Yahoo! is an example, have voluntarily signed pledges in support of Chinese censorship policies, and therefore offer a limited service in order to remain accessible. Search engines must weigh the cost and benefits of no accessibility versus limited accessibility.

13.7 LIBRARY CLASSIFICATION SCHEMES

During the 20th century, libraries underwent a transformation in their classification and presentation of books. The Dewey decimal classification (DDC) system, introduced in 1876 by Melvin Dewey, for the library at Amherst College, was revised and refined, so that today in its 21st edition, it is one of two popular classification systems in use. The other alternative system is the Library of Congress classification (LC) system. Because these systems enjoy worldwide use—for example, the Dewey decimal system is currently used in over 135 countries—it's natural to think of classifying webpages in a similar manner. Some groups are trying to encourage users to use either the DDC numbers or LC numbers in **metatags**. Yet, if a strong connection between webpages and traditional library classification systems is to develop, the job will probably fall on the crawlers and indexers of web search engines. If DDC or LC numbers are associated with each webpage in the future, then surfers are a short link away from accessing Amazon or digital libraries for information on related books.

ASIDE: Google's Digital Library Initiative

In December of 2004, Google announced its decade-long initiative to scan millions of books from the collections of major research universities. Harvard, Michigan, Stanford, and Oxford are among the cooperating universities, as well as the nonacademic New York Public Library. The ultimate goal is to allow surfers to search through text in books online. For books still under copyright protection, only brief snippets of text and reference information will appear.

However, several publishing companies are not excited about Google's new initiative. These companies prefer that their books and series not be included in the collection. Scanning a book is a clear violation of copyright law, and is allowed only with permission. Most publishers will grant such permission, however, they just want be asked first. In effect, the publishers are sending Google a warning message, that the search giant needs to respect the rules of this long-standing profession. In the meantime, Google has a huge stack of "May I" permission letters that need to be signed.

13.8 DATA FUSION

A new type of web retrieval application based on maps is the latest technology. The Where 2.0 conference assembles researchers and developers in location-based technology. The idea is to layer advanced user-friendly interactive search features on top of the familiar visual of a map. For example, the Swiss search engine, search.ch, which recently won the Best of the Swiss Web Prize, places icons of restaurants, movie theatres, bus stops, parking garages, hotels, and the like on satellite maps of Switzerland. Scrolling over an icon shows details, such as the number of minutes until the next bus, the number of open seats in the theatre, the number of open spots in a parking garage, ticket prices, and phone numbers. To achieve such up-to-date information, the engine periodically crawls the associated websites for the relevant information. By fusing data from other sources, such as phone directories and restaurant guides, search.ch provides a handy visual tool. In fact, visiting `www.map.search.ch` allows you to take a virtual tour of the country. With eventual cell phone and PDA accessibility, travel especially will be easy.

Chapter Fourteen

Resources for Web Information Retrieval

14.1 RESOURCES FOR GETTING STARTED

If you're a student or a researcher new to the field, you'll find these resources helpful for getting started. The datasets are small and manageable, the code simple, and the algorithms run quickly.

14.1.1 Datasets

There are several small web graphs that are available for download. The table below provides details.

Table 14.1 Small web graphs

Dataset	# pages	# links	Available at
movies	451	713	website 1
censorship	562	736	website 1
abortion	1693	4325	website 1
genetics	2952	6485	website 1
EPA	4772	8965	website 2
Hollins	6012	23875	website 3
California	9664	16150	website 2

Most of these webpages also contain other graphs that are similar in size and source. For example, Panayiotis Tsaparas hosts a nice webpage (website 4) that contains more graphs (and some C code).

Website 1: `http://www.cs.toronto.edu/~tsap/experiments/datasets/index.html`
Website 2: `http://www.cs.cornell.edu/Courses/cs685/2002fa/`
Website 3: `http://www.math.vt.edu/people/kemassey/ir/`
Website 4: `http://www.cs.toronto.edu/~tsap/experiments/download/download.html`

14.1.2 Crawlers

On page 17, we provided Cleve Moler's Matlab code for creating your own datasets. This m-file can be downloaded from the website for Cleve's new book *Numerical Computing with Matlab*, `http://www.mathworks.com/moler/ncmfilelist.html`. This m-file routine can be used to create small, tailored datasets. However, it can be slow and it does have some documented problems, e.g., it can stall waiting to download pages with images or data files.

14.1.3 Code

Matlab is a great tool for programming algorithms and testing ideas on reasonably sized datasets. This book contains Matlab code for many algorithms, such as the PageRank and HITS algorithms. Other programmers have also produced Matlab code for these link analysis problems. See, for example, the following websites:

- `http://www.stanford.edu/~sdkamvar/research.html#Data`
- `http://math.cofc.edu/ langvillea/PRDataCode/index.html`

14.1.4 References

Extensive lists of references, some hyperlinked, are available at:

- `http://www.cs.cornell.edu/Courses/cs685/2002fa/`
- `http://linkanalysis.wlv.ac.uk/`
- `http://math.cofc.edu/~langvillea/#Current%20Research`

In addition, each year the World Wide Web Conference has several papers related to link analysis.

14.2 RESOURCES FOR SERIOUS STUDY

When you are ready to move on to bigger problems, consider the tools cited in this section.

14.2.1 Datasets

Much larger datasets are available for those interested in more serious study of link analysis. Table 14.2 gives information for some representative datasets.

Website 5: `http://www.stanford.edu/~sdkamvar/research.html#Data`
Website 6: `http://cybermetrics.wlv.ac.uk/database/`

Table 14.2 Large web graphs

Dataset	# pages	# links	Available at
Stanford University sites	.28 million	2.3 million	website 5
Stanford-Berkeley sites	.68 million	7.6 million	website 5
23 U.S. University sites	3.0 million	23.9 million	website 6
38 Australian University sites	2.3 million	19.8 million	website 6

14.2.2 Crawlers

There are several nice tools for crawling and collecting link information for large datasets. For example, try the following tools:

- SocSciBot3: `http://socscibot.wlv.ac.uk/`
- WebBot: information and directions for downloading are available at `http://www.math.vt.edu/people/kemassey/ir/`
- Stanford WebBase Project: `http://www-diglib.stanford.edu/~testbed/doc2/WebBase/`
- WebGraph Graph Compression Tools: `http://webgraph.dsi.unimi.it/`

14.2.3 Code

Any serious study of algorithms, one aimed at creating production code, must implement algorithms in fortran, C, or C++ rather than a more user-friendly but high-level language such as Matlab. In order to compute ranking vectors, many of the link analysis methods in this book use classic numerical algorithms. Fortunately, effective, efficient code is readily available for such classic algorithms. For example, the Netlib repository (`http://www.netlib.org/`) contains various implementations of the power method or other eigenvector methods written in several of the most popular programming languages.

Chapter Fifteen

The Mathematics Guide

Appreciating the subtleties of PageRank, HITS, and other ranking schemes requires knowledge of some mathematical concepts. In particular, it's necessary to understand some aspects of linear algebra, discrete Markov chains, and graph theory. Rather than presenting a comprehensive survey of these areas, our purpose here is to touch on only the most relevant topics that arise in the mathematical analysis of Web search concepts. Technical proofs are generally omitted.

The common ground is linear algebra, so this is where we start. The reader that wants more detail or simply wants to review elementary linear algebra to an extent greater than that given here should consult [127].

15.1 LINEAR ALGEBRA

In the context of Web search the matrices encountered are almost always real, but because real matrices can generate complex numbers (e.g., eigenvalues) it's often necessary to consider complex numbers, vectors, and matrices. Throughout this chapter real numbers, real vectors, and real matrices are respectively denoted by $\Re$, $\Re^n$, and $\Re^{m\times n}$, while complex numbers, vectors, and matrices are respectively denoted by $\mathcal{C}$, $\mathcal{C}^n$, and $\mathcal{C}^{m\times n}$. The following basic concepts of arise in the mathematical analysis of Web search problems.

Norms

The most common way to measure the magnitude of a row (or column) vector $\mathbf{x} = (x_1, x_2, \ldots, x_n)$ of real or complex numbers is by means of the euclidean norm (sometimes called the 2-norm) that is defined by

$$\|\mathbf{x}\|_2 = \left(\sum_{i=1}^{n} |x_i|^2\right)^{1/2}.$$

However, in the applications involving PageRank and Markov chains, it's more natural (and convenient) to use the vector 1-norm defined by

$$\|\mathbf{x}\|_1 = \sum_{i=1}^{n} |x_i|$$

because, for example, if $\mathbf{p}$ is a PageRank (or probability) vector, (i.e., a nonnegative vector with components summing to one) then $\|\mathbf{p}\|_1 = 1$. Occasionally the vector ∞-norm

$$\|\mathbf{x}\|_\infty = \max_i |x_i|$$

is used. All norms satisfy the three properties

$$\|\mathbf{x}\| \geq 0 \quad \text{where} \quad \|\mathbf{x}\| = 0 \quad \text{if and only if} \quad \mathbf{x} = \mathbf{0},$$
$$\|\alpha\mathbf{x}\| = |\alpha| \; \|\mathbf{x}\| \quad \text{for all scalars } \alpha,$$
$$\|\mathbf{x}+\mathbf{y}\| \leq \|\mathbf{x}\| + \|\mathbf{y}\| \quad \text{(the triangle inequality).}$$

Associated with each vector norm is an *induced matrix norm.* If $\mathbf{A}$ is $m \times n$ and $\mathbf{x}$ is $n \times 1$, and if $\|*\|_\star$ is any vector norm, then the corresponding induced matrix norm is defined to be

$$\|\mathbf{A}\|_\star = \max_{\|\mathbf{x}\|_\star = 1} \|\mathbf{A}\mathbf{x}\|_\star\,.$$

The respective matrix norms that are induced by the 1- 2-, and ∞- vector norms are

$$\|\mathbf{A}\|_1 = \max_j \sum_i |a_{ij}| = \text{the largest absolute column sum},$$
$$\|\mathbf{A}\|_2 = \sqrt{\lambda_{\max}}, \quad \text{where } \lambda_{\max} = \text{largest eigenvalue of } \mathbf{A}^T\mathbf{A},$$
$$\text{(replace transpose by conjugate transpose if } \mathbf{A} \text{ is complex)},$$
$$\|\mathbf{A}\|_\infty = \max_i \sum_j |a_{ij}| = \text{the largest absolute row sum}.$$

The details surrounding these properties can be found in [127].

The nice thing about induced matrix norms is that each of them is *compatible* with its corresponding vector norm in the sense that

$$\|\mathbf{A}\mathbf{x}\|_\star \leq \|\mathbf{A}\|_\star \, \|\mathbf{x}\|_\star.$$

However, this compatibility condition holds only for right-hand matrix-vector multiplication. For left-hand vector-matrix multiplication, which is common in Markov chain applications, transposition is needed to convert back to right-hand matrix-vector multiplication, and this results in different compatibility rules. If $\mathbf{x}^T$ is $1 \times n$ and $\mathbf{A}$ is $m \times n$, then

$$\|\mathbf{x}^T\mathbf{A}\|_1 \leq \|\mathbf{x}^T\|_1 \, \|\mathbf{A}\|_\infty, \, \|\mathbf{x}^T\mathbf{A}\|_\infty \leq \|\mathbf{x}^T\|_\infty \, \|\mathbf{A}\|_1.$$

Sensitivity of Linear Systems

It is assumed that the reader is familiar with Gaussian elimination methods for solving a system $\mathbf{A}_{m\times n}\mathbf{x}_{n\times 1} = \mathbf{b}_{m\times 1}$ of m linear equations in n unknowns. If not, read [127]. Algorithms for solving $\mathbf{A}\mathbf{x} = \mathbf{b}$ are important, but the general behavior of a solution to small uncertainties or perturbations in the coefficients is particularly relevant, especially in light of the fact that the PageRank vector is the solution to a particular linear system.

While greater generality is possible, it suffices to consider a square nonsingular system $\mathbf{A}\mathbf{x} = \mathbf{b}$ in which both $\mathbf{A}$ and $\mathbf{b}$ are subject to uncertainties that might be the result of modeling error, numerical round-off error, measurement error, or small perturbations of any kind. How much uncertainty (or sensitivity) can the solution $\mathbf{x} = \mathbf{A}^{-1}\mathbf{b}$ exhibit?

An answer is provided by using calculus. Consider the entries of $\mathbf{A} = \mathbf{A}(t)$ and $\mathbf{b} = \mathbf{b}(t)$ to vary with a differentiable parameter t, and compute the relative size of the derivative of $\mathbf{x} = \mathbf{x}(t)$ by differentiating $\mathbf{b} = \mathbf{A}\mathbf{x}$ to obtain $\mathbf{b}' = (\mathbf{A}\mathbf{x})' = \mathbf{A}'\mathbf{x} + \mathbf{A}\mathbf{x}'$ (with $\star'$ denoting $d\star/dt$). Taking norms (the choice of norm is not important) yields

$$\begin{aligned}\|\mathbf{x}'\| &= \left\|\mathbf{A}^{-1}\mathbf{b}' - \mathbf{A}^{-1}\mathbf{A}'\mathbf{x}\right\| \leq \left\|\mathbf{A}^{-1}\mathbf{b}'\right\| + \left\|\mathbf{A}^{-1}\mathbf{A}'\mathbf{x}\right\| \\ &\leq \left\|\mathbf{A}^{-1}\right\| \|\mathbf{b}'\| + \left\|\mathbf{A}^{-1}\right\| \|\mathbf{A}'\| \|\mathbf{x}\|.\end{aligned}$$

Consequently,

$$\begin{aligned}\frac{\|\mathbf{x}'\|}{\|\mathbf{x}\|} &\leq \frac{\left\|\mathbf{A}^{-1}\right\| \|\mathbf{b}'\|}{\|\mathbf{x}\|} + \left\|\mathbf{A}^{-1}\right\| \|\mathbf{A}'\| \\ &\leq \|\mathbf{A}\| \left\|\mathbf{A}^{-1}\right\| \frac{\|\mathbf{b}'\|}{\|\mathbf{A}\| \|\mathbf{x}\|} + \|\mathbf{A}\| \left\|\mathbf{A}^{-1}\right\| \frac{\|\mathbf{A}'\|}{\|\mathbf{A}\|} \\ &\leq \kappa \frac{\|\mathbf{b}'\|}{\|\mathbf{b}\|} + \kappa \frac{\|\mathbf{A}'\|}{\|\mathbf{A}\|} = \kappa \left(\frac{\|\mathbf{b}'\|}{\|\mathbf{b}\|} + \frac{\|\mathbf{A}'\|}{\|\mathbf{A}\|} \right),\end{aligned}$$

where $\kappa = \|\mathbf{A}\| \left\|\mathbf{A}^{-1}\right\|$. The terms $\|\mathbf{x}'\| / \|\mathbf{x}\|$, $\|\mathbf{b}'\| / \|\mathbf{b}\|$ and $\|\mathbf{A}'\| / \|\mathbf{A}\|$ represent the respective relative sensitivities of $\mathbf{x}$, $\mathbf{b}$, and $\mathbf{A}$ to small changes. Because κ represents a magnification of the sum of the relative sensitivities in $\mathbf{b}$, and $\mathbf{A}$, κ is called a *condition number* for $\mathbf{A}$. The situation can summarize the situation as follows.

Sensitivity of Linear Systems

For a nonsingular system $\mathbf{A}\mathbf{x} = \mathbf{b}$, the relative sensitivity of $\mathbf{x}$ to uncertainties or perturbations in $\mathbf{A}$ and $\mathbf{b}$ is never more than the sum of the relative changes in $\mathbf{A}$ and $\mathbf{b}$ magnified by the condition number $\kappa = \|\mathbf{A}\| \left\|\mathbf{A}^{-1}\right\|$.

A Practical Rule of Thumb. If Gaussian elimination with partial pivoting is used to solve a well-scaled (row norms in $\mathbf{A}$ are approximately one) nonsingular system $\mathbf{A}\mathbf{x} = \mathbf{b}$ using t-digit floating-point arithmetic, and if κ is of order 10^p, then, assuming no other source of error exists, the computed solution can be expected to be accurate to at least $t - p$ significant digits, more or less. In other words, one expects to lose roughly p significant figures. This doesn't preclude the possibility of getting lucky and attaining a higher degree of accuracy—it just says that you shouldn't bet the farm on it.

Rank-One Updates

Suppose that $\mathbf{A} \in \Re^{n \times n}$ is the coefficient matrix of a nonsingular system $\mathbf{A}\mathbf{x} = \mathbf{b}$ that contains information that periodically requires updating, and each time new information is received, the system must be re-solved. Rather than starting from scratch each time, it makes sense to try to perturb the solution from the previous period in a simple but predictable way. Theoretically, the solution is always $\mathbf{x} = \mathbf{A}^{-1}\mathbf{b}$, so the problem of updating the solution to a linear system is equivalent to the problem of updating the inverse matrix $\mathbf{A}^{-1}$. If the new information can be formatted as a rank-one matrix $\mathbf{c}\mathbf{d}^T$, where $\mathbf{c}, \mathbf{d} \in \Re^{n \times 1}$, then there is a formula for updating $\mathbf{A}^{-1}$.

Sherman–Morrison Rank-One Updating Formula

If $\mathbf{A}_{n\times n}$ is nonsingular and if $\mathbf{c}$ and $\mathbf{d}$ are columns such that $1+\mathbf{d}^T\mathbf{A}^{-1}\mathbf{c}\neq 0$, then the sum $\mathbf{A}+\mathbf{c}\mathbf{d}^T$ is nonsingular, and

$$\left(\mathbf{A}+\mathbf{c}\mathbf{d}^T\right)^{-1}=\mathbf{A}^{-1}-\frac{\mathbf{A}^{-1}\mathbf{c}\mathbf{d}^T\mathbf{A}^{-1}}{1+\mathbf{d}^T\mathbf{A}^{-1}\mathbf{c}}. \tag{15.1.1}$$

The Sherman–Morrison formula makes it clear that when a nonsingular system $\mathbf{A}\mathbf{x}=\mathbf{b}$ is updated to produce another nonsingular system $(\mathbf{A}+\mathbf{c}\mathbf{d}^T)\mathbf{z}=\mathbf{b}$, where $\mathbf{b},\mathbf{c},\mathbf{d}\in\Re^{n\times 1}$, the solution of the updated system is

$$\begin{aligned}\mathbf{z}&=(\mathbf{A}+\mathbf{c}\mathbf{d}^T)^{-1}\mathbf{b}=\left(\mathbf{A}^{-1}-\frac{\mathbf{A}^{-1}\mathbf{c}\mathbf{d}^T\mathbf{A}^{-1}}{1+\mathbf{d}^T\mathbf{A}^{-1}\mathbf{c}}\right)\mathbf{b}\\&=\mathbf{A}^{-1}\mathbf{b}-\frac{\mathbf{A}^{-1}\mathbf{c}\mathbf{d}^T\mathbf{A}^{-1}\mathbf{b}}{1+\mathbf{d}^T\mathbf{A}^{-1}\mathbf{c}}=\mathbf{x}-\frac{\mathbf{A}^{-1}\mathbf{c}\mathbf{d}^T\mathbf{x}}{1+\mathbf{d}^T\mathbf{A}^{-1}\mathbf{c}}.\end{aligned}$$

The Sherman–Morrison formula is particularly useful when an update involves only one row or column of $\mathbf{A}$. For example, suppose that the only the ith row of $\mathbf{A}$ is affected—say row $\mathbf{A}_{i*}$ is updated to become $\mathbf{B}_{i*}$, and let $\boldsymbol{\epsilon}_i^T=\mathbf{B}_{i*}-\mathbf{A}_{i*}$. If $\mathbf{e}_i$ denotes the ith unit column (the ith column of the identity matrix $\mathbf{I}$), then the updated matrix can be written as

$$\mathbf{B}=\mathbf{A}+\mathbf{e}_i\boldsymbol{\epsilon}_i^T,$$

so that $\mathbf{e}_i$ plays the role of $\mathbf{c}$ in (15.1.1), and $\mathbf{A}^{-1}\mathbf{c}=\mathbf{A}^{-1}\mathbf{e}_i=[\mathbf{A}^{-1}]_{*i}$, the ith column of $\mathbf{A}^{-1}$. Consequently, $\mathbf{B}^{-1}$ can be constructed directly from the entries in $\mathbf{A}^{-1}$ and the perturbation vector $\boldsymbol{\epsilon}^T$ by writing.

$$\mathbf{B}^{-1}=\left(\mathbf{A}+\mathbf{e}_i\boldsymbol{\epsilon}_i^T\right)^{-1}=\mathbf{A}^{-1}-\frac{[\mathbf{A}^{-1}]_{*i}\boldsymbol{\epsilon}_i^T\mathbf{A}^{-1}}{1+\boldsymbol{\epsilon}_i^T[\mathbf{A}^{-1}]_{*i}}.$$

Eigenvalues and Eigenvectors

For a matrix $\mathbf{A}\in\mathcal{C}^{n\times n}$, the scalars λ and the vectors $\mathbf{x}_{n\times 1}\neq\mathbf{0}$ satisfying $\mathbf{A}\mathbf{x}=\lambda\mathbf{x}$ are the respective *eigenvalues* and *eigenvectors* for $\mathbf{A}$. A row vector $\mathbf{y}^T$ is a *left-hand eigenvector* if $\mathbf{y}^T\mathbf{A}=\lambda\mathbf{y}^T$.

The set $\sigma(\mathbf{A})$ of *distinct* eigenvalues is called the *spectrum* of $\mathbf{A}$, and the *spectral radius* of $\mathbf{A}$ is the nonnegative number

$$\rho(\mathbf{A})=\max_{\lambda\in\sigma(\mathbf{A})}|\lambda|.$$

The circle in the complex plane that is centered at the origin and has radius $\rho(\mathbf{A})$ is called the *spectral circle* , and it is a straightforward exercise to verify that

$$\rho(\mathbf{A})\leq\|\mathbf{A}\| \tag{15.1.2}$$

for all matrix norms.

The eigenvalues of $\mathbf{A}_{n\times n}$ are the roots of the characteristic polynomial $p(\lambda)=\det(\mathbf{A}-\lambda\mathbf{I})$, where $\det(\star)$ denotes determinant. The degree of $p(\lambda)$ is n, so, altogether,

$\mathbf{A}$ has n eigenvalues, but some may be complex numbers (even if the entries of $\mathbf{A}$ are real numbers), and some eigenvalues may be repeated. If $\mathbf{A}$ contains only real numbers, then its complex eigenvalues must occur in conjugate pairs—i.e., if $\lambda \in \sigma(\mathbf{A})$, then $\overline{\lambda} \in \sigma(\mathbf{A})$.

The *algebraic multiplicity* of an eigenvalue λ of $\mathbf{A}$ is the number of times that λ is repeated as a root of the characteristic equation. If $alg\ mult_{\mathbf{A}}(\lambda) = 1$, then λ is said to be a *simple eigenvalue.*

The *geometric multiplicity* of an eigenvalue λ of $\mathbf{A}$ is the number of linearly independent eigenvectors that are associated with λ. In more formal terms, $geo\ mult_{\mathbf{A}}(\lambda) = \dim N(\mathbf{A} - \lambda\mathbf{I})$, where $N(\star)$ denotes the nullspace or kernel of a matrix. It is always the case that $geo\ mult_{\mathbf{A}}(\lambda) \le alg\ mult_{\mathbf{A}}(\lambda)$. If $geo\ mult_{\mathbf{A}}(\lambda) = alg\ mult_{\mathbf{A}}(\lambda)$, then λ is said to be a *semisimple eigenvalue.*

The *index of an eigenvalue* $\lambda \in \sigma(\mathbf{A})$ is defined to be the smallest positive integer k such that $rank\left((\mathbf{A} - \lambda\mathbf{I})^k\right) = rank\left((\mathbf{A} - \lambda\mathbf{I})^{k+1}\right)$. It is understood that $index(\lambda) = 0$ when $\lambda \notin \sigma(\mathbf{A})$.

There are several different ways to characterize index. For $\lambda \in \sigma(\mathbf{A}_{n\times n})$, saying that $k = index(\lambda)$ is equivalent to saying that k is the smallest positive integer such that any of the following statements hold.

- $R\big((\mathbf{A} - \lambda\mathbf{I})^k\big) = R\big((\mathbf{A} - \lambda\mathbf{I})^{k+1}\big)$, where $R(\star)$ denotes range.
- $N\big((\mathbf{A} - \lambda\mathbf{I})^k\big) = N\big((\mathbf{A} - \lambda\mathbf{I})^{k+1}\big)$, where $N(\star)$ denotes nullspace (or kernel).
- $R\big((\mathbf{A} - \lambda\mathbf{I})^k\big) \cap N\big((\mathbf{A} - \lambda\mathbf{I})^k\big) = \mathbf{0}$.
- $\mathcal{C}^n = R\big((\mathbf{A} - \lambda\mathbf{I})^k\big) \oplus N\big((\mathbf{A} - \lambda\mathbf{I})^k\big)$, where $\oplus$ denotes direct sum.

The Jordan Form

Eigenvalues and eigenvectors are for matrices what DNA is for biological entities, and the Jordan form for a square matrix $\mathbf{A}$ completely characterizes the eigenstructure of $\mathbf{A}$. The theoretical basis for why the Jordan form looks as it does is somewhat involved, but the "form" itself is easy to understand, and that's all you need to deal with the issues that arise in understanding Web searching concepts.

Given a matrix $\mathbf{A}_{n\times n}$, a *Jordan block* associated with an eigenvalue $\lambda \in \sigma(\mathbf{A})$ is defined to be a matrix of the form

$$\mathbf{J}_\star(\lambda) = \begin{pmatrix} \lambda & 1 & & \\ & \ddots & \ddots & \\ & & \ddots & 1 \\ & & & \lambda \end{pmatrix}. \tag{15.1.3}$$

A *Jordan segment* $\mathbf{J}(\lambda)$ associated with $\lambda \in \sigma(\mathbf{A})$ is defined to be a block-diagonal matrix containing one or more Jordan blocks. In other words, a Jordan segment looks like

$$\mathbf{J}(\lambda) = \begin{pmatrix} \mathbf{J}_1(\lambda) & \mathbf{0} & \cdots & \mathbf{0} \\ \mathbf{0} & \mathbf{J}_2(\lambda) & \cdots & \mathbf{0} \\ \vdots & \vdots & \ddots & \vdots \\ \mathbf{0} & \mathbf{0} & \cdots & \mathbf{J}_t(\lambda) \end{pmatrix} \quad \text{with each } \mathbf{J}_\star(\lambda) \text{ being a Jordan block.}$$

The *Jordan canonical form* (or simply the *Jordan form*) for $\mathbf{A}$ is a block-diagonal matrix composed of the Jordan segments for each distinct eigenvalue. In other words, if $\sigma(\mathbf{A}) = \{\lambda_1, \lambda_2, \ldots, \lambda_s\}$, then the Jordan form for $\mathbf{A}$ is

$$\mathbf{J} = \begin{pmatrix} \mathbf{J}(\lambda_1) & \mathbf{0} & \cdots & \mathbf{0} \\ \mathbf{0} & \mathbf{J}(\lambda_2) & \cdots & \mathbf{0} \\ \vdots & \vdots & \ddots & \vdots \\ \mathbf{0} & \mathbf{0} & \cdots & \mathbf{J}(\lambda_s) \end{pmatrix}. \tag{15.1.4}$$

There is only one Jordan segment for each eigenvalue, but each segment can contain several Jordan blocks of varying size. The formula that governs the sizes and numbers of Jordan blocks is given in the following complete statement concerning the Jordan form.

Jordan's Theorem

For every $\mathbf{A} \in \mathcal{C}^{n \times n}$ there is a nonsingular matrix $\mathbf{P}$ such that

$$\mathbf{P}^{-1}\mathbf{A}\mathbf{P} = \mathbf{J} \tag{15.1.5}$$

is the Jordan form (15.1.4) that is characterized by the following features.

- $\mathbf{J}$ contains one Jordan segment $\mathbf{J}(\lambda)$ for each distinct eigenvalue $\lambda \in \sigma(\mathbf{A})$.
- Each segment $\mathbf{J}(\lambda)$ contains $t = \dim N(\mathbf{A} - \lambda\mathbf{I})$ Jordan blocks.
- The number of $i \times i$ Jordan blocks in $\mathbf{J}(\lambda)$ is given by

  $\nu_i(\lambda) = r_{i-1}(\lambda) - 2r_i(\lambda) + r_{i+1}(\lambda)$, where $r_i(\lambda) = rank\left((\mathbf{A} - \lambda\mathbf{I})^i\right)$.
- The largest Jordan block in each segment $\mathbf{J}(\lambda)$ is $k \times k$, where $k = index(\lambda)$.

The structure of $\mathbf{J}$ is unique in the sense that the number and sizes of the Jordan blocks in each segment is uniquely determined by the entries in $\mathbf{A}$. Two $n \times n$ matrices $\mathbf{A}$ and $\mathbf{B}$ are *similar* (i.e., $\mathbf{B} = \mathbf{Q}^{-1}\mathbf{A}\mathbf{Q}$ for some nonsingular $\mathbf{Q}$) if and only if $\mathbf{A}$ and $\mathbf{B}$ have the same Jordan form.

The matrix $\mathbf{P}$ in (15.1.5) is not unique, but its columns always form *Jordan chains* (or *generalized eigenvectors*) in the following sense. For each Jordan block $\mathbf{J}_\star(\lambda)$, there is a set of columns $\mathbf{P}_\star$ of corresponding size and position in $\mathbf{P} = \left[\cdots \,|\, \mathbf{P}_\star \,|\, \cdots\right]$ such that

$$\mathbf{P}_\star = \left[(\mathbf{A} - \lambda\mathbf{I})^i \mathbf{x}_\star \,\middle|\, (\mathbf{A} - \lambda\mathbf{I})^{i-1} \mathbf{x}_\star \,\middle|\, \cdots \,\middle|\, (\mathbf{A} - \lambda\mathbf{I}) \mathbf{x}_\star \,\middle|\, \mathbf{x}_\star \right]_{(i+1)\times n}$$

for some i and some $\mathbf{x}_\star$, where $(\mathbf{A} - \lambda\mathbf{I})^i \mathbf{x}_\star$ is a particular eigenvector associated with λ. Formulas exist for determining i and $\mathbf{x}_\star$ [127, p. 594], but the computations can be complicated. Fortunately, we rarely need to compute $\mathbf{P}$.

An important corollary of Jordan's theorem (15.1.5) is the following statement concerning the diagonalizability of a square matrix.

Diagonalizability

Each of the following statements is equivalent to saying that $\mathbf{A} \in \mathcal{C}^{n\times n}$ is similar to a diagonal matrix—i.e., $\mathbf{J}$ is diagonal (all Jordan blocks are 1×1).

- *index* $(\lambda) = 1$ for each $\lambda \in \sigma(\mathbf{A})$ (i.e., every eigenvalue is semisimple).
- *alg mult*$_{\mathbf{A}}(\lambda) =$ *geo mult*$_{\mathbf{A}}(\lambda)$ for each $\lambda \in \sigma(\mathbf{A})$.
- $\mathbf{A}$ has a complete set of n linearly independent eigenvectors (i.e., each column of $\mathbf{P}$ is an eigenvector for $\mathbf{A}$).

Functions of a Matrix

An important use of the Jordan form is to define functions of $\mathbf{A} \in \mathcal{C}^{n\times n}$. That is, given a function $f : \mathcal{C} \to \mathcal{C}$, what should $f(\mathbf{A})$ mean? The answer is straightforward. Suppose that $\mathbf{A} = \mathbf{PJP}^{-1}$, where $\mathbf{J} = \begin{pmatrix} \ddots & & \\ & \mathbf{J}_\star & \\ & & \ddots \end{pmatrix}$ is in Jordan form with the $\mathbf{J}_\star$'s representing the Jordan blocks described in (15.1.3) It's natural to define the value of f at $\mathbf{A}$ to be

$$f(\mathbf{A}) = \mathbf{P}f(\mathbf{J})\mathbf{P}^{-1} = \mathbf{P}\begin{pmatrix} \ddots & & \\ & f(\mathbf{J}_\star) & \\ & & \ddots \end{pmatrix}\mathbf{P}^{-1}, \tag{15.1.6}$$

but the trick is correctly defining $f(\mathbf{J}_\star)$. It turns out that right way to do this is by setting

$$f(\mathbf{J}_\star) = f\begin{pmatrix} \lambda & 1 & & \\ & \ddots & \ddots & \\ & & \ddots & 1 \\ & & & \lambda \end{pmatrix} = \begin{pmatrix} f(\lambda) & f'(\lambda) & \frac{f''(\lambda)}{2!} & \cdots & \frac{f^{(k-1)}(\lambda)}{(k-1)!} \\ & f(\lambda) & f'(\lambda) & \ddots & \vdots \\ & & \ddots & \ddots & \frac{f''(\lambda)}{2!} \\ & & & f(\lambda) & f'(\lambda) \\ & & & & f(\lambda) \end{pmatrix}. \tag{15.1.7}$$

Matrix Functions

Let $\mathbf{A} \in \mathcal{C}^{n\times n}$ with $\sigma(\mathbf{A}) = \{\lambda_1, \lambda_2, \ldots, \lambda_s\}$, and let $f : \mathcal{C} \to \mathcal{C}$ be such that $f(\lambda_i), f'(\lambda_i), \ldots, f^{(k_i-1)}(\lambda_i)$ exist for each i, where $k_i =$ *index* (λ_i). Define

$$f(\mathbf{A}) = \mathbf{P}f(\mathbf{J})\mathbf{P}^{-1} = \mathbf{P}\begin{pmatrix} \ddots & & \\ & f(\mathbf{J}_\star) & \\ & & \ddots \end{pmatrix}\mathbf{P}^{-1}, \tag{15.1.8}$$

where $\mathbf{J}$ is the Jordan form for $\mathbf{A}$ and $f(\mathbf{J}_\star)$ is given by (15.1.7).

There are at least two other equivalent and useful ways to view functions of matrices. The first of these is called the *spectral theorem for matrix functions,* and this arises by expanding the product on the right-hand side of (15.1.8) expand to yield the following.

Spectral Theorem for General Matrices

If $\mathbf{A} \in \mathcal{C}^{n\times n}$ with $\sigma(\mathbf{A}) = \{\lambda_1, \lambda_2, \ldots, \lambda_s\}$, then

$$f(\mathbf{A}) = \sum_{i=1}^{s}\sum_{j=0}^{k_i-1} \frac{f^{(j)}(\lambda_i)}{j!}(\mathbf{A} - \lambda_i\mathbf{I})^j\mathbf{G}_i, \tag{15.1.9}$$

where each $\mathbf{G}_i$ has the following properties.

- $\mathbf{G}_i$ is a projector (i.e., $\mathbf{G}_i^2 = \mathbf{G}_i$) onto $N\big((\mathbf{A}-\lambda_i\mathbf{I})^{k_i}\big)$ along $R\big((\mathbf{A}-\lambda_i\mathbf{I})^{k_i}\big)$.
- $\mathbf{G}_1 + \mathbf{G}_2 + \cdots + \mathbf{G}_s = \mathbf{I}$.
- $\mathbf{G}_i\mathbf{G}_j = \mathbf{0}$ when $i \neq j$.
- $(\mathbf{A}-\lambda_i\mathbf{I})\mathbf{G}_i = \mathbf{G}_i(\mathbf{A}-\lambda_i\mathbf{I})$ is nilpotent of index k_i.

The $\mathbf{G}_i$'s are called the *spectral projectors* associated with matrix $\mathbf{A}$.

Another useful way to deal with functions of a matrix is by means of infinite series.

Infinite Series Representations

If $\sum_{j=0}^{\infty} c_j(z-z_0)^j$ converges to $f(z)$ at each point in a circle $|z-z_0| = r$, and if $|\lambda - z_0| < r$ for each eigenvalue $\lambda \in \sigma(\mathbf{A})$, then $\sum_{j=0}^{\infty} c_j(\mathbf{A}-z_0\mathbf{I})^j$ converges, and

$$f(\mathbf{A}) = \sum_{j=0}^{\infty} c_j(\mathbf{A} - z_0\mathbf{I})^j.$$

If $\mathbf{A}$ is diagonalizable—i.e., if is similar to a diagonal matrix

$$\mathbf{A} = \mathbf{P}\begin{pmatrix} \lambda_1\mathbf{I} & \mathbf{0} & \cdots & \mathbf{0} \\ \mathbf{0} & \lambda_2\mathbf{I} & \cdots & \mathbf{0} \\ \vdots & \vdots & \ddots & \vdots \\ \mathbf{0} & \mathbf{0} & \cdots & \lambda_s\mathbf{I} \end{pmatrix}\mathbf{P}^{-1},$$

then

$$f(\mathbf{A}) = \mathbf{P}\begin{pmatrix} f(\lambda_1)\mathbf{I} & \mathbf{0} & \cdots & \mathbf{0} \\ \mathbf{0} & f(\lambda_2)\mathbf{I} & \cdots & \mathbf{0} \\ \vdots & \vdots & \ddots & \vdots \\ \mathbf{0} & \mathbf{0} & \cdots & f(\lambda_s)\mathbf{I} \end{pmatrix}\mathbf{P}^{-1},$$

and formula (15.1.9) yields the following spectral theorem for diagonalizable matrices

Spectral Theorem for Diagonalizable Matrices

If $\mathbf{A}$ is diagonalizable with with $\sigma(\mathbf{A}) = \{\lambda_1, \lambda_2, \ldots, \lambda_s\}$, then

$$\mathbf{A} = \lambda_1 \mathbf{G}_1 + \lambda_2 \mathbf{G}_2 + \cdots + \lambda_s \mathbf{G}_s, \tag{15.1.10}$$

and

$$f(\mathbf{A}) = f(\lambda_1)\mathbf{G}_1 + f(\lambda_2)\mathbf{G}_2 + \cdots + f(\lambda_s)\mathbf{G}_s, \tag{15.1.11}$$

where the spectral projectors $\mathbf{G}_i$ have the following properties.

- $\mathbf{G}_i = \mathbf{G}_i^2$ is the projector onto the eigenspace $N(\mathbf{A} - \lambda_i \mathbf{I})$ along $R(\mathbf{A} - \lambda_i \mathbf{I})$,
- $\mathbf{G}_1 + \mathbf{G}_2 + \cdots + \mathbf{G}_s = \mathbf{I}$,
- $\mathbf{G}_i \mathbf{G}_j = \mathbf{0}$ when $i \neq j$,
- $\mathbf{G}_i = \prod_{\substack{j=1 \\ j \neq i}}^{k} (\mathbf{A} - \lambda_j \mathbf{I}) \Big/ \prod_{\substack{j=1 \\ j \neq i}}^{k} (\lambda_i - \lambda_j) \quad \text{for } i = 1, 2, \ldots, k.$
- If λ_i happens to be a simple eigenvalue, then

$$\mathbf{G}_i = \mathbf{x}\mathbf{y}^* / \mathbf{y}^* \mathbf{x} \tag{15.1.12}$$

in which $\mathbf{x}$ and $\mathbf{y}^*$ are respective right-hand and left-hand eigenvectors associated with λ_i.

Powers of Matrices and Convergence

A fundamental issue in analyzing PageRank concerns convergence of powers of matrices. It follows from (15.1.8) that each power of $\mathbf{A} \in \mathcal{C}^{n \times n}$ is given by

$$\mathbf{A}^k = \mathbf{P}\mathbf{J}^k\mathbf{P}^{-1} = \mathbf{P}\begin{pmatrix} \ddots & & \\ & \mathbf{J}_\star^k & \\ & & \ddots \end{pmatrix}\mathbf{P}^{-1}, \quad \text{where} \quad \mathbf{J}_\star = \begin{pmatrix} \lambda & 1 & \\ & \ddots & \ddots \\ & & \lambda \end{pmatrix},$$

and

$$\mathbf{J}_\star^k = \begin{pmatrix} \lambda^k & \binom{k}{1}\lambda^{k-1} & \binom{k}{2}\lambda^{k-2} & \cdots & \binom{k}{m-1}\lambda^{k-m+1} \\ & \lambda^k & \binom{k}{1}\lambda^{k-1} & \ddots & \vdots \\ & & \ddots & \ddots & \binom{k}{2}\lambda^{k-2} \\ & & & \lambda^k & \binom{k}{1}\lambda^{k-1} \\ & & & & \lambda^k \end{pmatrix}_{m \times m}. \tag{15.1.13}$$

This observation leads to the following limiting properties.

Convergence to Zero and The Neumann Series

For $\mathbf{A} \in \mathcal{C}^{n\times n}$, the following statements are equivalent.

- $\rho(\mathbf{A}) < 1$. (15.1.14)
- $\lim_{k\to\infty} \mathbf{A}^k = \mathbf{0}$. (15.1.15)
- The *Neumann series* series $\sum_{k=0}^{\infty} \mathbf{A}^k$ converges to $(\mathbf{I} - \mathbf{A})^{-1}$. (15.1.16)

It may be the case that the powers $\mathbf{A}^k$ converge, but not to the zero matrix. The complete story concerning $\lim_{k\to\infty} \mathbf{A}^k$ is as follows.

Limits of Powers

For $\mathbf{A} \in \mathcal{C}^{n\times n}$, $\lim_{k\to\infty} \mathbf{A}^k$ exists if and only if $\rho(\mathbf{A}) < 1$, in which case $\lim_{k\to\infty} \mathbf{A}^k = \mathbf{0}$, or else $\rho(\mathbf{A}) = 1$, with $\lambda = 1$ being semisimple and the only eigenvalue on the unit circle. When it exists,

$$\lim_{k\to\infty} \mathbf{A}^k = \mathbf{G} = \text{the projector onto } N(\mathbf{I} - \mathbf{A}) \text{ along } R(\mathbf{I} - \mathbf{A}). \tag{15.1.17}$$

Averages and Summability

With each scalar sequence $\{\alpha_1, \alpha_2, \alpha_3, \ldots\}$ there is an associated sequence of averages $\{\mu_1, \mu_2, \mu_3, \ldots\}$ in which

$$\mu_1 = \alpha_1, \quad \mu_2 = \frac{\alpha_1 + \alpha_2}{2}, \quad \ldots, \quad \mu_n = \frac{\alpha_1 + \alpha_2 + \cdots + \alpha_n}{n}.$$

This sequence of averages is called the *Cesàro sequence*, and when $\lim_{n\to\infty} \mu_n = \alpha$, we say that $\{\alpha_n\}$ is *Cesàro summable* (or merely *summable*) to α. It can be proven that if $\{\alpha_n\}$ converges to α, then $\{\mu_n\}$ converges to α, but not conversely. In other words, convergence implies summability, but summability doesn't insure convergence. To see that a sequence can be summable without being convergent, notice that the oscillatory sequence $\{0, 1, 0, 1, \ldots\}$ doesn't converge, but it is summable to $1/2$, the mean value of $\{0, 1\}$. Averaging has a smoothing effect, so oscillations that prohibit convergence of the original sequence tend to be smoothed away or averaged out in the Cesàro sequence.

Similar statements hold for sequences of vectors and matrices, but Cesàro summability is particularly interesting when it is applied to the sequence $\mathcal{P} = \{\mathbf{A}^k\}_{k=0}^{\infty}$ of powers of a square matrix $\mathbf{A}$.

Summability

$\mathbf{A} \in \mathcal{C}^{n\times n}$ is Cesàro summable if and only if $\rho(\mathbf{A}) < 1$ or else $\rho(\mathbf{A}) = 1$ with each eigenvalue on the unit circle being semisimple. When it exists, the limit

$$\lim_{k\to\infty} \frac{\mathbf{I} + \mathbf{A} + \cdots + \mathbf{A}^{k-1}}{k} = \mathbf{G} \tag{15.1.18}$$

is the projector onto $N(\mathbf{I} - \mathbf{A})$ along $R(\mathbf{I} - \mathbf{A})$.

Notice that $\mathbf{G} \neq \mathbf{0}$ if and only if $1 \in \sigma(\mathbf{A})$, in which case $\mathbf{G}$ is the spectral projector associated with $\lambda = 1$. Furthermore, if $\lim_{k\to\infty} \mathbf{A}^k = \mathbf{G}$, then $\mathbf{A}$ is summable to $\mathbf{G}$, but not conversely.

The Power Method

Google's original method of choice for computing the PageRank vector was the *power method*, which is an iterative technique for computing a dominant eigenpair $(\lambda_1, \mathbf{x})$ of a diagonalizable matrix $\mathbf{A} \in \Re^{m\times m}$ with eigenvalues

$$|\lambda_1| > |\lambda_2| \geq |\lambda_3| \geq \cdots \geq |\lambda_k|.$$

For the Google matrix, the dominant eigenvalue is $\lambda_1 = 1$, but since the analysis of the power method is not dependent on this fact, we will allow λ_1 to be more general. However, notice that the hypothesis $|\lambda_1| > |\lambda_2|$ implies λ_1 is real—otherwise $\overline{\lambda}_1$ (the complex conjugate) is another eigenvalue with the same magnitude as λ_1. Consider the function $f(z) = (z/\lambda_1)^n$, and use the spectral representation (15.1.11) along with $|\lambda_i/\lambda_1| < 1$ for $i = 2, 3, \ldots, k$ to conclude that

$$\begin{aligned}\left(\frac{\mathbf{A}}{\lambda_1}\right)^n &= f(\mathbf{A}) = f(\lambda_1)\mathbf{G}_1 + f(\lambda_2)\mathbf{G}_2 + \cdots + f(\lambda_k)\mathbf{G}_k \\ &= \mathbf{G}_1 + \left(\frac{\lambda_2}{\lambda_1}\right)^n \mathbf{G}_2 + \cdots + \left(\frac{\lambda_k}{\lambda_1}\right)^n \mathbf{G}_k \to \mathbf{G}_1 \text{ as } n \to \infty. \end{aligned} \tag{15.1.19}$$

For every $\mathbf{x}_0$ we have $(\mathbf{A}^n\mathbf{x}_0/\lambda_1^n) \to \mathbf{G}_1\mathbf{x}_0 \in N(\mathbf{A} - \lambda_1\mathbf{I})$, so, if $\mathbf{G}_1\mathbf{x}_0 \neq \mathbf{0}$, then $\mathbf{A}^n\mathbf{x}_0/\lambda_1^n$ converges to an eigenvector associated with λ_1. This means that the direction of $\mathbf{A}^n\mathbf{x}_0$ tends toward the direction of an eigenvector because λ_1^n acts only as a scaling factor to keep the length of $\mathbf{A}^n\mathbf{x}_0$ under control. Rather than using λ_1^n, we can scale $\mathbf{A}^n\mathbf{x}_0$ with something more convenient. For example, $\|\mathbf{A}^n\mathbf{x}_0\|$ (for any vector norm) is a reasonable scaling factor, but there are better choices. For vectors $\mathbf{v}$, let $m(\mathbf{v})$ denote the component of maximal magnitude, and if there is more than one maximal component, let $m(\mathbf{v})$ be the *first* maximal component—e.g., $m(1, 3, -2) = 3$, and $m(-3, 3, -2) = -3$. The power method can be summarized as follows.

Power Method

Start with an arbitrary guess $\mathbf{x}_0$. (Actually it can't be completely arbitrary because you need $\mathbf{x}_0 \notin R(\mathbf{A} - \lambda_1\mathbf{I})$ to ensure $\mathbf{G}_1\mathbf{x}_0 \neq \mathbf{0}$, but it's highly unlikely that randomly chosen vector $\mathbf{x}_0$ will satisfy $\mathbf{G}_1\mathbf{x}_0 = \mathbf{0}$.) It can be shown [127, p. 534] that if we set

$$\mathbf{y}_n = \mathbf{A}\mathbf{x}_n, \quad \nu_n = m(\mathbf{y}_n), \quad \mathbf{x}_{n+1} = \frac{\mathbf{y}_n}{\nu_n}, \quad \text{for } n = 0, 1, 2, \ldots, \tag{15.1.20}$$

then $\mathbf{x}_n \to \mathbf{x}$ and $\nu_n \to \lambda_1$, where $\mathbf{A}\mathbf{x} = \lambda_1\mathbf{x}$.

There are several reasons why the power method might be attractive for computing Google's PageRank vector.

- Each iteration requires only one matrix-vector product, and this can be exploited to reduce the computational effort when $\mathbf{A}$ is large and sparse (mostly zeros), as is the case in Google's application.
- Computations can be done in parallel by simultaneously computing inner products of rows of $\mathbf{A}$ with $\mathbf{x}_n$.
- It's clear from (15.1.19) that, for a diagonalizable matrix, the rate at which (15.1.20) converges depends on how fast $(\lambda_2/\lambda_1)^n \to 0$. As discussed in section 4.7, Google can regulate $|\lambda_2|$ through the choice of the Google parameter α, so they can control the rate of convergence (it's just assumed that Google's matrix is diagonalizable).
- Since $\lambda_1 = 1$ for Google's PageRank problem, there is no need for the scaling factor ν_n. In other words, the iterations are simply $\mathbf{x}_{n+1} = \mathbf{A}\mathbf{x}_n$.

Linear Stationary Iterations

Solving systems of linear equations $\mathbf{A}_{n\times n}\mathbf{x} = \mathbf{b}$ is a frequent necessity for Web search applications, but the magnitude of n is usually too large for direct solution methods based on Gaussian elimination to be effective. Consequently, iterative techniques are often the only choice, and, because of size, sparsity, and memory considerations, the preferred algorithms are the simpler methods based on matrix-vector products that require no additional storage beyond that of the original data. Linear stationary iterative methods are the most common.

Linear Stationary Iterations

Let $\mathbf{Ax} = \mathbf{b}$ be a linear system that is square but otherwise arbitrary. Writing $\mathbf{A}$ as $\mathbf{A} = \mathbf{M} - \mathbf{N}$ in which $\mathbf{M}^{-1}$ exists is called a *splitting* of $\mathbf{A}$, and the product $\mathbf{H} = \mathbf{M}^{-1}\mathbf{N}$ is called the associated *iteration matrix*. For $\mathbf{d} = \mathbf{M}^{-1}\mathbf{b}$ and for an initial vector $\mathbf{x}(0)$, the sequence defined by

$$\mathbf{x}(k) = \mathbf{Hx}(k-1) + \mathbf{d} \qquad k = 1, 2, 3, \ldots \tag{15.1.21}$$

is called a *linear stationary iteration*. The primary result governing the convergence of (15.1.21) is the fact that if $\rho(\mathbf{H}) < 1$, then $\mathbf{A}$ is nonsingular, and

$$\lim_{k\to\infty} \mathbf{x}(k) = \mathbf{x} = \mathbf{A}^{-1}\mathbf{b} \quad \text{(the solution to } \mathbf{Ax} = \mathbf{b}\text{) for every } \mathbf{x}(0). \tag{15.1.22}$$

In theory, the convergence rate of (15.1.21) is governed by the size of $\rho(\mathbf{H})$ along with the index of its associated eigenvalue—look at (15.1.13). But for practical work an indication of how many digits of accuracy can be expected to be gained per iteration is needed. Suppose that $\mathbf{H}_{n\times n}$ is diagonalizable with

$$\sigma(\mathbf{H}) = \{\lambda_1, \lambda_2, \ldots, \lambda_s\}, \quad \text{where} \quad 1 > |\lambda_1| > |\lambda_2| \geq |\lambda_3| \geq \cdots \geq |\lambda_s|$$

(which is frequently the case in applications), and let $\boldsymbol{\epsilon}(k) = \mathbf{x}(k) - \mathbf{x}$ denote the error after the kth iteration. Subtracting $\mathbf{x} = \mathbf{Hx} + \mathbf{d}$ (the limiting value in (15.1.21)) from $\mathbf{x}(k) = \mathbf{Hx}(k-1) + \mathbf{d}$ produces (for large k)

$$\boldsymbol{\epsilon}(k) = \mathbf{H}\boldsymbol{\epsilon}(k-1) = \mathbf{H}^k\boldsymbol{\epsilon}(0) = (\lambda_1^k\mathbf{G}_1 + \lambda_2^k\mathbf{G}_2 + \cdots + \lambda_s^k\mathbf{G}_s)\boldsymbol{\epsilon}(0) \approx \lambda_1^k\mathbf{G}_1\boldsymbol{\epsilon}(0),$$

where the $\mathbf{G}_i$'s are the spectral projectors occurring in the spectral decomposition (15.1.11) of $\mathbf{H}^k$. Similarly, $\boldsymbol{\epsilon}(k-1) \approx \lambda_1^{k-1}\mathbf{G}_1\boldsymbol{\epsilon}(0)$, so comparing the ith components of $\boldsymbol{\epsilon}(k-1)$ and $\boldsymbol{\epsilon}(k)$ reveals that after several iterations,

$$\left|\frac{\epsilon_i(k-1)}{\epsilon_i(k)}\right| \approx \frac{1}{|\lambda_1|} = \frac{1}{\rho(\mathbf{H})} \quad \text{for each} \quad i = 1, 2, \ldots, n.$$

To understand the significance of this, suppose for example that

$$|\epsilon_i(k-1)| = 10^{-q} \quad \text{and} \quad |\epsilon_i(k)| = 10^{-p} \quad \text{with} \quad p \geq q > 0,$$

so that the error in each entry is reduced by $p - q$ digits per iteration, and we have

$$p - q = \log_{10}\left|\frac{\epsilon_i(k-1)}{\epsilon_i(k)}\right| \approx -\log_{10}\rho(\mathbf{H}).$$

Below is a summary.

Asymptotic Convergence Rate

The number $R = -\log_{10}\rho(\mathbf{H})$, called the *asymptotic convergence rate* for (15.1.21), is used to compare different linear stationary iterative algorithms because it is an indication of the number of digits of accuracy that can be expected to be eventually gained on each iteration of $\mathbf{x}(k) = \mathbf{Hx}(k-1) + \mathbf{d}$.

Each different splitting $\mathbf{A} = \mathbf{M} - \mathbf{N}$ produces a different iterative algorithm, but there are three particular splittings that have found widespread use.

The Three Classical Splittings

- **Jacobi's method** is the result of splitting $\mathbf{A} = \mathbf{D} - \mathbf{N}$, where $\mathbf{D}$ is the diagonal part of $\mathbf{A}$ (assuming each $a_{ii} \neq 0$), and $(-\mathbf{N})$ is the matrix containing the off-diagonal entries of $\mathbf{A}$. The Jacobi iteration is $\mathbf{x}(k) = \mathbf{D}^{-1}\mathbf{N}\mathbf{x}(k-1) + \mathbf{D}^{-1}\mathbf{b}$.

- **The Gauss-Seidel method** is the result of splitting $\mathbf{A} = (\mathbf{D} - \mathbf{L}) - \mathbf{U}$, where $\mathbf{D}$ is the diagonal part of $\mathbf{A}$ (assuming each $a_{ii} \neq 0$), and where $(-\mathbf{L})$ and $(-\mathbf{U})$ contain the entries occurring below and above the diagonal of $\mathbf{A}$, respectively. The iteration matrix is $\mathbf{H} = (\mathbf{D} - \mathbf{L})^{-1}\mathbf{U}$, and $\mathbf{d} = (\mathbf{D} - \mathbf{L})^{-1}\mathbf{b}$. The Gauss-Seidel iteration is $\mathbf{x}(k) = (\mathbf{D} - \mathbf{L})^{-1}\mathbf{U}\mathbf{x}(k-1) + (\mathbf{D} - \mathbf{L})^{-1}\mathbf{b}$.

- **The successive overrelaxation (SOR) method** incorporates a *relaxation parameter* $\omega \neq 0$ into the Gauss-Seidel method to build a splitting $\mathbf{A} = \mathbf{M} - \mathbf{N}$, where $\mathbf{M} = \omega^{-1}\mathbf{D} - \mathbf{L}$ and $\mathbf{N} = (\omega^{-1} - 1)\mathbf{D} + \mathbf{U}$.

It can be shown that Jacobi's method as well as the Gauss-Seidel method converge when $\mathbf{A}$ is *diagonally dominant* (i.e., when $|a_{ii}| > \sum_{j \neq i} |a_{ij}|$ for each $i = 1, 2, \ldots, n$.) This along with other convergence details can be found in [127].

M-matrices

Because the PageRank vector can be view as the solution to a Markov chain, and because $\mathbf{I} - \mathbf{P}$ is an M-matrix whenever $\mathbf{P}$ is a probability transition matrix, it's handy to know a few facts about M-matrices (named in honor Hermann Minkowski).

M-matrices

A square (real) matrix $\mathbf{A}$ is called an M-matrix whenever there exists a matrix $\mathbf{B} \geq \mathbf{0}$ (i.e., $b_{ij} \geq 0$) and a real number $r \geq \rho(\mathbf{B})$ such that $\mathbf{A} = r\mathbf{I} - \mathbf{B}$.

If $r > \rho(\mathbf{B})$ in the above definition then $\mathbf{A}$ is a *nonsingular* M-matrix. Below are some of the important properties of nonsingular M-matrices.

- $\mathbf{A}$ is a nonsingular M-matrix if and only if $a_{ij} \leq 0$ for all $i \neq j$ and $\mathbf{A}^{-1} \geq \mathbf{0}$.

- If $\mathbf{A}$ is a nonsingular M-matrix, then $\text{Re}(\lambda) > 0$ for all $\lambda \in \sigma(\mathbf{A})$. Conversely, all matrices with nonpositive off-diagonal entries whose spectrums are in the right-hand halfplane are nonsingular M-matrices.

- Principal submatrices of nonsingular M-matrices are also nonsingular M-matrices.

- If $\mathbf{A}$ is an M-matrix, then all of its principal minors are nonnegative. If $\mathbf{A}$ is a nonsingular M-matrix, then all principal minors are positive.

- All matrices with nonpositive off-diagonal entries whose principal minors are nonnegative are M-matrices. All matrices with nonpositive off-diagonal entries whose principal minors are positive are nonsingular M-matrices.
- If $\mathbf{A} = \mathbf{M} - \mathbf{N}$ is a splitting of a nonsingular M-matrix for which $\mathbf{M}^{-1} \geq \mathbf{0}$, then the linear stationary iteration (15.1.21) converges for all initial vectors $\mathbf{x}(0)$ and for all right-hand sides $\mathbf{b}$. In particular, Jacobi's method converges.

15.2 PERRON–FROBENIUS THEORY

At a mathematics conference held a few years ago our friend Hans Schneider gave a memorable presentation titled "Why I Love Perron–Frobenius" in which he made the case that the Perron–Frobenius theory of nonnegative matrices is not only among the most elegant theories in mathematics, but it is also among the most useful. One might sum up Hans's point by saying that Perron–Frobenius is a testament to the fact that beautiful mathematics eventually tends to be useful, and useful mathematics eventually tends to be beautiful. The applications involving PageRank, HITS, and other ranking schemes [103] help to underscore this principle.

A matrix $\mathbf{A}$ is said to be *nonnegative* when each entry is a nonnegative number (denote this by writing $\mathbf{A} \geq \mathbf{0}$). Similarly, $\mathbf{A}$ is a *positive matrix* when each $a_{ij} > 0$ (write $\mathbf{A} > \mathbf{0}$). For example, the hyperlink matrix $\mathbf{H}$ and the stochastic matrix $\mathbf{S}$ (from Chapter 4) that are at the foundation of PageRank are nonnegative matrices, and the Google matrix $\mathbf{G}$ is a positive matrix. Consequently, properties of positive and nonnegative matrices govern the behavior of PageRank, and the Perron–Frobenius theory reveals these properties by describing the nature of the dominant eigenvalues and eigenvectors of positive and nonnegative matrices.

Perron

So much of the mathematics of PageRank, HITS, and associated ideas involves nonnegative matrices and graphs. This section provides you with the needed ammunition to handle these concepts. Perron's 1907 theorem provides the insight for understanding the eigenstructure of positive matrices. Perron's theorem for positive matrices is stated below, and the proof is in [127].

Perron's Theorem for Positive Matrices

If $\mathbf{A}_{n\times n} > \mathbf{0}$ with $r = \rho(\mathbf{A})$, then the following statements are true.

1. $r > 0$.
2. $r \in \sigma(\mathbf{A})$ (r is called the *Perron root*).
3. $alg\ mult_{\mathbf{A}}(r) = 1$ (the Perron root is simple).
4. There exists an eigenvector $\mathbf{x} > \mathbf{0}$ such that $\mathbf{A}\mathbf{x} = r\mathbf{x}$.
5. The *Perron vector* is the unique vector defined by

$$\mathbf{A}\mathbf{p} = r\mathbf{p}, \qquad \mathbf{p} > \mathbf{0}, \|\mathbf{p}\|_1 = 1,$$

   and, except for positive multiples of $\mathbf{p}$, there are no other nonnegative eigenvectors for $\mathbf{A}$, regardless of the eigenvalue.

6. r is the only eigenvalue on the spectral circle of $\mathbf{A}$.
7. $r = \max_{\mathbf{x}\in\mathcal{N}} f(\mathbf{x})$, (the Collatz–Wielandt formula),

$$\text{where } f(\mathbf{x}) = \min_{\substack{1\le i\le n\\ x_i\neq 0}} \frac{[\mathbf{A}\mathbf{x}]_i}{x_i} \text{ and } \mathcal{N} = \{\mathbf{x} \,|\, \mathbf{x} \geq \mathbf{0} \text{ with } \mathbf{x} \neq \mathbf{0}\}.$$

Extensions to Nonnegative Matrices

Perron's theorem for positive matrices is a powerful result, so it's only natural to ask what happens when zero entries creep into the picture. Not all is lost if we are willing to be flexible. The next theorem (the proof of which is in [127]) says that a portion of Perron's theorem for positive matrices can be extended to nonnegative matrices by sacrificing the existence of a positive eigenvector for a nonnegative one.

Perron's Theorem for Nonnegative Matrices

For $\mathbf{A}_{n\times n} \geq \mathbf{0}$ with $r = \rho(\mathbf{A})$, the following statements are true.

- $r \in \sigma(\mathbf{A})$, (but $r = 0$ is possible).
- There exists an eigenvector $\mathbf{x} \geq \mathbf{0}$ such that $\mathbf{A}\mathbf{x} = r\mathbf{x}$.
- The Collatz–Wielandt formula remains valid.

Frobenius

This is as far as Perron's theorem can be generalized to nonnegative matrices without additional hypothesis. For example, $\mathbf{A} = \begin{pmatrix} 0 & 1 \\ 0 & 0 \end{pmatrix}$ shows that properties 1, 3, and 4 in Perron's theorem for positive matrices do not hold for general nonnegative matrices, and

$\mathbf{A} = \begin{pmatrix} 0 & 1 \\ 1 & 0 \end{pmatrix}$ shows that property 6 is also lost. Rather than accepting that the major issues concerning spectral properties of nonnegative matrices had been settled, F. G. Frobenius had the insight in 1912 to look below the surface and see that the problem doesn't stem just from the existence of zero entries, but rather from the positions of the zero entries. For example, properties 3 and 4 in Perron's theorem do not hold for

$$\mathbf{A} = \begin{pmatrix} 1 & 0 \\ 1 & 1 \end{pmatrix}, \text{ but they are valid for } \mathbf{B} = \begin{pmatrix} 1 & 1 \\ 1 & 0 \end{pmatrix}.$$

Frobenius's genius was to see that the difference between **A** and **B** is in terms of matrix reducibility (or irreducibility) and to relate these ideas to spectral properties of nonnegative matrices. The next section introduces these ideas.

Graph and Irreducible Matrices

A *graph* is a set of nodes $\{N_1, N_2, \ldots, N_n\}$ and a set of edges $\{E_1, E_2, \ldots, E_k\}$ between the nodes. A *connected graph* is one in which there is a sequence of edges linking any pair of nodes. For example, the graph shown on the right-hand side of Figure 15.1 is undirected and connected.

A *directed graph* is a graph containing directed edges. A directed graph is said to be *strongly connected* if for each pair of nodes (N_i, N_k) there is a sequence of directed edges leading from N_i to N_k. The graph on the left-hand side of Figure 15.1 is directed but *not* strongly connected (e.g., you can't get from N_3 to N_1).

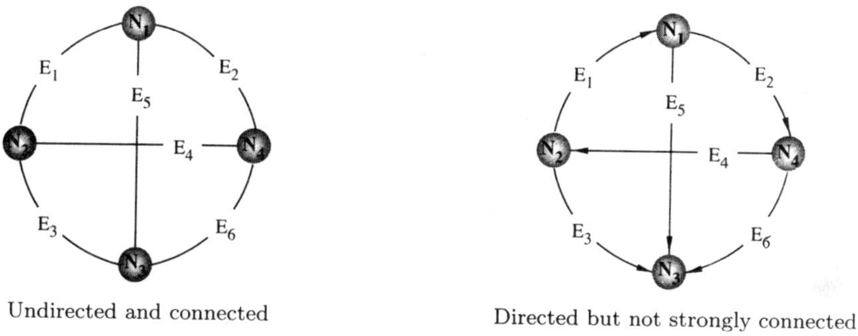

Figure 15.1

Each graph defines two useful matrices—an *adjacency matrix* and an *incidence matrix*. For a graph $\mathcal{G}$ containing nodes $\{N_1, N_2, \ldots, N_n\}$, the *adjacency matrix* $\mathbf{L}_{n\times n}$ is the $(0, 1)$-matrix having

$$l_{ij} = \begin{cases} 1 & \text{if there is an edge from } N_i \text{ to } N_j, \\ 0 & \text{otherwise.} \end{cases}$$

If $\mathcal{G}$ is undirected, then its adjacency matrix $\mathbf{L}$ is symmetric (i.e., $\mathbf{L} = \mathbf{L}^T$). For example, the adjacency matrices for the two graphs shown in Figure 15.1 are

$$\mathbf{L}_1 = \begin{array}{c} \\ N_1 \\ N_2 \\ N_3 \\ N_4 \end{array} \!\!\! \begin{array}{c} \begin{array}{cccc} N_1 & N_2 & N_3 & N_4 \end{array} \\ \begin{pmatrix} 0 & 1 & 1 & 1 \\ 1 & 0 & 1 & 1 \\ 1 & 1 & 0 & 1 \\ 1 & 1 & 1 & 0 \end{pmatrix} \end{array} \quad \mathbf{L}_2 = \begin{array}{c} \\ N_1 \\ N_2 \\ N_3 \\ N_4 \end{array} \!\!\! \begin{array}{c} \begin{array}{cccc} N_1 & N_2 & N_3 & N_4 \end{array} \\ \begin{pmatrix} 0 & 0 & 1 & 1 \\ 1 & 0 & 1 & 0 \\ 0 & 0 & 0 & 0 \\ 0 & 1 & 1 & 0 \end{pmatrix} \end{array}$$

For an undirected graph $\mathcal{G}$ with nodes $\{N_1, N_2, \ldots, N_n\}$ and edges $\{E_1, E_2, \ldots, E_k\}$, the *incidence matrix* $\mathbf{C}_{n \times k}$ is the $(0,1)$-matrix having

$$c_{ij} = \begin{cases} 1 & \text{if node } N_i \text{ touches edge } E_j, \\ 0 & \text{otherwise.} \end{cases}$$

If $\mathcal{G}$ is a directed graph, then its incidence matrix is the $(0,-1,1)$-matrix having

$$c_{ij} = \begin{cases} 1 & \text{if edge } E_j \text{ is directed } \textit{toward} \text{ node } N_i, \\ -1 & \text{if edge } E_j \text{ is directed } \textit{away from} \text{ node } N_i, \\ 0 & \text{if edge } E_j \text{ neither begins nor ends at node } N_i. \end{cases}$$

For example, the incidence matrices for the two graphs shown in Figure 15.1 are

$$\mathbf{C}_1 = \begin{array}{c} \\ N_1 \\ N_2 \\ N_3 \\ N_4 \end{array} \!\!\! \begin{array}{c} \begin{array}{cccccc} E_1 & E_2 & E_3 & E_4 & E_5 & E_6 \end{array} \\ \begin{pmatrix} 1 & 1 & 0 & 0 & 1 & 0 \\ 1 & 0 & 1 & 1 & 0 & 0 \\ 0 & 0 & 1 & 0 & 1 & 1 \\ 0 & 1 & 0 & 1 & 0 & 1 \end{pmatrix} \end{array} \text{ and } \mathbf{C}_2 = \begin{array}{c} \\ N_1 \\ N_2 \\ N_3 \\ N_4 \end{array} \!\!\! \begin{array}{c} \begin{array}{cccccc} E_1 & E_2 & E_3 & E_4 & E_5 & E_6 \end{array} \\ \begin{pmatrix} 1 & -1 & 0 & 0 & -1 & 0 \\ -1 & 0 & -1 & 1 & 0 & 0 \\ 0 & 0 & 1 & 0 & 1 & 1 \\ 0 & 1 & 0 & -1 & 0 & -1 \end{pmatrix} \end{array}.$$

There is a direct connection between the connectivity of a directed graph and the rank of its incidence matrix.

Connectivity and Rank

A directed graph with n nodes and incidence matrix $\mathbf{C}$ is connected if and only if

$$rank\,(\mathbf{C}) = n - 1. \tag{15.2.1}$$

For undirected graphs, arbitrarily assign directions to the edges to make the graph directed and apply (15.2.1) [127, p. 203].

Instead of starting with a graph to build a matrix, we can also do it in reverse—i.e., start with a matrix and build a graph. Given a matrix $\mathbf{A}_{n \times n}$, the graph of $\mathbf{A}$ is defined to be the *directed* graph $\mathcal{G}(\mathbf{A})$ on a set of nodes $\{N_1, N_2, \ldots, N_n\}$ in which there is a directed edge leading *from* N_i *to* N_j if and only if $a_{ij} \neq 0$. For example, if $\mathbf{A} = \begin{pmatrix} 1 & 0 \\ 2 & 3 \end{pmatrix}$, then the graph $\mathcal{G}(\mathbf{A})$ looks like this:

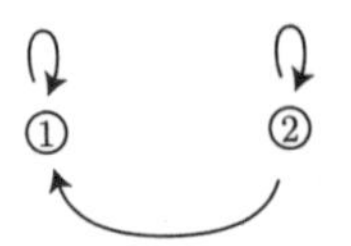

Any product of the form $\mathbf{P}^T\mathbf{AP}$ in which $\mathbf{P}$ is a permutation matrix (a matrix obtained from the identity matrix $\mathbf{I}$ by permuting its rows or columns) is called a *symmetric permutation* of $\mathbf{A}$. The effect of a symmetric permutation to a matrix is to interchange rows in the same way as columns are interchanged. The effect of a symmetric permutation on the graph of a matrix is to relabel the nodes. Consequently, the directed graph of a matrix in invariant under a symmetric permutation. In other words, $\mathcal{G}(\mathbf{P}^T\mathbf{AP}) = \mathcal{G}(\mathbf{A})$ whenever $\mathbf{P}$ is a permutation matrix. For example, if $\mathbf{P}$ is the permutation matrix $\mathbf{P} = \begin{pmatrix} 0 & 1 \\ 1 & 0 \end{pmatrix}$, and if we again use $\mathbf{A} = \begin{pmatrix} 1 & 0 \\ 2 & 3 \end{pmatrix}$, then

$$\mathbf{P}^T\mathbf{AP} = \begin{pmatrix} 3 & 2 \\ 0 & 1 \end{pmatrix}, \tag{15.2.2}$$

and the graph $\mathcal{G}(\mathbf{P}^T\mathbf{AP})$ looks like this:

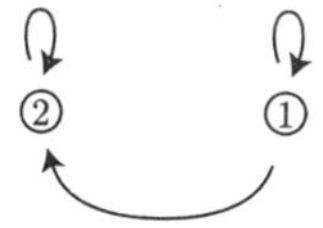

Matrix $\mathbf{A}_{n\times n}$ is said to be a *reducible matrix* when there exists a permutation matrix $\mathbf{P}$ such that

$$\mathbf{P}^T\mathbf{AP} = \begin{pmatrix} \mathbf{X} & \mathbf{Y} \\ \mathbf{0} & \mathbf{Z} \end{pmatrix}, \quad \text{where } \mathbf{X} \text{ and } \mathbf{Z} \text{ are both square.} \tag{15.2.3}$$

For example, the matrix $\mathbf{A}$ in (15.2.2) is clearly reducible. Naturally, an *irreducible matrix* is a matrix that is not reducible.

As the following theorem shows, the concepts of matrix irreducibility (or reducibility) and strong connectivity (or lack thereof) are intimately related.

Irreducibility and Connectivity

A square matrix $\mathbf{A}$ is irreducible if and only if its directed graph is strongly connected. In other words, $\mathbf{A}$ is irreducible if and only if for each pair of indices (i, j) there is a sequence of entries in $\mathbf{A}$ such that $a_{ik_1}a_{k_1k_2}\cdots a_{k_tj} \neq 0$. Equivalently, $\mathbf{A}$ is irreducible if for all permutation matrices $\mathbf{P}$,

$$\mathbf{P}^T\mathbf{AP} \neq \begin{pmatrix} \mathbf{X} & \mathbf{Y} \\ \mathbf{0} & \mathbf{Z} \end{pmatrix}, \quad \text{where } \mathbf{X} \text{ and } \mathbf{Z} \text{ are square.}$$

For example, can you determine if

$$\mathbf{A} = \begin{pmatrix} 0 & 1 & 2 & 0 & 0 \\ 0 & 0 & 0 & 7 & 0 \\ 2 & 0 & 0 & 0 & 0 \\ 0 & 9 & 2 & 0 & 4 \\ 0 & 0 & 0 & 1 & 0 \end{pmatrix}$$

is reducible or irreducible? It would be a mistake to try to use the definition because deciding on whether or not there exists a permutation matrix $\mathbf{P}$ such that (15.2.3) holds by sorting through all 6×6 permutation matrices is pretty hard. However, the above theorem makes the question easy. Examining $\mathcal{G}(\mathbf{A})$ reveals that it is strongly connected (every node is accessible by some sequence of paths from every other node), so $\mathbf{A}$ must be irreducible.

The Perron–Frobenius Theorem

Frobenius's contribution was to realize that while properties 1, 3, 4, and 6 in Perron's theorem for positive matrices can be lost when zeros creep into the picture (i.e., for nonnegative matrices), the trouble is not simply the existence of zero entries, but rather the problem is the location of the zero entries. In other words, Frobenius realized that the lost properties 1, 3, and 4 are in fact *not lost* when the zeros are in just the right locations—namely the locations that ensure that the matrix is irreducible. Unfortunately irreducibility alone still does not save property 6—it remains lost (more about this issue later).

Below is the formal statement of the Perron–Frobenius theorem—the details concerning the proof can be found in [127].

Perron–Frobenius Theorem

If $\mathbf{A}_{n\times n} \geq \mathbf{0}$ is irreducible, then each of the following is true.

1. $r = \rho(\mathbf{A}) > 0$.
2. $r \in \sigma(\mathbf{A})$ (r is the *Perron root*).
3. $alg\ mult_{\mathbf{A}}(r) = 1$. (the Perron root is simple).
4. There exists an eigenvector $\mathbf{x} > \mathbf{0}$ such that $\mathbf{A}\mathbf{x} = r\mathbf{x}$.
5. The *Perron vector* is the unique vector defined by
$$\mathbf{A}\mathbf{p} = r\mathbf{p}, \qquad \mathbf{p} > \mathbf{0}, \|\mathbf{p}\|_1 = 1,$$
and, except for positive multiples of $\mathbf{p}$, there are no other nonnegative eigenvectors for $\mathbf{A}$, regardless of the eigenvalue.
6. r need not be the only eigenvalue on the spectral circle of $\mathbf{A}$.
7. $r = \max_{\mathbf{x}\in\mathcal{N}} f(\mathbf{x})$, (the Collatz–Wielandt formula),
$$\text{where } f(\mathbf{x}) = \min_{\substack{1\leq i\leq n\\ x_i\neq 0}} \frac{[\mathbf{A}\mathbf{x}]_i}{x_i} \text{ and } \mathcal{N} = \{\mathbf{x} \mid \mathbf{x} \geq \mathbf{0} \text{ with } \mathbf{x} \neq \mathbf{0}\}.$$

Primitive Matrices

The only property in Perron's theorem for positive matrices on page 168 that irreducibility is not able to salvage is the sixth property, which states that there is only one eigenvalue on the spectral circle. Indeed, $\mathbf{A} = \begin{pmatrix} 0 & 1 \\ 1 & 0 \end{pmatrix}$ is nonnegative and irreducible, but the eigenvalues ± 1 are both on the unit circle. The property of having (or not having) only one eigenvalue on the spectral circle divides the set of nonnegative irreducible matrices into two important classes.

Primitive Matrices

- A matrix $\mathbf{A}$ is defined to be a *primitive matrix* when $\mathbf{A}$ is a nonnegative irreducible matrix that has only one eigenvalue, $r = \rho(\mathbf{A})$, on its spectral circle.
- A nonnegative irreducible matrix having $h > 1$ eigenvalues on its spectral circle is said to be *imprimitive,* and h is called the *index of imprimitivity.*
- If $\mathbf{A}$ is imprimitive, then the h eigenvalues on the spectral circle are

$$\{r, r\omega, r\omega^2, \ldots, r\omega^{h-1}\}, \quad \text{where} \quad \omega = e^{2\pi i/h}.$$

  In other words, they are the hth roots of $r = \rho(\mathbf{A})$, and they are uniformly spaced around the circle. Furthermore each eigenvalue $r\omega^k$ on the spectral circle is simple.

So what's the big deal about having only one eigenvalue on the spectral circle? Well, primitivity is important because it's precisely what determines whether or not the powers of a normalized nonnegative irreducible matrix will have a limiting value, and this is the fundamental issue concerning the existence of the PageRank vector. The precise wording of the theorem is as follows.

Limits and Primitivity

A nonnegative irreducible matrix $\mathbf{A}$ with $r = \rho(\mathbf{A})$ is primitive if and only if $\lim_{k\to\infty}(\mathbf{A}/r)^k$ exists, in which case

$$\lim_{k\to\infty}\left(\frac{\mathbf{A}}{r}\right)^k = \frac{\mathbf{p}\mathbf{q}^T}{\mathbf{q}^T\mathbf{p}} > \mathbf{0}, \tag{15.2.4}$$

where $\mathbf{p}$ and $\mathbf{q}^T$ are the respective right-hand and left-hand Perron vectors for $\mathbf{A}$.

If $\mathbf{A}_{n\times n} \geq \mathbf{0}$ is irreducible but imprimitive so that there are $h > 1$ eigenvalues on the spectral circle, then it can be demonstrated [127] that each of these eigenvalues is simple and that they are distributed uniformly on the spectral circle in the sense that they are the hth roots of $r = \rho(\mathbf{A})$—i.e., the eigenvalues on the spectral circle are given by

$$\{r, r\omega, r\omega^2, \ldots, r\omega^{h-1}\}, \quad \text{where} \quad \omega = e^{2\pi i/h}.$$

Given a nonnegative matrix, do we really have to compute the eigenvalues and count how many fall on the spectral circle to check for primitivity? No! There are simpler tests.

Tests for Primitivity

For a square nonnegative matrix $\mathbf{A}$, each of the following is true.

- $\mathbf{A}$ is primitive if $\mathbf{A}$ is irreducible and has at least one positive diagonal element.
- $\mathbf{A}$ is primitive if and only if $\mathbf{A}^m > \mathbf{0}$ for some $m > 0$.

The first test above only provides a sufficient condition for primitivity, while the second condition is both necessary and sufficient—the first test is cheaper but not conclusive, while the second is more expensive, but absolutely conclusive. For example, to determine whether or not the irreducible matrix $\mathbf{A} = \begin{pmatrix} 0 & 1 & 0 \\ 0 & 0 & 2 \\ 3 & 4 & 0 \end{pmatrix}$ is primitive, the first test doesn't apply because the diagonal of $\mathbf{A}$ is entirely zeros, so we are forced to apply the second test by computing powers of $\mathbf{A}$. But the job is simplified by noticing that if $\mathbf{B}$ is the Boolean matrix defined by

$$b_{ij} = \begin{cases} 1 & \text{if } a_{ij} > 0, \\ 0 & \text{if } a_{ij} = 0, \end{cases}$$

then $[\mathbf{B}^k]_{ij} > 0$ if and only if $[\mathbf{A}^k]_{ij} > 0$ for every $k > 0$. Therefore, we only need to compute powers of $\mathbf{B}$ (it can be shown that no more than $n^2 - 2n + 2$ powers are required), and these powers require only Boolean operations *AND* and *OR*. The matrix $\mathbf{A}$ in this example is primitive because the powers of $\mathbf{B}$ are

$$\mathbf{B} = \begin{pmatrix} 0 & 1 & 0 \\ 0 & 0 & 1 \\ 1 & 1 & 0 \end{pmatrix}, \ \mathbf{B}^2 = \begin{pmatrix} 0 & 0 & 1 \\ 1 & 1 & 0 \\ 0 & 1 & 1 \end{pmatrix}, \ \mathbf{B}^3 = \begin{pmatrix} 1 & 1 & 0 \\ 0 & 1 & 1 \\ 1 & 1 & 1 \end{pmatrix}, \ \mathbf{B}^4 = \begin{pmatrix} 0 & 1 & 1 \\ 1 & 1 & 1 \\ 1 & 1 & 1 \end{pmatrix}, \ \mathbf{B}^5 = \begin{pmatrix} 1 & 1 & 1 \\ 1 & 1 & 1 \\ 1 & 1 & 1 \end{pmatrix}.$$

While we might prefer our matrices to be primitive, Mother Nature doesn't always cooperate. Mathematical models of physical phenomena that involve oscillations generally produce imprimitive matrices, where the number of eigenvalues on the spectral circle (the index of imprimitivity) corresponds to the period of oscillation. Consequently, it's worthwhile to have a grasp on the index of imprimitivity. While the powers of an irreducible matrix $\mathbf{A} \geq \mathbf{0}$ can tell us if $\mathbf{A}$ has more than one eigenvalue on its spectral circle, the powers of $\mathbf{A}$ provide no clue to the number of such eigenvalues. The issue is more complicated—the following theorem is the primary theoretical aid in determining the index of imprimitivity short of actually computing all eigenvalues.

Index of Imprimitivity

If $c(x) = x^n + c_{k_1}x^{n-k_1} + c_{k_2}x^{n-k_2} + \cdots + c_{k_s}x^{n-k_s} = 0$ is the characteristic equation of an imprimitive matrix $\mathbf{A}_{n\times n}$ in which only the terms with nonzero coefficients are listed (i.e., each $c_{k_j} \neq 0$, and $n > (n-k_1) > \cdots > (n-k_s)$), then the index of imprimitivity h is the greatest common divisor of $\{k_1, k_2, \ldots, k_s\}$.

Finally, it is often useful to decompose an imprimitive matrix, and the *Frobenius form* is the standard way of doing so.

Frobenius Form

For each imprimitive matrix $\mathbf{A}$ with index of imprimitivity $h > 1$, there exists a permutation matrix $\mathbf{P}$ such that

$$\mathbf{P}^T\mathbf{AP}=\begin{pmatrix} \mathbf{0} & \mathbf{A}_{12} & \mathbf{0} & \cdots & \mathbf{0} \\ \mathbf{0} & \mathbf{0} & \mathbf{A}_{23} & \cdots & \mathbf{0} \\ \vdots & \vdots & \ddots & \ddots & \vdots \\ \mathbf{0} & \mathbf{0} & \cdots & \mathbf{0} & \mathbf{A}_{h-1,h} \\ \mathbf{A}_{h1} & \mathbf{0} & \cdots & \mathbf{0} & \mathbf{0} \end{pmatrix}, \qquad (15.2.5)$$

where the zero blocks on the main diagonal are square.

15.3 MARKOV CHAINS

The mathematical component of Google's PageRank vector is the stationary distribution of a discrete-time, finite-state Markov chain. So, to understand and analyze the mathematics of PageRank, it's necessary to have an appreciation of Markov chain concepts, and that's the purpose of this section. Let's begin with some definitions.

- A *stochastic matrix* is a nonnegative matrix $\mathbf{P}_{n\times n}$ in which each row sum is equal to 1. Some authors say "row-stochastic" to distinguish this from the case when each column sum is 1.

- A *stochastic process* is a set of random variables $\{X_t\}_{t=0}^{\infty}$ having a common range $\{S_1, S_2, \ldots, S_n\}$, which is called the *state space* for the process. Parameter t is generally thought of as time, and X_t represents the state of the process at time t. For example, consider the process of surfing the Web by successively clicking on links to move from one Web page to another. The state space is the set of all Web pages, and the random variable X_t is the Web page being viewed at time t.

  - To emphasize that time is considered discretely rather than continuously the phrase "*discrete-time* process" is often used, and the phrase "*finite-state* process" can be used to emphasize that the state space is finite rather than infinite. Our discussion is limited to discrete-time finite-state processes.

- A *Markov chain* is a stochastic process that satisfies the *Markov property*

  $$P(X_{t+1} = S_j \,|\, X_t{=}S_{i_t},\, X_{t-1}{=}S_{i_{t-1}},\, \ldots, X_0{=}S_{i_0}) = P(X_{t+1} = S_j \,|\, X_t = S_{i_t})$$

  for each $t = 0, 1, 2, \ldots$. The notation $P(E\,|\,F)$ denotes the conditional probability that event E occurs given event F occurs—a review some elementary probability is in order if this is not already a familiar concept.

  - The Markov property asserts that the process is memoryless in the sense that the state of the chain at the next time period depends only on the current state and not on the past history of the chain. For example, the process of surfing the Web is a Markov chain provided that the next page that the Web surfer visits doesn't depend on the pages that were visited in the past—the choice depends only on the current page. In other words, if the surfer randomly selects a link on the current page in order to get to the next Web page, then the process is a Markov chain. This kind of chain is referred to as a *random walk* on the link structure of the Web.

- The *transition probability* $p_{ij}(t) = P(X_t = S_j \mid X_{t-1} = S_i)$ is the probability of being in state S_j at time t given that the chain is in state S_i at time $t-1$, so think of this simply as the probability of moving from S_i to S_j at time t.
- The *transition probability matrix* $\mathbf{P}_{n\times n}(t) = [p_{ij}(t)]$ is clearly a nonnegative matrix, and a little thought should convince you that each row sum must be 1. In other words, $\mathbf{P}(t)$ is a stochastic matrix for each t.
- A *stationary Markov chain* is a chain in which the transition probabilities do not vary with time—i.e., $p_{ij}(t) = p_{ij}$ for all t. Stationary chains are also known as *homogeneous chains*.
  - In this case the transition probability matrix is a constant stochastic matrix $\mathbf{P} = [p_{ij}]$. Stationarity is assumed in the sequel.
  - In such a way, every Markov chain defines a stochastic matrix, but the converse is also true—every stochastic matrix $\mathbf{P}_{n\times n}$ defines an n-state Markov chain because the entries p_{ij} define a set of transition probabilities that can be interpreted as a stationary Markov chain on n states.
- An *irreducible Markov chain* is a chain for which the transition probability matrix $\mathbf{P}$ is an irreducible matrix. A chain is said to be *reducible* when $\mathbf{P}$ is a reducible matrix.
  - A *periodic Markov chain* is an irreducible chain whose transition probability matrix $\mathbf{P}$ is an imprimitive matrix. These chains are called periodic because each state can be occupied only at periodic points in time, where the period is the index of imprimitivity. For example, consider an irreducible chain whose index of imprimitivity is $h = 3$. The Frobenius form (15.2.5) means that the states can be reorder (relabeled) to create three clusters of states for which the transition matrix and its powers have the form

$$\mathbf{P}=\begin{pmatrix} 0 & \star & 0 \\ 0 & 0 & \star \\ \star & 0 & 0 \end{pmatrix},\ \mathbf{P}^2=\begin{pmatrix} 0 & 0 & \star \\ \star & 0 & 0 \\ 0 & \star & 0 \end{pmatrix},\ \mathbf{P}^3=\begin{pmatrix} \star & 0 & 0 \\ 0 & \star & 0 \\ 0 & 0 & \star \end{pmatrix},\ \mathbf{P}^4=\begin{pmatrix} 0 & \star & 0 \\ 0 & 0 & \star \\ \star & 0 & 0 \end{pmatrix}\cdots,$$

    where this pattern continues indefinitely. If the chain begins in a state in cluster i, then this periodic pattern ensures that the chain can occupy a state in cluster i only at the end of every third step—see transient properties on page 179.
  - An *aperiodic Markov chain* is an irreducible chain whose transition probability matrix $\mathbf{P}$ is a primitive matrix.
- A *probability distribution vector* (or "probability vector" for short) is defined to be a nonnegative row vector $\mathbf{p}^T = (p_1, p_2, \ldots, p_n)$ such that $\sum_k p_k = 1$. (Every row in a stochastic matrix is probability vector.)
- A *stationary probability distribution vector* for a Markov chain whose transition probability matrix is $\mathbf{P}$ is a probability vector $\boldsymbol{\pi}^T$ such that $\boldsymbol{\pi}^T\mathbf{P} = \boldsymbol{\pi}^T$.

- The kth *step probability distribution vector* for an n-state chain is defined to be

$$\mathbf{p}^T(k) = \big(p_1(k), p_2(k), \ldots, p_n(k)\big), \quad \text{where} \quad p_j(k) = P(X_k = Sj).$$

  In other words, $p_j(k)$ is the probability of being in the jth state after the kth step, but before the $(k+1)^{st}$ step.

- The *initial distribution vector* is

$$\mathbf{p}^T(0) = \big(p_1(0), p_2(0), \ldots, p_n(0)\big), \quad \text{where} \quad p_j(0) = P(X_0 = Sj).$$

  In other words, $p_j(0)$ is the probability that the chain starts in S_j.

To illustrate these concepts, consider the tiny three-page web shown in Figure 15.2,

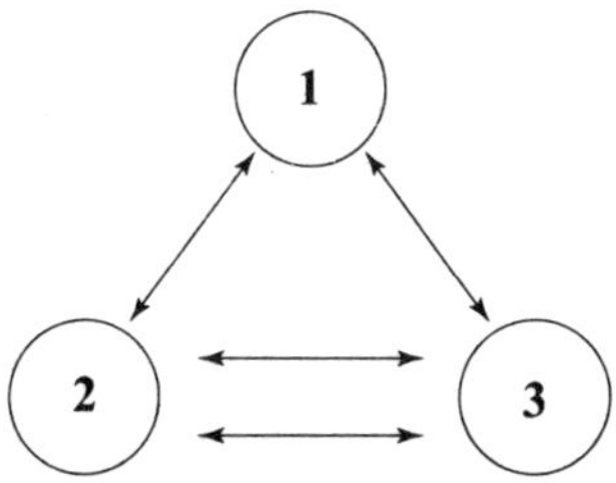

Figure 15.2

where the arrows indicate links—e.g., page 2 contains two links to page 3, and vice versa. The Markov chain defined by a random walk on this link structure evolves as a Web surfer clicks on a randomly selected link on the page currently being viewed, and the transition probability matrix for this chain is the irreducible stochastic matrix

$$\mathbf{H} = \begin{pmatrix} 0 & 1/2 & 1/2 \\ 1/3 & 0 & 2/3 \\ 1/3 & 2/3 & 0 \end{pmatrix}.$$

In this example $\mathbf{H}$ (the *hyperlink matrix*) is stochastic, but if there had been a dangling node (a page containing no links to click on), then $\mathbf{H}$ would have a zero row, in which case $\mathbf{H}$ would not be stochastic and the process would not be a Markov chain. [1]

If our Web surfer starts on page 2 in Figure 15.2, then the initial distribution vector for the chain is $\mathbf{p}^T(0) = (0,1,0) = \mathbf{e}_2^T$. But if the surfer simply selects an initial page at random, then $\mathbf{p}^T(0) = (1/3, 1/3, 1/3) = \mathbf{e}^T/3$ is the *uniform distribution vector.* A standard eigenvalue calculation reveals that $\sigma(\mathbf{H}) = \{1, -1/3, /, -2/3\}$, so it's apparent that $\mathbf{H}$ is a nonnegative matrix having spectral radius $\rho(\mathbf{H}) = 1$.

The fact that $\rho(\mathbf{H}) = 1$ is a feature of all stochastic matrices $\mathbf{P}_{n\times n}$ because having row sums equal to 1 means that $\|\mathbf{P}\|_\infty = 1$ or, equivalently, $\mathbf{Pe} = \mathbf{e}$, where $\mathbf{e}$ is the column of all 1's. Because $(1, \mathbf{e})$ is an eigenpair for every stochastic matrix, and because $\rho(\star) \leq \|\star\|$ for every matrix norm, it follows that it follows that

$$1 \leq \rho(\mathbf{P}) \leq \|\mathbf{P}\|_\infty = 1 \implies \rho(\mathbf{P}) = 1. \qquad (15.3.1)$$

[1] As explained earlier, this is why Google alters the raw hyperlink matrix before computing PageRank.

Furthermore, $\mathbf{e}$ is a positive eigenvector associated with $\rho(\mathbf{P}) = 1$. But be careful! This doesn't mean that you necessarily can call $\mathbf{e}$ the Perron vector for $\mathbf{P}$ because $\mathbf{P}$ might not be irreducible, [2] e.g., consider $\mathbf{P} = \begin{pmatrix} .5 & .5 \\ 0 & 1 \end{pmatrix}$.

Almost all Markovian analysis revolves around questions concerning the transient behavior of the chain as well as the limiting behavior, and standard goals are as follows.

- Describe the kth step distribution $\mathbf{p}^T(k)$ for any initial distribution vector $\mathbf{p}^T(0)$.
- Determine if $\lim_{k\to\infty} \mathbf{p}^T(k)$ exists, and, if so, find the value of $\lim_{k\to\infty} \mathbf{p}^T(k)$.
- When $\lim_{k\to\infty} \mathbf{p}^T(k)$ doesn't exist, determine if the Cesàro limit

$$\lim_{k\to\infty} \left[\frac{\mathbf{p}^T(0) + \mathbf{p}^T(1) + \cdots + \mathbf{p}^T(k-1)}{k} \right]$$

exists, and, if so, find its value and interpret its meaning.

Transient Behavior

Given an initial distribution vector $\mathbf{p}^T(0) = \big(p_1(0), p_2(0), \ldots, p_n(0)\big)$, the first aim is to calculate the probability of being in any given state after the first transition (but before the second)—i.e., determine $\mathbf{p}^T(1) = \big(p_1(1), p_2(1), \ldots, p_n(1)\big)$. Let $\wedge$ and $\vee$ respectively denote *AND* and *OR*. It follows from elementary probability theory that for each j,

$$\begin{aligned} p_j(1) &= P(X_1{=}S_j) = P\Big[X_1{=}S_j \wedge (X_0{=}S_1 \vee X_0{=}S_2 \vee \cdots \vee X_0{=}S_n)\Big] \\ &= P\Big[(X_1{=}S_j \wedge X_0{=}S_1) \vee (X_1{=}S_j \wedge X_0{=}S_2) \vee \cdots \vee (X_1{=}S_j \wedge X_0{=}S_n)\Big] \\ &= \sum_{i=1}^{n} P\Big[X_1{=}S_j \wedge X_0{=}S_i\Big] = \sum_{i=1}^{n} P\Big[X_0 = S_i\Big] P\Big[X_1 = S_j \,|\, X_0 = Si\Big] \\ &= \sum_{i=1}^{n} p_i(0) p_{ij}. \end{aligned}$$

In other words, $\mathbf{p}^T(1) = \mathbf{p}^T(0)\mathbf{P}$, which describes the evolution from the initial distributions to the distribution after one step. The "no memory" Markov property provides the state of affairs at the end of two steps—it says to simply start over but with $\mathbf{p}^T(1)$ as the initial distribution. Consequently, $\mathbf{p}^T(2) = \mathbf{p}^T(1)\mathbf{P}$, and $\mathbf{p}^T(3) = \mathbf{p}^T(2)\mathbf{P}$, etc., and successive substitution yields

$$\mathbf{p}^T(k) = \mathbf{p}^T(0)\mathbf{P}^k, \tag{15.3.2}$$

which is simply a special case of the power method (15.1.20) except that left-hand vector-matrix multiplication is used. Furthermore, if $\mathbf{P}^k = \big[p_{ij}^{(k)}\big]$, then setting $\mathbf{p}^T(0) = \mathbf{e}_i^T$ in (15.3.2) yields $p_j(k) = p_{ij}^{(k)}$ for each $i = 1, 2, \ldots, n$. Below is a summary.

---

[2]The need to force irreducibility is another reason why Google modifies the raw hyperlink matrix.

Transient Properties

If $\mathbf{P}$ is the transition probability matrix for a Markov chain on states $\{S_1, S_2, \ldots, S_n\}$, then each of the following is true.

- The matrix $\mathbf{P}^k$ represents the *k-step transition probability matrix* in the sense that its (i,j)-entry $[\mathbf{P}^k]_{ij} = p_{ij}^{(k)}$ is the probability of moving from S_i to S_j in exactly k steps.
- The kth step distribution vector is given by $\mathbf{p}^T(k) = \mathbf{p}^T(0)\mathbf{P}^k$.

Limiting Behavior

Analyzing limiting properties of Markov chains requires that the class of stochastic matrices (and hence the class of stationary Markov chains) be divided into four mutually exclusive categories.

(1)	$\mathbf{P}$ is irreducible with $\lim_{k\to\infty} \mathbf{P}^k$ existing	(i.e., $\mathbf{P}$ is primitive).
(2)	$\mathbf{P}$ is irreducible with $\lim_{k\to\infty} \mathbf{P}^k$ not existing	(i.e., $\mathbf{P}$ is imprimitive).
(3)	$\mathbf{P}$ is reducible with $\lim_{k\to\infty} \mathbf{P}^k$ existing.	
(4)	$\mathbf{P}$ is reducible with $\lim_{k\to\infty} \mathbf{P}^k$ not existing.	

In case (1) (an aperiodic chain) $\lim_{k\to\infty} \mathbf{P}^k$ can be easily evaluated. The Perron vector for $\mathbf{P}$ is $\mathbf{e}/n$ (the uniform distribution vector), so if $\boldsymbol{\pi} = (\pi_1, \pi_2, \ldots, \pi_n)^T$ is the Perron vector for $\mathbf{P}^T$, (i.e., $\boldsymbol{\pi}^T\mathbf{P} = \boldsymbol{\pi}^T$) then, by (15.2.4),

$$\lim_{k\to\infty} \mathbf{P}^k = \frac{(\mathbf{e}/n)\boldsymbol{\pi}^T}{\boldsymbol{\pi}^T(\mathbf{e}/n)} = \frac{\mathbf{e}\boldsymbol{\pi}^T}{\boldsymbol{\pi}^T\mathbf{e}} = \mathbf{e}\boldsymbol{\pi}^T = \begin{pmatrix} \pi_1 & \pi_2 & \cdots & \pi_n \\ \pi_1 & \pi_2 & \cdots & \pi_n \\ \vdots & \vdots & & \vdots \\ \pi_1 & \pi_2 & \cdots & \pi_n \end{pmatrix} > \mathbf{0}. \tag{15.3.3}$$

Therefore, if $\mathbf{P}$ is primitive, then a limiting probability distribution exists and is given by

$$\lim_{k\to\infty} \mathbf{p}^T(k) = \lim_{k\to\infty} \mathbf{p}^T(0)\mathbf{P}^k = \mathbf{p}^T(0)\mathbf{e}\boldsymbol{\pi}^T = \boldsymbol{\pi}^T. \tag{15.3.4}$$

Notice that because $\sum_k p_k(0) = 1$, the term $\mathbf{p}^T(0)\mathbf{e}$ drops away, so the value of the limit is *independent* of the value of the initial distribution $\mathbf{p}^T(0)$, which isn't too surprising.

In case (2), where $\mathbf{P}$ is irreducible but imprimitive, (15.2.4) insures that $\lim_{k\to\infty} \mathbf{P}^k$ cannot exist, and hence $\lim_{k\to\infty} \mathbf{p}^T(k)$ cannot exist (otherwise taking $\mathbf{p}^T(0) = \mathbf{e}_i^T$ for each i would insure that $\mathbf{P}^k$ has a limit). However, the results on page 173 insure that the eigenvalues of $\mathbf{P}$ lying on the unit circle are each simple, so, by (15.1.18), $\mathbf{P}$ is Cesàro summable to the spectral projector $\mathbf{G}$ associated with the eigenvalue $\lambda = 1$. By recalling (15.1.12) and using the fact that $\mathbf{e}/n$ is the Perron vector for $\mathbf{P}$, it follows that if

$\boldsymbol{\pi}^T = (\pi_1, \pi_2, \ldots, \pi_n)$ is the left-hand Perron vector, then

$$\lim_{k\to\infty} \frac{\mathbf{I}+\mathbf{P}+\cdots+\mathbf{P}^{k-1}}{k} = \frac{(\mathbf{e}/n)\boldsymbol{\pi}^T}{\boldsymbol{\pi}^T(\mathbf{e}/n)} = \frac{\mathbf{e}\boldsymbol{\pi}^T}{\boldsymbol{\pi}^T\mathbf{e}} = \mathbf{e}\boldsymbol{\pi}^T = \begin{pmatrix} \pi_1 & \pi_2 & \cdots & \pi_n \\ \pi_1 & \pi_2 & \cdots & \pi_n \\ \vdots & \vdots & & \vdots \\ \pi_1 & \pi_2 & \cdots & \pi_n \end{pmatrix},$$

which is exactly the same form as the limit (15.3.3) for the primitive case. Consequently, the kth step distributions have a Cesàro limit given by

$$\lim_{k\to\infty} \left[\frac{\mathbf{p}^T(0)+\mathbf{p}^T(1)+\cdots+\mathbf{p}^T(k-1)}{k}\right] = \lim_{k\to\infty} \mathbf{p}^T(0)\left[\frac{\mathbf{I}+\mathbf{P}+\cdots+\mathbf{P}^{k-1}}{k}\right]$$
$$= \mathbf{p}^T(0)\mathbf{e}\boldsymbol{\pi}^T = \boldsymbol{\pi}^T,$$

and, just as in the primitive case (15.3.4), this Cesàro limit is independent of the initial distribution. To interpret the meaning of this Cesàro limit, focus on one state, say S_j, and let $\{Z_k\}_{k=0}^{\infty}$ be random variables that count the number of visits to S_j by setting

$$Z_0 = \begin{cases} 1 & \text{if the chain starts in } S_j, \\ 0 & \text{otherwise,} \end{cases}$$

and for $i > 1$,

$$Z_i = \begin{cases} 1 & \text{if the chain is in } S_j \text{ after the } i^{th} \text{ move,} \\ 0 & \text{otherwise.} \end{cases}$$

Notice that $Z_0 + Z_1 + \cdots + Z_{k-1}$ counts the number of visits to S_j before the kth move, so $(Z_0 + Z_1 + \cdots + Z_{k-1})/k$ represents the fraction of times that S_j is hit before the kth move. The expected (or mean) value of each Z_i is

$$E[Z_i] = 1 \cdot P(Z_i{=}1) \;+\; 0 \cdot P(Z_i{=}0) = P(Z_i{=}1) = p_j(i).$$

Since expectation is linear, the expected fraction of times that S_j is hit before move k is

$$E\left[\frac{Z_0 + Z_1 + \cdots + Z_{k-1}}{k}\right] = \frac{E[Z_0] + E[Z_1] + \cdots + E[Z_{k-1}]}{k}$$
$$= \frac{p_j(0) + p_j(1) + \cdots + p_j(k-1)}{k} = \left[\frac{\mathbf{p}^T(0)+\mathbf{p}^T(1)+\cdots+\mathbf{p}^T(k-1)}{k}\right]_j$$
$$\to \pi_j.$$

In other words, the long-run fraction of time that the chain spends in S_j is π_j, which is the jth component of the Cesàro limit or, equivalently, the jth component of the left-hand Perron vector for $\mathbf{P}$. When $\lim_{k\to\infty} \mathbf{p}^T(k)$ exists, it is easily argued that

$$\lim_{k\to\infty} \mathbf{p}^T(k) = \lim_{k\to\infty} \left[\frac{\mathbf{p}^T(0)+\mathbf{p}^T(1)+\cdots+\mathbf{p}^T(k-1)}{k}\right]$$

so the interpretation of the limiting distribution $\lim_{k\to\infty} \mathbf{p}^T(k)$ for the primitive case is exactly the same as the interpretation of the Cesàro limit in the imprimitive case. Below is a summary of irreducible chains.

Irreducible Markov Chains

Let $\mathbf{P}$ be the transition probability matrix for an irreducible Markov chain on states $\{S_1, S_2, \ldots, S_n\}$, and let $\boldsymbol{\pi}^T$ be the left-hand Perron vector for $\mathbf{P}$ (i.e., $\boldsymbol{\pi}^T\mathbf{P} = \boldsymbol{\pi}^T$, $\|\boldsymbol{\pi}\|_1 = 1$). The following hold for every initial distribution $\mathbf{p}^T(0)$.

- The kth step transition matrix is $\mathbf{P}^k$. In other words, the (i, j)-entry in $\mathbf{P}^k$ is the probability of moving from S_i to S_j in exactly k steps.
- The kth step distribution vector is given by $\mathbf{p}^T(k) = \mathbf{p}^T(0)\mathbf{P}^k$.
- If $\mathbf{P}$ is primitive (so the chain is aperiodic), and if $\mathbf{e}$ is the column of all 1's, then

$$\lim_{k\to\infty} \mathbf{P}^k = \mathbf{e}\boldsymbol{\pi}^T \quad \lim_{k\to\infty} \mathbf{p}^T(k) = \boldsymbol{\pi}^T.$$

- If $\mathbf{P}$ is imprimitive (so the chain is periodic), then

$$\lim_{k\to\infty} \frac{\mathbf{I} + \mathbf{P} + \cdots + \mathbf{P}^{k-1}}{k} = \mathbf{e}\boldsymbol{\pi}^T$$

and

$$\lim_{k\to\infty} \left[\frac{\mathbf{p}^T(0) + \mathbf{p}^T(1) + \cdots + \mathbf{p}^T(k-1)}{k}\right] = \boldsymbol{\pi}^T.$$

- Regardless of whether $\mathbf{P}$ is primitive or imprimitive, the jth component π_j of $\boldsymbol{\pi}^T$ represents the long-run fraction of time that the chain is in S_j.
- The vector $\boldsymbol{\pi}^T$ is the unique *stationary distribution vector* for the chain because it is the unique probability distribution vector satisfying $\boldsymbol{\pi}^T\mathbf{P} = \boldsymbol{\pi}^T$.

Reducible Markov Chains

The Perron–Frobenius theorem is not directly applicable to reducible chains (chains for which $\mathbf{P}$ is a reducible matrix), so the strategy for analyzing reducible chains is to deflate the situation, as much as possible, back to the irreducible case. If $\mathbf{P}$ is reducible, then, by definition, there is a permutation matrix $\mathbf{Q}$ and square matrices $\mathbf{X}$ and $\mathbf{Z}$ such that

$$\mathbf{Q}^T\mathbf{P}\mathbf{Q} = \begin{pmatrix} \mathbf{X} & \mathbf{Y} \\ \mathbf{0} & \mathbf{Z} \end{pmatrix}. \text{ For convenience, denote this by writing } \mathbf{P} \sim \begin{pmatrix} \mathbf{X} & \mathbf{Y} \\ \mathbf{0} & \mathbf{Z} \end{pmatrix}.$$

If $\mathbf{X}$ or $\mathbf{Z}$ is reducible, then another symmetric permutation can be performed to produce

$$\begin{pmatrix} \mathbf{X} & \mathbf{Y} \\ \mathbf{0} & \mathbf{Z} \end{pmatrix} \sim \begin{pmatrix} \mathbf{R} & \mathbf{S} & \mathbf{T} \\ \mathbf{0} & \mathbf{U} & \mathbf{V} \\ \mathbf{0} & \mathbf{0} & \mathbf{W} \end{pmatrix}, \quad \text{where } \mathbf{R}, \mathbf{U}, \text{ and } \mathbf{W} \text{ are square.}$$

Repeating this process eventually yields

$$\mathbf{P} \sim \begin{pmatrix} \mathbf{X}_{11} & \mathbf{X}_{12} & \cdots & \mathbf{X}_{1k} \\ \mathbf{0} & \mathbf{X}_{22} & \cdots & \mathbf{X}_{2k} \\ \vdots & & \ddots & \vdots \\ \mathbf{0} & \mathbf{0} & \cdots & \mathbf{X}_{kk} \end{pmatrix}, \quad \text{where each } \mathbf{X}_{ii} \text{ is irreducible or } \mathbf{X}_{ii} = [0]_{1\times 1}.$$

Finally, if there exist rows having nonzero entries only in diagonal blocks, then symmetrically permute all such rows to the bottom to produce

$$\mathbf{P} \sim \left(\begin{array}{cccc|cccc} \mathbf{P}_{11} & \mathbf{P}_{12} & \cdots & \mathbf{P}_{1r} & \mathbf{P}_{1,r+1} & \mathbf{P}_{1,r+2} & \cdots & \mathbf{P}_{1m} \\ \mathbf{0} & \mathbf{P}_{22} & \cdots & \mathbf{P}_{2r} & \mathbf{P}_{2,r+1} & \mathbf{P}_{2,r+2} & \cdots & \mathbf{P}_{2m} \\ \vdots & & \ddots & \vdots & \vdots & \vdots & \cdots & \vdots \\ \mathbf{0} & \mathbf{0} & \cdots & \mathbf{P}_{rr} & \mathbf{P}_{r,r+1} & \mathbf{P}_{r,r+2} & \cdots & \mathbf{P}_{rm} \\ \hline \mathbf{0} & \mathbf{0} & \cdots & \mathbf{0} & \mathbf{P}_{r+1,r+1} & \mathbf{0} & \cdots & \mathbf{0} \\ \mathbf{0} & \mathbf{0} & \cdots & \mathbf{0} & \mathbf{0} & \mathbf{P}_{r+2,r+2} & \cdots & \mathbf{0} \\ \vdots & \vdots & \cdots & \vdots & \vdots & \vdots & \ddots & \vdots \\ \mathbf{0} & \mathbf{0} & \cdots & \mathbf{0} & \mathbf{0} & \mathbf{0} & \cdots & \mathbf{P}_{mm} \end{array}\right), \tag{15.3.5}$$

where each $\mathbf{P}_{11}, \ldots, \mathbf{P}_{rr}$ is either irreducible or $[0]_{1\times 1}$, and $\mathbf{P}_{r+1,r+1}, \ldots, \mathbf{P}_{mm}$ are irreducible (they can't be zero because each has row sums equal to 1). As mentioned on page 171, the effect of a symmetric permutation is simply to relabel nodes in $\mathcal{G}(\mathbf{P})$ or, equivalently, to reorder the states in the chain. When the states of a chain have been reordered so that $\mathbf{P}$ assumes the form on the right-hand side of (15.3.5), we say that $\mathbf{P}$ is in the *canonical form for reducible matrices.*

The results on page 173 guarantee that if an irreducible stochastic matrix $\mathbf{P}$ has h eigenvalues on the unit circle, then these h eigenvalues are the hth roots of unity, and each is a simple eigenvalue for $\mathbf{P}$. The same can't be said for reducible stochastic matrices, but (15.3.5) leads to the next best result (the proof of which is in [127]).

Unit Eigenvalues

The *unit eigenvalues* are those eigenvalues that are on the unit circle. For every stochastic matrix $\mathbf{P}_{n\times n}$, the following statements are true.

- Every unit eigenvalue of $\mathbf{P}$ is semisimple.
- Every unit eigenvalue has form $\lambda = e^{2k\pi i/h}$ for some $k < h \le n$.
- In particular, $\rho(\mathbf{P}) = 1$ is always a semisimple eigenvalue of $\mathbf{P}$.

The discussion on page 163 says that a matrix $\mathbf{A}_{n\times n}$ is Cesàro summable if and only if $\rho(\mathbf{A}) < 1$ or $\rho(\mathbf{A}) = 1$ with each eigenvalue on the unit circle being semisimple. Since the result above says that the latter holds for all stochastic matrices $\mathbf{P}$, we have the following powerful realization concerning all stochastic matrices.

All Stochastic Matrices Are Summable

Every stochastic matrix $\mathbf{P}$ is Cesàro summable in the sense that

$$\lim_{k\to\infty} \frac{\mathbf{I} + \mathbf{P} + \cdots + \mathbf{P}^{k-1}}{k} = \mathbf{G}$$

always exists and, as discussed on page 163, the value of the limit is the spectral projector $\mathbf{G}$ onto $N(\mathbf{I} - \mathbf{P})$ along $R(\mathbf{I} - \mathbf{P})$.

The structure and interpretation of the Cesàro limit when $\mathbf{P}$ is an irreducible stochastic matrix was developed on page 181 so to complete the picture all that remains is to analyze the nature of $\lim_{k\to\infty}(\mathbf{I}+\mathbf{P}+\cdots+\mathbf{P}^{k-1})/k$ for the reducible case.

Suppose that $\mathbf{P}=\begin{pmatrix}\mathbf{T}_{11} & \mathbf{T}_{12}\\ \mathbf{0} & \mathbf{T}_{22}\end{pmatrix}$ is a reducible stochastic matrix that is in the canonical form (15.3.5), where

$$\mathbf{T}_{11}=\begin{pmatrix}\mathbf{P}_{11} & \cdots & \mathbf{P}_{1r}\\ & \ddots & \vdots\\ & & \mathbf{P}_{rr}\end{pmatrix},\ \mathbf{T}_{12}=\begin{pmatrix}\mathbf{P}_{1,r+1} & \cdots & \mathbf{P}_{1m}\\ \vdots & & \vdots\\ \mathbf{P}_{r,r+1} & \cdots & \mathbf{P}_{rm}\end{pmatrix},\ \mathbf{T}_{22}=\begin{pmatrix}\mathbf{P}_{r+1,r+1} & & \\ & \ddots & \\ & & \mathbf{P}_{mm}\end{pmatrix}.$$

Because each row in $\mathbf{T}_{11}$ has a nonzero off-diagonal block, it follows that $\rho(\mathbf{P}_{kk})<1$ for each $k=1,2,\ldots,r$. Consequently, $\rho(\mathbf{T}_{11})<1$, and

$$\lim_{k\to\infty}\frac{\mathbf{I}+\mathbf{T}_{11}+\cdots+\mathbf{T}_{11}^{k-1}}{k}=\lim_{k\to\infty}\mathbf{T}_{11}^{k}=\mathbf{0}.$$

Furthermore, $\mathbf{P}_{r+1,r+1},\ldots,\mathbf{P}_{mm}$ are each irreducible stochastic matrices, so if $\boldsymbol{\pi}_j^T$ is the left-hand Perron vector for $\mathbf{P}_{jj}$, $r+1\le j\le m$, then (15.1.12) combined with (15.1.18) yields

$$\lim_{k\to\infty}\frac{\mathbf{I}+\mathbf{T}_{22}+\cdots+\mathbf{T}_{22}^{k-1}}{k}=\begin{pmatrix}\mathbf{e}\boldsymbol{\pi}_{r+1}^T & & \\ & \ddots & \\ & & \mathbf{e}\boldsymbol{\pi}_m^T\end{pmatrix}=\mathbf{E}.$$

It's clear from (15.2.4) that $\lim_{k\to\infty}\mathbf{T}_{22}^k$ exists if and only if $\mathbf{P}_{r+1,r+1},\ldots,\mathbf{P}_{mm}$ are each primitive, in which case $\lim_{k\to\infty}\mathbf{T}_{22}^k=\mathbf{E}$. Therefore, the limits, be they Cesàro or ordinary (if it exists), all have the form

$$\lim_{k\to\infty}\frac{\mathbf{I}+\mathbf{P}+\cdots+\mathbf{P}^{k-1}}{k}=\begin{pmatrix}\mathbf{0} & \mathbf{Z}\\ \mathbf{0} & \mathbf{E}\end{pmatrix}=\mathbf{G}=\lim_{k\to\infty}\mathbf{P}^k\ \text{(when it exists)}.$$

To determine the precise nature of $\mathbf{Z}$, use the fact that $R(\mathbf{G})=N(\mathbf{I}-\mathbf{P})$ (because $\mathbf{G}$ is the projector onto $N(\mathbf{I}-\mathbf{P})$ along $R(\mathbf{I}-\mathbf{P})$) to write

$$(\mathbf{I}-\mathbf{P})\mathbf{G}=\mathbf{0}\implies\begin{pmatrix}\mathbf{I}-\mathbf{T}_{11} & -\mathbf{T}_{12}\\ \mathbf{0} & \mathbf{I}-\mathbf{T}_{22}\end{pmatrix}\begin{pmatrix}\mathbf{0} & \mathbf{Z}\\ \mathbf{0} & \mathbf{E}\end{pmatrix}=\mathbf{0}\implies(\mathbf{I}-\mathbf{T}_{11})\mathbf{Z}=\mathbf{T}_{12}\mathbf{E}.$$

Since $\mathbf{I}-\mathbf{T}_{11}$ is nonsingular (because $\rho(\mathbf{T}_{11})<1$), it follows that

$$\mathbf{Z}=(\mathbf{I}-\mathbf{T}_{11})^{-1}\mathbf{T}_{12}\mathbf{E},$$

and thus the following results concerning limits of reducible chains are produced.

Reducible Markov Chains

If the states in a reducible Markov chain have been ordered to make the transition matrix assume the canonical form

$$\mathbf{P} = \begin{pmatrix} \mathbf{T}_{11} & \mathbf{T}_{12} \\ \mathbf{0} & \mathbf{T}_{22} \end{pmatrix}$$

that is described in (15.3.5), and if π_j^T is the left-hand Perron vector for $\mathbf{P}_{jj}$ $(r+1 \leq j \leq m)$, then $\mathbf{I} - \mathbf{T}_{11}$ is nonsingular, and

$$\lim_{k\to\infty} \frac{\mathbf{I}+\mathbf{P}+\cdots+\mathbf{P}^{k-1}}{k} = \begin{pmatrix} \mathbf{0} & (\mathbf{I}-\mathbf{T}_{11})^{-1}\mathbf{T}_{12}\mathbf{E} \\ \mathbf{0} & \mathbf{E} \end{pmatrix},$$

where

$$\mathbf{E} = \begin{pmatrix} \mathbf{e}\pi_{r+1}^T & & \\ & \ddots & \\ & & \mathbf{e}\pi_m^T \end{pmatrix}.$$

Furthermore, $\lim_{k\to\infty} \mathbf{P}^k$ exists if and only if the stochastic matrices $\mathbf{P}_{r+1,r+1}, \ldots, \mathbf{P}_{mm}$ in (15.3.5) are each primitive, in which case

$$\lim_{k\to\infty} \mathbf{P}^k = \begin{pmatrix} \mathbf{0} & (\mathbf{I}-\mathbf{T}_{11})^{-1}\mathbf{T}_{12}\mathbf{E} \\ \mathbf{0} & \mathbf{E} \end{pmatrix}. \tag{15.3.6}$$

Transient and Ergodic Classes

When the states of a chain are reordered so that $\mathbf{P}$ is in canonical form (15.3.5), the subset of states corresponding to $\mathbf{P}_{kk}$ for $1 \leq k \leq r$ is called the kth *transient class* because once left, a transient class can't be reentered. The subset of states corresponding to $\mathbf{P}_{r+j,r+j}$ for $j \geq 1$ is called the jth *ergodic class*. Each ergodic class is an irreducible Markov chain unto itself that is imbedded in the larger reducible chain. From now on, we will assume that the states in reducible chains have been ordered so that $\mathbf{P}$ is in canonical form (15.3.5).

Every reducible chain eventually enters one of the ergodic classes, but what happens after that depends on whether or not the ergodic class is primitive. If $\mathbf{P}_{r+j,r+j}$ is primitive, then the chain settles down to a steady state defined by the left-hand Perron vector of $\mathbf{P}_{r+j,r+j}$, but if $\mathbf{P}_{r+j,r+j}$ is imprimitive, then the process will oscillate in the jth ergodic class forever. There is not much more that can be said about the limit, but there are still important questions concerning which ergodic class the chain will end up in and how long it takes to get there. This time the answer depends on where the chain starts—i.e., on the initial distribution.

For convenience, let $\mathcal{T}_i$ denote the ith transient class, and let $\mathcal{E}_j$ be the jth ergodic class. Suppose that the chain starts in a particular transient state—say we start in the pth state of $\mathcal{T}_i$. Since the question at hand concerns only which ergodic class is hit but not what happens after it's entered, we might as well convert every state in each ergodic class into a trap by setting $\mathbf{P}_{r+j,r+j} = \mathbf{I}$ for each $j \geq 1$ in (15.3.5). The transition matrix for this modified chain is $\widetilde{\mathbf{P}} = \begin{pmatrix} \mathbf{T}_{11} & \mathbf{T}_{12} \\ \mathbf{0} & \mathbf{I} \end{pmatrix}$, and it follows from (15.3.6) that $\lim_{k\to\infty} \widetilde{\mathbf{P}}^k$ exists and has the form

$$\lim_{k\to\infty} \widetilde{\mathbf{P}}^k = \begin{pmatrix} 0 & (\mathbf{I}-\mathbf{T}_{11})^{-1}\mathbf{T}_{12} \\ 0 & \mathbf{I} \end{pmatrix} = \left(\begin{array}{cccc|cccc} 0 & 0 & \cdots & 0 & \mathbf{L}_{1,1} & \mathbf{L}_{1,2} & \cdots & \mathbf{L}_{1s} \\ 0 & 0 & \cdots & 0 & \mathbf{L}_{2,1} & \mathbf{L}_{2,2} & \cdots & \mathbf{L}_{2s} \\ \vdots & & \ddots & \vdots & \vdots & \vdots & \cdots & \vdots \\ 0 & 0 & \cdots & 0 & \mathbf{L}_{r,1} & \mathbf{L}_{r,2} & \cdots & \mathbf{L}_{rs} \\ \hline 0 & 0 & \cdots & 0 & \mathbf{I} & \mathbf{0} & \cdots & \mathbf{0} \\ 0 & 0 & \cdots & 0 & \mathbf{0} & \mathbf{I} & \cdots & \mathbf{0} \\ \vdots & \vdots & \cdots & \vdots & \vdots & \vdots & \ddots & \vdots \\ 0 & 0 & \cdots & 0 & \mathbf{0} & \mathbf{0} & \cdots & \mathbf{I} \end{array}\right).$$

Consequently, the (p, q)-entry in block $\mathbf{L}_{ij}$ represents the probability of eventually hitting the qth state in $\mathcal{E}_j$ given that we start from the pth state in $\mathcal{T}_i$. Therefore, if $\mathbf{e}$ is the vector of all 1's, then the probability of eventually entering somewhere in $\mathcal{E}_j$ is given by

$$P(\text{absorption into } \mathcal{E}_j \,|\, \text{start in } p^{th} \text{ state of } \mathcal{T}_i) = \sum_k \left[\mathbf{L}_{ij}\right]_{pk} = \left[\mathbf{L}_{ij}\mathbf{e}\right]_p.$$

If $\mathbf{p}_i^T(0)$ is an initial distribution for starting in the various states of $\mathcal{T}_i$, then

$$P\big(\text{absorption into } \mathcal{E}_j \,|\, \mathbf{p}_i^T(0)\big) = \mathbf{p}_i^T(0)\mathbf{L}_{ij}\mathbf{e}.$$

The expected number of steps required to first hit an ergodic state is determined as follows. Count the number of times the chain is in transient state S_j given that it starts in transient state S_i by reapplying the argument given in on page 180. That is, given that the chain starts in S_i, let

$$Z_0 = \begin{cases} 1 & \text{if } S_i = S_j, \\ 0 & \text{otherwise,} \end{cases} \quad Z_k = \begin{cases} 1 & \text{if the chain is in } S_j \text{ after step } k, \\ 0 & \text{otherwise.} \end{cases}$$

Since

$$E[Z_k] = 1 \cdot P(Z_k{=}1) \; + \; 0 \cdot P(Z_k{=}0) = P(Z_k{=}1) = \left[\mathbf{T}_{11}^k\right]_{ij},$$

and since $\sum_{k=0}^{\infty} Z_k$ is the total number of times the chain is in S_j, we have

$$\begin{aligned} E[\#\text{ times in } S_j \,|\, \text{ start in } S_i] &= E\left[\sum_{k=0}^{\infty} Z_k\right] = \sum_{k=0}^{\infty} E\left[Z_k\right] = \sum_{k=0}^{\infty} \left[\mathbf{T}_{11}^k\right]_{ij} \\ &= \left[(\mathbf{I}-\mathbf{T}_{11})^{-1}\right]_{ij} \quad (\text{because } \rho\left(\mathbf{T}_{11}\right) < 1). \end{aligned}$$

Summing this over all transient states produces the expected number of times the chain is in *some* transient state, which is the same as the expected number of times before first hitting an ergodic state. In other words,

$$E[\#\text{ steps until absorption} \,|\, \text{start in } i^{th} \text{ transient state}] = \left[(\mathbf{I}-\mathbf{T}_{11})^{-1}\mathbf{e}\right]_i.$$

It's often the case in practical applications that there is only one transient class, and the ergodic classes are just single absorbing states (states such that once they are entered, they are never left). If the single transient class contains r states, and if there are s absorbing states, then the canonical form for the transition matrix is

$$\mathbf{P} = \left(\begin{array}{ccc|ccc} p_{11} & \cdots & p_{1r} & p_{1,r+1} & \cdots & p_{1s} \\ \vdots & & \vdots & \vdots & & \vdots \\ p_{r1} & \cdots & p_{rr} & p_{r,r+1} & \cdots & p_{rs} \\ \hline 0 & \cdots & 0 & 1 & \cdots & 0 \\ \vdots & & \vdots & \vdots & \ddots & \vdots \\ 0 & \cdots & 0 & 0 & \cdots & 1 \end{array}\right). \tag{15.3.7}$$

In this case, $\mathbf{L}_{ij} = \left[(\mathbf{I}-\mathbf{T}_{11})^{-1}\mathbf{T}_{12}\right]_{ij}$, and the earlier development specializes to say that every absorbing chain must eventually reach one of its absorbing states. The absorption probabilities and absorption times are included in the following summary.

Absorption Probabilities and Absorption Times

For a reducible chain whose transition matrix $\mathbf{P} = \begin{pmatrix} \mathbf{T}_{11} & \mathbf{T}_{12} \\ \mathbf{0} & \mathbf{T}_{22} \end{pmatrix}$ is in the canonical form (15.3.5), let $\mathcal{T}_i$ and $\mathcal{E}_j$ be the ith and j^{th} transient and ergodic classes, respectively, and let $\mathbf{p}_i^T(0)$ be an initial distribution for starting in the various states of $\mathcal{T}_i$. If $(\mathbf{I}-\mathbf{T}_{11})^{-1}\mathbf{T}_{12}$ is partitioned as

$$(\mathbf{I}-\mathbf{T}_{11})^{-1}\mathbf{T}_{12} = \begin{pmatrix} \mathbf{L}_{1,1} & \mathbf{L}_{1,2} & \cdots & \mathbf{L}_{1s} \\ \mathbf{L}_{2,1} & \mathbf{L}_{2,2} & \cdots & \mathbf{L}_{2s} \\ \vdots & \vdots & \cdots & \vdots \\ \mathbf{L}_{r,1} & \mathbf{L}_{r,2} & \cdots & \mathbf{L}_{rs} \end{pmatrix},$$

then

- $P\big(\text{absorption into } \mathcal{E}_j \,|\, \mathbf{p}_i^T(0)\big) = \mathbf{p}_i^T(0)\mathbf{L}_{ij}\mathbf{e}$,
- $P(\text{absorption into } \mathcal{E}_j \,|\, \text{start in } p^{th} \text{ state of } \mathcal{T}_i) = \sum_k \left[\mathbf{L}_{ij}\right]_{pk} = \left[\mathbf{L}_{ij}\mathbf{e}\right]_p$,
- $E[\#\text{ steps until absorption} \,|\, \text{start in } i^{th} \text{ transient state}] = \left[(\mathbf{I}-\mathbf{T}_{11})^{-1}\mathbf{e}\right]_i$.

When there is only one transient class and each ergodic class is a single absorbing state ($\mathcal{E}_j = S_{r+j}$), $\mathbf{P}$ has the form (15.3.7). If S_i and S_j are transient states, then

- $P(\text{absorption into } S_{r+j} \,|\, \text{start in } S_i) = \left[(\mathbf{I}-\mathbf{T}_{11})^{-1}\mathbf{T}_{12}\right]_{ij}$,
- $E[\#\text{ steps until absorption} \,|\, \text{start in } S_i] = \left[(\mathbf{I}-\mathbf{T}_{11})^{-1}\mathbf{e}\right]_i$,
- $E[\#\text{ times in } S_j \,|\, \text{start in } S_i] = \left[(\mathbf{I}-\mathbf{T}_{11})^{-1}\right]_{ij}$.

15.4 PERRON COMPLEMENTATION

The theory of stochastic complementation in section 15.5 concerns the development of methods that allow the stationary distribution of a large irreducible Markov chain to be obtained by gluing together stationary distributions of smaller chains. The concepts are based on the theory of Perron complementation, which describes how the Perron vector of a large irreducible matrix can be expressed in terms of Perron vectors of smaller matrices.

Perron Complements

Partition an irreducible $\mathbf{A}_{n\times n} \geq \mathbf{0}$ with spectral radius $\rho(\mathbf{A}) = r$, as

$$\mathbf{A} = \begin{pmatrix} \mathbf{A}_{11} & \mathbf{A}_{12} & \cdots & \mathbf{A}_{1k} \\ \mathbf{A}_{21} & \mathbf{A}_{22} & \cdots & \mathbf{A}_{2k} \\ \vdots & \vdots & \ddots & \vdots \\ \mathbf{A}_{k1} & \mathbf{A}_{k2} & \cdots & \mathbf{A}_{kk} \end{pmatrix}, \tag{15.4.1}$$

where all diagonal blocks are square. The *Perron complement* of the ith diagonal block $\mathbf{A}_{ii}$is defined to be the matrix

$$\mathbf{P}_i = \mathbf{A}_{ii} + \mathbf{A}_{i\star}(r\mathbf{I} - \mathbf{A}_i^\star)^{-1}\mathbf{A}_{\star i}, \tag{15.4.2}$$

where $\mathbf{A}_{i\star}$ and $\mathbf{A}_{\star i}$ are, respectively, the ith row and the ith column of blocks with $\mathbf{A}_{ii}$ removed, and $\mathbf{A}_i^\star$ is the principal submatrix of $\mathbf{A}$ obtained by deleting the ith row and i^{th} column of blocks. The nonsingularity of $r\mathbf{I} - \mathbf{A}_i^\star$ is discussed on page 188.

For example, if $\mathbf{A} = \begin{pmatrix} \mathbf{A}_{11} & \mathbf{A}_{12} \\ \mathbf{A}_{21} & \mathbf{A}_{22} \end{pmatrix} \geq \mathbf{0}$ is irreducible with $\rho(\mathbf{A}) = r$, then the two Perron complements are

$$\mathbf{P}_1 = \mathbf{A}_{11} + \mathbf{A}_{12}(r\mathbf{I} - \mathbf{A}_{22})^{-1}\mathbf{A}_{21}\mathbf{P}_2 = \mathbf{A}_{22} + \mathbf{A}_{21}(r\mathbf{I} - \mathbf{A}_{11})^{-1}\mathbf{A}_{12}.$$

If $\mathbf{A}$ is partitioned as $\mathbf{A} = \begin{pmatrix} \mathbf{A}_{11} & \mathbf{A}_{12} & \mathbf{A}_{13} \\ \mathbf{A}_{21} & \mathbf{A}_{22} & \mathbf{A}_{23} \\ \mathbf{A}_{31} & \mathbf{A}_{32} & \mathbf{A}_{33} \end{pmatrix}$, then there are three Perron complements, and the second one is

$$\mathbf{P}_2 = \mathbf{A}_{22} + \begin{pmatrix} \mathbf{A}_{21} & \mathbf{A}_{23} \end{pmatrix} \begin{pmatrix} r\mathbf{I} - \mathbf{A}_{11} & -\mathbf{A}_{13} \\ -\mathbf{A}_{31} & r\mathbf{I} - \mathbf{A}_{33} \end{pmatrix}^{-1} \begin{pmatrix} \mathbf{A}_{12} \\ \mathbf{A}_{32} \end{pmatrix},$$

with the other two complements, $\mathbf{P}_1$ and $\mathbf{P}_3$, being similarly formed.

For $\mathbf{A} = \begin{pmatrix} \mathbf{A}_{11} & \mathbf{A}_{12} \\ \mathbf{A}_{21} & \mathbf{A}_{22} \end{pmatrix}$, the more familiar *Schur complements* are defined [127] to be

$$\mathbf{A}_{11} - \mathbf{A}_{12}\mathbf{A}_{22}^{-1}\mathbf{A}_{21}\mathbf{A}_{22} - \mathbf{A}_{21}\mathbf{A}_{11}^{-1}\mathbf{A}_{12},$$

so, while they are not the same, the Perron complements are related to the Schur complements by the following construction.

1. Shift $\mathbf{A}$ by $r\mathbf{I}$ by constructing $\mathbf{A} - r\mathbf{I}$.
2. Form Schur complements $\mathbf{C}_i$.
3. Shift the results back by constructing $r\mathbf{I} + \mathbf{C}_i$.

This is not the only reason for the terminology "Perron complement"—the other reasons will become evident as other developments unfold. The salient feature of all Perron complements is that they inherit "Perron properties" from their parent matrix in the sense that if $\mathbf{A}$ is nonnegative and irreducible, then so is each Perron complement $\mathbf{P}_i$ that is derived from $\mathbf{A}$. Furthermore, if $\rho(\mathbf{A}) = r$, then $\rho(\mathbf{P}_i) = r$ for each i. And, most importantly, the Perron vectors of the $\mathbf{P}_i$'s combine to form the Perron vector of the parent matrix $\mathbf{A}$. Before these things can be understood, some preliminary results are needed. The first such result is the converse to part of the Perron–Frobenius Theorem on page 172.

Irreducibility Revisited

$\mathbf{A}_{n\times n} \geq \mathbf{0}$ is irreducible if and only if $\mathbf{A}$ has a simple positive eigenvalue $\lambda > 0$ that is associated with a positive right-hand eigenvector $\mathbf{p} > \mathbf{0}$ as well as a positive left-hand eigenvector $\mathbf{q}^T > \mathbf{0}$.

Proof. Suppose that $\mathbf{A}$ has a simple eigenvalue $\lambda > 0$ associated right-hand and left-hand eigenvectors $\mathbf{p} > \mathbf{0}$ and $\mathbf{q}^T > \mathbf{0}$, respectively. If $\mathbf{D} = \text{diag}\,(p_1, p_2, \ldots, p_n)$, then

$$\mathbf{P} = \frac{\mathbf{D}^{-1}\mathbf{A}\mathbf{D}}{\lambda} \tag{15.4.3}$$

is a stochastic matrix that is irreducible if and only if $\mathbf{A}$ is irreducible. And 1 is a simple eigenvalue of $\mathbf{P}$ associated with the respective right-hand and left-hand eigenvectors $\mathbf{D}^{-1}\mathbf{p} = \mathbf{e} > \mathbf{0}$ and $\mathbf{q}^T\mathbf{D} > \mathbf{0}$. Consequently, $\mathbf{P}$ is Cesàro summable to the spectral projector $\mathbf{G}$ onto $N\,(\mathbf{I} - \mathbf{P})$ (page 182). The simplicity of $1 \in \sigma\,(\mathbf{P})$ means that

$$\mathbf{G} = \frac{\mathbf{D}^{-1}\mathbf{p}\mathbf{q}^T\mathbf{D}}{\mathbf{q}^T\mathbf{p}} > 0 \qquad \text{(recall (15.1.12) on page 161).}$$

This ensures that $\mathbf{P}$ (and hence $\mathbf{A}$) is irreducible. Otherwise, $\left[\mathbf{P}^k\right]_{ij} = 0$ for some $i \neq j$ and for all k, so

$$\left[\frac{\mathbf{I} + \mathbf{P} + \cdots + \mathbf{P}^{k-1}}{k}\right]_{ij} = 0 \text{ for } k = 1, 2, \ldots \implies \mathbf{G}_{ij} = 0. \quad \blacksquare$$

In order for a Perron complement $\mathbf{P}_i = \mathbf{A}_{ii} + \mathbf{A}_{i\star}(r\mathbf{I} - \mathbf{A}_i^\star)^{-1}\mathbf{A}_{\star i}$ to be well defined, the existence of $(r\mathbf{I} - \mathbf{A}_i^\star)^{-1}$ must be ensured. This, along with the fact that $(r\mathbf{I} - \mathbf{A}_i^\star)^{-1} > \mathbf{0}$, is the point of the next theorem.

Principal Submatrices

Let $\mathbf{A}_{n\times n} \geq \mathbf{0}$ be irreducible with $\rho(\mathbf{A}) = r$, and partition $\mathbf{A}$ as in (15.4.1). If $\mathbf{A}_i^\star$ is the principal submatrix of $\mathbf{A}$ obtained by deleting the ith row and i^{th} column of blocks, then

$$\rho(\mathbf{A}_i^\star) < r, \tag{15.4.4}$$

$$(r\mathbf{I} - \mathbf{A}_i^\star) \text{ is nonsingular, and } (r\mathbf{I} - \mathbf{A}_i^\star)^{-1} > \mathbf{0}. \tag{15.4.5}$$

In other words, $r\mathbf{I} - \mathbf{A}_i^\star$ is an M-matrix as described on page 166.

Proof. To prove that $\rho(\mathbf{A}_i^\star) < r$, suppose to the contrary that $r \le \rho(\mathbf{A}_i^\star)$. If $\mathbf{Q}$ is the permutation matrix such that

$$\mathbf{Q}^T\mathbf{A}\mathbf{Q} = \begin{pmatrix} \mathbf{A}_i^\star & \mathbf{A}_{\star i} \\ \mathbf{A}_{i\star} & \mathbf{A}_{ii} \end{pmatrix} = \widetilde{\mathbf{A}}, \quad \text{and if} \quad \widetilde{\mathbf{B}} = \begin{pmatrix} \mathbf{A}_i^\star & 0 \\ 0 & 0 \end{pmatrix}, \tag{15.4.6}$$

then $\rho(\widetilde{\mathbf{A}}) = \rho(\mathbf{A}) = r \le \rho(\mathbf{A}_i^\star) = \rho(\widetilde{\mathbf{B}})$. Furthermore $\widetilde{\mathbf{A}} \ge \widetilde{\mathbf{B}} \ge \mathbf{0}$ ensures that $\rho(\widetilde{\mathbf{A}}) \ge \rho(\widetilde{\mathbf{B}})$ [127, pg 619], so $r = \rho(\widetilde{\mathbf{B}}) = \rho(\mathbf{A}_i^\star)$. But this impossible because Perron's theorem for nonnegative matrices (page 168) guarantees the existence of a vector $\mathbf{v} \ge \mathbf{0}$, $\mathbf{v} \ne \mathbf{0}$, such that $\mathbf{A}_i^\star\mathbf{v} = r\mathbf{v}$, so $\mathbf{z} = (\mathbf{v}\ \ \mathbf{0})^T$ is a nonnegative nonzero vector $\mathbf{v}$ such that $\widetilde{\mathbf{B}}\mathbf{z} = r\mathbf{z}$. It follows from $\widetilde{\mathbf{A}} \ge \widetilde{\mathbf{B}}$ that $\widetilde{\mathbf{A}}\mathbf{z} \ge \widetilde{\mathbf{B}}\mathbf{z} = r\mathbf{z}$, and it's a straightforward exercise [127, pg 674] to show that this implies $\widetilde{\mathbf{A}}\mathbf{z} = r\mathbf{z}$ with $\mathbf{z} > \mathbf{0}$, which is a contradiction. Thus $\rho(\mathbf{A}_i^\star) < r$. The fact that $(r\mathbf{I} - \mathbf{A}_i^\star)$ is nonsingular and $(r\mathbf{I} - \mathbf{A}_i^\star)^{-1} > \mathbf{0}$ can be deduced from the Neumann series expansion (15.1.16) on page 162. ■

As discussed below, Perron complements inherit most of the useful properties that their parent matrix possesses.

Inherited Perron Properties

If $\mathbf{A}_{n\times n} \ge \mathbf{0}$ is an irreducible matrix with $\rho(\mathbf{A}) = r$ that is partitioned as in (15.4.1), and if $\mathbf{P}_i = \mathbf{A}_{ii} + \mathbf{A}_{i\star}(r\mathbf{I} - \mathbf{A}_i^\star)^{-1}\mathbf{A}_{\star i}$ is the ith Perron complement as defined in (15.4.2), then

$$\mathbf{P}_i \ge \mathbf{0} \text{ for every } i, \tag{15.4.7}$$

$$\mathbf{P}_i \text{ is irreducible for every } i, \tag{15.4.8}$$

$$\rho(\mathbf{P}_i) = r \text{ for every } i. \tag{15.4.9}$$

Proof. $\mathbf{P}_i \ge \mathbf{0}$ because $(r\mathbf{I}-\mathbf{A}_i^\star)^{-1} > \mathbf{0}$, and all of the other terms in $\mathbf{P}_i$ are nonnegative. To see that $\mathbf{P}_i$ is irreducible, let $\widetilde{\mathbf{p}} = \begin{pmatrix} \mathbf{x} \\ \mathbf{y} \end{pmatrix}$ be the partitioned right-hand Perron vector for the nonnegative irreducible matrix $\widetilde{\mathbf{A}}$ in (15.4.6) so that $(r\mathbf{I} - \widetilde{\mathbf{A}})\widetilde{\mathbf{p}} = \mathbf{0}$. The lower part of

$$\begin{pmatrix} r\mathbf{I} - \mathbf{A}_i^\star & -\mathbf{A}_{\star i} \\ -\mathbf{A}_{i\star} & r\mathbf{I} - \mathbf{A}_{ii} \end{pmatrix}\begin{pmatrix} \mathbf{x} \\ \mathbf{y} \end{pmatrix} = \begin{pmatrix} \mathbf{0} \\ \mathbf{0} \end{pmatrix} \Longrightarrow \begin{pmatrix} \mathbf{I} & \mathbf{0} \\ \mathbf{A}_{i\star}(r\mathbf{I} - \mathbf{A}_i^\star)^{-1} & \mathbf{I} \end{pmatrix}\begin{pmatrix} r\mathbf{I} - \mathbf{A}_i^\star & -\mathbf{A}_{\star i} \\ -\mathbf{A}_{i\star} & r\mathbf{I} - \mathbf{A}_{ii} \end{pmatrix}\begin{pmatrix} \mathbf{x} \\ \mathbf{y} \end{pmatrix} = \begin{pmatrix} \mathbf{0} \\ \mathbf{0} \end{pmatrix}$$

yields

$$(r\mathbf{I} - \mathbf{P}_i)\mathbf{y} = \mathbf{0}, \tag{15.4.10}$$

and thus $(r, \mathbf{y})$ is a right-hand eigenpair for $\mathbf{P}_i$ with $\mathbf{y} > \mathbf{0}$. A similar argument shows that there is also a left-hand eigenpair $(r, \mathbf{z}^T)$ for $\mathbf{P}_i$ with $\mathbf{z}^T > \mathbf{0}$. Furthermore, r is a simple eigenvalue of $\mathbf{P}_i$ because Perron–Frobenius insures that r is a simple eigenvalue of $\mathbf{A}$, as well as $\widetilde{\mathbf{A}}$, so this together with

$$\begin{pmatrix} \mathbf{I} & \mathbf{0} \\ \mathbf{A}_{i\star}(r\mathbf{I} - \mathbf{A}_i^\star)^{-1} & \mathbf{I} \end{pmatrix}\begin{pmatrix} r\mathbf{I} - \mathbf{A}_i^\star & -\mathbf{A}_{\star i} \\ -\mathbf{A}_{i\star} & r\mathbf{I} - \mathbf{A}_{ii} \end{pmatrix}\begin{pmatrix} \mathbf{I} & (r\mathbf{I} - \mathbf{A}_i^\star)^{-1}\mathbf{A}_{\star i} \\ \mathbf{0} & \mathbf{I} \end{pmatrix} = \begin{pmatrix} r\mathbf{I} - \mathbf{A}_i^\star & \mathbf{0} \\ \mathbf{0} & r\mathbf{I} - \mathbf{P}_i \end{pmatrix}$$

and the fact that $(r\mathbf{I} - \mathbf{A}_i^\star)$ is nonsingular produces

$$1 = \dim N(r\mathbf{I}-\widetilde{\mathbf{A}}) = \dim N(r\mathbf{I}-\mathbf{A}_i^\star) + \dim N(r\mathbf{I}-\mathbf{P}_i) = \dim N(r\mathbf{I}-\mathbf{P}_i). \tag{15.4.11}$$

Since $\mathbf{P}_i$ can be transformed into a stochastic matrix without altering multiplicities as described in (15.4.3), and since that the spectral radius of a stochastic matrix is semisimple

(p. 182), it follows that r is a semisimple eigenvalue for $\mathbf{P}_i$. Hence (15.4.11) insures that r is a simple eigenvalue for $\mathbf{P}_i$. The irreducibility of $\mathbf{P}_i$ is now a consequence of the result on page 188. Finally, part of the Perron–Frobenius theorem (p. 172) states that a nonnegative irreducible matrix can have no nonnegative eigenvectors other than multiples of the positive Perron vector associated with the spectral radius. Therefore, since $(r, \mathbf{y})$ is an eigenpair for $\mathbf{P}_i$ with $\mathbf{y} > \mathbf{0}$, it follows that $\rho(\mathbf{P}_i) = r$, where $\mathbf{z}_i = \mathbf{y}/\|\mathbf{y}\|_1$ is the associated Perron vector. ∎

The above proof is more important than it might first appear to be because it reveals a significant relationship between the Perron vector of $\mathbf{A}$ and the Perron vector of $\mathbf{P}_i$. If the Perron vector for $\mathbf{A}$ is partitioned conformably with the partition in (15.4.1) as

$$\mathbf{p} = \begin{pmatrix} \mathbf{p}_1 \\ \mathbf{p}_2 \\ \vdots \\ \mathbf{p}_k \end{pmatrix},$$

then the nature of the permutation in (15.4.6) makes it clear that $\mathbf{p}_i = \mathbf{y}$, where $\mathbf{y} > \mathbf{0}$ is the vector in (15.4.10). Consequently, the Perron vector for $\mathbf{P}_i$ is

$$\mathbf{z}_i = \frac{\mathbf{y}}{\|\mathbf{y}\|_1} = \frac{\mathbf{y}}{\mathbf{e}^T\mathbf{y}} = \frac{\mathbf{p}_i}{\mathbf{e}^T\mathbf{p}_i}$$

or, equivalently,

$$\mathbf{p}_i = \xi_i \mathbf{z}_i, \quad \text{where} \quad \xi_i = \mathbf{e}^T\mathbf{p}_i. \tag{15.4.12}$$

In other words, the Perron vectors $\mathbf{z}_i$ of smaller Perron complements can be glued together to build the Perron vector of $\mathbf{A}$ by writing

$$\mathbf{p} = \begin{pmatrix} \xi_1\mathbf{z}_1 \\ \xi_2\mathbf{z}_2 \\ \vdots \\ \xi_k\mathbf{z}_k \end{pmatrix}. \tag{15.4.13}$$

This looks like a nice result until you realize that the glue is the set of scalars $\xi_i = \mathbf{e}^T\mathbf{p}_i$, so we are going in circles if we need to use the components of $\mathbf{p}$ in order to compute the components $\mathbf{p}$. Fortunately, there's a clever way out of this dilemma by manufacturing the glue from the Perron vector of a *coupling matrix* $\mathbf{C}$, which is yet another matrix that inherits its Perron properties from the parent matrix $\mathbf{A}$. The following theorem brings everything together.

The Coupling Theorem

Suppose $\mathbf{A}_{n\times n} \geq \mathbf{0}$ is irreducible with $\rho(\mathbf{A}) = r$ that is partitioned into k levels as in (15.4.1). Let $\mathbf{p}$ and $\mathbf{z}_i$ be the respective Perron vectors of $\mathbf{A}$ and the Perron complement $\mathbf{P}_i$ defined in (15.4.2). The matrix

$$\mathbf{C} = \begin{pmatrix} \mathbf{e}^T\mathbf{A}_{11}\mathbf{z}_1 & \cdots & \mathbf{e}^T\mathbf{A}_{1k}\mathbf{z}_k \\ \vdots & \ddots & \vdots \\ \mathbf{e}^T\mathbf{A}_{k1}\mathbf{z}_1 & \cdots & \mathbf{e}^T\mathbf{A}_{kk}\mathbf{z}_k \end{pmatrix}_{k\times k}$$

is called the *coupling matrix* , and it has the following properties.

- $\mathbf{C}$ is nonnegative and irreducible.
- $\rho(\mathbf{C}) = r$.
- The Perron vector for $\mathbf{C}$, called the *coupling vector,* is given by $\boldsymbol{\xi} = \begin{pmatrix} \xi_1 \\ \xi_2 \\ \vdots \\ \xi_k \end{pmatrix}$, where $\xi_i = \mathbf{e}^T\mathbf{p}_i$ is as defined in (15.4.12).
- The Perron vector for $\mathbf{A}$ is given by $\mathbf{p} = \begin{pmatrix} \mathbf{p}_1 \\ \mathbf{p}_2 \\ \vdots \\ \mathbf{p}_k \end{pmatrix} = \begin{pmatrix} \xi_1\mathbf{z}_1 \\ \xi_2\mathbf{z}_2 \\ \vdots \\ \xi_k\mathbf{z}_k \end{pmatrix}$.

Proof. $\mathbf{C} \geq \mathbf{0}$ because each term $c_{ij} = \mathbf{e}^T\mathbf{A}_{ij}\mathbf{z}_j$ is nonnegative. $\mathbf{C}$ is irreducible because $c_{ij} = 0 \iff \mathbf{A}_{ij} = \mathbf{0}$ (if $\mathbf{C}$ could be permuted to a block triangular form, then so could $\mathbf{A}$). To prove the rest of the theorem, notice that $\mathbf{C} = \mathbf{RAL}$, where $\mathbf{R}$ and $\mathbf{L}$ are given by

$$\mathbf{R} = \begin{pmatrix} \mathbf{e}^T & \mathbf{0} & \cdots & \mathbf{0} \\ \mathbf{0} & \mathbf{e}^T & \cdots & \mathbf{0} \\ \vdots & \vdots & \ddots & \vdots \\ \mathbf{0} & \mathbf{0} & \cdots & \mathbf{e}^T \end{pmatrix}_{k\times n} \qquad \mathbf{L} = \begin{pmatrix} \mathbf{z}_1 & \mathbf{0} & \cdots & \mathbf{0} \\ \mathbf{0} & \mathbf{z}_2 & \cdots & \mathbf{0} \\ \vdots & \vdots & \ddots & \vdots \\ \mathbf{0} & \mathbf{0} & \cdots & \mathbf{z}_k \end{pmatrix}_{n\times k}.$$

We know from (15.4.12) that $\mathbf{L}\boldsymbol{\xi} = \mathbf{p}$ and $\mathbf{Rp} = \boldsymbol{\xi}$, so

$$\mathbf{C}\boldsymbol{\xi} = \mathbf{RAL}\boldsymbol{\xi} = \mathbf{RAp} = \mathbf{R}(r\mathbf{p}) = r\boldsymbol{\xi}.$$

Furthermore, $\boldsymbol{\xi} > \mathbf{0}$ (because $\mathbf{p}_i > \mathbf{0}$ for each i), and $\mathbf{e}^T\boldsymbol{\xi} = \mathbf{e}^T\mathbf{Rp} = \mathbf{e}^T\mathbf{p} = 1$. It now follows that $r = \rho(\mathbf{C})$ and $\boldsymbol{\xi}$ is the Perron vector for $\mathbf{C}$. The conclusion that $\mathbf{p} = \begin{pmatrix} \xi_1\mathbf{z}_1 \\ \xi_2\mathbf{z}_2 \\ \vdots \\ \xi_k\mathbf{z}_k \end{pmatrix}$ comes from (15.4.13). ∎

The matrices $\mathbf{R}$ and $\mathbf{L}$ in the above proof are special cases of transformations known respectively as ***restriction*** and ***prolongation*** operations because when $n > k$, $\mathbf{R}$ "restricts" n-tuples down to k-tuples while $\mathbf{L}$ "prolongates" k-tuples back up to n-tuples in an inverse-like manner since $\mathbf{RL} = \mathbf{I}$. Restriction-prolongation techniques like the one above are popular tools in applied and numerical work.

To solidify the concepts of Perron complementation, consider the following example. The matrix

$$\mathbf{A} = \left(\begin{array}{cc|cc} 2 & 1 & 0 & 3 \\ 4 & 2 & 3 & 0 \\ \hline 0 & 3 & 2 & 4 \\ 3 & 0 & 1 & 2 \end{array}\right) = \begin{pmatrix} \mathbf{A}_{11} & \mathbf{A}_{12} \\ \mathbf{A}_{21} & \mathbf{A}_{22} \end{pmatrix}$$

is irreducible with $\rho(\mathbf{A}) = 7$, and the two Perron complements are

$$\mathbf{P}_1 = \mathbf{A}_{11} + \mathbf{A}_{12}(7\mathbf{I} - \mathbf{A}_{22})^{-1}\mathbf{A}_{21} = \tfrac{1}{7}\begin{pmatrix} 29 & 10 \\ 40 & 29 \end{pmatrix}, \quad \text{with } \rho(\mathbf{P}_1) = 7,$$

and

$$\mathbf{P}_2 = \mathbf{A}_{22} + \mathbf{A}_{21}(7\mathbf{I} - \mathbf{A}_{11})^{-1}\mathbf{A}_{12} = \tfrac{1}{7}\begin{pmatrix} 29 & 40 \\ 10 & 29 \end{pmatrix}, \quad \text{with } \rho(\mathbf{P}_2) = 7.$$

The respective Perron vectors for $\mathbf{P}_1$ and $\mathbf{P}_2$ are

$$\mathbf{z}_1 = \begin{pmatrix} 1/3 \\ 2/3 \end{pmatrix} \mathbf{z}_2 = \begin{pmatrix} 2/3 \\ 1/3 \end{pmatrix},$$

and the coupling matrix is

$$\mathbf{C} = \begin{pmatrix} \mathbf{e}^T\mathbf{A}_{11}\mathbf{z}_1 & \mathbf{e}^T\mathbf{A}_{12}\mathbf{z}_2 \\ \mathbf{e}^T\mathbf{A}_{21}\mathbf{z}_1 & \mathbf{e}^T\mathbf{A}_{22}\mathbf{z}_2 \end{pmatrix} = \begin{pmatrix} 4 & 3 \\ 3 & 4 \end{pmatrix}, \quad \text{with } \rho(\mathbf{C}) = 7.$$

The coupling vector (the Perron vector of $\mathbf{C}$) is $\boldsymbol{\xi} = \begin{pmatrix} 1/2 \\ 1/2 \end{pmatrix}$, so the Perron vector of $\mathbf{A}$ is

$$\mathbf{p} = \begin{pmatrix} (1/2)\mathbf{z}_1 \\ (1/2)\mathbf{z}_2 \end{pmatrix} = \frac{1}{6}\begin{pmatrix} 1 \\ 2 \\ 2 \\ 1 \end{pmatrix}.$$

Knowledge of $\rho(\mathbf{A})$ is required to form the Perron complements of $\mathbf{A}$, and this can be a bottleneck in some situations. However, there are important applications in which the spectral radius is known in advance. A notable example is the theory of finite Markov chains as described in section 15.3 because $\rho(\mathbf{P}) = 1$ for all transition probability matrices $\mathbf{P}$. The next section is devoted to showing how Perron complementation is applied in the theory of Markov chains.

15.5 STOCHASTIC COMPLEMENTATION

When the concept of Perron complementation is applied to irreducible stochastic matrices, some useful aspects of Markov chains are produced. In particular, the Perron complementation idea applied to Markov chains results in a technique for reducing a chain with a large number of states to a smaller chain without losing important characteristics.

Consider an n-state irreducible Markov chain, and let

$$\mathbf{P} = \begin{pmatrix} \mathbf{P}_{11} & \mathbf{P}_{12} & \cdots & \mathbf{P}_{1k} \\ \mathbf{P}_{21} & \mathbf{P}_{22} & \cdots & \mathbf{P}_{2k} \\ \vdots & \vdots & \ddots & \vdots \\ \mathbf{P}_{k1} & \mathbf{P}_{k2} & \cdots & \mathbf{P}_{kk} \end{pmatrix} \quad \text{(with square diagonal blocks)} \qquad (15.5.1)$$

be a partition of the associated transition probability matrix. We know that $\mathbf{P}$ is an irreducible stochastic matrix with $\rho(\mathbf{P}) = 1$ (p. 177), so the associated Perron complements are given by

$$\mathbf{S}_i = \mathbf{P}_{ii} + \mathbf{P}_{i\star}(\mathbf{I} - \mathbf{P}_i^\star)^{-1}\mathbf{P}_{\star i}.$$

As we will see, these complements $\mathbf{S}_i$ have additional stochastic properties, so they are alternately referred to as *stochastic complements* in the context of Markov chains. Properties (15.4.7)–(15.4.9) on page 189 guarantee that each $\mathbf{S}_i$ is also a nonnegative irreducible matrix with $\rho(\mathbf{S}_i) = 1$. Furthermore,

$$\begin{aligned} \mathbf{Pe} = \mathbf{e} \quad &\Longrightarrow \quad \mathbf{P}_{ii}\mathbf{e} + \mathbf{P}_{i\star}\mathbf{e} = \mathbf{e} \quad \text{and} \quad \mathbf{P}_{\star i}\mathbf{e} + \mathbf{P}_i^\star\mathbf{e} = \mathbf{e} \\ &\Longrightarrow \quad \mathbf{P}_{ii}\mathbf{e} + \mathbf{P}_{i\star}\mathbf{e} = \mathbf{e} \quad \text{and} \quad \mathbf{e} = (\mathbf{I} - \mathbf{P}_i^\star)^{-1}\mathbf{P}_{\star i}\mathbf{e} \\ &\Longrightarrow \quad \mathbf{S}_i\mathbf{e} = \mathbf{e}. \end{aligned}$$

In other words, every stochastic complement $\mathbf{S}_i$ is itself the transition probability matrix of some smaller Markov chain.

To understand the relationship between the smaller chain defined by $\mathbf{S}_i$ and the parent chain associated with $\mathbf{P}$, consider the simpler (but equivalent) situation where the set of states $\{1, 2, \ldots, n\}$ is partitioned into two clusters,

$$\mathcal{S}_1 = \{1, 2, \ldots, r\}\mathcal{S}_2 = \{r+1,\, r+2, \ldots, n\},$$

so that

$$\mathbf{P} = \begin{array}{c} 1 \\ \vdots \\ r \\ r+1 \\ \vdots \\ n \end{array} \overset{\begin{array}{cc} 1 \cdots r & r+1 \cdots n \end{array}}{\left(\begin{array}{c|c} \mathbf{P}_{11} & \mathbf{P}_{12} \\ \hline \mathbf{P}_{21} & \mathbf{P}_{22} \end{array}\right)}, \quad \text{and} \quad \begin{aligned} \mathbf{S}_1 &= \mathbf{P}_{11} + \mathbf{P}_{12}(\mathbf{I} - \mathbf{P}_{22})^{-1}\mathbf{P}_{21}, \\ \mathbf{S}_2 &= \mathbf{P}_{22} + \mathbf{P}_{21}(\mathbf{I} - \mathbf{P}_{11})^{-1}\mathbf{P}_{12}. \end{aligned} \tag{15.5.2}$$

Focus on one of these complements—say, the second one—and interpret the (i, j)-entry $[\mathbf{S}_2]_{ij} = [\mathbf{P}_{22}]_{ij} + [\mathbf{P}_{21}(\mathbf{I} - \mathbf{P}_{11})^{-1}\mathbf{P}_{12}]_{ij}$. Notice that $[\mathbf{P}_{22}]_{ij}$ is simply the probability of moving from state $r + i \in \mathcal{S}_2$ to state $r + j \in \mathcal{S}_2$ in one step, while

$$[\mathbf{P}_{21}(\mathbf{I} - \mathbf{P}_{11})^{-1}\mathbf{P}_{12}]_{ij} = \sum_{k=1}^{r}[\mathbf{P}_{21}]_{ik}[(\mathbf{I} - \mathbf{P}_{11})^{-1}\mathbf{P}_{12}]_{kj}.$$

The term $[\mathbf{P}_{21}]_{ik}$ is the probability of moving from $r + i \in \mathcal{S}_2$ to $k \in \mathcal{S}_1$ in one step, while $[(\mathbf{I} - \mathbf{P}_{11})^{-1}\mathbf{P}_{12}]_{kj}$ is the probability of hitting state $r + j \in \mathcal{S}_2$ the first time the chain enters $\mathcal{S}_2$ when the process starts from $k \in \mathcal{S}_1$. This can be seen by considering the states in $\mathcal{S}_2$ to be absorbing so as to artificially force the process to stop as soon as the chain enters $\mathcal{S}_2$. It follows from the results on absorbing chains (p. 186) that $[(\mathbf{I} - \mathbf{P}_{11})^{-1}\mathbf{P}_{12}]_{ij}$ is the probability of entering $\mathcal{S}_2$ at state $r + j$ when the chain starts in $k \in \mathcal{S}_1$. Consequently, $[\mathbf{P}_{21}]_{ik}[(\mathbf{I} - \mathbf{P}_{11})^{-1}\mathbf{P}_{12}]_{kj}$ is the probability of moving directly from $r+i \in \mathcal{S}_2$ to $k \in \mathcal{S}_1$ and then, perhaps after several steps inside of $\mathcal{S}_1$, reentering $\mathcal{S}_2$ at state $r + j$ (without regard to what happened while the process was in $\mathcal{S}_1$). Therefore,

$$[\mathbf{S}_2]_{ij} = [\mathbf{P}_{22}]_{ij} + \sum_{k=1}^{r}[\mathbf{P}_{21}]_{ik}[(\mathbf{I} - \mathbf{P}_{11})^{-1}\mathbf{P}_{12}]_{kj}$$

is the probability of moving from $r + i \in \mathcal{S}_2$ to $r + j \in \mathcal{S}_2$ in a single step or else by moving directly from $r+i \in \mathcal{S}_2$ to somewhere inside of $\mathcal{S}_1$ (perhaps staying there for awhile) and then hitting state $r+j$ upon first reentry into $\mathcal{S}_2$. In other words, $\mathbf{S}_2$ is the transition probability matrix for a chain that records the location of the process only when the process is visiting states in $\mathcal{S}_2$, and visits to states in $\mathcal{S}_1$ are simply ignored or *censored out.*

15.6 CENSORING

Censored Markov Chains

For an n-state irreducible Markov chain with transition probability matrix $\mathbf{P}$ that is partitioned as in (15.5.1), let $\mathcal{S}$ denote the collection of states that correspond to the row (or column) indices of the ith diagonal block $\mathbf{P}_{ii}$, and let $\overline{\mathcal{S}}$ denote the complementary set of states. The *censored Markov chain* associated with $\mathcal{S}$ is defined to be the Markov chain that records the location of the parent chain (defined by $\mathbf{P}$) only when the parent chain visits states in $\mathcal{S}$. Visits to states in $\overline{\mathcal{S}}$ are ignored. The transition probability matrix for this censored chain is the stochastic complement

$$\mathbf{S}_i = \mathbf{P}_{ii} + \mathbf{P}_{i\star}(\mathbf{I} - \mathbf{P}_i^\star)^{-1}\mathbf{P}_{\star i}. \tag{15.6.1}$$

Property (15.4.8) guarantees that every stochastic complement $\mathbf{S}_i$ is an irreducible matrix, so every censored chain is an irreducible Markov chain. Consequently each censored chain has an associated stationary probability distribution, $\mathbf{s}_i^T$, such that

$$\mathbf{s}_i^T\mathbf{S}_i = \mathbf{s}_i^T, \qquad \mathbf{s}_i^T > \mathbf{0}, \mathbf{s}_i^T\mathbf{e} = 1 \qquad \text{(as summarized on p. 181).}$$

In the language of matrix theory $\mathbf{s}_i^T$ is the left-hand Perron vector for $\mathbf{S}_i$, but in the context of Markov chains $\mathbf{s}_i^T$ is called a *censored probability distribution.*

To interpret the meaning of a censored distribution, suppose that the state space for an n-state Markov chain is partitioned into clusters as

$$\{1,2,\ldots,n\} = \mathcal{S}_1 \cup \mathcal{S}_2 \cup \cdots \cup \mathcal{S}_k, \quad \text{where} \quad \mathcal{S}_i = \{\sigma_{i1}, \sigma_{i2}, \ldots, \sigma_{in_i}\}, \tag{15.6.2}$$

and partition the tth step distribution and the stationary distribution in accord with (15.6.2) as

$$\mathbf{p}^T(t) = \left(\mathbf{p}_1^T(t) \,|\, \mathbf{p}_2^T(t) \,|\, \cdots \,|\, \mathbf{p}_k^T(t)\right) \boldsymbol{\pi}^T = \left(\boldsymbol{\pi}_1^T \,|\, \boldsymbol{\pi}_2^T \,|\, \cdots \,|\, \boldsymbol{\pi}_k^T\right). \tag{15.6.3}$$

To ensure that limits exist assume the chain is primitive (page 181). Let X_t be the state of the chain after the tth step, and let Y_t be the cluster that contains X_t after the tth step. The probability of being in state σ_{ij} (the jth state of the ith cluster) after t steps is

$$P(X_t = \sigma_{ij}) = \left[\mathbf{p}_i^T(t)\right]_j \quad \text{(the } j^{th} \text{ component of } \mathbf{p}_i^T(t)\text{),}$$

and the limiting probability of being in σ_{ij} is

$$\lim_{t\to\infty} P(X_t = \sigma_{ij}) = \lim_{t\to\infty} \left[\mathbf{p}_i^T(t)\right]_j = \left[\boldsymbol{\pi}_i^T\right]_j \quad \text{(the } j^{th} \text{ component of } \boldsymbol{\pi}_i^T\text{).}$$

Similarly, the probability of being inside cluster $\mathcal{S}_i$ after t steps is

$$P(Y_t = i) = \mathbf{p}_i^T(t)\mathbf{e},$$

and the limiting probability of being somewhere in $\mathcal{S}_i$ is

$$\lim_{t\to\infty} P(Y_t = i) = \lim_{t\to\infty} \mathbf{p}_i^T(t)\mathbf{e} = \boldsymbol{\pi}_i^T\mathbf{e}. \tag{15.6.4}$$

Since $\boldsymbol{\pi}^T$ the left-hand Perron vector for the transition probability matrix $\mathbf{P}$, it follows from the left-hand interpretation of (15.4.12) that the jth component of ith censored distribution $\mathbf{s}_i^T$ with respect to the partition (15.6.2) is

$$\left[\mathbf{s}_i^T\right]_j = \frac{\left[\boldsymbol{\pi}_i^T\right]_j}{\boldsymbol{\pi}_i^T\mathbf{e}} = \lim_{t\to\infty} \frac{\left[\mathbf{p}_i^T(t)\right]_j}{\mathbf{p}_i^T(t)\mathbf{e}} = \lim_{t\to\infty} \frac{P(X_t = \sigma_{ij})}{P(Y_t = i)} = \lim_{t\to\infty} P(X_t = \sigma_{ij} \mid Y_t = i).$$

In other words, $\left[\mathbf{s}_i^T\right]_j$ is the limiting conditional probability of being in σ_{ij} given that the process is somewhere in $\mathcal{S}_i$. Below is a summary.

Censored Probability Distributions

Consider an n-state irreducible Markov chain whose transition probability matrix $\mathbf{P}$, stationary distribution $\boldsymbol{\pi}^T = (\boldsymbol{\pi}_1^T \mid \boldsymbol{\pi}_2^T \mid \cdots \mid \boldsymbol{\pi}_k^T)$, and state space are partitioned according to

$$\{1, 2, \ldots, n\} = \mathcal{S}_1 \cup \mathcal{S}_2 \cup \cdots \cup \mathcal{S}_k \quad \text{where} \quad \mathcal{S}_i = \{\sigma_{i1}, \sigma_{i2}, \ldots, \sigma_{in_i}\}.$$

The ***censored probability distributions*** are the stationary distributions $\mathbf{s}_i^T$ of the censored Markov chains defined by the stochastic complements $\mathbf{S}_i$ given in (15.6.1) so that $\mathbf{s}_i^T\mathbf{S}_i = \mathbf{s}_i^T$, where $\mathbf{s}_i^T > \mathbf{0}$ and $\mathbf{s}_i^T\mathbf{e} = 1$. Censored distributions have the following additional properties.

$$\mathbf{s}_i^T = \boldsymbol{\pi}_i^T / \boldsymbol{\pi}_i^T\mathbf{e} \quad \text{for each } i = 1, 2, \ldots k. \tag{15.6.5}$$

- If $\mathbf{P}$ is primitive, then the jth component of $\mathbf{s}_i^T$ is the limiting conditional probability of being in the jth state of cluster $\mathcal{S}_i$ given that the process is somewhere in $\mathcal{S}_i$. In other words,

$$\left[\mathbf{s}_i^T\right]_j = \lim_{t\to\infty} P(X_t = \sigma_{ij} \mid Y_t = i),$$

where X_t and Y_t are the respective state and cluster number of the chain after the tth step.

15.7 AGGREGATION

Now specialize the coupling theorem for Perron complements given on page 191 to Markov chains. Vectors are on the left-hand side of matrices for Markov chain applications, so, for the partition of $\mathbf{P}$ in (15.5.1) that corresponds to the partition of the state space in (15.6.2), the coupling matrix on page 191 takes the form

$$\mathbf{A} = \begin{pmatrix} \mathbf{s}_1^T\mathbf{P}_{11}\mathbf{e} & \cdots & \mathbf{s}_1^T\mathbf{P}_{1k}\mathbf{e} \\ \vdots & \ddots & \vdots \\ \mathbf{s}_k^T\mathbf{P}_{k1}\mathbf{e} & \cdots & \mathbf{s}_k^T\mathbf{P}_{kk}\mathbf{e} \end{pmatrix} = \begin{pmatrix} \mathbf{s}_1^T & \cdots & \mathbf{0} \\ \vdots & \ddots & \vdots \\ \mathbf{0} & \cdots & \mathbf{s}_k^T \end{pmatrix} \begin{pmatrix} \mathbf{P}_{11} & \cdots & \mathbf{P}_{1k} \\ \vdots & \ddots & \vdots \\ \mathbf{P}_{k1} & \cdots & \mathbf{P}_{kk} \end{pmatrix} \begin{pmatrix} \mathbf{e} & \cdots & \mathbf{0} \\ \vdots & \ddots & \vdots \\ \mathbf{0} & \cdots & \mathbf{e} \end{pmatrix}$$

$$= \mathbf{L}_{k\times n}\mathbf{P}_{n\times n}\mathbf{R}_{n\times k}, \tag{15.7.1}$$

where the $\mathbf{s}_i^T$'s in $\mathbf{L}$ are the censored distributions, and the $\mathbf{e}$'s in $\mathbf{R}$ are columns of 1's of appropriate size. (We switched the notation for the coupling matrix from $\mathbf{C}$ to $\mathbf{A}$ for reasons that soon will be apparent.) Remarkably, $\mathbf{A}$ also defines an irreducible Markov chain—but this chain has only k states. The nonnegativity and irreducibility of $\mathbf{A}$ are guaranteed by the coupling theorem on page 191, and $\mathbf{A}$ is stochastic because

$$\mathbf{Ae} = \mathbf{LPRe} = \mathbf{LPe} = \mathbf{Le} = \mathbf{e}.$$

To understand the nature of the chain defined by $\mathbf{A}$ along with its stationary distribution $\boldsymbol{\alpha}^T$, let's interpret the individual entries $a_{ij} = \mathbf{s}_i^T\mathbf{P}_{ij}\mathbf{e}$ in $\mathbf{A}$ as probabilities. As before, let X_t and Y_t be the respective state and cluster number of the chain after the tth step, and let $\wedge$ and $\vee$ denote *AND* and *OR*, respectively.

Given that the process is in cluster $\mathcal{S}_i$ after t steps, consider the the probability of moving to cluster $\mathcal{S}_j$ on the next step. In other words, consider

$$P(Y_{t+1} = j \mid Y_t = i) = \frac{P(Y_t = i \wedge Y_{t+1} = j)}{P(Y_t = i)}. \tag{15.7.2}$$

To determine this conditional probability, suppose that

$$\mathbf{P} = \begin{pmatrix} \mathbf{P}_{11} & \cdots & \mathbf{P}_{1k} \\ \vdots & \ddots & \vdots \\ \mathbf{P}_{k1} & \cdots & \mathbf{P}_{kk} \end{pmatrix}, \quad \mathbf{p}^T(t) = (\,\mathbf{p}_1^T(t) \mid \cdots \mid \mathbf{p}_k^T(t)\,), \boldsymbol{\pi}^T = (\,\boldsymbol{\pi}_1^T \mid \cdots \mid \boldsymbol{\pi}_k^T\,)$$

are partitioned in accord with (15.6.2), and compute the numerator in (15.7.2) as

$$\begin{aligned}
P(Y_t &= i \wedge Y_{t+1} = j) \\
&= P\big([X_t = \sigma_{i1} \vee \cdots \vee X_t = \sigma_{in_i}] \wedge [X_{t+1} = \sigma_{j1} \vee \cdots \vee X_{t+1} = \sigma_{jn_j}]\big) \\
&= P\big([X_t = \sigma_{i1} \wedge X_{t+1} = \sigma_{j1}] \vee \cdots \vee [X_t = \sigma_{in_i} \wedge X_{t+1} = \sigma_{jn_j}]\big) \\
&= \sum_{g=1}^{n_i}\sum_{h=1}^{n_j} P(X_t = \sigma_{ig} \wedge X_{t+1} = \sigma_{jh}) \\
&= \sum_{g=1}^{n_i}\sum_{h=1}^{n_j} P(X_t = \sigma_{ig})\,P(X_{t+1} = \sigma_{jh} \mid X_t = \sigma_{ig}) \\
&= \sum_{g=1}^{n_i} \left[\mathbf{p}_i^T(t)\right]_g \sum_{h=1}^{n_j} [\mathbf{P}_{ij}]_{gh} = \sum_{g=1}^{n_i} \left[\mathbf{p}_i^T(t)\right]_g [\mathbf{P}_{ij}\mathbf{e}]_g \\
&= \mathbf{p}_i^T(t)\mathbf{P}_{ij}\mathbf{e}.
\end{aligned}$$

The denominator in (15.7.2) is $P(Y_t = i) = \mathbf{p}_i^T(t)\mathbf{e}$, and thus

$$P(Y_{t+1} = j \mid Y_t = i) = \frac{\mathbf{p}_i^T(t)\mathbf{P}_{ij}\mathbf{e}}{\mathbf{p}_i^T(t)\mathbf{e}}. \tag{15.7.3}$$

It follows from (15.6.5) on page 195 that [3]

$$\mathbf{s}_i^T = \frac{\pi_i^T}{\pi_i^T \mathbf{e}} = \lim_{t\to\infty} \frac{\mathbf{p}_i^T(t)}{\mathbf{p}_i^T(t)\mathbf{e}},$$

and therefore, by (15.7.3), the entries in $\mathbf{A}$ are given by

$$a_{ij} = \mathbf{s}_i^T \mathbf{P}_{ij}\mathbf{e} = \lim_{t\to\infty} \frac{\mathbf{p}_i^T(t)\mathbf{P}_{ij}\mathbf{e}}{\mathbf{p}_i^T(t)\mathbf{e}} = \lim_{t\to\infty} P(Y_{t+1} = j \mid Y_t = i). \tag{15.7.4}$$

An irreducible chain is said to be in *equilibrium* at time (step) t if the process is at steady state in the sense that $\mathbf{p}^T(t) = \pi^T$. Consequently, (15.7.4) means that a_{ij} is the transition probability of moving from cluster $\mathcal{S}_i$ to cluster $\mathcal{S}_j$ after the process has achieved equilibrium. Below is a summary of these observations.

Aggregation Theorem for Markov Chains

An irreducible Markov chain whose states are partitioned into k clusters

$$\{1, 2, \ldots, n\} = \mathcal{S}_1 \cup \mathcal{S}_2 \cup \cdots \cup \mathcal{S}_k$$

can be compressed into a smaller k-state *aggregated chain* whose states are the individual clusters $\mathcal{S}_i$.

- The transition probability matrix $\mathbf{A}$ of the aggregated chain is the coupling matrix described on page 191. That is,

$$\mathbf{A} = \begin{pmatrix} \mathbf{s}_1^T\mathbf{P}_{11}\mathbf{e} & \cdots & \mathbf{s}_1^T\mathbf{P}_{1k}\mathbf{e} \\ \vdots & \ddots & \vdots \\ \mathbf{s}_k^T\mathbf{P}_{k1}\mathbf{e} & \cdots & \mathbf{s}_k^T\mathbf{P}_{kk}\mathbf{e} \end{pmatrix}_{k\times k}, \tag{15.7.5}$$

  where $\mathbf{P}_{ij}$ is the (i, j) block in the partitioned transition matrix $\mathbf{P}$ of the unaggregated chain, and $\mathbf{s}_i^T$ is the censored distribution of the ith stochastic complement derived from $\mathbf{P}$.

- If Y_t is the cluster that the unaggregated chain occupies after t steps, then, for primitive chains, the *aggregated transition probability* $a_{ij} = \mathbf{s}_i^T\mathbf{P}_{ij}\mathbf{e}$ can be expressed as

$$a_{ij} = \lim_{t\to\infty} P(Y_{t+1} = j \mid Y_t = i).$$

In other words, transitions between states in the aggregated chain correspond to transitions between clusters in the unaggregated chain when the unaggregated chain is in equilibrium.

As an example of the utility of aggregation in Markov chains consider the problem of determining the eventual probability that the chain is somewhere inside cluster $\mathcal{S}_i$ (the individual state in $\mathcal{S}_i$ that the process might eventually occupy is irrelevant) without directly computing the stationary probabilities for the chain. In other words, if Y_t is the cluster in which the process resides after t steps, the problem is to determine $\lim_{t\to\infty} P(Y_t = i)$.

[3]For these limits to exist, $\mathbf{P}$ must be assumed to be primitive.

Of course, there is no problem if the stationary probabilities are known because, as pointed out in (15.6.4), if $\mathbf{p}^T(t) = \left(\mathbf{p}_1^T(t) \,|\, \cdots \,|\, \mathbf{p}_k^T(t)\right)$ and $\boldsymbol{\pi}^T = \left(\boldsymbol{\pi}_1^T \,|\, \cdots \,|\, \boldsymbol{\pi}_k^T\right)$, then the limiting probability of being somewhere in $\mathcal{S}_i$ is

$$\alpha_i = \lim_{t\to\infty} P(Y_t = i) = \lim_{t\to\infty} \mathbf{p}_i^T(t)\mathbf{e} = \boldsymbol{\pi}_i^T\mathbf{e}. \tag{15.7.6}$$

But computing all of $\boldsymbol{\pi}^T$ in a large chain just to find $\boldsymbol{\pi}_i^T$ can be wasted effort. Since transitions in the aggregated chain correspond to transitions between the clusters $\mathcal{S}_i$ in the unaggregated chain at equilibrium, we expect the ith component of stationary distribution for the aggregated chain to be the limiting probability of being in $\mathcal{S}_i$, and this is true.

- In other words, if the stationary distribution of the aggregated chain defined by $\mathbf{A}$ in (15.7.5) is $\boldsymbol{\alpha}^T = (\alpha_1, \alpha_2, \ldots, \alpha_k)$, then $\alpha_i = \boldsymbol{\pi}_i^T\mathbf{e} = \lim_{t\to\infty} P(Y_t = i)$.

15.8 DISAGGREGATION

When interpreted in the context of Markov chains, the coupling theorem on page 191 represents an expansion or *disaggregation process.* Below is the formal statement of the disaggregation theorem.

Disaggregation in Markov Chains

Consider an irreducible Markov chain along with the associated aggregated chain for which the respective transition probability matrices are

$$\mathbf{P} = \begin{pmatrix} \mathbf{P}_{11} & \mathbf{P}_{12} & \cdots & \mathbf{P}_{1k} \\ \mathbf{P}_{21} & \mathbf{P}_{22} & \cdots & \mathbf{P}_{2k} \\ \vdots & \vdots & \ddots & \vdots \\ \mathbf{P}_{k1} & \mathbf{P}_{k2} & \cdots & \mathbf{P}_{kk} \end{pmatrix}_{n\times n} \quad \text{and } \mathbf{A} = \begin{pmatrix} \mathbf{s}_1^T\mathbf{P}_{11}\mathbf{e} & \cdots & \mathbf{s}_1^T\mathbf{P}_{1k}\mathbf{e} \\ \vdots & \ddots & \vdots \\ \mathbf{s}_k^T\mathbf{P}_{k1}\mathbf{e} & \cdots & \mathbf{s}_k^T\mathbf{P}_{kk}\mathbf{e} \end{pmatrix}_{k\times k},$$

where $\mathbf{s}_i^T$ is the ith censored distribution (the stationary distribution of the ith stochastic complement $\mathbf{S}_i = \mathbf{P}_{ii} + \mathbf{P}_{i\star}(\mathbf{I} - \mathbf{P}_i^\star)^{-1}\mathbf{P}_{\star i}$). If $\boldsymbol{\alpha}^T = (\alpha_1, \alpha_2, \ldots, \alpha_k)$ is the stationary distribution of the aggregated chain defined by $\mathbf{A}$, then the stationary distribution for the unaggregated chain defined by $\mathbf{P}$ is

$$\boldsymbol{\pi}^T = \left(\alpha_1\mathbf{s}_1^T \,|\, \alpha_2\mathbf{s}_2^T \,|\, \cdots \alpha_k\mathbf{s}_k^T\right).$$

In other words, the censored distributions $\mathbf{s}_i^T$ can be pasted together to form the global distribution $\boldsymbol{\pi}^T$, and the α_i's provide the glue to do the job.

It's clear that disaggregation as stated above can serve as an algorithm for computing the stationary probabilities of any irreducible chain. But while the aggregation-disaggregation results are beautiful theoretical theorems, their straightforward implementation usually doesn't result in a computational advantage over more standard methods. Computing the stochastic complements $\mathbf{S}_i$ in order to determine the censored distributions $\mathbf{s}_i^T$ is generally a computationally intensive task, so as far as computation is concerned, the goal is to somehow exploit special structure exhibited by the chain to judiciously implement the aggregation/disaggregation procedure.

When someone is seeking, it happens quite easily that he sees only the thing that he is seeking; that he is unable to find anything, unable to absorb anything, because he is only thinking of the thing he is seeking, because he has a goal, because he is obsessed with his goal.

Seeking means: to have a goal; but finding means: to be free, to be receptive, to have no goal. You, O worthy one, are perhaps indeed a seeker, for in striving towards your goal, you do not see many things that are under your nose.

— Siddhartha speaking to his friend Govinda
in Hermann Hesse's *Siddhartha* [95]

Chapter Sixteen

Glossary

anchor text text used in the hyperlink when linking from one webpage to another

arc a link between two nodes in a graph

authority a webpage with many inlinks; a good authority has inlinks from pages with high hub scores

authority matrix the matrix $\mathbf{L}^T\mathbf{L}$ created in the HITS method; its dominant right-hand eigenvector is the authority vector, which is used to give a ranking of webpages by their authoritativeness

authority score the numerical score assigned to a webpage that gives a measure of that page's authoritativeness

authority vector a vector that gives the authoritativeness of webpages; the ith component is the authority score for page i

blog a webpage that represents an online diary on a particular topic, which typically has postings sorted by time and many hyperlinks but little textual content

Boolean model a classic model in traditional information retrieval that uses the Boolean operators AND, OR, and NOT to answer queries

co-citation a term in bibliometrics that is used when two papers are cited by the same paper; on the Web it is used when two webpages have inlinks from the same page

content index the part of a search engine devoted to storing information about the content of a webpage

content score the information retrieval score assigned to each page; it is computed from traditional information retrieval factors such as similarity of the page to the query, use of query terms in the title, and the number of times the query terms are used in the page.

co-reference a term in bibliometrics that is used when two papers cite the same paper; on the Web it is used when two webpages have outlinks to the same page

crawler the part of the search engine that sends spiders to travel the Web, gathering new and updated webpages for the engine's indexes

cycle a path in the Web's graph that always returns back to its origin, e.g., a trivial cycle occurs when page A points only to page B and page B points only back to A; the random surfer of the PageRank model can get stuck in a cycle and circle indefinitely in the pages on the path, which causes convergence problems for PageRank

dangling node a webpage with no outlinks, which creates a $\mathbf{0}^T$ row in the PageRank matrix; causes a problem for the random surfer of the PageRank model because the random surfer is trapped whenever he enters a dangling node

dangling node vector the vector $\mathbf{a}$ that has a 1 if page i is a dangling node and 0 otherwise; used to help give the random surfer an outlet whenever he reaches a dangling node

fundamental matrix the matrix $(\mathbf{I} - \alpha bS)^{-1}$ that appears in many PageRank computations

Google bomb a way to spam Google by using the anchor text of a hyperlink to boost the rank of a target page; bomb detonates whenever a query on the terms in the anchor text is submitted and enough pages have the appropriate anchor text for a hyperlink pointing to the target page; invented by Adam Mathes in 2001 as a prank against his friend Andy Pressman

Google dance the shuffling of pages in the ranked list that occurs during the monthly (it's speculated) updating of PageRank

Google matrix the matrix used to determine the PageRank importance scores for webpages; its dominant left-hand eigenvector is the PageRank vector; the Google matrix is given by $\mathbf{G} = \alpha\mathbf{S} + (1 - \alpha)\mathbf{e}\mathbf{v}^T$

Googleopoly Google's dominance of the search market

HITS link analysis model that defines webpages as hubs and authorities and uses the graph structure of the web to rank webpages; developed by Jon Kleinberg in 1998; used by the Teoma search engine; acronym for Hypertext Induced Topic Search

hub a webpage with many outlinks; a good hub has outlinks to pages with high authority scores

hub matrix the matrix $\mathbf{L}\mathbf{L}^T$ created in the HITS method; its dominant right-hand eigenvector is the hub vector, which is used to give a ranking of webpages by their quality as portal pages

hub score the numerical score assigned to a webpage that gives a measure of that page's "hubbiness", which is a measure of the page's quality as a portal page

hub vector a vector that gives the "hubbiness" of webpages; the ith component is the hub score for page i

hyperlink a link in a webpage that allows a reader to automatically jump to another page; creates a directed arc in the web graph

indexer the part of the search engine that compresses a webpage from the crawler into an abbreviated Cliff Notes version; pulls off the essential elements of the page such as title, description, date, images, and tables

indexes where the search engine stores all its webpage information; often a search engine has several different indexes such as an image index, structure index, and inverted index

inlink a link into a webpage

intelligent agent a software robot designed to retrieve specific information automatically

intelligent surfer replaces the random surfer; the intelligent surfer follows the hyperlinks on the Web but does not randomly decide which page to visit next; rather he chooses the page that best fits his needs and interests

inverted file index the search engine's largest index; next to each term in the engine's database there is a list of all pages that use the term; similar to an index in the back of a book

Jon Kleinberg Cornell University computer science professor; inventor of the HITS algorithm

link analysis using the hyperlink structure of the Web to improve search engine rankings

link farm a link spamming technique for boosting a page's rank; a set of webpages that are densely connected

link spamming a type of spamming that uses the Web's hyperlinks to fool search engines

meta-search engine a search engine that combines the results of several independent search engines into one unified list

metatag hidden tag that is embedded in the HTML source code of a webpage to help spiders locate title, description, and keyword information in the page

modified HITS a modification to the standard HITS method that guarantees the existence and uniqueness of the HITS authority and hub vectors; uses the matrices $\xi\mathbf{L}^T\mathbf{L} + (1-\xi)/n\,\mathbf{e}\mathbf{e}^T$ and $\xi\mathbf{L}\mathbf{L}^T + (1-\xi)/n\,\mathbf{e}\mathbf{e}^T$ in place of $\mathbf{L}^T\mathbf{L}$ and $\mathbf{L}\mathbf{L}^T$, the standard authority and hub matrices

neighborhood graph the graph created in the first step of the HITS method; includes all pages that use the query terms as well as pages that link to and from the relevant pages

netizen a citizen of the Internet

node a vertex in a graph; webpages are nodes in the web graph

nondangling node a webpage with at least one outlink; any page that is not dangling

outlink a link from a webpage

overall score the final query-dependent relevancy score given to a page; a combination of the popularity score and the content score

PageRank link analysis model that uses an enormous Markov chain to rank webpages by importance; invented by Brin and Page in 1998; now part of Google

page repository where new or updated pages are temporarily stored after they are retrieved by the crawler module and before they are sent to the indexer

personalization vector the probability vector $\mathbf{v}^T > \mathbf{0}$ in the PageRank model; used to fix the problems of rank sinks and cycles faced by the random surfer; can be used to create personalized PageRank vectors that are biased toward a particular user's interests

polysemy occurs when a word has multiple meanings, e.g., bank

popularity score the score given to each webpage that measures the relative importance or popularity of that page; created from the Web's hyperlink structure

precision a measure of the quality of search results, specifically the ratio of the number of relevant documents to the total number of retrieved documents

primitivity fix the adjustment to the PageRank model that artificially adds direct (although small in weight) connections between every page on the Web; guarantees the existence and uniqueness of the PageRank vector and the convergence of the power method to that vector

probabilistic model a traditional information retrieval model that uses probability and odds ratios to identify the relevance of documents to the query

PR0 an abbreviation for the lowest PageRank score; it's believed that sometimes the pages of spammers are set to PR0 by Google

pure link a page returned in the search results whose ranking is pure in the sense that the page's owner did not pay the search engine for an improved ranking

query information request that is sent to a search engine

query-dependent a measure or model that depends on the query and is computed for each individual query

query-independent any measure or model that is computed regardless of the query; one measure that holds for all queries

query processing the part of the search engine that transforms the user's query into numbers that the system can handle

random surfer a surfer who follows the hyperlink structure of the Web indefinitely by choosing the next page to visit at random from among the outlinking pages of the current page; a convenient way of describing the PageRank model

rank sink a webpage or set of webpages that continue to suck in PageRank during the iterative PageRank computation; once the random surfer enters this set of pages, there is no escape route

real-time an adjective for a process that responds in a short and predictable time frame; the time frame is usually measured in vague units such as a user's patience threshold

recall a measure of the quality of search results, specifically the ratio of number of relevant documents retrieved to the total number of relevant documents in the collection

relevance feedback a refining and tuning technique used by many information retrieval systems; a user selects a subset of retrieved documents that are deemed useful, and with this additional information, a revised set of generally more useful documents is retrieved

relevance scoring a numerical score of a document's relevance to the query that is provided by most information retrieval systems

SALSA link analysis model that combines properties of PageRank and HITS to rank webpages as hubs and authorities; developed by Ronny Lempel and Shlomo Moran in 2000; acronym for Stochastic Approach to Link Structure Analysis

search engine optimization the process of changing a webpage to optimize its potential for high rankings by search engines; includes both ethical and unethical means of boosting rank

Sergey Brin and Larry Page former Ph.D. candidates at Stanford University who developed the PageRank system for ranking webpages by importance; cofounders and co-owners of Google

spam any act meant to intentionally deceive a search engine; spam includes using white text on a white background, link spamming, cloaking, misleading meta-tag descriptions, and Google bombing

special-purpose index the part of a search engine that is devoted to storing special purpose information such as images, PDF files, etc.

spider part of a search engine's crawler module that crawls the Web in search of new and updated pages

sponsored link a page returned in the search results whose owner has paid the search engine company for an improved ranking

stochasticity adjustment the adjustment to the original PageRank model that artificially forces the PageRank matrix to be stochastic; allows the random surfer to teleport to a new page immediately after entering a dangling node

structure index the part of a search engine that stores information about the link structure of the Web

synonymy occurs when two words have the same meaning, e.g., car and automobile

teleport a periodic action taken by the random surfer whereby he stops following the Web's hyperlink structure and immediately jumps to a new page at random; also occurs immediately after the random surfer enters a dangling node

traditional information retrieval the field that studies search within nonlinked document collections

TrafficRank link analysis model that uses optimization and entropy to rank webpages by their traffic flow; developed by John Tomlin in 2003

vector space model a traditional information retrieval model that thinks of documents as vectors in high-dimensional space and uses the angle between vectors to determine the similarity of documents to the query

web graph the graph created by the Web's hyperlink structure; the nodes in the graph are webpages and the arcs are hyperlinks

web information retrieval the field that studies search within the world's largest linked collection, the World Wide Web

Bibliography

[1] Caslon Analytics net metrics and statistics guide.
http://www.caslon.com.au/metricsguide.htm.

[2] Clever—IBM Corporation Almaden Research Center.
http://www.almaden.ibm.com/cs/k53/clever.html.

[3] Text REtrieval Conference. http://trec.nist.gov/.

[4] World Wide Web Conference. http://www2004.org.

[5] How much information, 2003. http://www.sims.berkeley.edu/how-much-info-2003.

[6] Medlars test collection, December 2003. Available at
http://www.cs.utk.edu/~lsi/.

[7] Why does my page's rank keep changing? Google PageRank information. http://www.google.com/webmasters/4.html, 2003.

[8] Eytan Adar, Li Zhang, Lada A. Adamic, and Rajan M. Lukose. Implicit structure and the dynamics of blogspace. In *The Thirteenth International World Wide Web Conference*, New York, 2004. ACM Press.

[9] Arvind Arasu, Junghoo Cho, Hector Garcia-Molina, Andreas Paepcke, and Sriram Raghavan. Searching the Web. *ACM Transactions on Internet Technology*, 2001.

[10] Arvind Arasu, Jasmine Novak, Andrew Tomkins, and John Tomlin. PageRank computation and the structure of the Web: Experiments and algorithms. In *The Eleventh International WWW Conference*, New York, May 2002. ACM Press.

[11] Konstantin Avrachenkov and Nelly Litvak. Decomposition of the Google PageRank and optimal linking strategy. Technical report, INRIA, January 2004.

[12] Konstantin Avrachenkov and Nelly Litvak. The effect of new links on Google PageRank. Technical report, INRIA, July 2004.

[13] Ricardo Baeza-Yates and Emilio Davis. Web page ranking using link attributes. In *The Thirteenth International World Wide Web Conference*, pages 328–29, New York, 2004. ACM Press. Poster.

[14] Ricardo Baeza-Yates and Berthier Ribeiro-Neto. *Modern Information Retrieval.* ACM Press, New York, 1999.

[15] Ziv Bar-Yossef, Andrei Z. Broder, Ravi Kumar, and Andrew Tomkins. Sic transit gloria telae: Towards an understanding of the Web's decay. In *The Thirteenth International World Wide Web Conference*, New York, 2004. ACM Press.

[16] Albert-Laszlo Barabasi. *Linked: The New Science of Networks*. Plume, 2003.

[17] Albert-Laszlo Barabasi, Reka Albert, and Hawoong Jeong. Scale-free characteristics of random networks: The topology of the World-Wide Web. *Physica A*, 281:69–77, 2000.

[18] R. Barrett, M. Berry, T. F. Chan, J. Demmel, J. Donato, J. Dongarra, V. Eijkhout, R. Pozo, C. Romine, and H. Van der Vorst. *Templates for the Solution of Linear Systems: Building Blocks for Iterative Methods*. SIAM, Philadelphia, 2nd edition, 1994.

[19] Luiz Andre Barroso, Jeffrey Dean, and Urs Holzle. Web search for a planet: The Google cluster architecture. *IEEE Micro*, pages 22–28, 2003.

[20] Gely P. Basharin, Amy N. Langville, and Valeriy A. Naumov. The life and work of A. A. Markov. *Linear Algebra and Its Applications*, (386):3–26, 2004.

[21] Abraham Berman and Robert J. Plemmons. *Nonnegative Matrices in the Mathematical Sciences*. Academic Press, 1979.

[22] Michael W. Berry, editor. *Computational Information Retrieval*. SIAM, Philadelphia, 2001.

[23] Michael W. Berry and Murray Browne. *Understanding Search Engines: Mathematical Modeling and Text Retrieval*. SIAM, Philadelphia, 2nd edition, 2005.

[24] Michael W. Berry, Zlatko Drmac, and Elizabeth R. Jessup. Matrices, vector spaces and information retrieval. *SIAM Review*, 41:335–62, 1999.

[25] Krishna Bharat, Andrei Broder, Monika Henzinger, Puneet Kumar, and Suresh Venkatasubramanian. The connectivity server: Fast access to linkage information on the Web. In *The Seventh World Wide Web Conference*, pages 469–77, Brisbane, Australia, 1998.

[26] Krishna Bharat and Monika R. Henzinger. Improved algorithms for topic distillation in hyperlinked environments. In *21st International ACM SIGIR Conference on Research and Development in Information Retrieval (SIGIR)*, pages 104–11, 1998.

[27] Krishna Bharat, Farzin Maghoul, and Raymie Stata. The term vector database: Fast access to indexing terms for webpages. *Computer Networks*, 33:247–255, 2000.

[28] Monica Bianchini, Marco Gori, and Franco Scarselli. PageRank: A circuital analysis. In *The Eleventh International WWW Conference*, May 2002.

[29] Monica Bianchini, Marco Gori, and Franco Scarselli. Inside PageRank. *ACM Transactions on Internet Technology*, 5(1), 2005. To appear.

[30] Nancy Blachman, Eric Fredricksen, and Fritz Schneider. *How to Do Everything with Google*. McGraw-Hill, 2003.

[31] Paolo Boldi, Massimo Santini, and Sebastiano Vigna. Do your worst to make the best: Paradoxical effects in PageRank incremental computations. In *Proceedings of WAW 2004, Lecture Notes in Computer Science*, number 3248, pages 168–80. Springer-Verlag, 2004.

[32] Paolo Boldi, Massimo Santini, and Sebastiano Vigna. PageRank as a function of the damping factor. In *The Fourteenth International World Wide Web Conference*, New York, 2005. ACM Press.

[33] Paolo Boldi and Sebastiano Vigna. The WebGraph framework II: Codes for the World Wide Web. Technical Report 294-03, Universita di Milano, Dipartimento di Scienze dell' Informazione Engineering, 2003.

[34] Paolo Boldi and Sebastiano Vigna. The WebGraph framework I: Compression techniques. In *The Thirteenth International World Wide Web Conference*, pages 595–602, New York, 2004. ACM Press.

[35] Jorge Luis Borges. *The Library of Babel.* David R. Godine, 2000. Translated by Andrew Hurley.

[36] Allan Borodin, Gareth O. Roberts, Jeffrey S. Rosenthal, and Panayiotis Tsaparas. Finding authorities and hubs from link structures on the World Wide Web. *The Eleventh International World Wide Web Conference*, pages 415–29, 2001.

[37] P. Bradley. Multi-search engines–a comparison. webpage, January 2002. `http://www.philb.com/msengine.htm`.

[38] Sergey Brin, Rajeev Motwani, Lawrence Page, and Terry Winograd. What can you do with a Web in your pocket? *Data Engineering Bulletin*, 21:37–47, 1998.

[39] Sergey Brin and Lawrence Page. The anatomy of a large-scale hypertextual Web search engine. *Computer Networks and ISDN Systems*, 33:107–17, 1998.

[40] Sergey Brin, Lawrence Page, R. Motwami, and Terry Winograd. The PageRank citation ranking: Bringing order to the Web. Technical Report 1999-0120, Computer Science Department, Stanford University, 1999.

[41] Andrei Broder, Ravi Kumar, and Marzin Maghoul. Graph structure in the Web. In *The Ninth International World Wide Web Conference*, pages 309–320, New York, May 2000. ACM Press.

[42] Andrei Broder, Ronny Lempel, Farzin Maghoul, and Jan Pedersen. Efficient PageRank approximation via graph aggregation. In *The Thirteenth International World Wide Web Conference*, pages 484–85, New York, 2004. ACM Press. Poster.

[43] Vannevar Bush. As we may think. *Atlantic Monthly*, 176(1):101–8, 1945.

[44] Tara Calishain and Rael Dornfest. *Google Hacks: 100 Industrial-Strength Tips and Tricks*. O'Reilly, 2003.

[45] Lord John Campbell. *The Lives Of the Chief Justices of England*, volume 3. John Murray, Albemarle Street, London, 1868.

[46] Steven Campbell and Carl D. Meyer. *Generalized Inverses of Linear Transformations*. Pitman, San Francisco, 1979.

[47] Yen-Yu Chen, Qingqing Gan, and Torsten Suel. I/O-efficient techniques for computing PageRank. In *Proceedings of the Eleventh International Conference on Information and Knowledge Management (CIKM'02)*, pages 549–557, Virginia, 2002.

[48] Steve Chien, Cynthia Dwork, Ravi Kumar, and D. Sivakumar. Towards exploiting link evolution. In *Workshop on Algorithms and Models for the Web Graph*, 2001.

[49] Grace E. Cho and Carl D. Meyer. Markov chain sensitivity measured by mean first passage times. *Linear Algebra and Its Applications*, 313:21–28, 2000.

[50] Grace E. Cho and Carl D. Meyer. Comparison of perturbation bounds for the stationary distribution of a Markov chain. *Linear Algebra and Its Applications*, 335(1–3):137–150, 2001.

[51] Grace E. Cho and Carl D. Meyer. Aggregation/disaggregation errors for nearly uncoupled Markov chains. Technical report, NCSU Tech. Report #102301, 2003.

[52] Junghoo Cho and Hector Garcia-Molina. The evolution of the Web and implications for an incremental crawler. In *Proceedings of the Twenty-sixth International Conference on Very Large Databases*, pages 200–209, New York, 2000. ACM Press.

[53] David Cohn and Huan Chang. Learning to probabilistically identify authoritative documents. In *Proceedings of the 17th International Conference on Machine Learning*, pages 167–174, Stanford, CA, 2000.

[54] Thomas H. Cormen, Charles E. Leiserson, Ronald L. Rivest, and Clifford Stein. *Introduction to Algorithms*. MIT Press, 2001.

[55] G. M. Del Corso, A. Gulli, and F. Romani. Exploiting Web matrix permutations to speedup PageRank computation. Technical Report IIT TR-04/2004, Istituto di Informatica e Telematica, May 2004.

[56] P. J. Courtois. *Decomposability*. Academic Press, New York, 1977.

[57] James W. Demmel. *Applied Numerical Linear Algebra*. SIAM, 1997.

[58] Michelangelo Diligenti, Marco Gori, and Marco Maggini. Web page scoring systems for horizontal and vertical search. In *The Eleventh International World Wide Web Conference*, pages 508–516, Honolulu, HI, 2002. ACM Press.

[59] Chris Ding, Xiaofeng He, Parry Husbands, Hongyuan Zha, and Horst Simon. Link analysis: Hubs and authorities on the World Wide Web. Technical Report 47847, Lawrence Berkeley National Laboratory, May 2001.

[60] Chris Ding, Xiaofeng He, Hongyuan Zha, and Horst Simon. PageRank, HITS and a unified framework for link analysis. In *Proceedings of the 25th ACM SIGIR Conference*, pages 353–354, Tampere, Finland, August 2002.

[61] Chris H. Q. Ding, Hongyuan Zha, Xiaofeng He, Parry Husbands, and Horst D. Simon. Link analysis: Hubs and authorities on the World Wide Web. *SIAM Review*, 46(2):256–68, 2004.

[62] Martin Dodge and Rob Kitchins. *Atlas of Cyberspace*. Addison-Wesley, 2001.

[63] Debora Donato, Luigi Laura, Stefano Leonardi, and Stefano Millozzi. Large scale properties of the webgraph. *The European Physical Journal B*, 38:239–43, 2004.

[64] Susan T. Dumais. Improving the retrieval of information from external sources. *Behavior Research Methods, Instruments and Computers*, 23:229–236, 1991.

[65] Cynthia Dwork, Ravi Kumar, and Moni Naor and D. Sivakumar. Rank aggregation methods for the Web. In *The Tenth International World Wide Web Conference*, New York, 2001. ACM Press.

[66] Nadav Eiron, Kevin S. McCurley, and John A. Tomlin. Ranking the Web frontier. In *The Thirteenth International World Wide Web Conference*, New York, 2004. ACM Press.

[67] Ronald Fagin, Anna R. Karlin, Jon Kleinberg, Prabhakar Raghavan, Sridhar Rajagopalan, Ronitt Rubinfeld, Madhu Sudan, and Andrew Tomkins. Random walks with "back buttons". In *32nd ACM Symposium on Theory of Computing*, 2000.

[68] Ronald Fagin, Ravi Kumar, Kevin S. McCurley, Jasmine Novak, D. Sivakumar, John A. Tomlin, and David P. Williamson. Searching the workplace web. In *The Twelfth International World Wide Web Conference*, pages 366–75, New York, 2003. ACM Press.

[69] Ronald Fagin, Ravi Kumar, and D. Sivakumar. Comparing top k lists. In *ACM SIAM Symposium on Discrete Algorithms*, pages 28–36, 2003.

[70] Michalis Faloutsos, Petros Faloutsos, and Christos Faloutsos. On power-law relationships of the internet topology. In *SIGCOMM*, pages 251–62, 1999.

[71] Ayman Farahat, Thomas Lofaro, Joel C. Miller, Gregory Rae, F. Schaefer, and Lesley A. Ward. Modifications of Kleinberg's HITS algorithm using matrix exponentiation and web log records. In *ACM SIGIR Conference*, pages 444–45, September 2001.

[72] Ayman Farahat, Thomas Lofaro, Joel C. Miller, Gregory Rae, and Lesley A. Ward. Authority rankings from HITS, PageRank, and SALSA: Existence, uniqueness, and effect of initialization. *SIAM Journal on Scientific Computing*, 27(4):1181–201, 2006.

[73] Graham Farmelo. *It Must Be Beautiful: Great Equations of Modern Science*. Granta Books, 2002.

[74] Dennis Fetterly, Mark Manasse, Marc Najork, and Janet L. Wiener. A large-scale study of the evolution of web pages. In *The Twelfth International World Wide Web Conference*, 2003.

[75] William B. Frakes and Ricardo Baeza-Yates. *Information Retrieval: Data Structures and Algorithms*. Prentice Hall, Englewood Cliffs, NJ, 1992.

[76] Robert E. Funderlic and Carl D. Meyer. Sensitivity of the stationary distribution vector for an ergodic Markov chain. *Linear Algebra and Its Applications*, 76:1–17, 1986.

[77] Robert E. Funderlic and Robert J. Plemmons. Updating LU factorizations for computing stationary distributions. *SIAM Journal on Algebraic and Discrete Methods*, 7(1):30–42, 1986.

[78] Sanjay Ghemawat, Howard Gobioff, and Shun-Tak Leung. The Google file system. In *Proceedings of the Nineteenth ACM symposium on Operating Systems Principles*, pages 29–43, New York, 2003.

[79] James Gillies and Robert Cailliau. *How the Web Was Born: The Story of the World Wide Web*. Oxford University Press, 2000.

[80] David Gleich, Leonid Zhukov, and Pavel Berkhin. Fast parallel PageRank: A linear system approach. In *The Fourteenth International World Wide Web Conference*, New York, 2005. ACM Press.

[81] Gene H. Golub and Chen Greif. Arnoldi-type algorithms for computing stationary distribution vectors, with application to PageRank. Technical Report SCCM-2004-15, Scientific Computation and Computational Mathematics, Stanford University, 2004.

[82] Gene H. Golub and Charles F. Van Loan. *Matrix Computations*. Johns Hopkins University Press, Baltimore, 1996.

[83] Gene H. Golub and Carl D. Meyer. Using the QR factorization and group inverse to compute, differentiate and estimate the sensitivity of stationary probabilities for Markov chains. *SIAM Journal on Algebraic and Discrete Methods*, 17:273–81, 1986.

[84] Zoltan Gyongyi and Hector Garcia-Molina. Web spam taxonomy. Technical report, Stanford University, 2004.

[85] D. J. Hartfiel and Carl D. Meyer. On the structure of stochastic matrices with a subdominant eigenvalue near 1. *Linear Algebra and Its Applications*, 272:193–203, 1998.

[86] Taher H. Haveliwala. Efficient computation of PageRank. Technical Report 1999-31, Computer Science Department, Stanford University, 1999.

[87] Taher H. Haveliwala. Efficient encodings for document ranking vectors. Technical report, Computer Science Department, Stanford University, November 2002.

[88] Taher H. Haveliwala. Topic-sensitive PageRank. In *The Eleventh International WWW Conference*, New York, May 2002. ACM Press.

[89] Taher H. Haveliwala. Topic-sensitive PageRank: A context-sensitive ranking algorithm for web search. *IEEE Transactions on Knowledge and Data Engineering*, 15(4):784–96, July/August 2003.

[90] Taher H. Haveliwala and Sepandar D. Kamvar. The second eigenvalue of the Google matrix. Technical Report 2003-20, Stanford University, 2003.

[91] Taher H. Haveliwala, Sepandar D. Kamvar, and Glen Jeh. An analytical comparison of approaches to personalizing PageRank. Technical report, Stanford University, 2003.

[92] Moshe Haviv. Aggregation/disaggregation methods for computing the stationary distribution of a Markov chain. *SIAM Journal on Numerical Analysis*, 22:952–66, 1987.

[93] Kevin Hemenway and Tara Calishain. *Spidering Hacks: 100 Industrial-Strength Tips and Tricks*. O'Reilly, 2003.

[94] Monika R. Henzinger, Hannes Marais, Michael Moricz, and Craig Silverstein. Analysis of a very large AltaVista query log. Technical Report 1998-014, Digital SRC, October 1998.

[95] Hermann Hesse. *Siddhartha*. New Directions Publishing Co., New York, 1951. Translated by Hilda Rosner.

[96] Jeffrey J. Hunter. Stationary distributions of perturbed Markov chains. *Linear Algebra and Its Applications*, 82:201–214, 1986.

[97] Ilse C. F. Ipsen and Steve Kirkland. Convergence analysis of a PageRank updating algorithm by Langville and Meyer. *SIAM Journal on Matrix Analysis and Applications*, 2005. To appear.

[98] Ilse C. F. Ipsen and Carl D. Meyer. Uniform stability of Markov chains. *SIAM Journal on Matrix Analysis and Applications*, 15(4):1061–74, 1994.

[99] Glen Jeh and Jennifer Widom. Scaling personalized web search. Technical report, Stanford University, 2002.

[100] Sepandar D. Kamvar and Taher H. Haveliwala. The condition number of the PageRank problem. Technical report, Stanford University, 2003.

[101] Sepandar D. Kamvar, Taher H. Haveliwala, Christopher D. Manning, and Gene H. Golub. Exploiting the block structure of the Web for computing PageRank. Technical Report 2003-17, Stanford University, 2003.

[102] Sepandar D. Kamvar, Taher H. Haveliwala, Christopher D. Manning, and Gene H. Golub. Extrapolation methods for accelerating PageRank computations. In *Twelfth International World Wide Web Conference*, New York, 2003. ACM Press.

[103] James P. Keener. The Perron-Frobenius theorem and the ranking of football teams. *SIAM Review*, 35(1):80–93, 1993.

[104] John G. Kemeny and Laurie J. Snell. *Finite Markov Chains*. D. Van Nostrand, New York, 1960.

[105] Maurice G. Kendall and B. Babington Smith. On the method of paired comparisons. *Biometrica*, 31, 1939.

[106] Jon Kleinberg. Authoritative sources in a hyperlinked environment. *Journal of the ACM*, 46, 1999.

[107] Robert R. Korfhage. *Information Storage and Retrieval*. Wiley, New York, 1997.

[108] Amy N. Langville and Carl D. Meyer. Deeper inside PageRank. *Internet Mathematics Journal*, 1(3):335–80, 2005.

[109] Amy N. Langville and Carl D. Meyer. A reordering for the PageRank problem. *SIAM Journal on Scientific Computing*, 2005. To appear.

[110] Amy N. Langville and Carl D. Meyer. A survey of eigenvector methods of web information retrieval. *The SIAM Review*, 47(1):135–61, 2005.

[111] Amy N. Langville and Carl D. Meyer. Updating the stationary vector of an irreducible Markov chain with an eye on Google's PageRank. *SIAM Journal on Matrix Analysis and Applications*, 27:968–987, 2006.

[112] Chris Pan-Chi Lee, Gene H. Golub, and Stefanos A. Zenios. A fast two-stage algorithm for computing PageRank and its extensions. Technical Report SCCM-2003-15, Scientific Computation and Computational Mathematics, Stanford University, 2003.

[113] Hyun Chul Lee and Allan Borodin. Perturbation of the hyperlinked environment. In *Lecture Notes in Computer Science: Proceedings of the Ninth International Computing and Combinatorics Conference*, volume 2697, Heidelberg, 2003. Springer-Verlag.

[114] Ronny Lempel and Shlomo Moran. The stochastic approach for link-structure analysis (SALSA) and the TKC effect. In *The Ninth International World Wide Web Conference*, New York, 2000. ACM Press.

[115] Ronny Lempel and Shlomo Moran. Rank-stability and rank-similarity of link-based web ranking algorithms in authority-connected graphs. In *Second Workshop on Algorithms and Models for the Web-Graph (WAW 2003)*, Budapest, Hungary, May 2003.

[116] Yizhou Lu, Benyu Zhang, Wensi Xi, Zheng Chen, Yi Liu, Michael R. Lyu, and Wei-Ying Ma. The PowerRank Web link analysis algorithm. In *The Thirteenth International World Wide Web Conference*, pages 254–55, New York, 2004. ACM Press. Poster.

[117] Michael S. Malone. The complete guide to Googlemania. *Wired*, 12.03, 2004.

[118] Bundit Manaskasemsak and Arnon Rungsawang. Parallel PageRank computation on a gigabit pc cluster. In *18th International Conference on Advanced Information Networking and Applications*, pages 273–277. IEEE, 2004.

[119] Fabien Mathieu and Mohamed Bouklit. The effect of the back button in a random walk: Application for PageRank. In *The Thirteenth International World Wide Web Conference*, pages 370–71, New York, 2004. Poster.

[120] Alberto O. Mendelzon and Davood Rafiei. An autonomous page ranking method for metasearch engines. In *The Eleventh International WWW Conference*, May 2002.

[121] Carl D. Meyer. The character of a finite Markov chain. *Linear Algebra, Markov Chains, and Queueing Models, IMA Volumes in Mathematics and Its Applications.*

[122] Carl D. Meyer. The role of the group generalized inverse in the theory of finite Markov chains. *SIAM Review*, 17:443–64, 1975.

[123] Carl D. Meyer. The condition of a finite Markov chain and perturbation bounds for the limiting probabilities. *SIAM Journal on Algebraic and Discrete Methods*, 1:273–83, 1980.

[124] Carl D. Meyer. Analysis of finite Markov chains by group inversion techniques. *Recent Applications of Generalized Inverses, Research Notes in Mathematics*, 66:50–81, 1982.

[125] Carl D. Meyer. Stochastic complementation, uncoupling Markov chains, and the theory of nearly reducible systems. *SIAM Review*, 31(2):240–72, 1989.

[126] Carl D. Meyer. Sensitivity of the stationary distribution of a Markov chain. *SIAM Journal on Matrix Analysis and Applications*, 15(3):715–28, 1994.

[127] Carl D. Meyer. *Matrix Analysis and Applied Linear Algebra*. SIAM, Philadelphia, 2000.

[128] Carl D. Meyer and Robert J. Plemmons. *Linear Algebra, Markov Chains, and Queueing Models*. Springer-Verlag, New York, 1993.

[129] Carl D. Meyer and James M. Shoaf. Updating finite Markov chains by using techniques of group matrix inversion. *Journal of Statistical Computation and Simulation*, 11:163–81, 1980.

[130] Carl D. Meyer and G. W. Stewart. Derivatives and perturbations of eigenvectors. *SIAM Journal on Numerical Analysis*, 25:679–691, 1988.

[131] Cleve Moler. The world's largest matrix computation. *Matlab News and Notes*, pages 12–13, October 2002.

[132] Cleve B. Moler. *Numerical Computing with MATLAB*. SIAM, 2004.

[133] Andrew Y. Ng, Alice X. Zheng, and Michael I. Jordan. Link analysis, eigenvectors and stability. In *The Seventh International Joint Conference on Artificial Intelligence*, 2001.

[134] Andrew Y. Ng, Alice X. Zheng, and Michael I. Jordan. Stable algorithms for link analysis. In *Proceedings of the 24th Annual International ACM SIGIR Conference*. ACM, 2001.

[135] Andrew Orlowski. Google founder dreams of Google implant in your brain. *The Register*, March 3, 2004.

[136] Gopal Pandurangan, Prabhakar Raghavan, and Eli Upfal. Using PageRank to characterize Web structure. In *The Eighth Annual International Computing and Combinatorics Conference (COCOON)*, 2002.

[137] Beresford N. Parlett. *The Symmetric Eigenvalue Problem*. SIAM, 1998.

[138] Luca Pretto. A theoretical analysis of google's PageRank. In *Proceedings of the Ninth International Symposium on String Processing and Information Retrieval*, pages 131–144, Lisbon, Portugal, September 2002.

[139] Sriram Raghavan and Hector Garcia-Molina. Compressing the graph structure of the Web. In *Proceedings of the IEEE Conference on Data Compression*, pages 213–22, March 2001.

[140] Sriram Raghavan and Hector Garcia-Molina. Towards compressing web graphs. In *Proceedings of the IEEE Conference on Data Compression*, pages 203–212, March 2001.

[141] Sriram Raghavan and Hector Garcia-Molina. Representing web graphs. In *Proceedings of the 19th IEEE Conference on Data Engineering*, Bangalore, India, March 2003.

[142] Matthew Richardson and Petro Domingos. The intelligent surfer: Probabilistic combination of link and content information in PageRank. *Advances in Neural Information Processing Systems*, 14:1441–8, 2002.

[143] Chris Ridings. PageRank explained: Everything you've always wanted to know about PageRank. `http://www.rankwrite.com/`. Accessed on May 22, 2002.

[144] Chris Ridings and Mike Shishigin. PageRank uncovered. `www.voelspriet2.nl/PageRank.pdf`. Accessed on September 19, 2002.

[145] Yousef Saad. *Iterative Methods for Sparse Linear Systems*. SIAM, 2003.

[146] Gerard Salton, editor. *The SMART Retrieval System: Experiments in Automatic Document Processing*. Prentice Hall, Englewood Cliffs, NJ, 1971.

[147] Gerard Salton and Chris Buckley. *Introduction to Modern Information Retrieval*. McGraw-Hill, New York, 1983.

[148] Eugene Seneta. Sensivity analysis, ergodicity coefficients, and rank-one updates for finite Markov chains. In William J. Stewart, editor, *Numerical Solution of Markov Chains*, pages 121–129. Marcel Dekker, 1991.

[149] Claude E. Shannon. A mathematical theory of communication. *The Bell System Technical Journal*, 27:379–423, 1948.

[150] Chris Sherman. Teoma vs. Google, round 2. *Silicon Valley Internet*, 2002. `http://dc.internet.com/news/print.php/1002061`.

[151] Herbert A. Simon and Albert Ando. Aggregation of variables in dynamic systems. *Econometrica*, 29:111–38, 1961.

[152] G. W. Stewart. *Matrix Algorithms*, volume 2. SIAM, 2001.

[153] G. W. Stewart and Ji-guang Sun. *Matrix Perturbation Theory*. Academic Press, 1990.

[154] William J. Stewart. *Introduction to the Numerical Solution of Markov Chains*. Princeton University Press, 1994.

[155] William J. Stewart and Wei Wu. Numerical experiments with iteration and aggregation for Markov chains. *ORSA Journal on Computing*, 4(3):336–50, 1992.

[156] Danny Sullivan. Searches per day. *Search Engine Watch*, 2003. `http://searchenginewatch.com/reports/article.php/2156461`.

[157] Marcin Sydow. Random surfer with back step. In *The Thirteenth International World Wide Web Conference*, pages 352–53, New York, 2004. Poster.

[158] Kristen Thorson. Modeling the Web and the computation of PageRank. Undergraduate thesis, Hollins University, 2004.

[159] John A. Tomlin. A new paradigm for ranking pages on the World Wide Web. In *The Twelfth International World Wide Web Conference*, New York, 2003. ACM Press.

[160] Michael Totty and Mylene Mangalindan. As Google becomes web's gatekeeper, sites fight to get in. *Wall Street Journal*, CCXLI(39), 2003. February 26.

[161] T. H. Wei. *The algebraic foundations of ranking theory*. PhD thesis, Cambridge University, 1952.

[162] James H. Wilkinson. *The Algebraic Eigenvalue Problem*. Clarendon Press, 1965.

[163] Ian H. Witten, Alistair Moffat, and Timothy C. Bell. *Managing Gigabytes: Compressing and Indexing Documents and Images*. Morgan Kaufmann, 1999.

[164] Hui Zhang, Ashish Goel, Ramesh Govindan, Kahn Mason, and Benjamin Van Roy. Making eigenvector-based reputation systems robust to collusion. In *Proceedings of WAW 2004, Lecture Notes in Computer Science*, number 3243, pages 92–104. Springer-Verlag, 2004.

[165] Xiaoyan Zhang, Michael W. Berry, and Padma Raghavan. Level search schemes for information filtering and retrieval. *Information Processing and Management*, 37:313–34, 2001.

Index

Essays on The Great Depression
Bernanke, Ben S.
ISBN: 978-81-224-1988-7, Original Edition Price: $24.95, Indian Edition Price: Rs. 395.00

Earthquakes in Human History
Boer, Jelle Zeilinga de
ISBN: 978-81-224-1883-5, Original Edition Price: $24.95, Indian Edition Price: Rs. 295.00

Econometrics
Hayashi, Fumio
ISBN: 978-81-224-2122-4, Original Edition Price: $85.00, Indian Edition Price: Rs. 295.00

Econometrics
Hayashi, Fumio
ISBN: 978-81-224-1711-1, Original Edition Price: $85.00, Indian Edition Price: Rs. 695.00

Financial Econometrics Problems, Models, and Methods
Gourieroux, Christian
ISBN: 978-81-224-2171-2, Original Edition Price: $67.50, Indian Edition Price: Rs. 295.00

Financial Econometrics Problems, Models, and Methods
Gourieroux, Christian
ISBN: 978-81-224-1697-8, Original Edition Price: $67.50, Indian Edition Price: Rs. 495.00

Google's Page Rank and Beyond
Amy N. Langville, Carl D. Meyer
ISBN: 978-81-224-3129-2, Original Edition Price: $39.50, Indian Edition Price: Rs. 395.00

Graphic Discovery
Wainer, Howard
ISBN: 978-81-224-1882-8, Original Edition Price: $29.95, Indian Edition Price: Rs. 295.00

Homological Algebra
Cartan, Henri
ISBN: 978-81-224-1997-9, Original Edition Price: $60.00, Indian Edition Price: Rs. 295.00

Hubbert's Peak: The Impending World Oil Shortage
Deffeyes, Kenneth S.
ISBN: 978-81-224-1708-6, Original Edition Price: $16.95, Indian Edition Price: Rs. 175.00

Interest Rate Models An Introduction
Andrew J.G. Cairns
ISBN: 978-81-224-3130-8, Original Edition Price: $49.95, Indian Edition Price: Rs. 200.00

Inflation Targeting
Bernanke, Ben S.
ISBN: 978-81-224-1989-4, Original Edition Price: $19.95, Indian Edition Price: Rs. 395.00

Infinity and the Mind
Rudy Rucker
ISBN: 978-81-224-2110-1, Original Edition Price: $19.95, Indian Edition Price: Rs. 295.00

Irrational Exuberance
Shiller, Robert. J.
ISBN: 978-81-224-1876-7, Original Edition Price: $27.95, Indian Edition Price: Rs. 395.00

Interest & Prices Foundations
Woodford, Michael
ISBN:978-81-224-1718-0, Original Edition Price: $ 75.00, Indian Edition Price: Rs. 795.00

Learning and Expectations in Macroeconomics
Evans, Honkapohja
ISBN: 978-81-224-3131-5, Original Edition Price: $61.00, Indian Edition Price: Rs. 495.00

Local Search in Combinatorial Optimization
Aarts, Emile
ISBN: 978-81-224-1999-3, Original Edition Price: $45.00, Indian Edition Price: Rs. 395.00

Liquid Crystals
Collings, Peter J.
ISBN: 978-81-224-1996-2, Original Edition Price: $42.00, Indian Edition Price: Rs. 395.00

Mathematical Techniques In Finance
Cerny, Ales
ISBN: 978-81-224-1715-9, Original Edition Price: $39.95, Indian Edition Price: Rs. 295.00

Microfoundations of Financial Economics
Lengwiler, Yvan
ISBN: 978-81-224-1698-5, Original Edition Price: $49.95, Indian Edition Price: Rs. 295.00

Neoclassical Finance
Ross, Stephen A
ISBN: 978-81-224-1881-1, Original Edition Price: $35.00, Indian Edition Price: Rs. 195.00

Optimization Insights and Applications
Jan Brinkhuis and Vladimir Tikhomirov
ISBN: 978-81-224-3132-2, Original Edition Price: $94.00, Indian Edition Price: Rs. 595.00

Plasma Physics for Astrophysics
Russell M. Kulsrud
ISBN: 978-81-224-3133-9, Original Edition Price: $60.00, Indian Edition Price: Rs. 295.00

Quadrangular Algebras
Richard M. Weiss
ISBN: 978-81-224-3134-6, Original Edition Price: $47.50, Indian Edition Price: Rs. 150.00

Quantitative Risk Management
Alexander J. McNeil, Rüdiger Frey, Paul Embrechts
ISBN: 978-81-224-3135-3, Original Edition Price: $85.00, Indian Edition Price: Rs. 495.00

Real Analysis Measure Theory, Integration, & Hilbert Spaces
Elias M Stein and Rami Shakarchi
ISBN: 978-81-224-3136-0, Original Edition Price: $70.00, Indian Edition Price: Rs. 495.00

Scientific Parallel Computing
L. Ridgway Scott, Terry Clark, Babak Bagheri
ISBN: 978-81-224-3137-7, Original Edition Price: $64.00, Indian Edition Price: Rs. 395.00

Strange Curves, Counting Rabbits, and other Mathematical Explorations
Ball, Keith
ISBN: 978-81-224-1878-1, Original Edition Price: $29.95, Indian Edition Price: Rs. 295.00

Small Worlds
Watts J. Duncan
ISBN: 978-81-224-1714-2, Original Edition Price: $24.95, Indian Edition Price: Rs. 195.00

The Structure and Dynamics of Networks
Mark Newman, Duncan J. Watts, Albert-Lászlá Barabási
ISBN: 978-81-224-3138-4, Original Edition Price: $69.00, Indian Edition Price: Rs. 595.00

Thermodynamics, A Dynamical Systems Approach
Wassim M. Haddad, V.S. Chellaboina and Sergey G. Nersesov
ISBN: 978-81-224-3139-1, Original Edition Price: $58.00, Indian Edition Price: Rs. 395.00

The Complexity of Cooperation
Axelrod, Robert
ISBN: 978-81-224-1709-8, Original Edition Price: $23.95, Indian Edition Price: Rs. 175.00

The Paradox of Asset Pricing
Bossaerts, Peter
ISBN: 978-81-224-2000-5, Original Edition Price: $32.95, Indian Edition Price: Rs. 295.00

The Econometrics of Financial Markets
Campbell, John Y.
ISBN: 978-81-224-2169-9, Original Edition Price: $95.00, Indian Edition Price: Rs. 395.00

The Econometrics of Financial Markets
Campbell, John Y.
ISBN: 978-81-224-1707-8, Original Edition Price: $95.00, Indian Edition Price: Rs. 595.00

The Future of Money
Cohen, Benjamin J.
ISBN: 978-81-224-1998-6, Original Edition Price: $19.95, Indian Edition Price: Rs. 295.00

The Calculus Gallery
Dunham, William
ISBN: 978-81-224-1880-4, Original Edition Price: $29.95, Indian Edition Price: Rs. 295.00

The Meaning of Relativity
Einstein, Albert
ISBN: 978-81-224-1817-0, Original Edition Price: $14.95, Indian Edition Price: Rs. 95.00

The Challenge of Global Capitalism
Gilpin, Robert
ISBN: 978-81-224-1713-5, Original Edition Price: $24.95, Indian Edition Price: Rs. 195.00

The New Division of Labor
Levy, Frank
ISBN: 978-81-224-1884-2, Original Edition Price: $39.95, Indian Edition Price: Rs. 195.00

The Theory of Incentives
Martimort David
ISBN: 978-81-224-1710-4, Original Edition Price: $34.95, Indian Edition Price: Rs. 295.00

The Company of Strangers A Natural History of Economic Life
Seabright, Paul
ISBN: 978-81-224-1877-4, Original Edition Price: $18.95, Indian Edition Price: Rs. 395.00

The New Financial Risk In the 21st Century Order
Shiller, Robert. J.
ISBN: 978-81-224-1716-6, Original Edition Price: $18.95, Indian Edition Price: Rs. 245.00

Why Stock Markets Crash
Didier, Sornette
ISBN: 978-81-224-1790-6, Original Edition Price: $19.95, Indian Edition Price: Rs. 275.00